Female
SEXUAL ABUSERS

THREE VIEWS

Patricia A. Davin • Julia C.R. Hislop • Teresa Dunbar

Safer Society Press

PO BOX 340 • BRANDON, VERMONT 05733

EDITOR: Euan Bear

DESIGN & COMPOSITION: Barbara Poeter, Pittsford, Vermont

PRINTING: BookCrafters, Chelsea, Michigan

ISBN: 1-884444-53-9

$22.00

ORDER FROM:

 **SaferSocietyPress**

PO BOX 340 • BRANDON, VERMONT 05733-0340

To receive a catalog or to place a phone order with your Visa or MasterCard, call 802-247-3132.

THE FEMALE SEXUAL ABUSER: Three Views

FOREWORD

The reality that women sexually abuse children has been acknowledged for quite some time, yet this particular group of sexual abusers seems to have evoked an approach-avoidance phenomenon within our field. At times there appears to be tremendous interest in identifying and treating female sexual abusers as a distinct group with special characteristics, while at others the whole idea of women as sexual abusers seems to go into hiding, along with the abuse they perpetrate and the victims they create. In the decade since Mathews, Matthews & Speltz (1989), Faller (1987), and Wolfe (1985) first published their groundbreaking studies, there has been no explosion in the literature on this particular group of sexual abusers, unlike the exponential growth we've seen in other areas of sexual abuse treatment literature. Maybe it is because we still think of "Mom" — along with apple pie and the American flag — as symbolic of a wholesome America, or maybe it is simply that we do not want to admit that the women who bring us into the world and nurture us could ever do anything to harm anyone.

Despite the dearth of literature, the Safer Society Foundation has tracked a growing number of programs in America treating female adolescent and adult sexual abusers. What models they are using and what differentiates their treatment of female abusers from that of male abusers remain largely undocumented; unfortunately, the literature on female sexual abusers has not kept up with the growth in programs treating them. There is still debate about typologies, treatment modalities most appropriate for treating female sexual abusers, and whether or not females should be treated in mixed groups with male sexual abusers.

In late winter of 1993, the late Fay Honey Knopp, founder and Director of the Safer Society Program & Press (now the Safer Society Foundation, Inc.) and I saw a need to convene the professionals in our field who were most knowledgeable in treating female sexual abusers and/or conducting research into this special population. We contacted Jim Brieling at the National Institute of Mental Health (NIMH) Violence and Traumatic Stress Research Branch, and suggested that our two organizations co-host the meeting. Jim was able to find funds and a date was set for June 25-26, 1993. Approximately 25 people — seasoned professionals, students, researchers, clinicians — attended that historic working conference, resulting in a much-needed exchange of information and perspectives and encouragement toward developing further research. We can't treat a population — or its constituent individuals — effectively when we know so little about its characteristics and motivations.

Among the exceptional and highly qualified professionals attending that meeting was a remarkable woman who had completed a dissertation on female sexual abusers: Julia Hislop. We also heard from two other remarkable women who had found us through their literature reviews or through the National Clearinghouse on Child Abuse and Neglect and were in the final stages of completing their research: Patricia Davin and Teresa Dunbar. We contacted these researchers and asked if they would be interested in publishing their dissertations through the Safer Society Press. All agreed, and this monograph is the result. It has taken us many more years than we planned to finish this project, but the material in these dissertations remains a valuable contribution to the field.

Each dissertation offers us a unique insight into the population of female sexual abusers. Through her analysis of extensive interviews with female inmates in seven different states, Dr. Patricia Davin's work in **Secrets Revealed** helps us understand some of the differences between women who sexually abuse as independent abusers versus those who abuse with a co-offender. We learn about the relationship between co-offenders and its impact on these women, including their probable motivations. Her study allows us to look into and better understand their backgrounds and the childhood abuses they experienced.

In **Women Who Sexually Molest Female Children,** Dr. Teresa Dunbar's analysis of six existing studies on female sexual abusers teaches us about similarities and differences between male and female etiologies for sexual abuse and possible gender-circumstantial differences that influence the development of adult molesting behavior. Her results emphasize the importance of the mother-daughter attachment (and its lack), among other factors, and its influence on later female molesting behavior, including the gender choice of victim. This research continues and confirms the importance of our understanding the issues of attachment, intimacy, and loneliness (emotional isolation).

By comparing the answers of female sexual abusers (both officially identified and self-identified under assurance of confidentiality) and other female offenders in prisons and patients in drug and alcohol rehabilitation and sexual abuse inpatient treatment programs, Dr. Julia Hislop's findings in **Female Child Molesters** challenge some common assumptions about why some women sexually abuse children. Among other conclusions, her study helps us better understand that female sexual abusers have serious dependency issues that should be addressed during the course of treatment. In addition, Dr. Hislop's research supports the existence of possible subtypes of female child molesters. An accepted typology of female sexual abusers has been elusive, a source of debate in recent years.

Together these three excellent research pieces provide an important contribution toward furthering our understanding of where female sexual abusers come from and why they abuse children. In a field that is still relatively young with a sub-population of clientele that needs further study, we are pleased to offer our readers another resource, an incremental increase in our knowledge that will eventually help us to make society safer for all our children.

We are grateful to the authors for agreeing to let the Safer Society Press publish their work, for their assistance in helping us make this project happen, and for their patience over the past five years while we completed the long journey toward finalizing this publication.

Robert E. Freeman-Longo, MRC, LPC
The Safer Society Foundation, Inc.
Brandon, Vermont

PART ONE

Secrets Revealed: A Study of Female Sex Offenders

PATRICIA A. DAVIN

CONTENTS

ACKNOWLEDGMENTS

To:

Dr. Ferguson for her consummate navigational skills throughout this incredible journey, JP Nims for his enduring support and exacting technical direction, Lorree for the supportive "jump starts" way back in the beginning of the journey, Jeanne for so many times providing the wind beneath my wings, Denise for her deep and abiding faith in me, Lisa for her impeccable art of balancing loving support with cracking the whip, and, most importantly, Mom and Dad for strongly, proudly standing beside me all the way.

ABSTRACT

This study examined 76 female sex offenders incarcerated in seven states for crimes of child sexual abuse. The women were classified into two groups: Co-Offenders (women who participated in the commission of the crime with a male codefendant) and Independent Offenders (women who perpetrated the crime without a codefendant). The overall purpose of the study was to examine these groups to provide clearer descriptions and a better analysis of these categories than had been done previously. This study also provided information regarding the relationship with a significant male in the commission of the crime. The MMPI-2 was administered to the women and they also participated in a Structured Interview with the researcher. The findings included characteristics of the female offenders, the offenses committed, and the Co-Offenders' relationships with their codefendants. The Independent Offenders are noticeably more psychologically disturbed than the Co-Offenders and suffered more severe sexual abuse as children. Over half the Co-Offenders were physically and psychologically abused as children. The subjects named mother as the principal abuser more often than father. Over three-quarters of the Co-Offenders described physically and psychologically abusive relationships with their codefendants. No clear relationship was found between chemical dependency and the commission of the offense for either group of offenders.

Chapter 1

Introduction

_____

Sexual abuse of children is recognized as one of this country's major problems. This is nearly universally interpreted as involving males abusing children. Few people are aware, though, that women are involved in as many as 37% of the reported cases (National Center for Child Abuse and Neglect, 1981). The American Humane Association study (AHA, 1978) described sexual abuse by a female acting on her own in 6% of the reported female victims' cases and in 14% of the reported male victims' cases.

Very little research has been done on female sex offenders. Relatively little is known about the characteristics of females who engage in sexually abusive behaviors, or the kinds of abusive sexual behaviors in which they engage. The few studies that have looked at this population have developed three rudimentary classification systems with suggestions of possible etiological factors (Faller, 1987; Mathews, Matthews, & Speltz, 1989; McCarty, 1986). The classification terms range from Polyincestuous Abuse to Noncustodial Abusers in the Faller study; from Teacher/Lover to Male-Coerced in the Mathews et al. study; and from Independent Offender to Accomplice in the McCarty study. This study focuses on offenders classified as Co-Offenders or Accomplices. Data collection on the nature and prevalence of these kinds of offenses is problematic. For example, the Uniform Crime Reports (U.S. Department of Justice) analyzes offense data by geographical areas as well as demographic variables such as age, race, and sex. In the past decade, women accounted for about 1% of total rape arrests.

Female participation in violent crimes (e.g., murder, forcible rape, robbery, and aggravated assault) in general increased 20.5% for 1975-78, and 38% for 1971-1985. Whether this is due to an actual increase in crime or in improved identification and reporting is unclear. Between 1971 and 1985, the arrest rate for females was much lower than that for males; however, it has risen faster. The base rate for female violent crime is so low that even minor annual variations can produce seemingly impressive percentage changes.

Until 1975, the Uniform Crime Reports did not include female arrests for forcible rape. Rape is perhaps contrary to the stereotype of female sexuality; however, women do commit rape and in much the same manner as men. Women may also commit other sex crimes (e.g., statutory sexual seduction, incest, indecent assault, assault with intent to rape, rape of a child or feeble-minded person); however, they most commonly are co-offenders or accomplices with male partners. Furthermore, a woman may be charged with rape if she aids or abets a male in such crimes. Because of the different kinds of statistics, it is impossible to determine incidence in any study area. Also, laws pertaining to female and male sexual abusers are defined and applied in various ways in different states.

REASONS FOR THE STUDY

Due to conflicting findings and reports, we need to investigate female sex offenders and their motivations. Their relationships have been described as dependent and passive with domineering and controlling men. The primary affiliation of mother with child is superseded in these cases. Further examination of the dynamics of these dependent relationships is needed.

The existing classification systems for female sexual offenders are vague, and a coherent system would improve our ability to identify and treat these women. We need to describe these women accurately and develop a workable classification system by studying different groups of female sexual offenders.

I am interested in investigating differences and similarities among offenders' personalities, development, and abuse-related behaviors and attitudes. Of particular interest to me is exploring the similarities and differences between Co-Offenders and Accomplices.

LOOKING AT WHERE WE'VE BEEN: OVERVIEW OF THE LITERATURE

The review focuses on literature pertaining to rape/sexual assault and child sexual abuse theories in the application of such concepts to women. Given the inadequate data about women sexual offenders, study of this population provides new insights into their psychological profiles and the dynamics of their interactions with male counterparts. The review includes a discussion of female sex offender and offense studies, as well as aspects of the offenders' lives. Because women seem to engage in child sexual abuse primarily with a male abuser, women's relationships with male partners are discussed from the perspectives of sex-role and socialization theories.

Various classification schemes for both male and female sexual offenders are examined. With the exception of one study, the results of female sex offender studies are based on clinical impressions and examination of records rather than systematic investigation, which results in vague and uncertain findings.

CHAPTER 2

Review of the Literature

Incidence of Child Sexual Abuse by Females

A starting point for the review is a landmark American Humane Association (AHA) effort that collected nationwide data on the incidence of child sexual abuse (American Humane Association, 1978). The AHA study described child sexual abuse by a female acting independently of a male in 6% of crimes with a reported female victim, and in 14% of those with a reported male victim. Three years later, the National Center for Child Abuse and Neglect (NCCAN, 1981) found that females sexually abused 13% of the reported female victims and 24% of the reported male victims.

Finkelhor and Russell (1984) reexamined the AHA data (1978) and the NCCAN data (1981) to attempt to estimate the incidence of female sexual abusers. They indicated that due to differing definitions in both studies, the figures are questionable. When the data were re-analyzed, separating females acting independently in the abuse from those who allowed the abuse, a dramatic decrease was found in the percentages of female independent sexual abusers.

In a national study of sexual abuse in 270 day care cases, Finkelhor and his colleagues reported that 40% of the abusers were women (Finkelhor, Williams, & Burns, 1988; Finkelhor, Williams, Burns, & Kalinowski, 1988). These women were described as intelligent, educated, and not likely to have histories of known deviant behavior.

There are methodological problems with this study. Although the authors required the abuse to be substantiated, it is uncertain that the cases are actually abuse cases rather than mistaken allegations. Thus, the sample includes a number of cases which resulted in dismissal or acquittals, or convictions which were later overturned. The McMartin case, for instance, which ended in dropped charges and acquittals, is included in this study.

Researchers have stated that there were barriers that have prevented the acknowledgment of female child sexual abuse. One barrier suggested is that the incest taboo is so strong that sexual abuse by women was considered to be extremely rare (Allen, 1990). Another barrier is disbelief that females actually are sexually abusive toward children (Banning, 1989).

Plummer (1981) asserted that there is a significant number of adult females who sexually abuse children. He contended that society denies the existence of sexuality in women, and that women are expected to have a certain amount of bodily contact with children. Therefore, any sexual abuse by women is hidden. It is difficult to accept Plummer's contention that women's sexuality is denied by today's society. One only needs to peruse any contemporary magazine such as Cosmopolitan to note that women's sexuality is in fact recognized in society.

It has also been suggested that mothers may be involved sexually with their sons in subtle ways that escape notice or legal intervention (Justice & Justice, 1979). Some examples include: sleeping with a son, caressing in a sexual manner, and emotionally binding him to her with implicit promises of sex — all of which could be disguised as "normal mothering" — hence artificially lowering the number of reported sexual crimes by women perpetrators.

In summary, the results obtained from the above studies are affected by the definitions of sexual abuse employed, the samples selected, and the methodologies used. Child sexual abuse by females may not be as rare as was once believed. It does occur.

Women and Sex Crimes

Society tends to perpetuate a belief that rape is a crime that is always committed by men. Rape is often thought to be a heterosexual crime, defined as an act of sexual intercourse, possibly due to the myth that the perpetrator desires sexual gratification, and to the ways state laws have defined the crime of rape. Rape has been changed to "sexual assault" in many states and encompasses more sexual behaviors, such as cunnilingus and fellatio, than just sexual intercourse.

Revisions of the legal terminology in states' rape statutes have included non-sexist language. Terms indicating the genders of the offender and the victim have been changed to the term "person," offering protection to male victims of this crime and providing for the inclusion of homosexual rape. These changes have resulted in more arrests of females on charges of rape. As an example, in a Massachusetts landmark case, Commonwealth v. Denise Whitehead (1974), the court found that a female accessory to male or female rape may also be charged with the crime of rape. If a woman aids or abets a male perpetrator by luring, restraining, or subduing a victim, she is an accessory and may be charged with rape. This decision further expanded the definition of rape to include circumstances where the victim and offender are female, and resulted in legislative changes to include such language in the law.

CHARACTERISTICS OF FEMALE SEXUAL OFFENDERS

Both offense and offender characteristics of females who rape have been examined by several researchers. In one study, seven women convicted and sentenced for rape in the New York State Prison System were evaluated (McCarthy, 1981). Unlike Finkelhor, McCarthy described these women as "unstable" psychologically, and at least one male accomplice was involved in each case. Another study examined data on 20 women charged with rape (Brown, Hull, & Panesis, 1984). The information was obtained from the files of the Office of the Massachusetts Commissioner of Probation and stated that in all of those cases, the offender knew her victim in the context of acquaintance, friend, or family member.

To understand why females are involved in sexually abusive behaviors, various studies explored facets of female sex offenders' lives (Marvasti, 1986; McCarty, 1986; Wolfe, 1985). One study presented case histories of five female sex offenders (Marvasti, 1986). In two of the cases the victims were sons, ages 2 and 17, and one case involved teenage male victims unrelated to the offender. In the remaining two cases, the victims were a teenage daughter and a 4-year-old daughter. This study revealed that: 1) women's sexual abuse is usually nonviolent; 2) power and authority issues, a psychodynamic factor noted in father-daughter incest, are not significantly present; and 3) no psychosis was found in either the mother or son in these cases (no mention was made of the daughters' mental health in this study).

Eight case histories of men who were sexually molested by their mothers as children were examined by Krug (1989). He found that the mothers seemed to be attempting to satisfy emotional and relationship needs via their sons. None of the mothers was believed to be psychotic.

Loneliness was identified as a significant motivating factor in a study of three cases of sexual abuse of an infant by a mother (Chasnoff, Burns, Schnoll, Burns, Chisum, & Kyle-Sproe, 1986). The mothers were all separated from their sexual partners and were described as socially alienated and isolated. Two of the three were diagnosed as having borderline personality disorder.

Nine case histories of women referred for evaluation and treatment at a forensic psychiatric clinic were examined by Travin, Cullin, & Protter (1990). All nine subjects were reported to exhibit low self-esteem and had histories of severe psychological, physical, and/or sexual abuse. Four had histories of serious psychopathology, including substance abuse and psychosis. The remaining five subjects were thought to have characterological deficiencies, but no history of psychosis.

A study composed of 12 female sexual offenders and male sexual offenders evaluated in an outpatient program specializing in the evaluation and treatment of sex offenders showed the following gender differences: 1) 50% of the women aided and abetted a male adult, which is rarely seen with male offenders; 2) some women rationalize their behavior in terms of dependency, a reason rarely heard from a male offender population; 3) both male and female offenders use denial, projection, and minimization; 4) physical force was rarely used by either male or female offenders; and 5) the victim was more apt to be a family member than not for both male and female offenders (Wolfe, 1985).

In another study, researchers examined 23 cases of women convicted of unlawful sexual intercourse and committed to Holloway Prison in England (O'Connor, 1987). Here, in a total of 23 cases, 21 women were aiding and abetting a man in committing the sexual offense. O'Connor corroborated Wolfe's conclusions about the powerful influence of the male partner in the relationship. Of particular interest is the high number of women involved with men in the execution of the sexual abuse. The women's roles were to assist the male perpetrators in the abusive situation.

Socialization Theory and Sex-Role Theory

The socialization process for women emphasizes a desire for affiliation and the perpetuation of a passive-dependent role. Discussion of sex-role theory in the literature on female criminality purports that there are gender differences in socialization as well as expectations of behavioral standards (Heidensohn, 1985;

Hoffman-Bustamante, 1973; Sears, 1989). Women's participation in violent crimes tends to be in ways that reflect gender role and socialization. Hoffman-Bustamante contended that "it appears that they have played secondary, supportive roles. ... Thus, women seem to commit crimes in roles auxiliary to men, in keeping with their sex roles and for lesser returns" (1973, p. 131).

Gender theory also addresses men's and women's different crime rates and presumes that purported personality differences exist between genders due to socialization processes (Naffin, 1985). Different socialization of women is noted then, not only in the kinds of offenses committed but also in nature of participation. The male personality is thought to predispose men to offend; women are viewed as inclined to conform rather than act (Naffin, 1985).

Women, Women Criminals, and Relationships

Female identity and women's needs to affiliate with or attach to others to receive love has been contrasted with men's identity in terms of autonomy and separation by Bardwick (1971). She asserted that a woman's positive self-concept is derived from stable important affiliations. She further believed that out of insecurity a woman would yield to her mate to continue to be affiliated. However, Bardwick's work was done with women raised in the 1950s and 1960s. Since that time, there has been a considerable amount of social change, particularly in female roles. How accurate her notions are regarding women raised in the 1960s and 1970s remains an open question.

Men characteristically acquire self-esteem in an autonomous way, whereas women may do so in a similar manner, but with an added part: affiliation (Notman, Zilbach, Baker-Miller, & Nadelson, 1986). Gilligan (1982) wrote in a similar vein in her description of women's sense of self as being derived partially from attachment with important others.

Early sex role and masculinity/femininity theorists believed that women are "dependent helpmates" to male offenders due to socially prescribed passivity (Klein, 1973; Smart, 1976; Veddar & Sommerville, 1975). More recently, the majority of theories on female criminality concur that women are driven by affiliative behavior. Female offenders have been described in their attachment to males as passive and dependent (Covington, 1985). Baldwin (1983) and Sears (1989) viewed female crimes as representative of sex-role behaviors: men lead and women follow in joint criminal activities.

Numerous studies support this notion by showing repeatedly that women participate in violent crime in a way that is consistent with traditional female roles, i.e., they assist the male perpetrators (Faller, 1987; Groth & Birnbaum, 1979; Mathews, Matthews, & Speltz, 1989; McCarty, 1986; O'Connor, 1987; Sears, 1989; Ward, Jackson, & Ward, 1980; Wolfe, 1985). These studies describe women as passive in their relationships with men and extremely dependent on them. Their individual need for acceptance far surpasses their recognition of their children's needs. Female sexual offenders appear to be willing to go to sexual behavioral extremes to maintain their relationships with their mates, and to avoid rejection, abuse, and abandonment.

Classification of Male Sexual Offenders

There have been attempts at classifications based on a variety of criteria to construct homogeneous groups of offenders and/or offenses. The different systems have focused on characteristics of the offender, the victim, and the sexual acts, as well as situational aspects. Offenders have been classified according to age, psychological diagnosis, type of sexual act, motivation for the act, relationship between the offender and victim, and other factors.

A classification system based on age distribution resulted in three groups (Mohr, Turner, & Jerry, 1964). They identified an adolescent group, distinguished by delayed development in sociosexual functioning; a middle-aged group, identified by regression to child partners in response to sexual and social failure; and an older group (mid- to late-50s) whose crimes were viewed as a means of dealing with social isolation and loneliness.

Another classification system (West, 1977) focused only on adolescents and is described in a way similar to that of Mohr, et al. (1964). In this study the adolescents are described as developmentally delayed in social and sexual areas, passive, and unable to relate well with peers. West believed this group to be unlikely to re-offend. This group is differentiated from the older offender in terms of a persistent pattern of attachment to children over time and the high likelihood of a repetition of offending behavior. West asserted that both groups are markedly different from a psychopathic group of offenders who tend to exhibit inappropriate sexual behavior and deviance in both sexual and non-sexual areas of life.

A commonly used typology for male child molesters is the one constructed by Groth (1978, 1982). His classification system is psychological and divided into two categories depending upon whether the sexual abuse is a persistent pattern (fixation), or whether the behavior is new or a change in sexual behavior or lifestyle (regression). He defined the fixated type as one "whose primary sexual orientation is towards children," and the regressed type as one "whose sexual involvement with a child is a clear departure, under stress, from a primary sexual orientation towards agemates" (1982, p. 133).

Groth (1978) also classified sex offenders according to the motivation for the crime. His two primary categories are sex-pressure offenses and sex-force offenses. These are differentiated primarily by whether aggression is involved in the sexual act. The sex-pressure offenses include use of nonaggressive techniques such as enticement and entrapment. Intimidation and physical force are used to accomplish the offender's goal in the sex-force offenses. Groth subclassified sex-force contacts into exploitive (victim resistance is dealt with by threat or force) and sadistic (the force is eroticized). While these offense categories are presented by Groth as descriptions of acts performed on victims, there is an indication that "sex-pressure" and "sex-force" may be characteristics of the offender. Therefore, this system may be thought of as an offender typology.

Another classification system divides male sexual offenders, including child molesters, into two groups: situational or preferential (Dietz, 1983). He described the situational offender as having no psychosexual mental disorder; however, he sexually offends against children due to situational factors such as "intoxication, social stressors, mood, and mental conditions" (p. 1489). He further described situational offenders as "reasonably well adjusted and nonparaphiliac men who committed first offenses while drinking heavily, after being fired, during their wives' pregnancies, following a divorce, or during a depressive, manic, or schizophrenic episode" (p. 1489).

The preferential type is depicted as a person "whose preferred or exclusive method of achieving sexual arousal involves unconventional mental imagery or acts" (p. 1489) and "is regarded by contemporary psychiatry as suffering from a diagnosable psychosexual disorder" (p. 1498).

From the descriptions provided by Dietz and Groth, it appears that there are similarities between the typologies presented. Dietz's situational offender may be synonymous with Groth's regressed type, and similarly, Dietz's preferential offender with Groth's fixated type.

Classification of Female Sexual Offenders

Three primary studies have produced classifications or typologies of female sexual offenders: McCarty (1986), Mathews, Matthews & Speltz (1989), and Faller (1987).

MCCARTY

McCarty (1986) studied the case records of 26 female sexual offenders in the Dallas Incest Treatment Program. Five mothers were considered accomplices due to their roles in enabling the abuse and were evaluated separately. As an example of enabling, one offender was aware of the abuse of her 15-year-old daughter from the beginning and made no attempts to prevent it. In fact, she ultimately took her daughter for an abortion. Another offender was also aware of the sexual abuse of her three daughters soon after it began; however, she stated in court that she considered this "good" for the girls. Nine mothers were co-offenders with a male, and 12 were independent offenders. Among the independent offenders, a male offender was associated in half of the situations.

As a result of the study, McCarty classified female sexual offenders in three groups: Independent Offenders, Co-Offenders, and Accomplices. These classifications were based on the nature of the offense. In addition, she seems to have based her classification scheme on earlier work by Groth (1982), who used similar terms in discussing mother-child incest. He stated: "The mother may be the offender or the co-offender, an active and participating accomplice in the sexual assault, or a passive bystander" (p. 230). These terms are:

INDEPENDENT OFFENDER. This offender is a sole perpetrator, typified as having a troubled childhood, including sexual abuse and marrying as a teenager. She maintains steady employment and is of average intelligence. She may be seriously emotionally disturbed and may abuse substances. Most often, her daughter is her victim, and she views her as an extension of herself.

CO-OFFENDER. This offender actively participates in the sexual abuse. She also has had a troubled childhood, including sexual abuse. She does not work outside her home and is of borderline intelligence. She married as a teenager and has been married several times. She is a neglectful parent, with a strong need to be taken care of superseding her children's needs. Her victim is as often her son as her daughter.

ACCOMPLICE. This offender may not be present, yet is aware of the sexual abuse; however, she takes no action to stop it, or may be assisting in it and/or procuring victims (active vs. passive accomplice). She works outside the home and married as a teenager. She is of average intelligence and has a powerful need to be cared for. Like the Co-Offender, this need supersedes children's needs. Most often, her teenaged daughter is her victim.

Strengths and Limitations of McCarty's Classification System

McCarty acknowledged the female sex offender's relationship with a spouse in descriptions of the Co-Offender and Accomplice. This is relevant in that McCarty believed a contributing factor in child sex abuse is the offender's dependence on her spouse.

A strength of McCarty's system of classification is that her terms (Independent Offender, Accomplice, and Co-Offender) offer a starting place for further refinement. If her terms were precisely defined, including subcategories (i.e., incest, family member victim, victim known or unfamiliar to the offender), the system would be more accurate.

One limitation of McCarty's system is that she did not clearly define her criteria for the classification of offenders. For example, while McCarty described the Accomplices' roles in the abuse as "enabling," she did not define what she meant by this term. The Co-Offenders' participation in the sexual abuse is not addressed. Was their involvement in the sexual abuse with the male voluntary or coerced? Was she appeasing the male to stop negative interaction directed toward her? It is also impossible to determine whether there is a difference between Co-Offenders and Accomplices.

Further, McCarty noted that of the 12 Independent Offenders, a male offender was associated with six. This raises the question: What is the difference between these six Independent Offenders and the Co-Offenders and/or Accomplices? McCarty's categories are therefore not mutually exclusive, which results in the classification system being inadequate.

In addition, McCarty's sample was derived from case records. Although this method provides important information to a study, there are no tests for differences and no statistically significant findings. The small sample size and lack of control over data gathering conditions are limitations.

The sample consisted of mothers identified by a child protective service in Texas. Her classification system focused exclusively on incest, and not sexual offenses in general. These findings cannot be assumed to be representative of female sexual offenders in general; therefore there are limitations to the findings' generalizability.

MATHEWS, MATTHEWS, & SPELTZ

Mathews et al. (1989) drew from a sample of 16 female sexual abusers in Minneapolis, Minnesota, who participated in the Genesis II Female Sex-

Offender Program from May 1985 through December 1987. The study was primarily qualitative due to the small number of subjects; however, quantitative data were compiled using the Minnesota Multiphasic Personality Inventory (MMPI), Tennessee Self-Concept Scale, and Family Adaptability and Cohesion Evaluation Scales (FACES). These instruments were administered to the women pre- and post-treatment.

From this work, Mathews, et al. delineated three types of female sex offenders: 1) Teacher/Lover, 2) Predisposed (intergenerational), and 3) Male-Coerced. These categories derive from a cluster of attributes relative to the crimes committed, the perpetrators' views of the victims, co-offender involvement, and similarities and differences among the offenders from a psychological perspective.

The Teacher/Lover offender is characterized as sexually involved with prepubescent and adolescent males for the purpose of teaching sexuality. She relates to her victims as peers.

The Predisposed offender has a history of long-standing and severe sexual abuse. When she became a perpetrator, she acted alone and initiated the sexual abuse on her victims, who are primarily her children. She is seen as attempting to experience emotional intimacy in a nonthreatening way.

The Male-Coerced offender also has a history of childhood sexual abuse. She acts in concert with a male who has a history of sexually abusing children. Five of the eight women acted only in conjunction with a male. Three were initially coerced by a male, but later initiated sexual abuse on their own. She is viewed as extremely dependent and nonassertive, and in time may initiate the sexual abuse. She sexually abuses her own children as well as children outside her family.

Strengths and Limitations of the Mathews et al. Classification System

Mathews et al. (1989) appropriately acknowledged the women's relationships with men in terms of passivity and dependence on males. Quantitative data were compiled (i.e., MMPI, Tennessee Self-Concept Scale); however, due to the limited sample size (N=16), qualitative methodologies were employed and the quantitative test scores (e.g., MMPI) were reported in the form of profiles with brief interpretations provided in each of their categories of classification.

The MMPI, Tennessee Self-Concept, and FACES instruments were administered pre- and post-treatment; however, data are presented only in a global fashion. A very small number of subjects completed the post-tests, and no data are reported for post-test results.

Categories devised by Mathews, et al. contain mixed types of sexual offenses. For example, in the Predisposed offender group, victims included their own children (male and female), other relatives, and children who were acquaintances. The dynamics involved in these varied types of victim-perpetrator relationships may be different.

In describing the Male-Coerced group, Mathews et al. noted that some of the women were abused physically and sexually, and that all were verbally abused. However, they do not include what specific types of coercion were used by the males. The fear of loss of or abandonment by the males may be different from fears for health, safety, and well-being. The manner in which the coercion was carried out by the males was not discussed by Mathews et al.

FALLER

A classification scheme was developed to describe women sexual offenders by categorizing cases of sexual abuse (Faller, 1987). From this study of 40 female perpetrators and their victims, Faller identified five primary case types: Polyincestuous Abuse, Single-parent Abuse, Psychotic Abusers, Adolescent Perpetrators, and Noncustodial Abusers.

Polyincestuous Abuse included 29 (72.5%) of the women in this study. This type of sexual abuse involves at least two perpetrators and usually two or more victims. Abusers and victims from outside the household are often involved also. At least one of the dyads in this type of intrafamily abuse is probably interfamily. Group sex with children of both sexes and multiple sexually abusive relationships constitute this type of abuse.

In 24 of the 29 Polyincestuous cases, the victims suggested that men initiated the abuse. In some cases the victim indicated that the female offender was complying with instructions from the male offender. Six (15%) of the female offenders were classified as Single Parents, and did not have current relationships with men. The victims included both sexes. Three (7.5%) women were labeled Psychotic Abusers. Four other women were not psychotic at the time of the abuse; however, they had histories of psychotic episodes. Three (7.5%) of the female perpetrators were Adolescents. In general, the sexual behavior was aimed at gratification for the perpetrator rather than the victim.

One female in this study was classified as a Noncustodial Abuser. A characteristic of this type of case is that the victim serves as an emotional gratifier for the perpetrator's loss of spouse, and an outlet for her anger toward the spouse.

Faller's findings suggest that women in polyincestuous situations may be at risk for becoming perpetrators. These situations are characterized by women being persuaded or coerced by a male offender into participating in the sexual abuse. Faller further related chemical dependency, poor parenting skills, and mental difficulties to an increased vulnerability that contributed to their perpetrating the sexual abuse.

Strengths and Limitations of Faller's Classification System

Faller aptly acknowledged the female perpetrator's involvement with a male perpetrator. She classified the offenders by the nature of the crime/types of cases. She called attention to the Single Parent and Noncustodial Abusers. These terms may overlap with McCarty's Independent Offender, and Polyincestuous abuse may overlap with McCarty's Co-Offender.

However, Faller's categories are not mutually exclusive. It seems plausible that a Psychotic Abuser could be an Adolescent Perpetrator, as well as a Noncustodial Abuser. As a result, her classification system could lead to overlap and confusion.

The female perpetrators' relationships with men were not discussed. She mentioned that when the women admitted to the sexual abuse, they described being coerced by the male perpetrators. Moreover, she did not define coercion, nor address how it was carried out by the male.

Faller provided demographic characteristics and information on the psychological and social functioning of her entire sample of female perpetrators (N=40), departing from her classification system. Unfortunately, it is unclear which characteristics predominate in which categories.

Finally, the method by which she evaluated the cases is not described and no standardized instruments are noted.

COMPARISON OF THE THREE CLASSIFICATION SYSTEMS

Three classification systems for female sex offenders have been presented and discussed. These systems include information pertinent to the offenders, victims, and offenses. A summary illustrating the similarities and differences among these classification schemes is presented in Table 1.

Table 1.
Classification Similarities and Differences

MATHEWS ET AL.	MCCARTY	FALLER
PREDISPOSED	**INDEPENDENT**	**SINGLE-PARENT ABUSE CASES**
History of childhood sexual abuse. As adults, nitiated child sex abuse.	History of childhood sexual abuse. As adults, initiated child sex abuse	Sexual abuse
History of sexual indiscretion/promiscuity.	History of sexual indiscretion/promiscuity.	
Substance abuse problem.	Substance abuse problem.	
Victim is most often a daughter.	Victim is most often a daughter.	Both male and female victims.
Explicit sexual acts with victims.	Male victims viewed as adult male substitutes.	Oldest child victim viewed as surrogate partner.
Believed to have an unstable employment history.	Described as able to maintain employment.	
Not seriously emotionally disturbed/psychotic.	Serious emotional disturbance.	
MALE-COERCED	**CO-OFFENDER**	**POLYINCESTUOUS CASES**
History of childhood sexual abuse (abused by more than one family member).	History of childhood sexual abuse, primarily by adult caretakers.	Coerced by male.
Coerced by male.	Coerced by male.	
Dependent on men.	Dependent on men.	
Strong need to be taken care of.	Strong need to be taken care of.	
Married at a young age.	Married at a young age.	
Not emotionally disturbed	Not emotionally disturbed.	

Need for Male and Female Systems of Classifications

There are difficulties with both male and female classification systems. Many female sexual offenders may well fit the categories regressed or situational; however, neither system takes into account whether the offender acted alone or with an accomplice. In addition, neither differentiates between the sexual abuse being intra- or interfamilial.

From the descriptions and classifications of male and female sexual offenders, there appear to be significant differences between groups of sexual perpetrators. Wolfe (1985) compared male and female sexual offenders and found the following differences: women offenders rarely attempt to coerce the victim into providing direct sexual stimulation; males rarely rationalize their behavior in terms of dependency; male offenders connect ejaculation with the offense, whereas few women associate orgasm with the sexual offense; women offenders also tend to be less educated than a comparable sample of male offenders.

For classification purposes, if most female sex abusers offend in concert with a male partner, female offenders may be more appropriately classified by whether they offended independently, co-offended, or were accomplices. Additionally, coercion and/or dependency variables must be considered for co-offenders and accomplices.

Neither the systems for classifying male sexual offenders nor those used to classify female sexual offenders are complete or precise. Given apparent differences in male and female sexual offenses, separate classification schemes are required for men and women. This study focuses on clarifying and expanding our knowledge of accomplices and co-offenders by providing analyses of these categories, building on the works of McCarty and Mathews et al.

CHAPTER 3

Statement of the Problem

Exploring Women's Motivations to Abuse

Theories of women's development indicate that women gain their sense of self via affiliations with others; for men, identity comes before intimacy (Bardwick, 1971; Gilligan, 1982; Notman, et al., 1986). Women were once, and some possibly still are, conforming to prescribed sex roles of dependency and passivity. Research into women's participation in violent crimes describes their roles as secondary and supportive, in keeping with their sex roles.

Female sexual offenders' relationships have been characterized as dependent and entered into with men who are dominating and controlling. In these dependent relationships, it has been suggested that women co-offend with men due to force, coercion, or persuasion to participate in the sexual abuse (Mathews, et al., 1989; Faller, 1987). Further investigation of the dynamics of these dependent relationships is warranted.

Research Questions

Current research in the area of female sexual offenders falls short of providing a precise and coherent system for classifying these women. Noticeably absent is a consensus about the ways in which Co-Offenders and Accomplices may be similar and/or different. Further, the variables of dependency and coercion have not been examined in relation to these two classifications, despite evidence that female perpetrators offend in concert with a male offender.

This study concentrates on groups of female sexual offenders classified as Co-Offenders and Accomplices. The overall purpose of the study is to examine these groups to provide clearer descriptions and better analysis of these categories than have been made previously. Second, this study may provide information about the relationship with a significant male in child sexual abuse. The contributory factors, if any, which are a part of the women's past and present relationships with men, are examined in a semi-structured interview, as well as through information obtained from a questionnaire.

The purpose of this study is to focus on the women who commit these crimes with male partners, with special attention to McCarty's classification system, though not accepting it as definitive. Her system is descriptive of the acts committed but does not provide psychological characteristics. The categories Accomplice and Co-Offender are examined to provide more precise descriptions in the classification of female sex offenders. This study focuses on the offense(s) the subjects were convicted of which led to their incarceration. Exploration of subjects' lifelong patterns was reserved as an option, should the data emerge in this direction. The Minnesota Multiphasic Personality Inventory (MMPI-2) was used to ascertain personality patterns and/or pathology, and to see if there are personality patterns that may preclude the type(s) of abuse a woman engages in that are more independent of demographic information.

This study may provide information about the women's relationships with significant males in child sexual abuse. This research asks the following questions:

1. What, if any, demographic, behavioral, and psychological charteristics depict female Co-Offenders and Accomplices?

2. What are the commonalities and differences between female Co-Offenders and Accomplices in cases of child sexual abuse?

3. Are there elements such as sexual abuse or physical abuse in the woman's current or past history that contribute to her involvement in a dependent relationship and involvement in the child sexual abuse?

4. What are the elements of coercion, force, and/or persuasion related to the commission of the child sexual abuse?

      a. Was the woman and/or child threatened with physical force and/or abandonment if she refused to comply?

      b. Was the woman and/or child assaulted?

      c. What type(s) of force was used?

      d. Was there emotional and/or economic reprisal involved?

      e. Were there bribes or enticements?

5. Was chemical dependency involved in the relationship between the female Co-Offender and the male Co-Defendant?

6. Was chemical dependency involved in the commission of the offense?

CHAPTER 4

Method

Subjects and Sampling Criteria

The subjects in this study were 76 female sexual offenders, incarcerated in seven states for crimes of child sexual abuse with minors under the age of 18. These offenses included as victims the subjects' own biological children as well as stepchildren and nonfamilial children.

The subjects were classified as Co-Offenders (women who actively participated in the sexual abuse) or Accomplices (women who facilitated/assisted in the sexual abuse, but did not actively participate in it) based on the crime(s) they were convicted of which led to their incarceration. During the subject selection process, it became clear that there were several incarcerated Independent Offenders; therefore, this classification was added to this research.

Inclusion criteria included:

1. The subjects must be at least 18 years of age.

2. The subjects must have privileges within the institution to allow for an interview without a correctional officer's presence.

3. The subjects must be able to read and speak English.

Exclusion criteria included:

1. Subjects who appear to be confused to the point of inability to provide reliable or reasonable information (as determined during the interview).

2. Subjects who are actively hallucinating and/or are violent (as determined via prison records or during the interview).

3. Subjects who appear to lack competency to give legal consent to participation (as determined by clinical judgment).

Special considerations must be addressed in studying an incarcerated population: 1) the prisoners' time constraints, as well as the prison system's; and 2) the importance of the prison administration and staff's willingness to create the time and space to conduct the study. In a prison setting, it is not feasible to conduct more than one extensive individual interview with each subject, as prisoners are unable to set their own schedules and create available time.

Participation in this study was voluntary, and the subjects' identities and any connection between the material and their identities is kept confidential. Due to the subjects' limited rights and limited free consent, the following provisions and assurances were given to obtain informed consent:

1. The subjects could withdraw from the study at any time without affecting their status or legal rights.

2. The researcher could conclude the interview early and not include the data in the study.

3. Subjects' participation or nonparticipation would not become a part of their institutional records.

4. Subjects' participation in this study would have no effect on decisions relating to their release, institutional treatment, housing, or other benefits.

5. All tests and materials would be maintained by the researcher outside of the institution, and at no time would materials be reviewed by prison personnel (refer to the Informed Consent Form in Appendix A).

Instruments

MMPI-2

The Minnesota Multiphasic Personality Inventory (MMPI-2, Hathaway & McKinley, 1989) was administered in a group setting to ascertain subjects' personality characteristics. This instrument consists of 567 items, to which subjects were asked to respond "true" or "false."

The normative data are based on a national sample of 1,138 male and 1,462 female clinical subjects, ranging in age from 18 to 84 and above. This normative sample is much larger and more nationally representative than that of the original MMPI.

Some of the items are taken from the original MMPI and others were designed to expand test coverage. A total of 84% of the MMPI items are found in the MMPI-2 in an original or revised form (Archer, 1992). Original items that contained sexist and/or obsolete language were reworded, and sentence structure was improved or simplified. The order of the items was changed so that all of the Basic Scales may be scored from the first 370 items.

The standard validity and clinical scales of the MMPI have been carried over into the MMPI-2. The MMPI-2 retains the statistical properties for reliability, validity, and standard error of the MMPI (Archer, 1992; Nichols, 1992). The reliability and validity for this instrument are satisfactory for the purposes of this study.

This test was scored by National Computer Systems and a report emerged in the form of a profile report, which contains plotted scale scores. These types of scores can be used for comparison within individuals as well as between them.

PRE-SENTENCING INVESTIGATION REPORTS

The subjects' Pre-Sentencing Investigation reports (PSI's) were examined to obtain the following:

1. Demographic information including age, race, age at time of offense, education, marital status, and co-offender information.

2. The nature of the offense, including a detailed description of the offense.

3. Information regarding the victim(s), including age, race, sex, and relationship to the perpetrator.

The consent to review the PSI's may be found in Appendix B.

STRUCTURED INTERVIEW

The Structured Interview (see Appendix C) was composed of questions created by the researcher, as well as some questions from other sources. This part of the interview included the following topics:

1. Demographic information containing subject's date of birth, race, education, number of children, and employment information.

2. The subject's history of physical and/or sexual abuse (adapted from Walker, 1984).

3. Family data, including the subject's personal history regarding sex and dating (adapted from Nims, 1979).

4. Information about the subject's relationship with the codefendant (adapted from Walker, 1984).

5. Information about the victim (e.g., the subject's relationship to the victim and the victim's age and sex).

6. The exact nature of the abuse (e.g., activity; time frame; frequency; means of force, coercion, and/or persuasion).

The results of this instrument were tabulated. This interview was conducted individually by the researcher, with no custodial personnel present.

Procedure

Wardens of the various prison systems were contacted to determine the specific procedures and contact persons necessary to conduct research in each institution. The Wardens also appointed a contact person to identify prospective subjects.

Prospective subjects met with the researcher in a group setting, at which time they completed Informed Consent forms. Whenever possible, the MMPI-2 was administered in a group setting.

Individual interviews were conducted by the researcher with 76 subjects in a structured interview format. The initial portion of the interview established demographic information. The interview proceeded with gathering information about the subjects' families, sex histories, and sexual experiences. Material specific to the subjects' histories of sexual and/or physical abuse was obtained. Information was collected regarding the subjects' relationships with the codefendants, as well as information specific to the offense.

The interviews took approximately 1 hour, and were conducted with only the subject and researcher present. Each subject was identified by a number only (no names) for scoring purposes and to ensure confidentiality.

Prior to the collection of data for this study, a pilot study was done using all of the instruments. This pilot study assisted with evaluating the content and structure of the questionnaire and the interview formats and topics, as well as evaluating their administration.

CHAPTER 5

Results

Data Analysis

The responses generated from the results of the MMPI-2 and the Structured Interview comprise the data for analysis in this study. Standard descriptive statistics were used initially on the data obtained from the MMPI-2 and the Structured Interview on three groups (Co-Offenders, Accomplices, and Independent Offenders) similar in age, race, and education. A first consideration was to determine whether the groups were different in any respect. To answer this question, t-test procedures were used for the ordinal value variables.

Chi-square tests were used for nominal value variables to assess group differences. Discriminant Analysis was used to define the personality characteristics (as measured by the MMPI-2) and the variables from the Structured Interview most helpful in distinguishing one group from the other. Such groupings would clarify differences between the samples.

Subject Demographics

This research was designed to study women in the Accomplice and Co-Offender categories. During the subject selection process in the various prison systems, it became clear that the number of incarcerated Independent Offenders was nearly equal to the number of Co-Offenders, and the number of Accomplices was small in comparison. The author decided to interview women who fit the descriptions of all three categories.

For purposes of clarity, the Co-Offender group was renamed Accomplice/Active (women who actively participated in the sexual abuse), and the Accomplice group was renamed Accomplice/Passive (women who facilitated/assisted in the sexual abuse, but did not actively participate in it).

The study sample consisted of 76 female sexual offenders, incarcerated in 12 prisons in seven states (representing West and East Coasts of the United States), for crimes of sexual abuse of minors under the age of 18. Of the 76 subjects, 30 were classified as Independent Offenders, 35 as Accomplice/Active Offenders, and 11 as Accomplice/Passive Offenders. Because the sample size is relatively small (fewer than 100 subjects), a change of one response would be more than 1%; therefore, the results should be interpreted with caution.

A total of 30 women denied paticipating in the offense (4 in the Accomplice/Passive group, 14 in the Accomplice/active group, and 12 in the Independent group) and maintained their denial through the trial and incarceration. Information obtained from these subjects in relation to the offense is based on the charges of which they were convicted and the contents of their Pre-Sentencing Investigation Reports.

Tables 2.1–2.6 illustrate the demographic information for the three groups: Accomplice/Passive, Accomplice/Active, and the Independent Offenders. The most recent statistics (1986) from a nationally representative sample of women incarcerated in State prisons are also included (U.S. Department of Justice, 1991).

AGE

The 35 participants in the Accomplice/Active group ranged in age from 25 to 67, with a mean age of 37. The women in this group are older than the women in the other groups. In general, women sex offenders are in their 30s (see Table 2.1).

ETHNICITY

Table 2.2 shows that the majority of the participants in this study are Caucasian. The category "other race" for the Independent Offenders Group is Native American. The national statistics show that the majority of women in prison are Black.

Table 2.1
Age

	ACCOMPLICE/ PASSIVE $n=11$	ACCOMPLICE/ ACTIVE $n=35$	INDEPENDENT $n=30$	NATIONAL $n=19,812$
RANGE				
	28–41	25–67	21–45	18–64
MEAN				
	33.5	37.0	31.8	31.1
SD				
	5.2	7.4	6.5	—

Note: For national statistics, 3.1 is an approximation of average age. SD is not available.

Table 2.2
Ethnicity

	ACCOMPLICE/ PASSIVE $n=11$	ACCOMPLICE/ ACTIVE $n=35$	INDEPENDENT $n=30$	NATIONAL $n=19,812$
BLACK				
	18.2%	8.6%	13.3%	46.2%
CAUCASIAN				
	72.7%	88.5%	73.3%	39.6%
HISPANIC				
	9.1%	2.9%	6.7%	11.7%
OTHER RACE				
	0.0%	0.0%	6.7%	2.5%
TOTAL				
	100.0%	100.0%	100.0%	100.0%

M=3.0 (response #3 caucasian)   SD=.05

EDUCATION

The level of education completed by the participants, shown in Table 2.3, indicates that nearly half of all groups (45.5% in the Accomplice/Passive group, 42.9% in the Accomplice/Active group, and 44.8% in the Independent group)

Table 2.3
Education

	ACCOMPLICE/ ACTIVE *n*=11	ACCOMPLICE/ PASSIVE *n*=35	INDEPENDENT *n*=30	NATIONAL *n*=19,812
8TH GRADE OR LESS				
27.2%	11.3%	17.2%	16.4%
SOME HIGH SCHOOL				
27.3%	22.9%	24.1%	40.4%
HIGH SCHOOL GRADUATE				
45.5%	42.9%	44.8%	28.4%
SOME COLLEGE OR >				
0.0%	22.9%	13.9%	14.8%
TOTAL				
100.0%	100.0%	100.0%	100.0%

M=11.2   SD=2.1

Note: M & SD not available for national statistics

completed the 12th grade, via actual attendance in school as well as completing the GED. In the Accomplice/Active group, 6 participants had taken some college courses, and 2 had Master's degrees. The women in the Accomplice/Active group have nearly twice as much college education as women in the Independent group. Of the participants in the Independent group, 4 had taken some college courses. The women in this study have more education than the women in the national sample.

MARITAL STATUS

Table 2.4 shows that marital status among the groups is diverse. Nearly half of the women in the Accomplice/passive group are divorced, and a little over a quarter are married. In the Accomplice/active group, nearly as many partici-

Table 2.4
Marital Status

	ACCOMPLICE/ ACTIVE *n=11*	ACCOMPLICE/ PASSIVE *n=35*	INDEPENDENT *n=30*	NATIONAL *n=19,812*
MARRIED				
	27.2%	11.3%	13.4%	20.1%
WIDOWED				
	0.0%	2.9%	3.3%	6.7%
DIVORCED				
	45.5%	37.1%	33.3%	20.5%
SEPARATED				
	9.1%	11.4%	0.0%	11.0%
NEVER MARRIED				
	18.2%	8.6%	50.0%	41.7%
TOTAL				
	100.0%	100.0%	10.0%	100.0%

Note: M & SD not available for national statistics

pants are divorced as are married. In the Independent Offender group, fewer than a quarter are married. Fifty percent of the participants in the Independent group had never been married. The national statistics also reflect a large number of women who never married. Because there were no available national comparison statistics for nonmarried relationships (either lesbian or heterosexual), those data were not collected for this study.

CHILDREN

The 76 participants have, in total, 190 children (including stepchildren), with a mean of 2.5. The average age of the children is 12.8 years (see Table 2.5). At the national level, 32% of the women have 1 child, and 29% have 2 to 4 children. National statistics regarding children's ages are not available.

Table 2.5
Children

	ACCOMPLICE/ PASIVE *n*=11	ACCOMPLICE/ ACTIVE *n*=35	INDEPENDENT *n*=30
NUMBER OF CHILDREN			
Mean	3.2	3.3	2.6
SD	1.3	1.5	1.4
Range	2–6	0–7	0–6
AGE			
Mean	11.5	14.0	10.5
SD	5.2	6.9	6.1
Range	1–32	2–38	1–25

Note: These figures include stepchildren

OCCUPATION

The longest period of time the participants held a job, shown in Table 2.6, ranged from zero (no job) to 25 years. The groups' participants are categorized in terms of types of jobs held, ranging from 1 to 5 (low-level to high-level job). Examples of low-level (level 1) jobs include: baby-sitting, factory work, fast food employee; level 2: retail sales, cashier, waitress/cook; level 3: assistant supervisory positions, sales, clerical/secretary; level 4: dental assistant, retail management; and high-level (level 5) jobs: teacher, Registered Nurse. The women in the Accomplice/Active group had higher level jobs than the women in the Independent Offender group. Most of the women in this study held low-level and semi-skilled jobs. There are no national statistics on offender employment levels.

Table 2.6
Employment

(1–5= low to high level jobs)	ACCOMPLICE/ PASSIVE *n*=11	ACCOMPLICE/ ACTIVE *n*=35	INDEPENDENT *n*=30
NO JOB			
	9.0%	5.7%	10.0%
1			
	45.5%	17.1%	46.7%
2			
	45.5%	34.3%	23.3%
3			
	0.0%	28.6%	10.0%
4			
	1.0%	5.7%	3.3%
5			
	0.0%	8.6%	6.7%
TOTAL			
	100.0%	100.0%	100.0%

M=20   SD=1.3

Comparison of Accomplice Groups

A one-way ANOVA found that on these demographic variables, as well as the MMPI-2, there are no significant differences between the Accomplice/Active and Accomplice/Passive groups. Examination of the data obtained from the Structured Interview also revealed very few differences between these groups. In some instances, the questions asked of the women in the Accomplice/Passive group did not apply to them. For example, several women in this group were not married to or living with the codefendant; therefore, questions regarding relationship with the codefendant were not applicable. As a result, the number of respondents was so low that meaningful analysis was not possible. No distinguishing differences emerged between these two groups in terms of demographics, histories, behaviors, or psychometrics.

Table 3
Family Data

	CO-OFFENDERS		INDEPENDENTS	
BIOLOGICAL PARENTS				
	26	56.5%	16	53.4%
MOTHER				
	1	2.2%	2	6.7%
FATHER				
	0	0.0%	1	3.3%
FOSTER				
	0	0.0%	1	3.3%
OTHER				
	19	41.3%	10	33.3%
TOTAL				
	100%	100.0%	30	100.0%

Statistics for Table 3

Statistic	DF	Value	Prob
Chi-Square	4	4.3	0.363

COMBINING ACCOMPLICE/PASSIVE AND ACCOMPLICE/ACTIVE GROUPS

The women in this study were categorized into three groups for the reader's convenience. As previously stated, no significant differences were found between the Accomplice/Passive and the Accomplice/Active groups. Conceptually, these two groups are both Co-Offenders — they are all women who offended with a male. The 76 participants in this study were raised by their biological parents

(Co-Offenders=56.5% and Independent Offenders=53.3%). Forty-one percent of the Co-Offenders and 33 percent of the Independent Offenders were raised by "other" than their biological parents (this category represents mixes of biological and stepparents).

Table 4.1
Relationship with Mother-Figure

N	MEAN	STD DEV	STD ERROR
CO-OFFENDER			
8	1.50	2.27	0.80
INDEPENDENT			
7	1.29	2.21	0.84

Variances	T	DF	Prob>|T|
Equal	0.1846	13.0	0.8564

For HO: Variances are equal
$F'=1.05$ $DF=(7, 6)$ Prob>F'=0.970

Table 4.2
Relationship with Father-Figure

N	MEAN	STD DEV	STD ERROR
CO-OFFENDER			
15	– 0.13	2.70	0.70
INDEPENDENT			
11	– 0.09	2.51	0.76

Variances	T	DF	Prob>|T|
Equal	– 0.0408	24.0	0.9678

For HO: Variances are equal
$F'=116$ $DF=(14, 10)$ Prob>F'=0.8359

Table 4.3
Relationship with Mother

N	MEAN	STD DEV	STD ERROR
CO-OFFENDER			
42	0.90	2.39	0.37
INDEPENDENT			
25	0.96	1.95	0.39

Variances	T	DF	Prob>|T|
Equal	– 0.0979	65.0	0.9223

For HO: Variances are equal
$F'=1.50$ $DF=(41, 24)$ $Prob>F'=0.2899$

Table 4.4
Relationship with Father

N	MEAN	STD DEV	STD ERROR
CO-OFFENDER			
33	0.82	2.47	0.43
INDEPENDENT			
23	1.30	2.24	0.47

Variances	T	DF	Prob>|T|
Equal	– 0.7522	54.0	0.4552

For HO: Variances are equal
$F'=1.21$ $DF=(32, 22)$ $Prob>F'=0.6514$

The researcher wondered about the women's relationships with guardians or their mothers and fathers. Information gathered in the Structured Interview (see Appendix C) regarding the women's perception of their relationships with their parents and/or guardians (ranked on a Likert-type scale from -3 negative to +3 positive) was analyzed. The resulting data (Tables 4.1-4.4) show no significant difference between the two groups in relating to their parent-figures.

SEXUAL EXPERIENCES

Both groups learned to masturbate via self-discovery or from friends. Table 5 shows that the Independent Offenders began masturbating at a younger age compared to the Co-Offenders.

Table 5
Age of First Masturbation

N	MEAN	STD DEV	STD ERROR
CO-OFFENDER			
40	16.3	8.5	1.3
INDEPENDENT			
26	14.6	6.1	1.2

Variances	T	DF	Prob>|T|
Equal	0.89	64.0	0.378

For HO: Variances are equal
$F'=1.94$ $DF=(39, 25)$ Prob>F'=0.083

DATING

While the Co-Offenders and Independent Offenders began dating at similar ages (mean 15.4 and 15.9, respectively), Table 6 indicates significant differences between the groups related to satisfaction with dating experiences. The Independent Offenders indicate more satisfaction with dating (1.56 mean on a scale ranging from -3 to +3) than the Co-Offenders (.60 mean). This difference is statistically significant at the .05 level.

SEXUAL EXPERIENCES WITH MEN

The initial data analysis indicated the Co-Offenders had an average of 47 male sexual partners, and the Independent Offenders had an average of 39. One Co-Offender reported 999 male sexual partners, attributing this number to her years in prostitution. One Independent Offender reported she had been a prostitute, claiming 400 male sexual partners. Two women in the Independent Offender group reported no peer heterosexual experiences. When the two extreme numbers and the two women with no heterosexual experiences were eliminated, the two groups appear nearly identical (Co-Offender Group Mean = 25.8 and Independent Offender Group Mean = 28.5).

Table 6
Satisfaction with Dating

N	MEAN	STD DEV	STD ERROR
CO-OFFENDER			
45	0.6	2.0	0.3
INDEPENDENT			
25	1.6	1.9	0.4

Variances	T	DF	Prob>|T|
Equal	– 1.94	68.0	0.056

For HO: Variances are equal
$F'=1.07$ $DF=(44, 24)$ $Prob>F'=0.8807$

Table 7 shows the report of the women's satisfaction with these sexual experiences. The Independent Offenders indicate a more positive satisfaction level compared to the Co-Offenders. This is an interesting finding in that although the Independent Offenders also report more satisfaction with dating, 50% never married.

HISTORY OF VIOLENCE

As we would expect, during childhood, most of the women had been physically and psychologically abused (see Table 8). The unexpected finding is that mothers were the primary abusers.

The Co-Offenders and Independent Offenders did not differ significantly regarding frequency of "spankings" received between birth and 18 years of age. The groups did significantly differ, however, with respect to the frequency they

Table 7
Satisfaction with Sexual Experiences with Men

N	MEAN	STD DEV	STD ERROR
CO-OFFENDER			
46	– 0.3	2.3	0.3
INDEPENDENT			
28	1.0	2.4	0.4

Variances	T	DF	Prob>|T|
Equal	– 2.3	72.0	0.026

For HO: Variances are equal
$F'=1.06$ $DF=(27, 45)$ Prob$>F'=0.8534$

Table 8
Physical and Psychological Abuse

	CO-OFFENDERS		OFFENDERS	
NONE				
	12	26.1%	13	43.3%
PSYCHOLOGICAL				
	9	19.6%	6	20.0%
PHYSICAL AND PSYCHOLOGICAL				
	25	54.3%	11	36.7%
TOTAL				
	46	100.0%	30	100.0%

Statistics for Table 8

Statistic	DF	Value	Prob
Chi–Square	2	2.8	0.241

Table 9
Frequency of Spanking with Objects

	CO-OFFENDERS		INDEPENDENTS	
NEVER				
	7	15.6%	11	36.7%
ONCE				
	3	6.7%	0	0.0%
2 OR 3 TIMES				
	7	15.6%	6	20.0%
> 2 OR 3 TIMES				
	11	24.3%	7	23.3%
OFTEN				
	16	35.6%	6	20.0%
NO RECALL				
	1	2.2%	0	0.0%
TOTAL				
	45	100.0%	30	100.0%

Note: In the Co-Offender Group, one response was recorded "n/a" rather than "never." That response was excluded.

Statistics for Table 9

Statistic	DF	Value	Prob
Chi-Square	5	7.7	0.173

were spanked with an object. Table 9 shows that the Co-Offenders were spanked far more often (82%) than the Independent Offenders (63%), and more often with objects. The Co-Offenders were punished more severely and more frequently. For both groups, the most commonly used object used is a belt.

SEXUAL ABUSE AS A CHILD

These findings are based on what the subjects were willing or able to report regarding their histories as victims of sex abuse in childhood. The majority of

Table 10
Sexual Abuse Victimization

	CO-OFFENDERS		INDEPENDENTS	
NO				
	10	22.2%	7	24.1%
YES				
	35	77.8%	22	75.9%
TOTAL				
	45	100.0%	29	100.0%

Note: One subject in each group (Co-Offenders and Independents) recorded "n/a" rather than "no." Those responses were excluded.

Statistics for Table 10

Statistic	DF	Value	Prob
Chi-Square	1	0.04	0.848

the individuals in both groups were reportedly sexually abused as children (77.8% and 75.9%, respectively). Table 10 shows these results.

Of those reporting a history of sexual abuse, over 60% were abused by male relatives (predominantly uncles and brothers). While none of the Co-Offenders reported being sexually abused by their mothers, 3 of the Independent Offenders were, and 1 woman was abused by her foster mother. Relationships of Co-Offenders and Independent Offenders who reported being sexually abused as children to their abusers are shown in Table 11.

Natural, step-, adoptive-, and foster fathers and mothers account for 54.4% of abusers reported by Independent Offenders, and 37.2% of abusers reported by Co-Offenders.

AGE AT ONSET OF SEXUAL ABUSE

There are no statistically significant differences between the groups regarding age at the beginning of their own sexual abuse. Table 12 shows these results.

Table 11
Sexual Abusers of
Women Offenders

	CO-OFFENDERS		INDEPENDENTS	
FATHER				
	8	22.9%	5	22.7%
MOTHER				
	0	0.0%	3	13.6%
MALE RELATIVE				
	24	68.6%	14	63.6%
FEMALE RELATIVE				
	1	2.9%	0	0.0%
MALE STRANGER				
	4	11.4%	0	0.0%
STEP-FATHER				
	5	14.3%	0	0.0%
ADOPTIVE FATHER				
	0	0.0%	1	4.5%
MALE ACQUAINTANCE				
	7	20.0%	5	22.7%
FOSTER MOTHER				
	0	0.0%	1	4.5%
FOSTER FATHER				
	0	0.0%	2	9.1%
TOTAL				
	49	140.1%	31	140.7%

Note: Totals exceed 100% because some subjects were victims of multiple abusers.

Table 12
Age at Onset of Sex Abuse

N	MEAN	STD DEV	STD ERROR
CO-OFFENDER			
12	7.3	1.7	0.5
INDEPENDENT			
16	6.3	2.0	0.5

Variances	T	DF	Prob>|T|
Equal	1.4	26.0	0.163

For HO: Variances are equal
$F'=0.5631$

DURATION OF THE SEXUAL ABUSE

Table 13 shows that the Co-Offenders and the Independent Offenders are essentially similar in terms of duration of their own sexually abusive experiences.

Table 13
Duration of Sex Abuse

N	MEAN	STD DEV	STD ERROR
CO-OFFENDER			
12	4.9	3.3	0.9
INDEPENDENT			
16	5.6	4.8	1.2

Variances	T	DF	Prob>|T|
Equal	– 0.439	26.0	0.665

For HO: Variances are equal
$F'=2.13$ $DF=(15, 11)$ Prob>$F'=0.2094$

SEXUAL ABUSE BEFORE AGE 10

No apparent differences were noted between the Co-Offenders and the Independent Offenders when they were initially asked about their histories of sexual abuse. There were also no initial apparent differences between groups regarding who sexually abused them. When these women were asked in detail about their histories of sexual abuse, differences between the groups began to emerge.

There are statistically significant differences between the groups related to sexual abuse occurring before the age of 10 and the severity of the abuse. Approximately half of the Independent Offenders reportedly experienced sexual abuse through acts that went beyond fondling, before age 10, but only a quarter of the Co-Offenders reported such experiences. Sexual abuse consisting of several acts of intercourse, beginning before age 10, was experienced by 30% of the Independent Offenders, compared to 10.8% of the Co-Offenders. A significant difference is evident between the groups related to the women experiencing sexual abuse in the form of several acts of oral sex, commencing before they were 10 years of age. Half of the Independent Offenders reported this type of sexual abuse; only 15% of the Co-Offenders reported this type of sexual abuse. Table 14 shows the differences between the two groups in relation to the types of sexual activities experienced as children before age 10.

Table 14
Acts of Sexual Abuse / Onset Before Age 10

CO-OFFENDER		INDEPENDENTS		PROB
No	Yes	No	Yes	Chi-Square
ACTS > FONDLING				
34	12	14	12	.016
73.9%	26.1%	46.7%	53.3%	
SEVERAL ACTS OF INTERCOURSE				
41	5	21	9	.035
89.1%	10.9%	70.0%	30.0%	
SEVERAL ACTS OF ORAL SEX				
39	7	15	15	.001
84.8%	15.2%	50.0%	50.0%	

Note: Totals may exceed 100% due to multiple responses.

In summary, the findings shown in Table 14 indicate that the Independent Offenders were significantly seriously sexually abused in duration and severity before age 10. This may explain the significant psychological differences between the groups as also shown in MMPI-2 results later in this chapter. Herman, Russell, and Trocki (1986) studied women and the effects of childhood sexual abuse and found that severe, prolonged sexual abuse in childhood resulted in negative effects with long-term psychological consequences. This finding is confirmed in this study.

Characteristics of the Crime

The characteristics of the crimes for which the subjects were convicted are as follows:

LOCATION

The majority (84.7%) of Co-Offenders' offenses occurred in their homes; only 50% in the Independent Offender group took place there. The others occurred in a relative's home or other private setting (e.g., neighbor's home, friend's home, child's home). Table 15 lists these statistics.

Table 15
Location of the Offense

CO-OFFENDER		INDEPENDENTS		PROB
HOME				
39	84.8%	15	50.0%	.001
RELATIVE'S HOME				
2	4.4%	3	10.0%	.331
PRIVATE SETTING				
6	13.0%	11	36.7%	.016
CAR				
2	4.4%	1	3.3%	.824
PUBLIC				
0	0.0%	2	6.7%	.076

Note: Totals may exceed 100% due to multiple locations.

SEXUAL
ACTIVITIES

Information regarding the types of sexually abusive behaviors was collected using data from the Structured Interview (Appendix C). The unit of analysis was each type of sexual behavior perpetrated by a given woman on each child. For instance, a woman may have repeatedly performed fellatio on a boy victim, but these acts would be considered one type of abuse. The sexual activities were categorized into 14 types, and the findings appear in Table 16.

The activities reported by the Co-Offenders are: oral sex (76%), the adult fondling the child (74%), the child fondling the adult (61%), and intercourse (41%). These figures represent the activities that reportedly occurred during the offense, which included a male codefendant; therefore, they are representative of the activities in general. They are not indicative of the activities of the female sole offender. However, these women reported they observed and/or assisted the codefendant in the abuse.

The sexually abusive activities reported by the Independent Offenders are: the adult fondled the child (83%), oral sex (74%), the child fondled the adult (47%), and digital penetration (50%). These figures are indicative of the acts by these women in that they acted alone in the commission of the offense.

Previous studies have indicated that fondling is the most common type of sexual abuse (Allen, 1991; Faller, 1987; Finkelhor, 1979; Russell, 1986). This study shows that fondling is the most common for the Independent Offenders; however, it ranks second among the Co-Offenders.

There are significant differences between the two groups of women offenders in terms of types of sexual activities. For instance, there are four offending behaviors that reportedly never occurred in the Independent Offender group, but did occur in the Co-Offender group. These include: child watches others have sex, others watch child have sex, group sex, and ritualistic sex. The only activity that did not occur in either group is satanic sex. The terms "ritualistic sex" and "satanic sex" were presented in the Structured Interview without definition. Only 6% of the Independent Offenders reported anal sex as a part of the sexual abuse, but 32% of the Co-Offenders reported this type. Sexual abuse involving intercourse was reported by over half the Co-Offenders, compared to 13% of the Independent Offenders (see Table 16). No analysis was done on any possible correlation between the type of activity and the age of the victim. The findings related to anal sex and intercourse should be viewed cautiously, as they were reportedly performed by the male partner.

Table 16
Offense — Sexual Activities

CO-OFFENDER		INDEPENDENTS		PROB CHI-SQUARE
FONDLED A TO C				
34	73.9%	25	83.3%	.335
FONDLED C TO A				
28	60.9%	14	46.7%	.224
CHILD WATCHES OTHERS HAVE SEX				
19	41.3%	0	0.0%	.000
OTHERS WATCH CHILD HAVE SEX				
9	19.6%	0	0.0%	.010
SEX WITH OTHER KIDS				
6	13.0%	2	6.7%	.376
GROUP SEX				
4	8.7%	0	0.0%	.097
VIDEOS/PHOTOS TAKEN				
9	19.6%	2	6.7%	.118
DIGITAL PENETRATION				
16	34.8%	15	50.0%	.187
S-M; BONDAGE				
3	6.5%	1	3.3%	.543
SATANIC SEX				
0	0.0%	0	0.0%	—
RITUALISTIC SEX				
1	2.2%^	0	0.0%	.416
ANAL SEX				
15	32.6%	2	6.7%	.008
ORAL SEX				
35	76.1%	22	73.3%	.786
INTERCOURSE MALE PARTNER				
27	58.7%	4	13.3%	.000

Note: Totals may exceed 100% due to multiple activities.

Table 17
Offense — Sexual Acts Performed by Female Offenders

CO-OFFENDER		INDEPENDENTS		TOTAL
ORAL SEX ADULT TO CHILD				
15	36.6%	21	65.5%	36
ORAL SEX CHILD TO ADULT				
16	39.0%	7	21.9%	23
INTERCOURSE WITH FEMALE OFFENDER				
10	24.4%	4	12.6%	14
TOTAL				
41	100.0%	32	100.0%	73

Statistics for Table 17

Statistic	DF	Value	Prob
Chi-Square	2	6.1	0.048

SEXUAL ACTIVITIES PERFORMED BY FEMALE OFFENDERS. Following a detailed examination of the data regarding oral sex and intercourse, Table 17 reveals additional significant differences between the groups. Well over half of the sexual activities reported by Independent Offenders involved performing oral sex on victims, compared to 37% of the Co-Offenders. Sexual intercourse performed by the Co-Offenders constituted nearly a quarter of these activities, compared to 12.6% for Independent Offenders.

NUMBER OF OCCURRENCES. Nearly half the Independent Offenders (43%) reported the sexual abuse occurred one time, but only 27% of the Co-Offenders reported a single occurrence. The groups show similar results, reporting the sexual abuse occurred more than five times (Co-Offenders= 32%, Independent Offenders= 36%). Table 18 shows these results.

DURATION

Table 19 reveals a significant difference in duration of abuse. The results indicate the sexual abuse took place during a 1-day period for 43% of Independent

Table 18
Number of Occurrences

	CO-OFFENDERS		INDEPENDENT	
1 TIME				
	12	27.9%	13	43.3%
2 TIMES				
	3	6.9%	1	3.3%
3 – 5 TIMES				
	14	32.6%	5	16.7%
>5 TIMES				
	14	32.6%	11	36.7%
TOTAL				
	43	100.0%	30	100.0%

Note: Three responses in the Co-Offender Group were given as "unknown"; they were excluded from the data.

Offenders and only 27% of the Co-Offenders. Particularly significant is the finding that 29.6% of the Co-Offenders indicate the sexual abuse took place over a period of 2-5 years, but no Independent Offenders reported sexually abusing any victims for this length of time.

VICTIMS

The women had a total of 135 victims (Co-Offenders= 93 victims, Independent Offenders= 42 victims). For the Co-Offenders, there were a total of 42 male victims and 51 female victims. For the Independent Offenders, there were a total of 15 male victims and 27 female victims. Table 20 shows these results.

For the Co-Offenders, 71.7% were mothers to their victims. In contrast, only 23.3% of the Independent Offenders were mothers to their victims. The majority of victims of the Independent Offenders are acquaintances, including children they were baby-sitting (36.7%). An interesting finding is there were no multiple victims for the Independent Offenders. The victims were not known to the Co-Offenders and the Independent Offenders in only 4.3% and 3.3.% of the cases, respectively. Table 21 reveals the results of the perpetrator-victim relationships.

Table 19
Duration of Sexually Abusive Activities

	CO-OFFENDERS		INDEPENDENT	
1 DAY				
	12	27.3%	14	46.7%
SEVERAL DAYS				
	2	4.6%	0	0.0%
1 WEEK				
	0	0.0%	1	3.3%
SEVERAL WEEKS				
	1	2.2%	1	3.3%
1 MONTH				
	4	9.1%	4	13.3%
SEVERAL MONTHS				
	9	20.5%	7	23.4%
1 YEAR				
	0	0.0%	3	10.0%
2 – 5 YEARS				
	13	29.5%	0	0.0%
OTHER				
	3	6.8%	0	0.0%
TOTAL				
	44	100.0%	30	100.0%

Note: For the Co-Offender Group, 2 responses were recorded as "unknown"; they were excluded from the data.

VICTIM MOTIVATION — WOMEN OFFENDERS' PERSPECTIVE

These results represent the women offenders'view of the child's motivation; however, the child' experience may be very different. Therefore, these results should be viewed with caution.

Table 20

Offense — Victims

	CO-OFFENDERS		INDEPENDENT	
MALE CHILDREN				
	42	45.2%	15	35.7%
FEMALE CHILDREN				
	51	54.8%	27	64.3%
TOTAL				
	93	100.0%	42	100.0%

Statistics for Table 20

Statistic	DF	Value	Prob
Chi_Square	1	1.058	0.304

The women offenders reported they believed the victims participated or went along with their abusers' requests or demands for a variety of reasons, including fear, affection, pleasure, obligation, and fun (game). These perceptions differ greatly between the Co-Offenders and the Independent Offenders. In the Co-Offender group, fear (68.9%) is the primary response given regarding the victims' participation in the sexual abuse, whereas, fun (game) (30%), affection (16.7%), and pleasure (16.7%) are the explanations offered most by the women in the Independent Offender group (see Table 22).

For the Co-Offenders, a question emerges: which of the offenders might the child have feared — the male or the female? It seems plausible the victims may have been fearful of the male rather than the female offenders. The Independent Offenders, for the most part, deny fear as a motivation for the child. These women's perceptions may be more self-serving than those of the Co-Offenders, but the behavior of the Independent Offenders may also have been less coercive and more seductive.

MEANS OF ELICITING VICTIM COOPERATION

The Co-Offenders describe threats and force as the main ways their codefendants elicited cooperation from victims, used on multiple victims and possibly more than once. For the Independent Offenders, threats and force

Table 21
Perpetrator-Victim Relationship

	CO-OFFENDERS		INDEPENDENT	
BIOLOGICAL CHILD				
	33	71.7%	7	23.3%
STEPCHILD				
	1	2.2%	0	0.0%
OTHER RELATIVE				
	3	6.5%	2	6.7%
NEIGHBOR				
	9	19.6%	5	16.7%
ACQUAINTANCE, INCLUDING BABYSITTER				
	1	2.2%	11	36.7%
STRANGER				
	2	4.3%	1	3.3%
OTHER				
	1	2.2%	4	13.3%
TOTAL				
	50	108.7%	30	100.0%

Note: Totals may exceed 100%; some in the Co-Offender Group have multiple victims.

represent a a small fraction (23.3%) of ways victim compliance or cooperation was elicted. The results, shown in Table 23, indicate that victims were never threatened with physical harm toward another by the Independent Offenders, while victims were never told the sexual abuse was an expression of love by the Co-Offenders.

The results show the Independent Offenders used very different tactics to elicit cooperation from victims. Acting as if the sexually abusive behaviors were a game accounted for 26.7% of the Independent Offender respondents. Of interest is that 20% of this group, compared with 9.1% of the Co-Offenders, indicated they did not know how they obtained cooperation from victims or they did not

Table 22
Victim Motivation — Women Offenders' Perspective

	CO-OFFENDERS		INDEPENDENT	
FEAR				
	31	68.9%	8	26.6%
AFFECTION				
	1	2.2%	5	16.7%
PLEASURE				
	2	4.4%	5	16.7%
OBLIGATION				
	5	11.1%	0	0.0%
FUN (GAME)				
	4	8.9%	9	30.0%
OTHER				
	5	11.1%	3	10.0%
TOTAL				
	48	106.6%	30	100.0%

Note: Totals may exceed 100% in the Co-Offender Group due to multiple responses.

do anything in particular. The Independent Offenders implied the children willingly went along with their requests.

For the Independent Offenders, 13.3% said they told the victim the sexual abuse was an expression of love. As stated previously, none of Co-Offenders told their victims this. The results indicate that less violent measures were taken by the Independent Offenders to elicit participation from their victims.

ATTEMPTS TO PREVENT VICTIMS FROM REPORTING THE SEXUAL ABUSE

Table 24 shows that over half the Independent Offenders (58%) did nothing to attempt to keep their victims from telling others about the sexual abuse. For the

Table 23
Ways of Eliciting Victim Cooperation — Women Offenders' Perspective

	CO-OFFENDERS		INDEPENDENT	
THREATENED DEATH				
	10	22.7%	1	3.3%
THREATENED PHYSICAL HARM TO THE CHILD				
	16	36.4%	3	10.0%
THREATENED PHYSICAL HARM TO OTHER				
	8	18.2%	0	0.0%
THREATENED LOSS OF LOVE				
	2	4.5%	0	0.0%
THREATENED ABANDONMENT				
	8	18.2%	1	3.3%
FORCE				
	5	11.4%	2	6.7%
BRIBES				
	7	15.9%	3	10.0%
EXPRESSION OF LOVE				
	0	0.0%	4	13.3%
TEACHING SEX				
	1	2.3%	2	6.7%
GAMES				
	6	13.6%	8	26.7%
OTHER				
	4	9.1%	6	20.0%
TOTAL				
	67	152.3%	30	100.0%

Note: Totals in the Co-Offender Group may exceed 100 due to multiple responses. "Other" reflects responses "did not" and "n/a."

Table 24
Ways of Preventing Victims from Telling —
Women Offenders' Perspective

	CO-OFFENDERS		INDEPENDENT	
THREATENED DEATH				
	10	31.1%	1	8.3%
THREATENED PHYSICAL HARM TO THE CHILD				
	12	37.5%	2	16.7%
THREATENED PHYSICAL HARM TO OTHER				
	6	18.8%	0	0.0%
THREATENED PUNISHMENT				
	1	3.1%	1	8.3%
THREATENED ABANDONMENT				
	6	18.8%	1	8.3%
DID NOT				
	4	12.5%	7	58.4%
TOTAL				
	39	122.0%	12	100.0%

Note: Totals may exceed 100 due to multiple responses.

Co-Offenders, threats were commonly used in an attempt to keep the victims from telling others. These results also indicate the Independent Offenders used significantly less violent tactics.

SUMMARY OF TABLES 22-24

A curious finding is noted after closely examining the number of times the response "fear" appeared in relation to the responses of "threats" and "force." When respondents were asked a general question about victim motivation for participation in the sexual abuse (Table 22), 31 responses indicated the Co-Offenders believed the victims participated out of "fear." For the Independent Offenders, eight responses to this question were "fear."

The next question sought more specific information by asking how cooperation was elicited from victims. For the Co-Offenders, a total of 49 responses included a combination of threats and force. Responses of threats and force totaled 7 for the Independent Offenders (see Table 23).

A total of 35 responses of "threats and force" is found for the Co-Offenders regarding their perspectives on ways to keep the victims from revealing the sexual abuse (see Table 24). The total number of responses "threats and force" is 5 for the Independent Offenders.

Table 25
Women Offenders' Motivation for the Sexual Abuse

	CO-OFFENDERS		INDEPENDENT	
THREATENED WITH DEATH				
	7	15.3%	0	0.0%
THREATENED WITH PHYSICAL HARM TO THE CHILD				
	5	10.9%	0	0.0%
THREATENED WITH PHYSICAL HARM TO OTHER				
	3	6.5%	0	0.0%
THREATENED WITH LOSS OF LOVE				
	2	4.3%	0	0.0%
THREATENED WITH ABANDONMENT				
	11	23.9%	0	0.0%
ACTUAL PHYSICAL HARM TO YOU				
	4	8.7%	0	0.0%
VOLUNTARILY PARTICIPATED				
	0	0.0%	18	60.0%
DENIED ACTS				
	14	30.4%	12	40.0%
TOTAL				
	46	100.0%	30	100.0%

The discrepancy noted for the Co-Offenders between responses to the general and specific questions about the women's views of victims' participation in the sexual abuse is puzzling. Using threats and force to elicit participation from victims possibly would instill fear in the victims. Yet the high number of responses "threats and force" to the specific questions from the Co-Offenders is not consistent with the low number of "fear" responses to the general question. One explanation for this discrepancy may be that the women are engaging in denial. This discrepancy is not found with the Independent Offenders.

WOMEN OFFENDERS' MOTIVATION FOR THE SEXUAL ABUSE

For Independent Offenders, 18 of the women voluntarily participated in the sexual abuse, and 12 denied the sexual abuse. For Co-Offenders, 14 of the women denied participation in the sexual activities. Fear of abandonment (23.9) and fear of death (15.3) ranked highest among the Co-Offenders' motivations for participation in the sexual abuse (see Table 25).

Table 26
Alcohol Use During the Offense

	CO-OFFENDERS		INDEPENDENT	
NO				
	35	76.1%	25	83.3%
YES				
	9	19.6%	5	16.7%
NOT SURE				
	2	4.3%	0	0.0%
TOTAL				
	46	100.0%	30	100.0%

Statistics for Table 26

Statistic	DF	Value	Prob
Chi-Square	2	1.5	0.470

USE OF SUBSTANCES DURING THE COMMISSION OF THE OFFENSE

Table 26 shows the results of alcohol and drug use during the commission of the offense. Alcohol use by the Co-Offenders and the Independent Offenders is quite low, 19.6% and 16.7%, respectively. Drug use is also low for the Independent Offenders, 16.7%; however, 30.4% of the Co-Offenders reported using drugs during the offense (see Table 27).

Table 27
Drug Use During the Offense

	CO-OFFENDERS		INDEPENDENT	
NO				
	30	65.2%	25	83.3%
YES				
	14	30.4%	5	16.7%
NOT SURE				
	2	4.4%	0	0.0%
TOTAL				
	46	100.0%	30	100.0%

Statistics for Table 27

Statistic	DF	Value	Prob
Chi-Square	2	3.5	0.173

SEXUAL GRATIFICATION: THE OFFENSE

Sexual gratification is not a motivating factor in the commission of the sexual offense for the Co-Offenders (5%). However, over a quarter of the Independent Offenders (27%) reported orgasms while offending. Table 28 indicates these results.

Table 28
Sexual Gratification — Offense

	CO-OFFENDERS		INDEPENDENT	
NO				
	38	95.0%	22	73.3%
YES				
	2	5.0%	8	26.7%
TOTAL				
	40	100.0%	30	100.0%

Statistics for Table 28

Statistic	DF	Value	Prob
Chi-Square	1	6.6	0.010

Table 29
Women Offenders' Ages — Offense

N	MEAN	STD DEV	STD ERROR
CO-OFFENDER			
46	29.8	6.5	1.0
INDEPENDENT			
30	26.9	6.2	1.1

Variances	T	DF	Prob>|T|
Equal	1.95	74.0	0.055

WOMEN OFFENDERS' AGE AT ONSET OF THE OFFENSE

The Co-Offenders were nearly 30 years old at the onset of the offense. The Independent Offenders were significantly younger, nearly 27 years old. These results are illustrated in Table 29.

Table 30.1
MMPI-2 Clinical Scales

	CO-OFFENDERS		INDEPENDENT		
	M	SD	M	SD	PROB
L					
	58.9	10.1	54.3	10.1	.065
F					
	62.0	18.5	73.3	22.4	.023
PD					
	62.8	11.6	68.9	13.9	.049
PT					
	52.0	12.0	61.4	15.6	.005
SC					
	57.3	15.0	67.1	17.6	.014

Table 30.2
MMPI-2 Supplementary Scales

	CO-OFFENDERS		INDEPENDENT		
	M	SD	M	SD	PROB
A					
	62.0	15.3	69.0	17.1	.071
R					
	51.6	13.1	61.4	16.8	.007
DO					
	47.5	9.6	57.1	14.0	.001
RE					
	54.8	13.2	61.8	17.6	.058
PS					
	56.8	17.1	63.2	14.8	.105
MAC-R					
	55.9	11.3	65.1	16.8	.007

Table 30.3
MMPI-2 Content Scales

| | CO-OFFENDERS | | INDEPENDENT | | |
	M	SD	M	SD	PROB
DEP					
	52.1	12.1	62.2	13.9	.002
HEA					
	52.2	10.3	59.3	15.1	.022
BIZ					
	52.3	11.2	59.9	12.9	.010
TPA					
	60.8	20.0	74.3	24.8	.013
LSE					
	59.8	8.7	65.5	15.5	.048
FAM					
	54.6	10.3	49.8	10.1	.052
TRT					
	42.6	10.9	37.5	7.4	.032

MMPI-2

MEAN SCALE SCORES

A total of 72 MMPI-2 Tests were computer-scored by the National Computer Systems Professional Assessment Services. Two subjects from each group refused to take this instrument, although they did participate in the Structured Interview.

The mean scores of the Co-Offenders and the Independent Offenders on the validity measures indicate valid profiles. Tables 30.1, 30.2, and 30.3 illustrate significant differences between the mean scale scores of the Co-Offenders and the Independent Offenders on the clinical, supplementary, and content scales. Both groups' mean scores on the *L* scale are indicative of a usual test-taking approach. The differences between the mean scores of the two groups indicate that the Independent Offenders are significantly more psychologically disturbed in comparison to the Co-Offenders. Tables 31.1, 31.2, and 31.3 show the groups' profiles and graphically illustrate the differences between the groups.

Co-Offenders

The Co-offenders generated relatively flat profiles on the clinical scales, indicative of scores well within normal limits. Several normal profiles emerged in this group, as well as a few with elevations. No extreme lows were found. This pattern seems to be common for this group of Co-offenders.

As a group, these individuals tend to view the world as a threatening place; they feel misunderstood and unfairly treated. They are distrustful, submissive, and easily influenced by others. The group score on the *TRT* scale (Negative Treatment Indicators) was *T*-42. This score shows that these individuals would be good candidates for treatment.

Independent Offenders

Several of these women had seriously elevated profiles, with no extreme lows. This pattern seems to be common, if not typical, for this group.

As a group, the Independent Offenders may be described as inhibited, self-critical, and overly sensitive to rejection. They tend to possess unusual beliefs, may exhibit bizarre actions, and are withdrawn and alienating. Their scores also indicate identity confusion and difficulties with thinking and concentration. These individuals may have problems with authority and their relationships with others tend to be superficial.

Scores on scales 4 (*PD* – Psychopathic Deviate) and 8 (*SC* – Schizophrenia) are elevated. This finding indicates that these individuals' problems began early, and relates to their basic attitude of distrust. As a group, the Independent Offenders scored *T*-38 on the *TRT* scale (Negative Treatment Indicators). This score shows that these women would be good candidates for treatment.

SUMMARY OF MMPI-2 RESULTS

Significant differences emerge between the Co-Offenders and the Independent Offenders via group mean scores on the MMPI. In general, the Independent Offenders are much more emotionally disturbed than the Co-Offenders. This is evidenced by significantly different mean scores on scales related to depression, social and emotional alienation, ego mastery, anxiety, repression, general addic-

Table 31.1
MMPI-2 Basic Validity and Clinical Scales

CO-OFFENDERS = SOLID LINE ━━━━
INDEPENDENTS = BROKEN LINE ------

▓▓ Scores falling in gray area are considered within normal limits

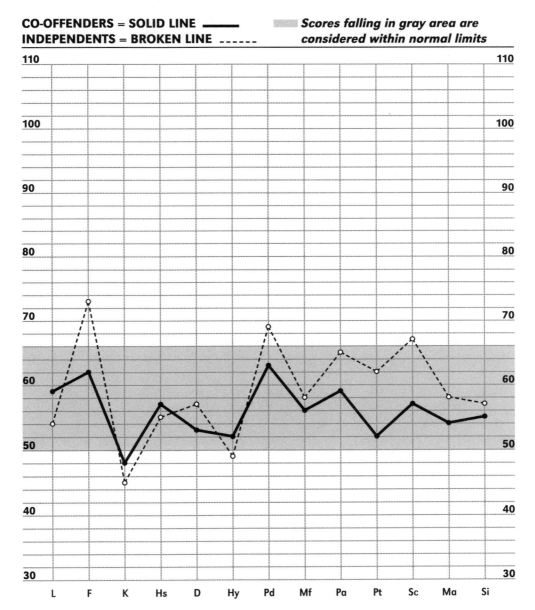

VALIDITY SCALES: L = Lie, F = Infrequency, K = Defensiveness

CONTENT SCALES: Hs = Hypochondriasis, D = Depression, Hy = Conversion Hysteria, Pd= Psychopathic Deviate, MF = Masculinity-Femininity, Pa = Paranoia, Pt = Psychasthenia, Sc = Schizophrenia, Ma = Hypomania, Si = Social Intervention

Table 31.2
MMPI-2 Supplementary Scales

CO-OFFENDERS = SOLID LINE ———   ▨ *Scores falling in gray area are*
INDEPENDENTS = BROKEN LINE ‑‑‑‑‑   *considered within normal limits*

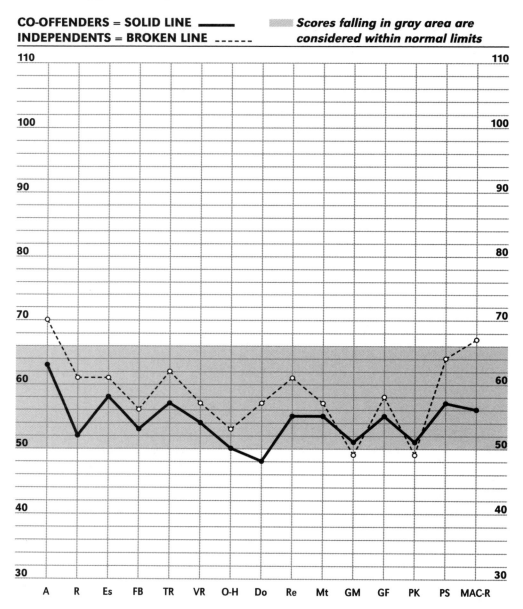

SUPPLEMENTARY SCALES: A = Anxiety, R = Repression, Es = Ego Strength, FB = Back F, TR = True Response,
VR = Variable Response, O-H = Overcontrolled Hostility, Do = Dominance, Re = Social Responsibility,
Mt = College Maladjustment, GM = Gender Role — Masculine, GF = Gender Role — Feminine,
PK = Post-Traumatic Stress Disorder — Keane, PS = Post-Traumatic Stress Disorder — Schlenger,
MAC-R = MacAndrew Alcoholism — Revised

Table 31.3
MMPI-2 Content Scales

CO-OFFENDERS = SOLID LINE ——— Scores falling in gray area are
INDEPENDENTS = BROKEN LINE ------ considered within normal limits

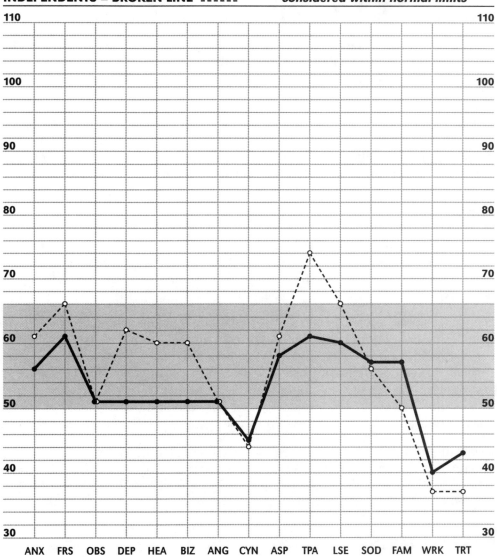

*CONTENT SCALES: ANX = Anxiety, FRS = Fears, OBS = Obsessiveness, DEP = Depression,
HEA = Health Concerns, BIZ = Bizarre Mentation, ANG = Anger, CYN = Cynicism,
ASP = Antisocial Practices, TPA = Type A, LSE = Low Self-Esteem, SOD = Social Discomfort,
FAM = Family Problems, WRK = Work Interference, TRT = Negative Treatment Indicators*

tion-proneness, dominance, social responsibility, and self-esteem. The Co-Offenders' scores reflect individuals who are realistic, sociable, and adventurous; the Independents' scores reflect unrealistic, isolated, and inhibited individuals.

Characteristics of Co-Offenders' Relationships

The following information was obtained solely from the women in the Co-Offender group ($n=40$). The Independent Offenders did not have codefendants. Very few of the Independent Offenders had continuing relationships at the time of the crime.

The Co-Offenders describe their relationships with the codefendants as abusive and overpowering. They commonly recall the "charm and sensitivity" these men possessed in the relationships' early stages. They recall the relationship changing from "very loving" to "controlling and abusive" over the course of time.

SUBSTANCE USE

These women report a very small percentage of drug use for themselves and their codefendants during their relationships. Cocaine and marijuana were the most commonly used drugs during the relationship; however, usage patterns were low for the male and the female.

Daily cocaine use accounted for 7.5% of this sample in describing their codefendants' drug use patterns, and 2.5% reported daily use for themselves. Marijuana use was also reportedly relatively low on a daily basis: 17.5% of the women described their codefendants' use on a daily basis, with 12.5% reportedly using almost every day. The women described their own marijuana use as infrequent. The results indicate 5% reported daily use, 7.5% used from nearly daily to about once a month, and 12.5% indicated they used only a couple of times a year.

Over a quarter of these women reported their codefendants drank to intoxication on a daily basis. None of the women in this sample reported this pattern of alcohol use for themselves. The results show that fewer than a quarter of these women drank to intoxication on a couple-of-times-a-year basis (see Table 32).

POWER DIFFERENCES

These relationships appear very unequal and controlled by the male codefendant. The results indicate that 75% of the women believed their codefendant

Table 32
Substance Abuse During Relationship

	LSD MALE	LSD FEMALE	MESCALINE MALE	MESCALINE FEMALE	HEROIN MALE	HEROIN FEMALE	COCAINE MALE	COCAINE FEMALE	MARIJUANA MALE	MARIJUANA FEMALE	ALCOHOL MALE	ALCOHOL FEMALE
NO	82.5	92.5	90.0	92.5	85.0	97.5	65.0	75.0	40.0	60.0	22.5	47.5
2 TIMES/YEAR	5.0	7.5	5.0	5.0	5.0	2.5	5.0	7.5	5.0	12.5	17.5	22.5
1 TIME/MONTH							5.0	5.0	5.0	7.5	7.5	7.5
ONE TIME/WEEK					2.5		5.0		10.0	7.5	7.5	10.0
2 – 3 TIMES/WEEK							2.5	2.5	2.5	7.5	2.5	5.0
NEAR DAILY							5.0	7.5	12.5		15.0	7.5
DAILY							7.5	2.5	17.5	5.0	27.5	
DON'T KNOW	12.5		5.0		7.5		5.0		7.5			

"always" knew where they were when they were not together. Forty-one percent of the Co-Offenders stated that the codefendant "always" won disagreements about major issues; fewer than 10% of these women felt compromise was achieved.

EXPRESSION OF ANGER

Table 33 clearly shows the women's perceived differences between their codefendants and themselves regarding how they handled anger in the relationships.

Table 33
Expressions of Anger — Women's Perspective

	MALE CO-DEFENDANTS	WOMEN CO-OFFENDERS
TRIED TO TALK IT OUT		
	28.2%	65.8%
SULKED, WITHDREW		
	43.6%	63.2%
CRIED		
	7.7%	57.9%
SWORE OR SHOUTED		
	76.9%	55.3%
DIRECTED ANGER TOWARD OBJECTS		
	66.7%	28.9%
DIRECTED ANGER TOWARD CHILDREN		
	41.0%	15.8%
THREATENED PHYSICAL VIOLENCE		
	56.4%	18.4%
USED PHYSICAL VIOLENCE WITH SPOUSE		
	76.9%	26.3%
USED PHYSICAL VIOLENCE WITH KIDS		
	28.2%	15.8%

Note: Totals may exceed 100% due to multiple responses

In these relationships, the women reportedly attempted discussion as their predominant method of dealing with anger nearly as often as they did sulking or withdrawing. About a quarter of the responses indicated the women chose to fight back against their codefendant with physical violence.

Over three-quarters of the women Co-Offenders' responses showed that their codefendants were physically violent with them. They indicated the codefendants often directed their anger toward objects as well as toward their children.

CHARACTERISTICS OF THE SEXUAL RELATIONSHIP

In their descriptions of aspects of their sexual relationships with their codefendants these women frequently described forced sex when the women did not desire it and being forced to engage in unwanted sexual activities. The women related that their codefendants frequently asked or forced them to engage in what they considered "unusual" sexual acts (e.g., anal sex, sex with others). More than half of the women Co-Offenders (54%) reported that their co-defendants desired sex after battering them. Table 34 contains the reports of the women Co-Offenders' descriptions of their sexual relationships with their codefendants.

Findings of the Research Questions

> *1. What, if any, demographic, behavioral, and psychological characteristics depict female Co-Offenders and Accomplices?*

No significantly distinguishing differences were found between the Co-Offenders and the Accomplices in terms of demographics, behaviors, or psychometrics. For purposes of clarification, the Co-Offenders were renamed Accomplices/Active, and the Accomplices were renamed Accomplices/Passive. The author combined these groups to form one group (Co-Offenders) and decided to proceed with the emerging data to ascertain if there were significant differences between Co-Offenders and Independent Offenders. The Co-Offenders and the Independent Offenders were examined for comparative purposes.

> *2. What are the similarities and differences between female Co-Offenders and Accomplices in cases of child sexual abuse?*

The female Co-Offenders and Accomplices are very similar along demographic, behavioral, and psychometric lines. No significant differences were found between these groups.

Table 34
The Sexual Relationship

	MALE CO-DEFENDANTS		WOMEN CO-OFFENDERS	
WANTED SEX TOO OFTEN				
	14	40.0%	6	24.0%
FORCED SEX				
	22	62.9%	2	8.0%
REFUSED SEX				
	16	45.7%	16	64.0%
COMPARED NEGATIVELY TO OTHERS				
	19	54.3%	4	16%
FORCED TO DO SEXUAL ACTS				
	22	62.9%	1	4.0%
INSENSITIVE TO SEXUAL NEEDS				
	28	80.0%	6	24.0%
DESIRED SEX AFTER A BATTERING				
	19	54.3%	0	0.0%

Note: Totals may exceed 100% due to multiple responses

> 3. *Are there elements such as sexual abuse or physical abuse in the woman's current or past history that contribute to her involvement in a dependent relationship and involvement in the child sexual abuse?*

Over half the female Co-Offenders had childhood histories of physical and psychological abuse. Their mothers were the predominant abusers. During the Structured Interview, most of these women spoke about the content of the psychological abuse, stating how much more damaging their mothers' words were to them, compared to the effects of the physical abuse they encountered. Commonly heard phrases by this researcher were: "You'll never amount to anything," "You're ugly and stupid," "You'll never find a man who will love you," and "You can't do anything right." The female Co-Offenders were severely and frequently physically abused as well. Nearly 36% of them were spanked with objects (predominantly belts) often between birth and age 13.

Nearly 78% of the women Co-Offenders were sexually abused as children, chiefly by uncles and brothers. The average age of the women at the onset of the sex abuse was seven.

Over three-quarters of the female Co-Offenders reported that their relationships with the men who are their Co-Defendants were physically and psychologically abusive. They reported how "loved" and "valued" they felt by these men in the early stages of the relationships, and how shocked they were when the abusive behaviors began. These women reportedly were dominated and controlled both physically and emotionally during the course of their relationships with their codefendants.

These female Co-Offenders related how intensely jealous their Co-Defendants were of their families, other women, other men, children, and friends. These women recounted that initially, they viewed the jealousy as an expression of love. Over time, these women noted the jealousy became more intense, and with this came increased possessiveness over the women and more intrusiveness into their lives.

These women stated that the male Co-Defendant frequently asked or forced them to perform what they considered unusual sex acts (e.g., anal sex, sex with others — including their own children). Even so, they commonly recalled the sensitivity these men expressed to them. Therefore, they continued to cling to what they knew the man was capable of expressing to them.

The female Co-Offenders related experiences of severe psychological abuse by the men they were in relationships with, predominantly in the form of criticism and verbal harassment. The women reported that in retrospect, they see the similarities between their codefendants' psychological abuse and the ways their mothers psychologically abused them.

4. *How are coercion, force, and/or persuasion related to the commission of the child sexual abuse?*

   a. Was the woman and/or child threatened with physical force and/or abandonment if she refused to comply?

   b. Was the woman and/or child assaulted?

   c. What type(s) of force was used?

   d. Was there emotional and/or economic reprisal involved?

   e. Were there bribes or enticements?

It is important to recall that of the 46 female Co-Offenders, 14 denied participation in the sexual abuse. Therefore, the information pertinent to the commission of the child sexual abuse is based on the responses of 32 female Co-Offenders.

The male codefendants reportedly used coercive techniques to engage the female Co-Offenders in the child sexual abuse. Some women related that the male codefendants threatened them and/or the child(ren) with death (15% of the responses) if they refused to comply with his wishes. Approximately 18% of the women indicated the male codefendant also backed up his threats by using a weapon.

Threats of physical force directed at the child(ren) and/or the woman comprised 17% of the responses. The male codefendant reportedly threatened the woman and/or the child(ren) with withdrawing his love and abandoning her and the family (28% of the responses) if they refused him. The results indicate the male codefendant did not often actually inflict physical harm to the woman (8.7%).

The coercive measures taken by the male codefendant in the form of threats appeared sufficient to engage the woman and the child(ren) in the sexually abusive activities. This is not a surprising finding in that it is common that battered women believe the man capable of carrying out his threats. This research found no evidence of bribes or enticements related to the sexual offense.

> *5. Was chemical dependency involved in the relationship between the female Co-Offender and the male Co-Defendant?*

The results indicate that excessive drug use in the relationship (including the woman and the male codefendant) was uncommon. While more than a quarter of the female Co-Offenders report excessive alcohol consumption by the male codefendant, the results show infrequent alcohol consumption for the women.

> *6. Was chemical dependency involved in the commission of the offense?*

Fewer than a quarter of the Independent Offenders reported drug use during the commission of the offense, compared to 30% of the Co-Offenders. Fewer than 20% of the women in both groups admitted to alcohol use during the sexual abuse. No clear relationship was found between chemical dependency and the commission of the offense. While some drug use was reported, it does not meet criteria for a chemical dependency diagnosis.

CHAPTER 6

Discussion

This study's original focus was on groups of female sexual offenders classified as Co-Offenders and Accomplices. The purpose was to examine these groups to provide clearer descriptions of their personality, development, and abuse-related behaviors and attitudes than had been done previously. This research further sought to investigate the relationship with a significant male in the commission of child sexual abuse.

The findings indicated that the offenders in the Accomplice group and the Co-Offender group did not differ significantly. For purposes of clarity, the Co-Offender group was renamed Accomplice/Active, and the Accomplice group was renamed Accomplice/Passive. The data from the Accomplice groups were collapsed to form the Co-Offender group. The focus of this research moved to a comparison between Co-Offenders and Independent Offenders.

Limitations of the Study

This study's findings are based on an incarcerated population; therefore, there are limitations to the findings' generalizability. These results cannot be assumed to be representative of women who sexually abuse children in the general population. Nonetheless, this research is substantially more ambitious than other such studies in terms of numbers and geographic areas represented. This study is perhaps more rigorous in its classification of female sex offenders, in that it separates groups that other studies have combined.

This research focused on the retrospective experiences of subjects who disclosed information about their histories, including all types of abuse, as well as the nature of the offense of which they were convicted. Therefore, these findings are based on the subjects' willingness and ability to recall traumatic life experiences.

Characteristics of the Female Sex Offenders

HISTORY OF PHYSICAL, PSYCHOLOGICAL AND SEXUAL ABUSE

Most of the women in both groups had suffered physical and psychological abuse during their childhoods; however, the Co-offenders were abused more severely and more frequently (physically and psychologically) than the Independent Offenders. Of particular interest is that mothers were reportedly the primary abusers. Previous studies have found depression and low self-esteem in child victims of physical abuse, and that as adults, the former child victims display aggressive or antisocial patterns (McCann, Sakheim, & Abrahamson, 1988; Sears, 1989). This study supports these findings.

The majority of the women in both groups were reportedly sexually abused as children. Over 60% of the molestations were perpetrated by the offenders' male relatives, predominantly uncles and brothers. Research conducted by Painter and Dutton (1985) determined that victims of childhood sexual abuse are apt to display "self-destructive" behavior or to engage in abusive relationships in adulthood. This study's findings concur.

The two groups are similar regarding age of onset and duration of the sexual abuse. The Independent Offenders were significantly more seriously sexually abused (before age 10) in terms of duration and severity of abuse, than the Co-Offenders. This may account for the severity of psychological disturbance found in the women in the Independent Offender group.

PSYCHOLOGICAL CHARACTERISTICS

The MMPI-2 was administered to both groups of female sex offenders. Statistically significant differences, at or below the .05 level, are found between the two groups on mean scale scores for scales L, F, Pd, Pt, and Sc. The Independent Offenders are notably more seriously disturbed, as a group, than the Co-Offenders. This is evidenced by mean scale score elevations on scales F and Sc, which may be indicative of psychotic processes and confusional states. The mean scale score on the MAC-R (a measure of general addiction-proneness) for this group is suggestive of substance abuse.

The Independent Offenders are emotionally regressed and naive. They severely lack a sense of boundaries, as well as the means to establish appropriate ones. These women have significant identity problems and lack ego strength and the ability to form age-appropriate relationships.

The Co-Offenders scored within normal limits on the clinical, supplementary, and content scales. This is a curious finding in that one wonders how women who molest their own children can appear "normal" on the MMPI-2. This may be a reflection of an inadequacy of the instrument in discerning characteristics of abuse dynamics, in terms of history of child abuse as well as current abuse. Another possible explanation for this group scoring within normal limits may be related to the women's denial systems. As a group, these women tend to be submissive, distrustful, and easily influenced by others. Their mean scale score on the MAC-R does not indicate substance abuse as a major problem.

Previous studies have yielded conflicting results regarding the psychological characteristics and/or functioning of female sex offenders. Faller (1987) reported that about half her sample had mental problems, including retardation and psychotic illness. The Independent Offenders in McCarty's (1986) study were described as "seriously emotionally disturbed." Mathews, et al. (1989) found that none of the female offenders was severely emotionally disturbed or psychotic. This study found a combination of both results reported from these prior studies. From the results of the MMPI-2, many of the Independent Offenders are seriously emotionally disturbed, while few of the Co-Offenders show evidence of severe psychological disturbance.

SUBSTANCE ABUSE

Mixed findings have been reported in previous studies related to female sex offenders' use or abuse of substances. Faller (1987) found that over half her sample had substance abuse problems. McCarty (1986) found similar results with Independent Offenders; however, the percentages decreased significantly regarding the Co-Offenders and Accomplices. Most of the female sex offenders in Allen's (1991) study reportedly were not substance abusers.

This study did not find a correlation between alcohol use or abuse in relation to the offense for either the Co-Offender or the Independent Offenders. A little over a quarter of the Co-Offenders admitted to drug use during the offense, and the majority of the Independent Offenders denied drug use. This is a curious finding in that the scores on the MAC-R scale of the MMPI-2 are somewhat suggestive of substance abuse for the Independent Offenders, but are contraindicative for the Co-Offenders. This may be a function of self-report bias.

Characteristics of the Crime

SEXUAL ACTIVITIES

Previous studies have reported that fondling is the most common type of sexual activity (Allen, 1991; Faller, 1987; Finkelhor, 1979; Russell, 1986). This study concurs with this finding regarding the Independent Offenders. Oral sex was the second most frequently reported activity. Oral sex was the most frequently reported activity by the Co-Offenders, followed by the adult fondling the child. Faller (1987) found that group sex was the most commonly reported activity. She stated that the majority of the women in her sample sexually offended with more than one male perpetrator (Co-Offender or Accomplice) and offered this as a possible reason for the difference between studies. In this study, the activity "group sex" was not reported at all for the Independent Offenders, and reportedly occurred on only four occasions for the Co-Offenders.

The Independent Offenders reportedly performed oral sex on their victims, but the Co-Offenders' victims performed the activity on them. A possible explanation for this difference may be a function of the different motivations found between the groups. The Independent Offenders used different strategies compared to the Co-Offenders. They predominantly set the stage for the offense from a position of fun (game), with the connotation of pleasure for the victim, as well as a means of showing affection. Fear was instilled in the Co-Offenders' victims, reportedly by the male codefendant, via threats of physical harm and/or abandonment. These women reported that the male codefendants orchestrated the sexual activities and instructed the victims to perform oral sex on the women.

ADMISSION OF GUILT

Despite their convictions for child sexual abuse, approximately 30% of the Co-Offenders and 40% of the Independent Offenders denied committing the offense. In this study, all of the subjects were treated as guilty, in that the researcher took the legal verdict at face value. It is not uncommon for convicted offenders, both male and female, to deny guilt of the offense for which they were convicted.

In general, minimization and denial are characteristic of child sexual abusers. Allen's (1991) comparative study of male and female sex offenders found that 27% of the female offenders ($n=65$) and 49% of the male offenders ($n=75$) admitted guilt. Therefore, he contended that female offenders are more apt to deny their abusive acts than male offenders.

VICTIMS

More female children than male children were sexually abused by both groups; however, the proportion of female to male victims was strikingly higher for the Independent Offenders. This finding supports an assertion made by other authors that female sex offenders are more likely to abuse girls than boys (Brown, Hull, & Panesis, 1984; Faller, 1987; Finkelhor & Russell, 1984). The difference in proportion of male and female victims between the groups may indicate availability of the victims, rather than a preference for one sex or the other.

The majority of the victims of the Co-Offenders were their biological children. This finding is also confirmed in other studies (e.g., Faller, 1987, Allen, 1991). For the Independent Offenders, victims were predominantly acquaintances (children they were baby-sitting). This may be because these women have fewer children than the Co-Offenders, as well as a function of victim availability.

WOMEN OFFENDERS' PERSPECTIVES REGARDING VICTIMS

Interesting differences emerge between the groups in terms of the women's beliefs about the victims' involvement in the offense. These include: 1) why the children went along with the abusers' requests or demands; 2) the ways in which victims' participation was elicited; and 3) the methods used to gain victims' silence about the sexual abuse.

More violent tactics (e.g., threats of death, physical harm to the child and/or other, abandonment, force) were reported by the Co-Offenders than by the Independent Offenders. The Co-Offenders reported that the male co-defendant delivered the threats to the children; therefore, it is likely that the victims were fearful of and threatened by the male.

The Independent Offenders were less coercive and used tactics such as promoting the sexual activities as a game or fun. These women displayed a sort of naïveté about the way they dealt with their victims. Nearly a quarter of this group indicated either they did not know how they elicited cooperation from the victims or they did not do anything at all. They intimated the victims were willing participants. Over half the Independent Offenders did not attempt to keep the victims from telling others of the sexual abuse.

Compared to the Co-Offenders, the Independent Offenders were less abusive in the sexual acts as well as in the ways they elicited victims' cooperation. The Independent Offenders may have primarily attempted to get their own emotional needs met by developing a relationship with the child victim. Compared to their own childhood sexual abuse, the sexual acts that constituted the offense they committed were less abusive than those reportedly done to them as children.

WOMEN OFFENDERS' IMPETUS FOR PARTICIPATION IN THE SEXUAL ABUSE

The Independent Offenders who admitted to their crimes voluntarily participated, in that they offended singularly, without a codefendant. Nearly a quarter of the Co-Offenders who acknowledged participation in the offense reported they feared abandonment by their significant other (the codefendant) if they did not participate. Threats of death and physical harm to the child or another were also noted among these women as motivations for their participation in the sexual abuse.

Sexual Gratification

Of the Independent Offenders, over a quarter reported they experienced orgasms while offending; however, this was not a motivating factor in the offense. Wolfe (1985) reported a similar finding; however, the subjects in her study were not categorized into types of offenders (e.g., women offending independently, women offending with a male codefendant). Rather, they were mixed, and no comparison may be drawn. In contrast, only 5% of the Co-Offenders reported orgasms during the offense.

A possible motivation for the Independent Offenders may have been the strong need to connect with another. This may be related to regressed behavior from the time they were abused as children.

Co-Offenders — Relationship Characteristics

The information regarding women offenders' relationships is specific to the Co-Offenders, in that the Independent Offenders did not have codefendants involved in their cases. Also, very few Independent Offenders were involved in relationships at the time of their offenses.

BATTERED WOMAN SYNDROME

This research found that over three-quarters of the Co-Offenders were involved in violent, abusive relationships with their codefendants. The physical and psychological abuse they experienced as children may have set the pattern for further abusive relationships. Their responses to questions about various aspects of the relationship were consistent with responses that accompany Battered Woman Syndrome (Walker, 1984).

The Co-Offenders recalled that they could not have imagined or predicted that the men they were involved with would ultimately become violent until after the violence actually occurred. They described the men in the early phases of the relationships as "charming and sensitive." Many reported they had never felt as special and loved before in their lives.

These relationships were fraught with coercive techniques used by the male, which also were carried into the sexually abusive behaviors with children. Examples of these coercive techniques included: 1) intense jealousy (on the male's part), which led to increased possessiveness of the woman and further intrusiveness into her life; 2) severe psychological abuse, which consisted of relentless criticism of the woman and numerous power struggles that the male always won; 3) threats of physical violence toward the woman and her significant others; 4) unusual and degrading sexual behaviors including anal sex, and sex with others (e.g., sex with the woman's children).

The Co-Offenders reported a very small incidence of drug use for themselves and their codefendants. Marijuana and cocaine were the drugs reportedly used; however, the incidence is very low for the women and the codefendants.

Walker's (1989) research found that 60% of the women she interviewed reported their abusive partners had drinking problems and often abused alcohol. This research supports her findings, in that over 50% of the Co-Offenders reported their codefendants had severe drinking problems.

SEX-ROLE THEORY AND MASCULINITY/FEMININITY THEORY

These theories were introduced as useful perspectives from which to examine the possible influence of significant male relationships in the crime of child sexual abuse. The theories are reintroduced at this point as they have proven valuable in understanding the women Co-Offenders' involvement in the sexual offense, and in terms of their affiliations with the male codefendants.

The various applications of sex-role theory found in the literature on female criminality share the notion that there are gender-related differences in socialization and expectations of behavioral standards. The findings of this research affirm the fundamental assumption of masculinity/femininity theory; there are personality differences between the genders discerned consistently in this sample of female Co-Offenders.

The more recent theories on female criminality suggest that women are motivated by affiliative behavior. These theories describe women in connection with men as passive and dependent (Covington, 1985), and their crimes suggestive of sex-role behaviors: men initiate and women follow in joint criminal endeavors (Baldwin, 1983; Sears, 1989).

Women with histories of physical and/or sexual abuse are found to behave in stereotypically feminine ways (Kuhl, 1984; Newman & Caplan, 1982; Painter & Dutton, 1985). Dependence, submissiveness, and passive-aggressiveness are personality characteristics that described this sample of female Co-Offenders and correspond to the tenets of the masculinity/femininity theory. These women were in relationships where they accepted a participatory role in child sexual abuse. It is unclear whether these personality characteristics emerged in response to stereotypical female criminal roles, or if they were previously in place and contributed to the assumption of the roles. More research is needed in this area.

Baldwin (1983) described women's roles in crime as helpers. She alleged they are led into, as opposed to leading, criminal acts. The findings pertinent to the women Co-Offenders in this study support Baldwin's theory.

The majority of the Co-Offenders in this study had been exposed to a significant amount of abuse before late adolescence. At the onset of the physical and emotional abuse in their adult relationships, they were already conditioned to respond with passive acceptance or, at best, minimal effort at self-protection.

History of Maternal Abuse

Research has almost exclusively focused on male abusers of females. We may have overlooked another equally damaging, if not more damaging, type of abuse — maternal abuse.

Many of the Co-Offenders in this study had a history of maternal physical and psychological abuse, and an absence of appropriate maternal modeling, suggesting a generational pattern. When the most primary of all bonds, the mother-child bond, becomes an abusive one, a distorted passive-dependence is habituated long before the woman reaches dating age. Through the earlier abuse, the woman is conditioned by her mother, as an infant and/or child, to be submissive. This submissiveness ultimately results in a connection between affiliation and exploitation and makes these women tend toward passive-dependent relationships with men. The passivity and dependency that permeate the relationships with men may also be components in the child sexual abuse with their male codefendants.

IMPLICATIONS FOR TREATMENT

As clinicians, we need to take careful histories of women who relate histories of child abuse, including physical, psychological, and sexual abuse. We need to pay special attention to the age of onset, duration, and degree of invasiveness of the sexual abuse to assist us in determining the potential psychological damage that may have resulted, as well as in developing appropriate treatment plans.

This study adds to our knowledge of the consequences of physical, psychological, and/or sexual abuse. It suggests earlier intervention with victims, before the victim becomes a perpetrator.

Social service agencies that serve families and investigate allegations of child sexual abuse have an opportunity to intervene in cases of child sexual abuse perpetrated by women. With proper training and the knowledge that women do sexually abuse children, with or without a male codefendant, such agencies may be able to identify a likely problem early and recommend intervention. This study suggests the importance of thorough and comprehensive family evaluations.

Counselors in correctional institutions may also benefit from these findings. This study suggests that women sex offenders are good candidates for treatment. By focusing their treatment toward examining the women's families of origin, where possible, and dealing with the denial and minimization, great strides may be made toward change. Based on knowledge of 12-step groups, this would raise the speculation that group therapy, initiated early in the woman's incarceration (a time of increased vulnerability) may assist in breaking through the denial. This may ultimately lead to the women accepting responsibility for their actions and provide a supportive atmosphere for change.

Additionally, treatment based on an appraisal of the Co-Offenders' relationships, and where possible, families of origin, may also promote the awareness necessary for change. Exposure to findings relative to Battered Woman Syndrome would be particularly useful to these women. These treatment aims could also be met via group therapy.

Suggestions for Future Research

This research was based on data from an incarcerated population. There may be an implicit assumption that these study subjects were more disturbed (and their crimes more serious) than other women who molested children but received probation, not incarceration. A possible avenue for further study may be to compare data from an incarcerated population with demographically matched data from the general population. Another possibility may be a comparative study of women who had been molested as children but do not molest as adults, and women who had been molested as children and do molest as adults.

This study suggests the potential for serious long-term damage from physical, psychological, and/or sexual abuse, as well as the perpetuation of abuse. Research is necessary to identify sexual abuse processes as well as the development of sexually abusive tendencies. For example, more research into young women at risk is needed to identify them earlier.

More information is needed about how these women dealt with their own child sexual abuse. Did they tell anyone about the abuse while it was occurring? Whom did they tell? What was the outcome? Did they receive treatment as children for their abuse? At what age? The answers to these questions may assist us in learning more about the generational pattern of sexual abuse, and in determining ways to intervene effectively.

Research that focuses on the needs of victims of female sexual perpetrators is needed, as is the development of appropriate treatment strategies. Some female sex offenders molest their own biological children, others molest children biologically unrelated to them. We need further information regarding the victim's needs. For instance, children who have been molested by their biological mothers may be affected differently from those molested by baby-sitters. More knowledge is necessary to develop appropriate treatment strategies for victims.

CHAPTER 7

Summary and Conclusion

The results of this research represent demographic, behavioral, and psychological characteristics of 76 incarcerated female sexual offenders. This sample spans both East and West Coasts in the United States and encompasses 12 State prisons. All of the women offended against children under age 18. Of these 76 subjects, 46 were classified as Co-Offenders and 30 as Independent Offenders.

This study sought to more clearly define these women in terms of personality characteristics, development, and abuse-related behaviors than previous studies. An additional research aim was to explore the relationship with a significant male (codefendant) in the commission of the crime. The basic assumptions of sex-role and masculinity/femininity theories were offered as useful starting points from which to understand and increase knowledge about female offenders who committed sexual offenses with a male codefendant.

The findings indicate that most female sexual offenders have suffered physical and psychological abuse, predominantly by their mothers, during childhood. The Co-Offenders were abused more frequently and physically and psychologically more severely than the Independent Offenders. This early abuse may be indicative of the women's maladaptive decisions as adults, not the least of which result in their abusive relationships with men.

The majority of the women in both groups were sexually abused as children, predominantly by male relatives (e.g., brothers and uncles). Statistically significant differences were found between Co-Offenders and Independent Offenders regarding the sexual abuse commencing before age 10 and the severity of the abuse. The Independent Offenders experienced more severe sexual abuse beginning before age 10 than the Co-Offenders. Previous research has indicated that severe and prolonged sexual abuse in early childhood results in lasting negative psychological effects on women. This is confirmed in this research.

Regarding psychological characteristics of female sex offenders, the Independent Offenders are strikingly more seriously disturbed (based on the MMPI-2) than the Co-Offenders. Few of the Co-Offenders show evidence of severe psychological disturbance.

This study found no relationship between alcohol abuse and the offense for both offender groups. Most of the Independent Offenders denied drug use, and roughly a quarter of the Co-Offenders admitted to using drugs during the offense. Group mean scores on the MAC-R scale of the MMPI-2 yielded the opposite results; substance abuse was contraindicated for the Co-Offenders, and suggestive for the Independent Offenders. This may be a function of self-report bias or possibly denial.

Differences emerge between the two groups of female offenders in location of the offense, the sex acts involved, and the strategies used on the victims. The Co-Offenders reported much more violent tactics with the victim(s) than the Independent Offenders. The Independent Offenders tended to be less coercive (e.g., promoting the sexual abuse as a game or something that would be fun) than the Co-Offenders. It is important to note the Co-Offenders reported that the male codefendant performed the coercive maneuvers on the victims. The majority of the Co-Offenders were battered women who feared abandonment as well as physical harm for themselves and/or their children if they refused to comply with codefendants' demands regarding the child sexual abuse.

Child sexual abuse by women does occur, and it may not be as rare as previous studies indicated. This study has shown that there are many different circumstances in which women may sexually abuse children, and in the circumstances that lead them to do so. Women sexually offend in concert with male partners, and they offend without partners.

REFERENCES

References

Allen, C.M. (1990). Women as perpetrators of child sexual abuse: Recognition barriers. In A.L. Horton, B.L. Johnson, L.M. Roundy, & D. Williams (Eds.). *The incest perpetrator: A family member no one wants to treat* (pp. 108-125). Newbury Park, CA: Sage.

Allen, C.M. (1991). *Women and men who sexually abuse children: A comparative analysis*. Orwell, VT: Safer Society Press.

American Humane Association. (1978). *National study on child neglect and abuse reporting*. Denver: Author.

Archer, R.P. (1992). Review of the Minnesota Multiphasic Personality Inventory-2. In J.J. Kramer & J.C. Conoley (Eds.), *The eleventh mental measurements yearbook* (pp. 558-561). Lincoln, NE: University of Nebraska Press.

Baldwin, J.I. (1983). The effects of women's liberation and socialization on delinquency and crime. *Humboldt Journal of Social Relations, 10,* 90-111.

Banning, A. (1989). Mother-son incest: Confronting a prejudice. *Child Abuse & Neglect, 13,* 563-570.

Bardwick, J.M. (1971). *Psychology of women: A study of bio-cultural conflicts*. New York: Harper & Row.

Brown, M., Hull, L., & Panesis, S. (1984). *Women who rape*. Boston, MA: Massachusetts Trial Court.

Chasnoff, I.J., Burns, W.J., Schnoll, S.H., Burns, K., Chisum, G., & Kyle-Sproe, L. (1986). Maternal-neonatal incest. *American Journal of Orthopsychiatry, 56,* 577-580.

Covington, J. (1985). Gender differences in criminality among heroin users. *Journal of Research in Crime and Delinquency, 22,* 329-353.

Dietz, P.E. (1983). Sex offenses: Behavioral aspects. In S.H. Kadish (Ed.), *Encyclopedia of crime and justice* (Vol. 4, pp.1485-1493). New York: Free Press.

Faller, K. (1987). Women who sexually abuse children. *Violence and Victims, 2,* 263-276.

Finkelhor, D. (1979). *Sexually victimized children*. New York: Free Press.

Finkelhor, D., & Russell, D. (1984). Women as perpetrators: Review of the evidence. In D. Finkelhor (Ed.), *Child sexual abuse: New theory and research* (pp. 171-187). New York: Free Press.

Finkelhor, D., Williams, L.M., & Burns, N. (1988). *Nursery crimes: Sexual abuse in day care.* Newbury Park, CA: Sage.

Finkelhor, D., Williams, L.M., Burns, N., & Kalinowski, M. (1988). *Sexual abuse in day care: A national study.* Study prepared under grant 90-CA-1155 from the National Center on Child Abuse and Neglect. University of New Hampshire: Family Research Laboratory.

Gilligan, C. (1982). *In a different voice.* Cambridge, MA: Harvard University Press.

Groth, A.N. (1978). Patterns of sexual assault against children and adolescents. In A.W. Burgess, A.N. Groth, L.L. Holmstrom, & S.M. Sgroi (Eds.), *Sexual assault of children and adolescents* (pp. 3-24). Lexington, MA: Heath.

Groth, A.N. (1982). The child molester: Clinical observations. In J.R. Conte & D.A. Shore (Eds.), *Social work and child sexual abuse.* New York: Hawthorn Press.

Hathaway, S.R., & McKinley, J.C. (1989). *Manual for the MMPI-2.* Minneapolis, MN: National Computer Systems.

Heidensohn, F. (1985). Women and crime: Questions for criminology. In P. Carlen & A. Worrall (Eds.), *Gender, crime and justice* (pp. 16-27). Philadelphia, PA: Open University.

Herman, J., Russell, D., & Trocki, K. (1986). Long-term effects of incestuous abuse in childhood. *American Journal of Psychiatry, 143,* 1293-1296.

Hoffman-Bustamante, D. (1973). The nature of female criminality. *Issues in Criminality, 8,* 117-136.

Justice, B., & Justice, R. (1979). *The broken taboo.* New York: Human Sciences Press.

Klein, D. (1973). The etiology of female crime: A review of the literature. In S.K. Datesman & F.R. Scarpitti (Eds.), *Women, crime and justice* (pp. 70-105). New York: Oxford University Press.

Krug, R.S. (1989). Adult male report of childhood sexual abuse by mothers: Case descriptions, motivations, and long-term consequences. *Child Abuse & Neglect, 13,* 111-120.

Kuhl, A.A. (1984). Personality traits of abused women: Masochism myth refuted. *Victimology: An International Journal, 9,* 450-463.

Marvasti, J. (1986). Incestuous mothers. *American Journal of Forensic Psychiatry, 7,* 63-69.

Mathews, R., Matthews, J., & Speltz, K. (1989). *Female sexual offenders: An exploratory study.* Orwell, VT: Safer Society Press.

McCann, I.L., Sakheim, D.K., & Abrahamson, D.J. (1988). Trauma and victimization: A model of psychological adaption. *The Counseling Psychologist, 16,* 531-593.

McCarthy, D. (1981). *Women who rape.* Unpublished manuscript.

McCarty, L. (1986). Mother-child incest: Characteristics of the offender. *Child Welfare, 65,* 447-458.

Mohr, J.W., Turner, R.W., & Jerry, M.B. (1964). *Pedophilia and exhibitionism.* Toronto: University of Toronto Press.

Naffin, N. (1985). The masculinity-femininity hypothesis: A consideration of gender-based personality theories of female crime. *British Journal of Criminology, 25,* 365-381.

National Center for Child Abuse and Neglect. (1981). *Study findings: National study of incidence and severity of child abuse and neglect.* Washington, DC: Department of Health, Education, and Welfare.

Newman, F., & Caplan, P.J. (1982). Juvenile female prostitution as gender consistent response to early deprivation. *International Journal of Women's Studies, 5,* 128-137.

Nichols, D.S. (1992). Review of the Minnesota Multiphasic Personality Inventory-2. In J.J. Kramer & J.C. Conoley (Eds.), *The eleventh mental measurements yearbook* (pp. 562-565).

Notman, M.T., Zilbach, J.J., Baker-Miller, J., & Nadelson, C.C. (1986). Themes in psychoanalytic understanding of women: Some reconsiderations of autonomy and affiliation. *Journal of the American Academy of Psychoanalysis, 14,* 241-253.

O'Connor, A. (1987). Female sex offenders. *British Journal of Psychiatry, 150,* 615-620.

Painter, S.L., & Dutton, D. (1985). Patterns of emotional bonding in battered women. *International Journal of Women's Studies, 8,* 363-375.

Plummer, K. (1981). Pedophilia: Constructing a psychological baseline. In M. Cook & K. Howells (Eds.), *Adult sexual interest in children*. London: Academic Press.

Russell, D. (1986). *The secret trauma: Incest in the lives of girls and women*. New York: Basic Books.

Sears, K. (1989). *The significance of relationships with important male "others" in the first conviction of female offenders*. Unpublished doctoral dissertation, The Fielding Institute, Santa Barbara, CA.

Smart, C. (1976). *Women, crime and criminology*. London: Routledge & Kegan Paul.

Travin, S., Cullin, K., & Protter, B. (1990). Female sex offenders: Severe victims and victimizers. *Journal of Forensic Sciences, 35,* 140-150.

U.S. Department of Justice, Bureau of Justice Statistics (1991, March). *Women in prison*. Rockville, MD: U.S. Government Printing Office.

U.S. Department of Justice. (1985). *FBI crime in the United States*. Washington, DC: U.S. Government Printing Office.

U.S. Department of Justice, Federal Bureau of Investigation. (1987). *Crime in the United States, 1986*. Washington, D.C.: U.S. Government Printing Office.

U.S. Department of Justice. *Uniform crime reports for the United States, 1975-78*. Washington, DC: Government Printing Office.

Veddar, C.B., & Sommerville, D.B. (1975). *The delinquent girl* (2nd ed.). Springfield, MO: Charles C. Thomas.

Walker, L.E. (1984). *The battered woman syndrome*. New York: Harper & Row.

Walker, L.E. (1989). *Terrifying love: Why battered women kill and how society responds*. New York: Harper & Row.

Ward, D., Jackson, M., & Ward, R. (1980). Crimes of violence by women. In S. Datesman & F. Scarfieti (Eds.), *Women, crime, and justice* (pp. 309-330). New York: Oxford University Press.

West, D.J. (1977). *Homosexuality re-examined*. London: Duckworth.

Wolfe, F. (1985, March). *Twelve female sexual offenders*. Presented at a conference on "Next steps in research on the assessment and treatment of sexually aggressive persons (paraphiliacs)," St. Louis, MO.

APPENDICES

INFORMED CONSENT

1. I understand that this study is of a research nature. It may offer no direct benefit to me.

2. The purpose of this study is to improve understanding of women who have been convicted of sex crimes involving children.

3. Participation in this study is voluntary. I may refuse to enter it or I may withdraw from it at any time without affecting my status or legal rights. The researcher may conclude the interview early and not include the data in the study. Participation or nonparticipation will not become a part of my institutional record. I understand that participation in this study will have no effect on decisions relating to release, institutional treatment, housing or other benefits.

4. As a participant in this study I will be asked to take part in the following procedures:
   a. Complete a simple paper-and-pencil text *(MMPI)*.
   b. Participate in a 1-1½ hour private interview with the researcher only.

5. Participation in this study will take approximately 3 hours of my time.

6. The risks, discomforts and inconvenience of the above procedures might be: I will be asked to reveal personal data that I may find to be stressful, embarrassing or upsetting. However, I am free to end the interview at any time. I may also be referred to the mental health staff of this facility, if I so request.

7. The possible benefits of the procedures might be:
   a. I may come to a better understanding of my own behavior.
   b. I will be helping to contribute to psychological science and human welfare.

8. I understand that the researcher will not reveal my name or any personal data to prison personnel or to the general public. All tests and materials will be maintained by the researcher outside of the prison. At no time will these materials be reviewed by prison personnel.

9. Notes will be taken during the individual (notes will not contain names) interview. At the end of the study, the notes will be destroyed.

10. I give permission for the researcher to read my Pre-Sentencing Investigation report.

11. I understand that there will be no custodial personnel posted inside the room during the interview.

12. Information about this study was discussed with me by the researcher, Patricia A. Davin, a doctoral student at the Fielding Institute.

13. I am not receiving any compensation for participating in this study.

If you are interested in the results of this study, please indicate below. A description of the study will be sent to you when the results are available.

I have read and understand all of the foregoing and I am executing this agreement freely and voluntarily and without threat or coercion from any person.

Date _____ Signature _____

Please send me a copy of the results _____

Address _____

_____

_____

Appendix B

CONSENT FOR RELEASE OF INFORMATION

DATE _____

I, _____ , give permission for the researcher, Patricia

A. Davin, to read my Pre-Sentencing Investigation Report.

SIGNED,

_____

Appendix C

STRUCTURED INTERVIEW

DEMOGRAPHICS

1. What is your date of birth? _____

2. What is your race?
      1 Asian _____
      2 Black _____
      3 Caucasian _____
      4 Hispanic _____
      5 Native American _____
      6 Other _____

3. What is the highest grade that you completed?
      Grade school 1 ____ 2 ____ 3 ____ 4 ____ 5 ____ 6 ____ 7 ____ 8 ____
      High school 9 ____ 10 ____ 11 ____ 12 ____
      College 13 ____ 14 ____ 15 ____ 16 ____
      Post-College 17 ____ 18 ____ 19 ____ 20 ____

4. Are you now
      1 Married _____
      2 Widowed _____
      3 Divorced _____
      4 Separated _____
or have you
      5 Never been married? _____

5. Please tell me the *age* and *sex* of biological, adopted, and/or stepchildren that you now have.

_____

6a. What is the longest period of time that you held a job?
      Years 1 ____ 2 ____ 3 ____ 4 ____ 5 ____ 6 ____ 7 ____ 8 ____ 9 ____ 10 ____
      Months 1 ____ 2 ____ 3 ____ 4 ____ 5 ____ 6 ____ 7 ____ 8 ____ 9 ____ 10 ____ 11 ____

6b. What kind of work did you do (occupation)? _____

_____

      Ranked 1–5 *(low level to high level job)* _____

FAMILY DATA

Now I'd like to find out about your family while you were growing up.

7. Who raised you (mostly)?

1 Biological parents_____	9 MGF_____
2 Mother_____	10 PGM_____
3 Father_____	11 PGF_____
4 Stepparents_____	12 Sister_____
5 Stepmother_____	13 Brother_____
6 Stepfather_____	14 Aunt_____
7 Foster parents_____	15 Uncle_____
8 MGM_____	16 Other_____

8. How was your relationship with the woman who mostly raised you?

Negative . . . . Positive

-3 -2 -1 0 1 2 3

9. How was your relationship with the man who mostly raised you?

Negative . . . . Positive

-3 -2 -1 0 1 2 3

10. How was your relationship with your Mother?

Negative . . . . Positive

-3 -2 -1 0 1 2 3

11. How was your relationship with your Father?

Negative . . . . Positive

-3 -2 -1 0 1 2 3

12. How often were you spanked from birth to 12 years of age?

1 Never_____

2 Less than 2–3 times a year_____

3 Less than once a month_____

4 2–3 times a month_____

5 2–3 times a week_____

6 Daily_____

7 Don't remember_____

13. How often were you spanked from 13 to 18 years of age?

1 Never_____

2 Less than 2–3 times a year_____

3 Less than once a month_____

4 2–3 times a month_____

5 2–3 times a week_____

6 Daily_____

7 Don't remember_____

14. How often were you hit or spanked with an object?

     1 Never_____

     2 Once_____

     3 Two or three times_____

     4 More than 2–3 times, but not often_____

     5 Often_____

     6 Don't remember_____

If Yes, what objects?

1 Shoes_____	5 Water Hose_____
2 Belt_____	6 Wet Towel_____
3 Board_____	7 Fly Swatter_____
4 Paddle_____	8 Switches_____

15a. Of the people who mostly raised you, who do you think most contributed to your knowledge of sex?

1 Biological parents_____	9 MGF_____
2 Mother_____	10 PGM_____
3 Father_____	11 PGF_____
4 Stepparents_____	12 Sister_____
5 Stepmother_____	13 Brother_____
6 Stepfather_____	14 Aunt_____
7 Foster parents_____	15 Uncle_____
8 MGM_____	16 N/A_____

15b. On this 7-point scale, how freely did he/she answer your questions about sex?

     Questions   Answered

     not answered . . . . freely

          -3 -2 -1 0 1 2 3

16. What do you think your mother's (woman who mostly raised you) attitude about sex was?

     Negative . . . . Positive

          -3 -2 -1 0 1 2 3

17 What do you think your Father's (man who mostly raised you) attitude about sex was?

     Negative . . . . Positive

          -3 -2 -1 0 1 2 3

18. What do you think their sex life was like?

     Negative . . . . Positive

          -3 -2 -1 0 1 2 3

19a. On a scale of -3 to +3, how encouraged or discouraged to date were you by the woman who mostly raised you?

     Discouraged . . . . Encouraged

          -3 -2 -1 0 1 2 3

19b. On a scale of -3 to +3, how encouraged or discouraged to date were you by the man who mostly raised you?

     Discouraged . . . . Encouraged

          -3 -2 -1 0 1 2 3

19c. On the same scale, how much control did the woman who mostly raised you have over your dating; that is, how strict were her rules?

Controlled . . . . Not Controlled

-3 -2 -1 0 1 2 3

19d. On the same scale, how much control did the man who mostly raised you have over your dating; that is, how strict were his rules?

Controlled . . . . Not Controlled

-3 -2 -1 0 1 2 3

20a. On this same scale, how encouraged or discouraged to have intercourse before marriage were you by the woman who mostly raised you?

Discouraged . . . . Encouraged

-3 -2 -1 0 1 2 3

20b. On this same scale, how encouraged or discouraged to have intercourse before marriage were you by the man who mostly raised you?

Discourage . . . . Encouraged

-3 -2 -1 0 1 2 3

20c. On the same scale, how much concern and fear did the woman who mostly raised you have about you having intercourse before marriage?

Not much   Much concern
concern and fear . . . . and fear

-3 -2 -1 0 1 2 3

20d. On the same scale, how much concern and fear did the man who mostly raised you have about you having intercourse before marriage?

Not much   Much concern
concern and fear . . . . and fear

-3 -2 -1 0 1 2 3

PERSONAL HISTORY

Now I'd like to find out about how you learned about sex.

21. How much of your knowledge of sex was obtained from:

    a. Parents (or people who mostly raised you)

Very Little . . . . A Lot

3 -2 -1 0 1 2 3

    b. Brothers and sisters

Very Little . . . . A Lot

-3 -2 -1 0 1 2 3

    c. Friends

Very Little . . . . A Lot

-3 -2 -1 0 1 2 3

    d. School

Very Little . . . . A Lot

-3 -2 -1 0 1 2 3

e. Church

Very Little . . . . A Lot

-3 -2 -1 0 1 2 3

f. Movies &/or TV

Very Little . . . . A Lot

-3 -2 -1 0 1 2 3

g. Books

Very Little . . . . A Lot

-3 -2 -1 0 1 2 3

Now I'd like to ask you some questions about sexual experiences.

22. How did you learn to masturbate? *(If Did not, skip to Question 26)*

1 Did not_____   5 Friend_____

2 Parents_____   6 School_____

3 Brother/sister_____   7 Movies/TV_____

4 Books_____   8 Self_____

23. How old were you when you began to masturbate?_____

24. When you were young, how comfortable or uncomfortable did you feel about masturbating?

Very uncomfortable . . . . Very comfortable

-3 -2 -1 0 1 2 3

25. How comfortable or uncomfortable do you currently feel about masturbating?

Very uncomfortable . . . . Very comfortable

-3 -2 -1 0 1 2 3

26. How old were you when you began to date?_____

27. How satisfied were you with your dating?

Very dissatisfied . . . . Very satisfied

-3 -2 -1 0 1 2 3

28a. When you were a teenager, did you pet on dates? *(If No, skip to Question 29)*

No_____

Yes_____

28b. When you petted on dates, did you *(in ascending order)*:

1 Deep kiss_____

2 Include breasts_____

3 Include genital stimulation by hand_____

4 Include mouth-genital stimulation_____

5 Include total nudity?_____

29a. *(If married)* Did you have intercourse before marriage? *(If No, skip to Queston 31)*

No_____

Yes_____

29b. *(If Yes)* **Did you have intercourse with:**

      1 Future spouse only?_____

      2 With love relationship only?_____

      3 Not necessarily with love relationship_____

30a. What are your present feelings about past non-marital sex?

      Very dissatisfied . . . . Very satisfied

                -3 -2 -1 0 1 2 3

30b. How comfortable or uncomfortable do you feel about past non-marital sex?

      Very uncomfortable . . . . Very comfortable

                -3 -2 -1 0 1 2 3

31. At what age did you first have intercourse?_____

32a. How many male sexual partners have you had?_____

32b. How satisfied have you been with these experiences?

      Very dissatisfied . . . . Very satisfied

                -3 -2 -1 0 1 2 3

32c. How many female sexual partners have you had?_____

32d. How satisfied have you been with these experiences?

      Very dissatisfied . . . . Very satisfied

                -3 -2 -1 0 1 2 3

32e. How many sexual experiences have you had with animals?_____

32f. How satisfied have you been with these experiences?

      Very dissatisfied . . . . Very satisfied

                -3 -2 -1 0 1 2 3

33. On a scale of -3 to +3, how important is sex to you?

      Unimportant . . . . Very important

                -3 -2 -1 0 1 2 3

HISTORY OF VIOLENCE

Now I'd like to find out about any abuse that happened in the home you grew up in. *(Hand subject card.)* **By** *ABUSE,* **I mean: any verbal or physical activity among family members that is different from typical family conflict. It includes things like the following:**

      1) Excessive possessiveness and/or jealousy.

      2) Extreme verbal harassment; derogatory comments — like "you are a bitch," "you are stupid," "you can't do anything right," etc.

      3) Restriction of activity through physical or psychological means — like not letting someone have the car or money so they can never go anywhere.

      4) Verbal or nonverbal threats of punishment or deprivation — like "I won't let you out of the house for a week."

      5) Actual physical attack (hitting, etc.) with or without injury.

34. With this definition in mind, would you say there was abuse while you were growing up? *(If No, skip to Question 36)*

        No _____ Yes _____

35a. Were *you* abused by anyone while you were growing up? *(If No, skip to Question 36)*

        No _____ Yes _____

35b. By whom? _____

35c. How often did this occur?

        1 Once _____
        2 Occasionally _____
        3 Frequently _____
        4 Don't know _____

35d. What type of abuse was it?

        1 Psychological only _____
        2 Physical & psychological _____

35e. Who was the abuse between that affected you the most? _____

_____

35f. How often did this occur?

        1 Once _____
        2 Occasionally _____
        3 Frequently _____
        4 Don't know _____

35g. What type of abuse was it?

        1 Psychological only _____
        2 Physical & psychological _____

HISTORY OF SEXUAL ABUSE

The following questions are about any sexual abuse you may have experienced as a child. I'll read a list of things. Tell me if any of them have ever happened to you:

36a. Did the MALE WHO RAISED YOU ever do any of these things to you?

        Who? _____

        (Woman's age) _____ to _____

	N/A	No	Attempted but resisted	Yes, single incident	Yes, several times
Fondled you	0	1	2	3	4
You fondled him	0	1	2	3	4
Oral sex	0	1	2	3	4
Sexual intercourse	0	1	2	3	4
Other	0	1	2	3	4

35b. Did the FEMALE WHO RAISED YOU ever do any of these things to you?

Who?_____

*(Woman's age)*_____ to _____

	N/A	No	Attempted but resisted	Yes, single incident	Yes, several times
Fondled you	0	1	2	3	4
You fondled her	0	1	2	3	4
Oral sex	0	1	2	3	4
Sexual intercourse	0	1	2	3	4
Other	0	1	2	3	

35c. Did ANY OTHER MALE RELATIVE ever do any of these things to you?

Who?_____

*(Woman's age)*_____ to _____

	N/A	No	Attempted but resisted	Yes, single incident	Yes, several times
Fondled you	0	1	2	3	4
You fondled him	0	1	2	3	4
Oral sex	0	1	2	3	4
Sexual intercourse	0	1	2	3	4
Other	0	1	2	3	4

35d. Did ANY OTHER FEMALE RELATIVE ever do any of these things to you?

Who?_____

*(Woman's age)*_____ to _____

	N/A	No	Attempted but resisted	Yes, single incident	Yes, several times
Fondled you	0	1	2	3	4
You fondled her	0	1	2	3	4
Oral sex	0	1	2	3	4
Sexual intercourse	0	1	2	3	4
Other	0	1	2	3	4

35e. Did ANYONE ELSE ever do any of these things to you?

Who?_____

*(Woman's age)*_____ to _____

	N/A	No	Attempted but resisted	Yes, single incident	Yes, several times
Fondled you	0	1	2	3	4
You fondled him	0	1	2	3	4
Oral sex	0	1	2	3	4
Sexual intercourse	0	1	2	3	4
Other	0	1	2	3	4

SUMMARY:

Was this woman sexually abused as a child?

No _____ Yes _____

By whom?

1 Father _____	7 Stepfather _____
2 Mother _____	8 Adoptive father _____
3 Male relative _____	9 Male Acquaintance _____
4 Female relative _____	10 Foster mother _____
5 Male stranger _____	11 Foster father _____
6 Female stranger _____	12 Stepmother _____

HISTORY OF SUBSTANCE ABUSE IN THE RELATIONSHIP

Now I'd like to know something about alcohol and/or substance use during you relationship with him/codefendant.

37. During your relationship with him, did HE use prescription drugs such as tranquilizers, pain killers, antidepressants? *(If No, skip to Question 38)*

No _____ Yes _____

If Yes, how often?

1 Only a couple of times a year _____
2 About once a month _____
3 About once a week _____
4 2–3 times a week _____
5 Almost every day _____
6 Every day _____
7 Don't know _____

Which ones did he use? _____

38. During your relationship with him, did YOU use prescription drugs? *(If No, skip to Question 39)*

No _____ Yes _____

If Yes, how often?

1 Only a couple of times a year _____
2 About once a month _____
3 About once a week _____
4 2–3 times a week _____
5 Almost every day _____
6 Every day _____
7 Don't know _____

Which ones did you use? _____

39.During your relationship, did HE use drugs such as:

a. LSD *(If No, skip to b)*

      Yes_____

      No_____

If Yes, how often?

      1 Only a couple of times a year_____

      2 About once a month_____

      3 About once a week_____

      4 2–3 times a week_____

      5 Almost every day_____

      6 Every day_____

      7 Don't know_____

b. Mescaline *(If No, skip to c)*

      Yes_____

      No_____

If Yes, how often?

      1 Only a couple of times a year_____

      2 About once a month_____

      3 About once a week_____

      4 2–3 times a week_____

      5 Almost every day_____

      6 Every day_____

      7 Don't know_____

c. Heroin *(If No, skip to d)*

      Yes_____

      No_____

If Yes, how often?

      1 Only a couple of times a year_____

      2 About once a month_____

      3 About once a week_____

      4 2–3 times a week_____

      5 Almost every day_____

      6 Every day_____

      7 Don't know_____

d. Cocaine *(If No, skip to e)*

Yes _____ No _____

If Yes, how often?

1 Only a couple of times a year _____

2 About once a month _____

3 About once a week _____

4 2–3 times a week _____

5 Almost every day _____

6 Every day _____

7 Don't know _____

e. Marijuana *(If No, skip to Question 40)*

Yes _____ No _____

If Yes, how often?

1 Only a couple of times a year _____

2 About once a month _____

3 About once a week _____

4 2–3 times a week _____

5 Almost every day _____

6 Every day _____

7 Don't know _____

40. During your relationship, did YOU use drugs such as:

a. LSD *(If No, skip to b)*

Yes _____ No _____

If Yes, how often?

1 Only a couple of times a year _____

2 About once a month _____

3 About once a week _____

4 2–3 times a week _____

5 Almost every day _____

6 Every day _____

7 Don't know _____

b. Mescaline *(If No, skip to c)*

Yes _____ No _____

If Yes, how often?

1 Only a couple of times a year _____

2 About once a month _____

3 About once a week _____

4 2–3 times a week _____

5 Almost every day _____

6 Every day _____

7 Don't know _____

c. Heroin *(If No, skip to d)*

        Yes _____ No _____

If Yes, how often?

        1 Only a couple of times a year _____
        2 About once a month _____
        3 About once a week _____
        4 2–3 times a week _____
        5 Almost every day _____
        6 Every day _____
        7 Don't know _____

d. Cocaine *(If No, skip to e)*

        Yes _____ No _____

If Yes, how often?

        1 Only a couple of times a year _____
        2 About once a month _____
        3 About once a week _____
        4 2–3 times a week _____
        5 Almost every day _____
        6 Every day _____
        7 Don't know _____

e. Marijuana *(If No, skip to Question 41)*

        Yes _____ No _____

If Yes, how often?

        1 Only a couple of times a year _____
        2 About once a month _____
        3 About once a week _____
        4 2–3 times a week _____
        5 Almost every day _____
        6 Every day _____
        7 Don't know _____

41. Did HE get drunk? *(If No, skip to Question 42)*

If Yes, how often?

        1 Only a couple of times a year _____
        2 About once a month _____
        3 About once a week _____
        4 2–3 times a week _____
        5 Almost every day _____
        6 Every day _____
        7 Don't know _____

42. Did YOU get drunk? *(If No, skip to Quesiton 43)*

If Yes, how often?

      1 Only a couple of times a year_____

      2 About once a month_____

      3 About once a week_____

      4 2–3 times a week_____

      5 Almost every day_____

      6 Every day_____

      7 Don't know_____

Now let's talk some about your relationship with him.

43. How often did HE know where you were when you were not together?

      1 Never_____

      2 Rarely_____

      3 Sometimes_____

      4 Usually_____

      5 Always_____

44. How often did you know where he was when you were not together?

      1 Never_____

      2 Rarely_____

      3 Sometimes_____

      4 Usually_____

      5 Always_____

45. Were there places that you would have liked to go, but didn't because you felt he wouldn't want you to go? If yes, how often did this happen?

      1 Never_____

      2 Rarely_____

      3 Sometimes_____

      4 Usually_____

      5 Always_____

46. Were there places you thought he might have liked to go, but didn't because he felt you wouldn't have wanted him to? If yes, how often did this happen?

      1 Never_____

      2 Rarely_____

      3 Sometimes_____

      4 Usually_____

      5 Always_____

47. In general, when you and he disagreed on major issues, who won?

    1 He always won _____

    2 He usually won _____

    3 About equal or compromise _____

    4 You usually won _____

    5 You always won _____

    6 Not resolved _____

    7 Other _____

48. When you were angry or mad at him, how did you show it? (Circle all that apply)

    1 Tried to talk it out _____

    2 Sulked, quit speaking, withdrew _____

    3 Cried _____

    4 Cursed, swore, or shouted _____

    5 Directed anger toward objects (threw something, hit or broke something) _____

    6 Directed anger toward children or pets _____

    7 Threatened physical violence _____

    8 Used physical violence with spouse _____

    9 Used physical violence with kids _____

49. When he was angry or mad at you, how did he show it? (Circle all that apply)

    1 Tried to talk it out _____

    2 Sulked, quit speaking, withdrew _____

    3 Cried _____

    4 Cursed, swore, or shouted _____

    5 Directed anger toward objects (threw something, hit or broke something) _____

    6 Directed anger toward children or pets _____

    7 Threatened physical violence _____

    8 Used physical violence with spouse _____

    9 Used physical violence with kids _____

50. Who generally initiated sex?

    1 Man _____

    2 Both _____

    3 You _____

51. Was sex with HIM ever unpleasant for you?

    1 Never _____

    2 Rarely _____

    3 Occasionally _____

    4 Frequently _____

    5 Most of the time _____

52. Were any of these a part of your sexual relationship?

1 He wanted sex too often _____

2 He forced me to have sex when I didn't want it _____

3 He refused to have sex when I wanted it _____

4 He compared me unfavorably to other women _____

5 He made me do things I didn't want to do _____

6 Insensitive to my sexual needs (not enough foreplay, didn't last long enough) _____

7 He had physical problems _____ _____

8 I had physical problems _____ _____

9 He wanted sex after a battering _____

53a. Was sex with YOU ever unpleasant for him?

1 Never _____

2 Rarely _____

3 Occasionally _____

4 Frequently _____

5 Most of the time _____

53b. Were any of these a part of your sexual relationship?

1 I wanted sex too often _____

2 I forced him to have sex when he didn't want it _____

3 I refused to have sex when he wanted i _____

4 I compared him unfavorably to other men _____

5 I made him do things he didn't want to do _____

6 Insensitive to his sexual needs (not enough foreplay, didn't last long enough) _____

7 I had physical problems _____

8 He had physical problems _____

9 I wanted sex after a battering _____

54. Was he ever JEALOUS about the possibility of YOUR having an affair?

1 Never _____

2 Rarely _____

3 Sometimes _____

4 Usually _____

5 Always _____

55. Were you ever JEALOUS about the possibility of HIS having an affair?

1 Never _____

2 Rarely _____

3 Sometimes _____

4 Usually _____

5 Always _____

56. Did your partner ever have a sexual relationship (an affair) with another while you were married or living together?

   1 Never_____

   2 Suspected, but not sure_____

   3 Once _____

   4 Yes, unsure how often_____

   5 2 or 3 times_____

   6 More than 2 or 3 times but not often_____

   7 Often_____

57. Did YOU ever have a sexual relationship (an affair) with another while you were married or living together?

   1 Never_____

   2 Yes, once_____

   3 Yes, 2 or 3 times_____

   4 More than 2 or 3 times but not often_____

   5 Often_____

58a. Did he ever ASK you or FORCE you to perform what you would consider to be unusual sex acts?

   No_____

   Yes_____

58b. If Yes, how often?

   1 Once_____

   2 Occasionally_____

   3 Frequently_____

c. What were these acts? *(Circle ALL that apply)*

   1 Oral sex_____

   2 Anal sex_____

   3 Insert objects_____

   4 Bondage; S-M_____

   5 Sex with others_____

   6 Sex with animals_____

   7 Other_____

59. Did he ever FORCE you to have intercourse (sex)?

   No_____

   Yes_____

If Yes, how often?

   1 Once_____

   2 2 or 3 times_____

   3 More than 2 or 3 times but not often_____

   4 Often_____

OFFENSE INFORMATION

INCIDENT # _____

I'd like to find out some information regarding the offense.

60. Where did the sexual abuse occur?

    a. Your home   No _____ Yes _____
    b. Relative's home   No _____ Yes _____
    c. Other private setting No _____ Yes _____
    d. Car   No _____ Yes _____
    e. Public setting   No _____ Yes _____
    f. Other   No _____ Yes _____   _____

61. What types of activities were involved?

    a. Child fondled   No _____ Yes _____
    b. Child fondles   No _____ Yes _____
    c. Child watches others have sex   No _____ Yes _____
    d. Others watch child have sex   No _____ Yes _____
    e. Sex with other children   No _____ Yes _____
    f. Group sex   No _____ Yes _____
    g. Videos/photos/polaroids   No _____ Yes _____
    h. Digital penetration   No _____ Yes _____
    i. S-M; bondage   No _____ Yes _____
    j. Satanic sex   No _____ Yes _____
    k. Ritualistic sex   No _____ Yes _____
    l. Anal sex   No _____ Yes _____
    m. Oral sex   No _____ Yes _____
    n. Intercourse   No _____ Yes _____
    o. Other   No _____ Yes _____   _____

62a. How many times did this occur?

    1 1 time _____
    2 2 times _____
    3 3-5 times _____
    4 >5 times _____

62b. Over how long a period of time did this occur?

    1 1 day _____
    2 Several days _____
    3 1 week _____
    4 Several weeks _____
    5 1 month _____
    6 Several months
    7 1 year _____
    8 2-5 years _____

9 Other_____ _____

63. How old were you when this activity first began?_____

64. Was there more than one child involved?

       No_____ Yes_____

65. Tell me the AGE, RACE and SEX of the child(ren)_____

_____

66. What was his/her/their relationship to you?

       1 Biological child_____
       2 Stepchild_____
       3 Adopted child_____
       4 Foster child_____
       5 Other relative_____
       6 Neighbor_____
       7 Acquaintance_____
       8 Stranger_____
       9 Other_____ _____

67. Why do you think he/she/they went along/participated?

       1 Fear_____
       2 Affection_____
       3 Pleasure_____
       4 Obligation_____
       5 Fun (game)_____
       6 Other_____ _____

68. How did you get him/her/them to go along?

       1 Threatened death_____
       2 Threatened physical harm to child_____
       3 Threatened physical harm to other_____
       4 Threatened punishment (other than physical harm)_____
       5 Threatened loss of love_____
       6 Threatened abandonment_____
       7 Force_____
       8 Bribes_____
       9 Told child it was expression of love_____
       10 Teaching sex to child_____
       11 Game_____
       12 Other_____ _____

69. Were you worried that the child(ren) might tell?

       No_____ Yes_____

70. Did he/she/they tell?

       No_____ Yes_____

71. How did you/codefendant keep the child(ren) from telling?
      1 Threatened death _____
      2 Threatened physical harm to child _____
      3 Threatened physical harm to other _____
      4 Threatened punishment (other than physical harm) _____
      5 Threatened loss of love _____
      6 Threatened abandonment _____
      7 Death _____
      8 Actual physical harm _____
      9 Other _____ _____

72. Did you directly participate in the sex abuse?
      No _____ Yes _____

73. How did you come to be involved in the sexual abuse?
      1 Threatened with death _____
      2 Threatened physical harm to child _____
      3 Threatened physical harm to other _____
      4 Threatened with loss of love _____
      5 Threatened with abandonment _____
      6 Actual physical harm to you _____
      7 Actual physical harm to child _____
      8 Actual physical harm to other _____
      9 Voluntarily participated _____
      10 Other _____ _____

74. Was a weapon used?
      No _____ Yes _____

If Yes, what kind of weapon was it?
      1 Household item _____
      2 Actual weapon _____

75. Was the co-offender using drugs during the offense?
      No _____ Yes _____ Not sure _____

76. Was the co-offender using alcohol during the offense?
      No _____ Yes _____

77. Were you using drugs during the offense?
      No _____ Yes _____ Not sure _____

78. Were you using alcohol during the offense?
      No _____ Yes _____ Not sure _____

79. Were you orgasmic while offending?
      No _____ Yes _____

80a. Did you fantasize during the offending?

        No _____ Yes _____

80b. If Yes, who did you fantasize about?

        1 Fantasized about the child _____

        2 Fantasized about the child as an adult _____

        3 Fantasized about the co-offender _____

        4 Other _____ _____

81a. As you think back to the offense, do you fantasize?

        No _____ Yes _____

81b. If Yes, who do you fantasize about?

        1 Fantasize about the child _____

        2 Fantasize about the child as an adult _____

        3 Fantasize about the co-offender _____

        4 Other _____ _____

81c. Do you masturbate?

        No _____ Yes _____

HISTORY OF SIGNIFICANT RELATIONSHIPS

82. Tell me about 2 of the most significant relationships (people you've been in love with) you have had with men and/or women.

[Quantify: #; exclusive with men, women, both; duration, degree of abuse]

_____

_____

_____

_____

_____

_____

FACTUAL QUESTIONS

Now I'd like to ask just a few more factual questions about you:

83. What is your height?   _____ Feet _____ Inches

84. What is your weight?   _____ lbs.

85. How many brothers and sisters do you have?

        Brothers _____ Sisters _____

86. Are your parents still alive?

        a. Mother   No _____ Yes _____

        If No, what was your age when she died? _____

        b. Father   No _____ Yes _____

        If No, what was your age when he died? _____

87. How many different men have you been married to or lived with?

        a. Number of marriages *(Include live-withs that resulted in marriage)* _____

        b. Number of just live-withs _____

88. How has this interview been for you? _____

_____

_____

89. Was there any part that was especially difficult for you? Describe. _____

_____

_____

_____

_____

_____

_____

PART TWO

FEMALE CHILD MOLESTERS

JULIA R.C. HISLOP

CONTENTS

This work is fondly dedicated
to my parents
Constance E. Baker Hislop, PhD
and David M. C. Hislop, MD.

ACKNOWLEDGMENTS

This dissertation could not have been completed without the efforts of numerous individuals. The women who participated in this study bravely provided very personal and often painful information in the interest of helping others, and their contributions are gratefully acknowledged.

Dozens of staff members at the 13 data collection sites used for this dissertation were involved in the process of approving this study, and in data collection. They are not being named in the interest of maintaining the confidentiality of the subjects in this study. Their contributions were invaluable, however, and are very deeply appreciated.

Several authors cited in this study helped me to locate copies of their articles and unpublished papers, and several agencies were helpful in providing me with reference lists related to the topic of this study. Their efforts are also greatly appreciated.

The efforts of the staff members at the National Institute of Mental Health in reviewing the application materials for the approval of this study are also very much appreciated.

The input of my committee members: Robert Bernstein, PhD, Michael Petrovich, PhD, and Merle Canfield, PhD was invaluable.

Lastly, I wish to express a deep appreciation for my family and friends who provided me with encouragement, support, and a sense of humor over the years that this study was in progress.

ABSTRACT

The present study included 43 females who had engaged in sexual activity with children or adolescents who were aged 15 or younger at the time of the sexual contacts. The subjects were drawn from prisons, sexual abuse treatment facilities, and residential drug and alcohol rehabilitation centers. A Confidentiality Certificate, issued by the Department of Health and Human Services was obtained for the protection of these subjects, ensuring that their identities could not be revealed. Thirty-five of the women described their sexual contacts with a total of 56 children.

Demographic and psychosocial history data is provided for the women, including detailed information concerning their own reported child sexual abuse histories. Information concerning the women's offenses against children is also provided.

The female child molesters' psychosocial histories suggested more dependency than was the case for control group subjects matched for age, education, race, and type of data collection facility. Contrary to expectation, female child molesters were not significantly different from a matched control group in terms of history of number of male sex partners, income, family-of-origin pathology, or severity of sexual abuse history.

An exploratory factor analysis provided support for the existence of possible subtypes of female child molester. A step-wise multiple regression analysis did not provide support for the hypothesis that the severity of childhood sexual abuse history, as modified by family-of-origin pathology, would predict the severity of the sexual abuse perpetrated by the female child molesters.

CHAPTER 1

Introduction

While females who have been in sexual contact with children have been all but ignored in clinical literature, recent studies have begun to find that the rates at which females have sexual contact with children are sufficiently high as to justify the study of this phenomenon (Allen, 1991; Condy, Templer, Brown, & Veaco, 1987; DeFrancis, 1969; Faller, 1987; Finkelhor, 1984; Fritz, Stoll, & Wagner, 1981; Fromuth, 1983; Gomes-Schwartz, Horowitz, & Cardeelli, 1990; Haugaard & Emery, 1989; Kercher & McShane, 1985; McCarty, 1986; Petrovich & Templer, 1984; Pierce & Pierce, 1987; Reinhart, 1987; Risin & Koss, 1987; Russell, 1983; Schultz & Jones, 1983). Information currently available on females who molest children is largely based on case study material (Forward & Buck, 1978; Lidz & Lidz, 1969; Margolis, 1977, 1984; Marvasti, 1986; Masters, 1963; Shengold, 1980; Wahl, 1960; Yorukoglu & Kemph, 1966). As such, many documented incidents of sexual contact describe cases where either the older female or the child with whom she has had sexual contact is disturbed in some way, while failing to give evidence that these are representative of other cases. Studies which have sought to systematically examine groups of female perpetrators have by and large examined groups of females who have come to the attention of authorities (Allen, 1991). Exceptions include a study by Sarrel and Masters (1982) which examined and categorized female offenders based upon the reports of males seeking sex therapy who had histories of molestation, and studies by Paiser (1992) and Swink (1989) which examined females' accounts of childhood molestation by their mothers. Further study is needed to include more diverse samples of females.

Existing literature concerning females who have sexual contacts with children is often contradictory. For example, while some authors have proposed that the female offender is most likely to act in concert with a male offender (Justice & Justice, 1979; Larson & Maison, 1987; Nielsen, 1983), others have claimed that the female offender is likely to be motivated by a lack of a male partner (Forward & Buck, 1978; Mayer, 1983; Rist, 1979). Some researchers developed categories of female offenders (Faller, 1988; Mathews, Matthews, & Speltz, 1989; McCarty, 1986; Sarrel & Masters, 1982). Categories of female offenders that have emerged, however, have not always been consistent. Variables thought to differentiate types of offenders are grouped differently according to various authors. Variables are combined into different categories largely on the basis of clinical impressions, yet to be subject to statistical confirmation.

The psychosocial histories of the female perpetrators previously researched indicate that a history of sexual abuse is common among females who have sexual contact with children (Condy et al., 1987; Faller, 1988; Fehrenbach & Monastersky, 1988; Groth, 1979a; Johnson, 1989; Justice & Justice, 1979; Knopp & Lackey, 1987; Larson & Maison, 1987; Marvasti, 1986; Mathews et al., 1989; McCarty, 1986; Meiselman, 1978; O'Connor, 1987; Wolfe, 1985). Largely, however, these reports have been from case studies, or from populations for which control groups were not available. No study has yet shown a correlational relationship between more severe sexual abuse in childhood and a greater capacity to have the same types of contacts with children in adulthood, or a more severe history among female sex offenders than among controls.

Females whose own history of sexual abuse is more severe tend to be found to be suffering from adverse effects, in general. Severity has been measured in terms of the total incidents of abuse (or frequency/duration), the nature of the acts which occurred, the relationship to the perpetrator, or the total number of perpetrators. It is yet to be determined whether greater severity of sexual abuse in childhood might lead to a greater propensity to molest children in later years.

Other factors have emerged in the psychosocial histories of females who have had sexual contact with children. Studies have noted physical abuse (Fehrenbach & Monastersky, 1988; Groth, 1979a; Johnson, 1989; Larson & Maison, 1987; Mathews et al., 1989; McCarty, 1986), various sorts of family-of-origin pathology (Groth, 1979a; Johnson, 1989; Justice & Justice, 1979; Kercher & McShane, 1985; Larson & Maison, 1987; Mathews et al., 1989; McCarty, 1986), emotional, mental and intellectual difficulties (Condy et al., 1987; Faller, 1987; Groth, 1979a; Lukianowicz, 1972; Maltz & Holman, 1987; Margolis, 1984; Marvasti, 1986; Masters, 1963; Mathews et al., 1989; McCarty, 1986; Meiselman, 1978; O'Connor, 1987; Shengold, 1980; Wahl, 1960; Wolfe, 1985), and difficulties in relationships with males (Groth, 1979a; Kercher & McShane, 1985; Larson & Maison, 1987; Lukianowicz, 1972; Maltz & Holman, 1987; Margolis, 1984; Marvasti, 1986; Masters, 1963; McCarty, 1986, Meiselman, 1978; O'Connor, 1987; Shengold, 1980; Wahl, 1960; Wolfe, 1985).

This study sought to support the findings of previous authors that females having sexual contact with children have psychosocial histories that include sexual abuse in childhood, pathology in their families-of-origin, low-incomes, dependency, and more male sex partners. It sought to expand upon previous findings by including populations of female child molesters other than those who have come to the attention of authorities. It sought to investigate whether these difficulties occur with greater frequency than is present in a matched control group. Additionally, this study explored whether severity of sexual abuse in childhood correlates with later propensity towards more severe acts of sexual contact with children, and whether family history variables might modify these effects. It also sought to explore whether or not there is statistical support for the subtyping of female child molesters. Because of the paucity of existing data concerning the nature of sexual contacts that females have with children, this study surveyed other demographic data concerning the female child molesters, and the types of sexual interactions that they report having with children. Such data may be useful in helping to identify females who have had sexual contact with children, and in identifying treatment needs of women known to have had such contact.

CHAPTER 2
Literature Review

Prevalence of Female-Perpetrated Child Sexual Abuse

SOCIETAL RELUCTANCE TO ACKNOWLEDGE FEMALE-PERPETRATED CHILD SEXUAL ABUSE

Very little has been written about females who engage in child sexual molestation (Banning, 1989; Knopp & Lackey, 1987; Krug, 1989; Paiser, 1992; Ramsey-Klawsnik, 1990; Sheldon & Sheldon, 1989; Travin, Cullen & Protter, 1990). Sexual offenses against children by females have only recently been acknowledged and tentatively explored in the psychological research literature. Researchers have commented that sexual abuse at the hands of females was previously thought to be rare (Banning, 1989; Masters, 1963), or to never occur (Finkelhor, 1984). Only recently have these beliefs begun to be questioned (Allen, 1991; Condy, 1985; Finkelhor, 1984; Petrovich & Templer, 1984; Ramsey-Klawsnik, 1990; Shrier & Johnson, 1988; Swink, 1989; Wolfe, 1985).

Interspersed among findings concerning other populations of primary study, such as male child molesters, or incest offenders, were occasional, incidental remarks that female child molesters had been discovered. Preliminary conclusions drawn from such available information were based on a limited number of cases, often from biased samples of subjects. While researchers have recently begun to investigate female sex offenders, there is still a paucity of information written on this topic. As such, little is available in terms of treatment for the female child molester. Additionally, a lack of acknowledgment and understanding of the female child molester places limitations upon the protection and treatment afforded the child who is sexually victimized by a female.

Contributing to the lack of research on the female child molester is the problem of child molesters being infrequently known to those other than their victims. Sexual abuse, in general, tends to be underreported. Rowan, Rowan and Langelier (1990) commented that a prepubescent victim may not report sexual abuse, and a postpubescent victim may not view the sexual behavior as abusive. Kendall-Tackett and Simon (1987) found that only 18 percent of adults molested as children who were entering treatment had reported the abuse. Russell (1983) in a random survey of 930 women in San Francisco found that only 2 percent of those reporting a history of intra-familial child sexual abuse, and 6 percent of those reporting a history of extrafamilial child sexual abuse cases had ever reported their abuse to the police. The vast majority of offenders in these cases of child sexual abuse were male. The crimes of female perpetrators may be even more widely ignored (Travin et al., 1990).

Female-perpetrated child sexual abuse is widely thought to be particularly underreported (Knopp & Lackey, 1987). Paiser (1992) remarked that available incident figures may not begin to approach the actual incident rates because female-perpetrated sexual abuse is so taboo. As early as 1944, Apfelberg, Sugar and Pfeffer remarked on the underreporting of female-perpetrated sexual abuse, stating:

> Cases have been known of women who exposed their genitals but were either not arrested or were charged with intoxication or disorderly conduct. We have seen no examples of such charges as impairing the morals of a minor among women although there are instances in which women have seduced minors. (p. 768)

What research is available supports the belief that children are reticent to admit to having been sexually abused by a female. Johnson and Shrier (1987) found that only 18 percent of 11 boys molested by females had reported the abuse. The 11 boys came to the attention of the interviewers in the course of a psychosexual interview which took place as a part of a routine physical examination of medical patients. Shrier and Johnson (1988) stated that while most of the molestations reported to them had occurred in the early school age years (M = 12, R = 5-17), no boy who was under the age of 14 admitted a history of such abuse to them. The average age at which the boys revealed a history of sexual abuse to the researchers was 18; young boys did not appear to be divulging information concerning sexual abuse until several years after the events. Similarly, of 216 college men identified by Risin and Koss (1987) as having been sexually abused in childhood (47% of whom were abused by a woman), 81 percent had told no one about the sexual abuse. Evert (cited in Vanderbilt, 1992) found that of 93 women and 9 men who were sexually abused by their mothers, 80 percent reported that the abuse was the most hidden part of their lives. Only 3 percent of the women, and none of the men, had told anyone of their childhood abuse.

The apparent reluctance of victims to report sexual abuse by a female is thought by some to be a particular difficulty when the victim is a male. Several researchers have commented on the particular reluctance of male victims in general to acknowledge having been sexually abused. Groth and Burgess (1980) concluded that men do not report rape by men because of stigma related to societal beliefs that men should defend themselves, the concern that their sexuality may become suspect, and the distress involved in making such a report. Faller (1989) also commented that boys do not report sexual abuse because they are socialized not to reveal doubts, weaknesses and fears. Finkelhor (1984) similarly remarked that boys are reluctant to report being victims of sexual abuse, as did Renvoize (1982), who noted that boys are reluctant to admit to having played a "passive" sexual role.

Nasjleti (1980) surveyed available literature and questioned adolescent males in group therapy and made similar conclusions concerning the cultural factors that keep males from reporting sexual abuse. According to Nasjleti, United States male children are generally socialized to be physically aggressive, self-reliant and independent; they are generally not socialized to be dependent on others, to be passive, or to spontaneously express feelings, such as fear, vulnerability, and helplessness. The male may fear being labeled as unmanly if he reports being victimized; if he is abused by a woman this may be a particular concern. Boys may fear that their reports will not be taken seriously, either because it is generally not believed that males can be sexually abused by females, or because of beliefs that such abuse is not harmful. Finally, males may fear physical retribution from reporting.

In cases where a mother sexually abuses a male child, additional difficulties may interfere with the disclosure of incest. Because mother-son incest has been viewed as the most taboo form of incest (Barry & Johnson, 1958; Renvoize, 1982; Rist, 1979), or because it may be embarrassing (Krug, 1989), sons may be particularly reluctant to report this type of sexual abuse. Krug (1989) also noted that such abuse may go undetected because males do not get pregnant, and because mothers are seen as being "all good." Additionally, he noted that male children may be viewed as having been unaffected by sexual abuse; reports of maternal abuse may be ignored, and therapists may not connect difficulties in therapy with a history of maternal sexual abuse. Nasjleti (1980) remarked that because mothers are viewed as nonsexual in this culture, boys molested by their mothers may assume responsibility for the sexual contact, or they may fear that the maternal incest is indicative of their having a mental illness.

The cultural perception of women as individuals incapable of committing sexual offenses has been examined by many authors as another reason why the population of female sex offenders remains unacknowledged and underresearched. Banning (1989) remarked upon the culturally based unwillingness to believe that women might commit such acts. Ramsey-Klawsnik (1990) also commented that sociocultural factors decrease the likelihood that children might report sexual abuse by a woman to authorities, as well as the likelihood that such reports are believed.

Several authors have pointed to the societal belief that women are asexual and nonaggressive as a factor which serves to protect female child molesters from identification. Larson and Maison (1987) stated:

> *Socially, we, as a culture, find it particularly disturbing to think that women would sexually abuse children. Our Judeo-Christian heritage places enormous emphasis on women as warm, nurturing mothers. Furthermore, we are, at best, culturally ambivalent about female sexuality. We struggle with the notion of women — particularly mothers — being sexual at all.* (p. 30)

Scavo (1989) commented that the patriarchal structure of society perpetuates the role of males as aggressive and dominant, and the view of females as passive and submissive; females are not seen as capable of threatening or intimidating a victim, and are, as such, not seen as potential sexual abusers of children. Allen (1991) commented upon the role of psychoanalytic thought in contributing to this societal perception of men's and women's sex-roles, with men being "predators," and women "docile recipients." He noted that the breach of the incest taboo by a woman is consequently viewed as a greater deviation than a similar act by a man. Mayer (1992) remarked, "Society does not perceive females as abusers; they are stereotyped as physically and psychologically incapable of victimizing" (p. 5).

In addition to the belief that women are asexual and nonaggressive, the cultural expectation that women have physical contact with children has been suggested by some as a factor that may mask the sexual abuse of children by females. Groth (1979a) commented that women may engage in sexually abusive behavior under the guise of caretaking activities. Plummer (1981) noted that the expectations of the female role simultaneously dictate that a woman have bodily contact with children, while denying the existence of sexuality in women, allowing for sexual abuse without detection. The boundary between appropriate touching and sexual abuse may be loosely defined where female caretakers are concerned. Mayer (1992) remarked that the demarcation between sexually abusive and nonabusive behavior is less clear for women, as more physical contact is expected of them. Rowan et al. (1990) remarked that given the traditional care-giving role of women, it is unlikely that typical psychosocial histories will include questions about sexual abuse by a woman, particularly if the interviewer is a female. They also commented that, given the role of woman as caregiver, a report of sexual abuse by a woman may not be believed.

When the female caretaker is a mother, the societal expectation that she have physical contact with her charges may be particularly strong and the boundary between appropriate touching and sexual abuse may be particularly difficult to discern. Goodwin and DiVasto (1979), as well as Barry and Johnson (1958) commented, for example, that in some cultures it is acceptable practice for mothers to actively masturbate their infants. Goodwin and DiVasto (1979) noted that in cases of mother-daughter incest, in particular, social tolerance of physical intimacy may cause difficulty in recognizing when incestuous contact has occurred, and may make it difficult for the child to recognize the mother's behavior as inappropriate. In a similar vein, Barry and Johnson (1958) suggested that there is less prohibition in our society against the expression of partially seductive attitudes of a mother towards her son, than for a father towards his daughter.

In addition to the cultural expectations based upon traditional sex-roles, cultural expectations based upon feminist ideology have been implicated by some as factors contributing to the masking of female-initiated child sexual abuse. Nielsen (1983) commented that the women's movement, largely responsible for bringing into awareness the concerns of rape and of child sexual abuse, largely focused on the victimization of females by males. The concern of males and children being sexually abused by women was not so loudly addressed. Paiser (1992) similarly remarked that the feminist model tends to associate only men as sexually abusive, towards only women. Finkelhor (1984) has stated a similar opinion. Allen (1991) also commented that the overextension of feminist explanations of child sexual abuse has contributed to the lack of recognition of child sexual abuse that is committed by females. He noted that the notion of women and children being victimized because of the socialization of men towards becoming dominant and aggressive, when women are socialized into a victim's role, contributes towards the understanding of sexual abuse. He cautioned, however, that when this is accepted as the only explanation for child sexual abuse, it may serve to mask child sexual abuse by women. Mayer (1992) speculated that feminists may be reluctant to acknowledge abusive behavior among females, as the cases may "be publicized disproportionately in order to minimize and justify male offenses" (p 6).

Because sexual abuse by female perpetrators is not widely recognized, inadequate provisions for the protection of female-molested children may be made. Petrovich and Templer (1984) remarked that women may have less fear of social retribution for sexual contact with children. This speculation was borne out in research by Wolfe (1985), who observed that of 12 female sex offenders seen in treatment (11 of whom offended against children), only two were incarcerated, and of these one was incarcerated in a work program. Similarly, Ramsey-Klawsnik (1990) remarked that only one of the female offenders identified by children who were referred by a social service agency for evaluation of sexual abuse was subjected to criminal prosecution; these included 83 cases of children for whom the abuse was confirmed by diagnostic evaluation. The women were not prosecuted in spite of the sadistic nature of many of the assaults; 56 percent of the abusive acts committed by the female perpetrators included burning, beating, biting or pinching the breasts or genitals of the children, or tying them during acts of sexual assault. In cases where females are prosecuted and convicted of child molestation, it is not always the case that they lose the custody of their children. Larson and Maison (1987) found that of 10 convicted and imprisoned sex offenders who were mothers, two lost the custody of some of their children, and only four lost the custody of all of their children.[1]

Recent evidence suggests that sexual offenses against children by females are rare in comparison to similar offenses committed by men (Allen, 1991; Rowan et al., 1990; Travin et al., 1990). However, in spite of the numerous factors which may serve to underestimate the incidence of reported female-initiated sexual assaults, recent studies have begun to find that the rates of female-initiated child sexual abuse are sufficiently high as to justify the study of this phenomenon (Condy et al., 1987; Cupoli & Sewell, 1988; DeFrancis, 1969; Faller, 1987; Finkelhor, 1984; Fritz et al., 1981; Gomes-Schwartz et al., 1990; Kercher & McShane, 1985; McCarty, 1986; Petrovich & Templer, 1984; Reinhart, 1987; Rowan et al.,1990; Russell, 1983; Schultz & Jones, 1983; Travin et al., 1990). Studies have examined the rates at which females engage in these activities through several means. These have included: reviewing the number of female offenders reported to law enforcement, child protection agencies, or sex abuse

---

[1] Allen (1991), however, noted that although only 51 percent of female sexual offenders had children in their care removed from their homes, they were nevertheless more likely than were male offenders to have them removed.

treatment or evaluation agencies; self-report studies of college students and medical patients; random telephone or face-to-face interviewing; and self-report from specialized populations such as prison inmates and clinical samples. Each of these methods reveals significant numbers of females engaging in sexual contact with children.

Initial Findings of Female-Perpetrated Child Sexual Abuse

With several barriers hindering the exploration of the phenomenon of women who sexually abuse children, knowledge in this area has accumulated slowly. It is only in the last decade that most of the very few studies which exist on this topic have come into existence. Prior to this, documentation proceeded at a snail's pace. In the 1930s some of the first documented cases of female sex offenses were written and largely ignored. Further documentation of the existence of the female offender appeared over the next several decades in isolated case studies, and among incidental reports on the existence of female offenders, often discovered in the course of research on the larger topics of incest or sexual abuse, and noted with little further remark.

In 1934, Wulffen briefly described over two dozen cases in which females acted out sexually against children. These included all manner of sexual abuse against children. The cases included caretakers who beat their charges for sexual gratification. Also included were cases of direct sexual contact between the older females and minors, such as the case of a grandmother who attempted to rape a 12-year-old boy, several cases of incest (mother-son, mother-daughter, aunt-nephew, sister-younger brother), a case of an 18-year-old female who encouraged sexual acts between an 8-year-old-boy and an 11-year-old girl and herself, cases of family friends molesting children, and cases of homosexual and heterosexual child molestation by a governess. One case included a 4-year-old female who acted out sexually against a younger brother. Cases of females indirectly sexually abusing minors were also reported, such as the case of a 44-year-old female allowing her 13-year-old daughter to be used for intercourse in the service of enticing the man involved, and a case of a 52-year-old woman who prostituted a 7-year-old boy. Two cases of a wife cooperating in her husband's rape of a younger girl, in one of the cases her own daughter, are also reported. Chideckel (1935) also briefly mentioned a case in which, at the solicitation of her parents, a female who was "guilty of many sexual crimes with boys" (p. 145) was committed to a corrective institution. The existence of teachers and police-women who had beaten children for sexual gratification was also noted by this author.

Kinsey, Pomeroy and Martin (1948) were also among those to first document the finding that preadolescent boys have sexual contact with adult females, though they did not systematically research this type of sexual contact. They wrote:

> Older persons are the teachers of younger people in all matters, including the sexual. The record includes some cases of pre-adolescent boys involved in sexual contacts with adult females, and still more cases of pre-adolescent boys involved with adult males. Data on this point were not systematically gathered from all histories, and consequently the frequency of contacts with adults cannot be calculated with precision. (p. 167)

Several subsequent authors have similarly reported incidental findings of female child molesters discovered in the course of research not primarily geared towards this population. Groth (1979a), a leading authority on male sex offenders, indicated that he had encountered three adult females who committed sexual assaults against children, and described additional cases wherein male sex offenders had recounted sexual abuse by females as children. Groth and Loredo (1981) noted a female babysitter among adolescent sex offenders in treatment. Justice and Justice (1979) noted two cases of mother-son incest in a survey of 112 families. Weinberg (cited in Masters, 1963) is reported to have found 37 cases of brother-sister incest (initiator unspecified) and two cases of mother-son incest, among "some two hundred cases in Illinois" (p. 66). Lukianowicz (1972) noted three cases of mother-son incest, and two cases of aunt-nephew incest, among 700 patients in several treatment facilities, and noted that there were also cases in which sisters initiated contact with their brothers. De Jong, Hervada, and Emmett (1983) noted four female assailants, all except one of whom offended with a male accomplice, among the records of 566 children under the age of 16 who presented to a pediatric sexual assault crisis center. Spencer and Dunklee (1986) discovered two female perpetrators, in one case a sister and in one a mother, who offended in conjunction with two male relatives, listed in the records of 140 boys who were seen for evaluation and medical treatment for sexual abuse. Hunt and Baird (1990) noted that females were among perpetrators found in sex rings that offended against 10 children seen for sexual abuse treatment.

Two research groups have counted female offenders and victims of female offenders among women seeking treatment for drug and alcohol abuse. Chasnoff et al. (1986) noted three cases of maternal-neonatal incest among the cases of 25 women seeking treatment for substance abuse. Benward and Densen-Gerber (1979) interviewed 118 women in a psychiatrically oriented residential therapeutic community treatment facility for substance abusers. These interviewers sought to examine preadult incest experiences. They found that 52 of these women reported a total of 93 incestuous partners, eight of whom were female. They noted that all of the women reporting incestuous relationships with a female also reported incestuous relationships with a male, although it is not noted if these relationships occurred in conjunction with one another.

Evidence of maternal incest with children is also found in a handful of case studies. Several early authors reported on cases of mother-son incest. Bender and Blau (1937) noted a 6-year-old inpatient male who had sexual contact with his mother, though responsibility for initiating the contact was placed with the child. Wahl (1960) reported on two cases of consummated mother-son incest. Forward and Buck (1978) described one case study involving mother-son incest, as did Raphling, Carpenter, and Davis (1967), and Margolis (1977, 1984). Yorukoglu and Kemph (1966) reported on a case in which a mother had sexual contact with both her son and daughter.

Other early authors remarked upon findings of incest where females, generally relatives, played the role of aggressor. Barry and Johnson (1958) reported that they had encountered cases of mother-daughter incest, grandmother-granddaughter incest and mother-father-daughter incest. They also noted that a colleague had encountered a case of mother-son incest, and described a seductive relationship with the mother in the history of a male client who was having sexual contact with his daughter. They reported that they had histories of several young males who had fondled their mothers' breasts. Masters (1963) noted a case of older sister-brother incest, and noted a case of mother-daughter incest, and of mother-adopted son incest that appeared in prior literature. Lidz and Lidz (1969) described three cases in which mothers had had "sensuous physical intimacies" with daughters. Butler (1978) described a case of a male who was molested by a foster mother's sister, and a case in which a female entered therapy after touching her infant son's genitals. Goodwin and DiVasto (1979) described six cases of mother-daughter incest and two cases of grandmother-granddaughter incest, from their files and from previous literature.

Additional accounts of individuals who have been molested by females have appeared in recent case study literature, within the past decade. These have also generally described incestuous relationships. Marvasti (1986) gave brief descriptions of five cases of incestuous mothers, and Catanzarite and Combs (1980) reported that two cases of mother-son incest were revealed in all-male encounter groups. Shengold (1980) reported on a single case of mother-son incest. Sugar (1983) described the case of a male (who himself had sexually abused children), and the case of a female, both of whom were sexually abused by an older female cousin, and also described a case in which a mother attempted sexual contact with her daughter. Korbin (1986) revealed aunt-nephew incest in the history of a woman imprisoned for killing her daughter. Sheldon and Sheldon (1989) described the case of an adult male inpatient who was being treated for sexual abuse at the hands of his mother.

One study examined incest in the homosexual population. Simari and Baskin (1982) examined incest occurring among a sample of homosexual individuals enlisted to participate in the study through a series of "social and friendship networks" covering the boroughs of New York City, and through gay and lesbian organizations. Of 29 lesbians, ranging in age from 22-65, four reported incestuous experiences with females. However, it is not clear what the age differences between the participants were, or which participant initiated the incest.

Recently, some authors have discussed their own sexual abuse by a female. Evert and Bijkerk (1987) described Evert's sexual abuse by her mother, and her subsequent treatment for this abuse. Dolan (1991) also described her own sexual abuse at the hands of her mother. Vanderbilt (1992) described sexual abuse by a female caretaker, as well as additional cases: three of mother-son incest, one case of the maternal sexual abuse of both a daughter and son, one case of daughter-mother incest, one case of granddaughter-grandmother incest, and one case of a female child, herself sexually abused, who sexually abused a foster sister.

Throughout the past several decades, documentation of the existence of female child molesters has largely disputed the notion that women are incapable of committing sexual offenses against children. More recently, with the tentative acknowledgment of the existence of the female offender, researchers have attempted to estimate rates at which females commit sexual offenses. Researchers have proceeded to estimate the rates at which females engage in sexual offenses against children using different definitions of "sexual abuse," and different populations which often include very specific samples. At best, current estimates concerning these rates of offense are preliminary. These difficulties notwithstanding, available evidence suggests that female offenders exist in numbers large enough to warrant their further study.

RATES AT WHICH WOMEN SEXUALLY OFFEND AGAINST CHILDREN

Percentages of Females Among Sex Offenders Known to Authorities

Cases of sexual abuse which are reported to authorities are likely to be more severe, more long term, more likely to conform to case workers' expectations, and more likely to involve family members (Finkelhor, 1984). De Francis (1969) was among the first to estimate the actual rates at which adult females have sexual contact with children based on reported cases of female sex offenders. He found that 3 percent of sex offenders against children were female. His study examined data from cases of sexual abuse gathered from a child protective agency in New York City; the females had previously come to the attention of the authorities. Because one of the objectives of his study was to evaluate the impact of court hearings on the victim and family, he excluded for study those cases in which prosecution was unlikely. He included data only on families for which an interview could be obtained.

In 1984, Finkelhor estimated larger rates of adult female contact with children, based on an examination of similar populations. He reported estimates on the prevalence of female-perpetrated child sexual abuse based on data gathered from two major studies completed in 1981: the American Humane Association Study and the National Incidence Study of Child Abuse and Neglect. These two studies were also based primarily on reports of women who had come to the attention of child protection agencies. On the basis of original figures provided by the National Incidence Study, which also included cases brought to the attention of other professionals, Finkelhor estimated that about 13 percent of the perpetrators against female children and 24 percent of perpetrators against male children were female. To arrive at these figures, he subtracted those females who had been included as female perpetrators for "permitting the abuse to occur"; with these females included, the data suggested that 46 percent of the offenders had been female. Finkelhor noted however, that his readjusted figures still included as perpetrators those women who may have been mistreating, neglecting, or inadequately supervising their children at the time when someone else had sexual contact with them, as well as women who offended against children in the presence of a male, who may have coerced them.

In his examination of data reported by the American Humane Association (AHA), Finkelhor also found that estimates of female perpetrators were inflated, as women who allowed the sexual abuse of their children to occur were listed as co-offenders, regardless of whether or not they had had sexual contact with the children. Original estimates by AHA indicated that in 41 percent of cases where males were sexually victimized, and in 31 percent of cases where females were sexually victimized, a female was cited as a perpetrator. Finkelhor was able to isolate cases of sexual abuse by a female in which the female was listed as the sole perpetrator. While this may have had the reverse effect of eliminating women who sexually co-offended with a male, he was able to provide estimates for female sex offenders acting alone. Based on the American Humane Association data, he estimated that 14 percent of the offenders against boys, and 6 percent of the offenders against girls were females.

After reviewing these studies, he approximated that women are the perpetrators in 5 percent of the cases of girls, and in 20 percent of cases of boys. He noted that larger numbers of girls than boys are victimized, and therefore concluded that greater numbers of females than males are molested by women, in spite of the fact that a greater percentage of male victims have been molested by female offenders.

Faller (1987) also studied a population primarily of reported cases in order to estimate the rates at which females commit sexual offenses against children. Two hundred and eighty-nine perpetrators were referred to the University of Michigan Interdisciplinary Project on Child Abuse and Neglect (IPCAN) between the years of 1978-1987. Of this total population of sexual perpetrators against children, 40 (14%) were women. These women were referred from child protection agencies (29 or 75% of cases), mental health agencies (4 or 10% of cases), the courts (4 or 10% of cases), or self-referral for molestation by a woman during childhood (3 cases or 7.5%).

Several other agencies providing treatment or evaluation services to sex offenders have reported smaller percentages of female perpetrators among the general child molester population. McCarty (1986) reported specifically on rates of reported cases of mother-child incest. Over the course of a 3-year period, 29 mothers constituted 4 percent of the offender population referred to the Dallas Incest Treatment Program, a child protective service of the Texas Department of Human Services. This number included five accomplices who were treated as offenders. Rowan et al. (1990) reported that female offenders accounted for 1.5 percent of offenders identified through sex offender evaluations done for the New Hampshire judicial system and similar evaluations done for Vermont social service agencies and courts. Four of the 200 New Hampshire cases and five of the 400 Vermont cases involved women perpetrators. Travin et al. (1990) described cases of females who acted out sexually against children and younger relatives. Five who had been convicted for sexual offenses and referred to their sex offender treatment program constituted 1 percent of such offenders referred for treatment. The authors believed that this is an underestimate of female-perpetrated sex offenses, and reported on an additional 2 cases of females who had molested children. Gomes-Schwartz et al. (1990) noted that 4 percent of the perpetrators discovered in a family treatment setting for sexual abuse were female.

Kercher and McShane (1985) reviewed data from a county Child Protective Services Agency (C.P.S.) (619 cases) and a District's Attorney's Office (495 cases). The C.P.S. cases were included only if they had been determined to be valid by the caseworker, and the District's Attorney's Office cases were included only if charges were filed. Females were found to be perpetrators in 3 percent of these cases.

Rates of female participation in sexual offenses against children have also been estimated among juvenile offender populations. Pierce and Pierce (1987) noted that 19 percent of 37 cases involving juvenile sex offenders, found through a review of open protective service records, involved a female offender. Grayson (1989) in a review of available literature noted two reports of adolescent treatment programs, and found that adolescent female offenders comprised 2 percent and 3 percent of the treatment populations, respectively. Smith and Israel (1987) found that in 25 families in which there were cases of sibling incest, 20 percent of the perpetrators were female.

Present estimates based on studies of offender populations that have come to the attention of authorities indicate that women constitute the minority of these sex offenders. Researchers have estimated that they comprise not more than 20 percent of the reported child molester population, and many authors have found that females constitute roughly 2-4 percent of this population. Estimates of the percentages of female child molesters who are among child molesters reported to authorities are not likely to accurately reflect the percentages of females among the child molester population at large. As previously noted, several factors are thought to preclude the detection and reporting of the female sex offender.

There was some trend among these studies for larger percentages of women to be found among populations of child molesters who had recently come to the attention of reporting agencies, as opposed to those populations where the molestation had been in some way validated by authorities or moved along in the system. Studies that examined cases that were farther along in the system were somewhat more likely to find that women constituted a comparatively smaller percentage of the child molesters. These included, for example, cases validated by a child protection agency, those thought to be good cases for prosecution, or those referred for specialized treatment or evaluation by the agency that first became aware of the abuse. Such would appear to support the contention of many authors that cases of female-initiated child sexual molestation are less likely to be taken seriously.

Most authors are quick to suggest that identifying the percentage of women found among reported child molesters is an inadequate means of estimating the total percentage of females among the child molester population at large. Because women are not generally viewed as capable of committing sexual offenses and their sexual abuse of children is likely to be underreported, only more disturbed offenders or those who have committed more blatantly abusive acts may come to the attention of the authorities. Travin et al. (1990) for example, noted that the sex crimes by females that were reported each involved bizarre or violent sexually deviant acts, more likely to be taken seriously by authorities. An additional two cases brought to their attention during the course of psychiatric evaluations involved disturbed individuals. Present rates, however, at which women are reported to authorities for having committed sexual offenses against children indicate that female offenders exist in numbers large enough to warrant their further study.

Female Perpetrators Identified by Child Victims Receiving Treatment

In addition to examining pools of known child molesters, in order to estimate the percentages of women among the child molester population, several authors have turned to populations of known child sex abuse victims. These studies typically reveal a larger estimate of the prevalence of women among this population.

Two authors have examined cases in which children suspected of having been sexually abused were evaluated by specialists. Faller (1989) noted that in a sample of 87 boys referred to a program of child sexual abuse specialists, seven (8%) had been molested by a female, and 25 (29%) had been molested by both a male and a female; among a similar sample of 226 girls, two (1%) were molested by a female and 40 (18%) by both a male and a female. These figures suggest that of the total 313 sexually abused children, nine (3%) were molested by a woman alone, 65 (21%) were molested by a woman and a man, and 74 (24%) in total were molested by a woman (regardless of whether they were also molested by a male).

Ramsey-Klawsnik (1990) reported on findings based on 117 children under the age of 12 referred by the Massachusetts Department of Social Services between 1984 and 1989 for an evaluation of suspected child sexual abuse. Eighty-three of the children were confirmed as sexual abuse victims. Twenty-three percent of the 83 children were abused by females only, and 29 percent were abused by both males and females. Two-thirds of the children abused by both sexes were abused by their mothers and fathers. Ramsey-Klawsnik did not suggest that these are reflective of incidence rates of female sexual offenders. Rather, she noted that the severity of the abuse in the cases that she examined would suggest that females come to the attention of authorities only when they exhibit higher levels of pathology than their male counterparts.

Two studies have estimated the percentages of female perpetrators among the offender population based on the reports of victims receiving a medical examination subsequent to having been sexually abused. Reinhart (1987) reviewed abuse records for 189 males who were sexual abuse victims referred to University of California (Davis) Medical Center, for child sexual abuse evaluations during 1983-1985, as well as for an age- and race-matched sample of female victims. He found that females were perpetrators 4 percent of the time against the males (8 cases), and that females were perpetrators against the females in four cases. Cupoli and Sewell (1988) noted that female perpetrators accounted for 26 episodes of child sexual abuse, or 2.3 percent of all episodes of child sexual abuse among those reported by 1059 children aged 3 months to 16 years receiving a Medical Examiner Sexual Abuse Exam. Such children were given this exam only if a law enforcement officer had made a determination of probable cause, and if the sexual abuse involved contact, as judged by the Department of Health and Rehabilitative Services and law enforcement.

Kendall-Tackett and Simon (1987) found that 3 percent of the offenders reported by adults who were molested as children were female. These adults were entering an AMAC (adults molested as children) treatment program.

Female Child Molesters Reported Retrospectively by College Students

Several studies have examined the rates of female sexual perpetration against children by polling college students regarding their history of sexual abuse in childhood; one study also asked college females about their history of sexual contacts with younger males. These self-report studies have generally found larger percentages of female perpetrators among child molesters than are generally found among those cases that have been reported to the authorities. Some studies of college students have reported the percentages of female offenders reported by men only, or by females only, or by both genders in combination.

Landis (1956) was among the first to report upon the sexual experiences in childhood reported by college students. The sexual experiences in this study are less comprehensively defined than is the case in subsequent studies. He surveyed 1800 university students, in part to determine the rates at which children have experiences with "adult sexual deviates." One hundred forty men reported 215 experiences. Of the 215 experiences, 0.4 percent involved interest in or attempted coitus. Of the women, 360 reported 531 experiences with "adult sexual deviates;" 1.5 percent reported a homosexual approach. Cases were discarded in which it was judged that minimal age differences may have caused the sexual interactions to be categorized as sex play or experimentation.

In more recent studies examining female child molesters, some have not differentiated between male and female victims in reporting the rates of female offenders. Two studies have found that when college men and women are combined, those reporting a history sexual abuse report that about 13 percent of the offenders were female. Schultz and Jones (1983) examined childhood sexual abuse histories among college students who had lived in West Virginia. Two hundred sixty-seven students were surveyed; 117 of these students reported that they had experienced sexual acts before the age of 12 with a person over the age of 16. Again, 13 percent of the offenders were reported to have been female. Haugaard and Emery (1989) similarly noted that of 1089 undergraduates surveyed, 101 reported wanted or unwanted sexual experiences before the age of 17 with an individual who was at least 16, and more than five years older. Of these, 13 percent reported a female perpetrator. These studies suggest that of college students (men and women considered together), between 1-5 percent overall have been sexually molested in childhood by a female.

Two studies have shown larger percentages of female perpetrators among the molesters reported by samples of college men; however, they have shown similar overall percentages of men to have been sexually abused in childhood by a female perpetrator. Risin and Koss (1987) surveyed 2,972 male students among 32 institutions of higher learning and found that 216 (7%) reported a sexually abusive incident before the age of 14. Offenders were women or girls in 43 percent of cases, and both a female and male in 4 percent. Almost half of the female perpetrators were babysitters between the ages of 14 and 17. Fritz et al. (1981), surveyed 952 psychology students at the University of Washington and found that of the 5 percent of males reporting a prepubescent physical contact of an overt sexual nature with a post-adolescent person, 60 percent reported the contacts to have been with females. These two studies suggest that approximately 3 percent of all college men have experienced sexual abuse by a female in childhood.

Condy et al. (1987) surveyed college students to determine the rates of occurrence of sexual acts in which the female was at least 5 years older than the male, and at least 16 years old at the time of contact, and in which the male was younger than 16 years of age. Among a sample of 359 college men, they found that 16 percent reported a history of such contact. These men had been forced into the activity 14 percent of the time, but had forced the woman 7 percent of the time. Of the men having contact, 79 percent reported more than one sexual contact, and 49 percent reported more than one partner.

Fromuth (1983) found that 5 percent of the perpetrators of child sexual abuse reported by 482 Auburn University female undergraduate psychology students were females. Sexual abuse included a variety of contact and noncontact sexual activities or sexual requests between either a girl younger than 13 with a partner who was 16 or older and at least 5 years her senior, or a girl age 13-16 with an offender 10 years her senior.

Condy et al. (1987) surveyed 636 college women concerning their experiences with children, and found that 3 women (0.5%) reported such contact with a male child. One female had more than one such contact.

When male and female college students are considered together, it has been consistently found that 13 percent of the students who have been sexually abused have been abused by females; between 1 and 5 percent of college students have experienced sexual abuse in childhood at the hands of a female perpetrator. Where males only are considered the percentage of victims reporting a female perpetrator is substantially higher (43-60%), with roughly 3 to 16 percent of all college men reporting a history of child sexual abuse by a female perpetrator. The percentage of females reporting a female perpetrator is lower, with 5 to 10 percent of perpetrators reported to be female; less than 1 percent of college women overall report sexual abuse in childhood by a woman.

Percentages of Female Child Molesters Among Child Molesters Identified by Victims in the Population at Large

Many researchers have surveyed the population at large and have reported on the percentage of female perpetrators described by victims. Based on a review of literature, Nielsen (1983) estimated that 12 percent of reported cases in which a boy is molested involve a mother as a sole perpetrator, while 5 percent of reported cases in which a female is molested involve a mother as the sole perpetrator.

Russell (1983) conducted a random dialing survey of 930 adult women in San Francisco. Fifty percent of those randomly contacted individuals took part in an interview concerning unwanted sexual contact. Among her findings, Russell discovered that 4 percent of intra-familial perpetrators of child sexual abuse (8 perpetrators) and 4 percent of extrafamilial child sexual abuse (17 perpetrators) were female. Perpetrators were included only if they had had actual physical contact with the female prior to her 18th birthday.

Finkelhor, Hotaling, Lewis and Smith (1990) conducted a nationwide study in conjunction with The Los Angeles Times Poll; 1,145 men and 1,481 women were questioned for one half hour on topics related to sexual abuse in a telephone interview. The respondents were asked if they had had any experience in childhood that they would now consider to be sexual abuse. Female offenders that were reported by the respondents accounted for 17 percent of the sexual abuse against males, and 1 percent of the abuse against females, prior to the age of 18.

Cameron et al. (1986) conducted a random survey in which participants were solicited door-to-door to complete a questionnaire. Several questions were asked to ascertain the extent to which the individuals had experienced sexual abuse in childhood. These included questions about adults who had solicited or obtained sexual activity from participants before they were 13, the number of individuals who had had sexual contact with or had been solicited by caretakers, and the number who had had their first sexual experiences with adults. Among the males in this survey, 9 percent reported a first experience with an adult female before the age of 18; 4 percent reported such an experience before the age of 16. Some of the women involved included wives (7%) and prostitutes (3%). Among the women, 0.1 percent stated that their first sexual experience was with a woman before the age of 16. Of the men, 7 percent reported advances by adult women when they were under the age of 13, and actual sexual contact with women when they were under the age of 13 was reported by 6 percent. Of the women, 0.6 percent reported sexual advances by women when they were under the age of 13, with 0.2 percent reporting sexual contact with an adult woman before the age of 13. First sexual experiences with both men and women were recorded.

First sexual experiences with women were reported to have occurred when the respondent was under the age of 13 by 2 percent of the men, and under the age of 16 by 11 percent of the men. First experiences with women were reported to have occurred while under the age of 13 by 0.5 percent of the women and while under the age of 16 by 1 percent of the women. These researchers also observed newspaper reports of child molestation in several newspapers for a period of 4 months; they observed that in 2 percent of cases where the gender of the offender could be ascertained, the offender was female.

Imprisoned Male Sex Offenders' Histories of Sexual Abuse by a Female

A handful of studies have examined the numbers of inmates having had sexual contact with a female in childhood. Gebhard, Gagnon, Pomeroy and Christenson (1965), using data collected in the early 1940s and early 1950s found that several convicted sex offenders had had sexual contact before puberty with a female who was at least five years older, and at least 15. Among male offenders against female children, 8 percent had experienced masturbation, mouth-genital, or anal contact with an older female, while 4 percent had experienced coitus. For male offenders against female minors, these figures were 14 percent and 5 percent respectively. For male offenders against female adults the figures were 9 percent and 2 percent. Figures for male aggressors against female victims were: against children 11 percent and 11 percent; against minors 0 percent in both categories; and against adults, 9 percent and 5 percent. For male incest offenders, percentages of offenders having had masturbation, oral-genital, or anal contact with an older female while prepubescent, or having had coitus were: for the offenders against children, 6 percent and 4 percent respectively; for male offenders against female minors, 6 percent and 4 percent respectively; and for male offenders against adults, 0 percent in both categories. For male offenders against same-gender children these figures were 8 percent and 4 percent respectively; for offenders against same-gender minors 7 percent and 4 percent; and for male offenders against same-gender adults 4 percent in both categories.

Groth (1979b) interviewed and reviewed the records of 348 convicted male rapists and child molesters. Among his findings were 44 cases in which these men reported they had suffered sexual victimization in childhood at the hands of a female. Sexual trauma between the ages of 1 and 15 at the hands of a female adult was noted in the developmental histories of 38 percent of the rapists reporting such trauma, and 18 percent of the child molesters who reported the same. Sexual trauma at the hands of a female peer was noted in 24 percent of the rapists with a history of sexual trauma, and 5 percent of the child molesters with the same. It was noted that rapists' victimizations were more incestuous in nature, and that female offenders against the rapists outnumbered male offenders. Petrovich and Templer (1984) found that 59 percent of 83 male incarcerated rapists had been heterosexually molested in childhood; twelve men had been molested by more than one female. Condy et al. (1987) found that among a sample of 212 male prison inmates, the rates of childhood sexual contact with an adult female were: 37 percent among the child molesters, 57 percent among the rapists, and 47 percent among the nonsex offenders. However, 3 percent of all the cases of prison men were cases where the boy had forced the woman to have sexual activity with him. Of the prison men reporting sexual contact, 88 percent reported more than one contact, and 71 percent reported more than one partner. Burgess and her colleagues (cited in Johnson, 1989) found that 56 percent of their sample of 41 male rapists were sexually abused in childhood; 40 percent of the perpetrators were female. Freeman-Longo, in 1987, noted that over 40 percent of the rapists that he had worked with had been sexually abused by women in childhood (cited in Allen, 1991). Allen (1991) found that male child molesters reported that 45 percent of their sexual abusers in childhood had been female (Allen also found that female child molesters reported that 6 percent of their molesters in childhood had been female).

Given the male offenders' reports of sexual contact by older females, it is interesting to note that among a sample of 172 female inmates surveyed by Condy et al. (1987), 8 percent reported having had such contact with a male minor; 62 percent of these women had had more than one contact, and 46 percent had had more than one partner.

Sexual Abuse by a Female in Daycare Populations

Some researchers have focused on sexual abuse by females in daycare settings, and in sex rings. Faller (1988) noted that of 48 children who were sexually abused in daycare settings, 2 percent were abused by a female, and 50 percent were abused by both a male and a female. Williams and Farrell (1990) found that of 58 alleged perpetrators reported to have sexually abused children in day care, 38 percent were female.

Summary of Estimates of the Percentage of Females Among the Child Molester Population

Allen (1991) has commented that while rates at which females commit sexual crimes against children are low when compared with rates at which men commit the same offenses, the actual numbers of children affected by these crimes are substantial. Estimating that 23 percent of females are sexually abused in childhood, and that an estimated 5 percent of the offenders are females, Allen used US Census Bureau figures to estimate that 1.5 million females may have been sexually abused by a woman. In a similar fashion, estimating that roughly 6.75 percent of males experience sexual abuse in childhood, and that 20 percent of those abused will have been abused by a female, he indicated that roughly 1.6 million males will have been abused by women. He cautioned that comparatively low relative rates of occurrence do not imply low absolute numbers of occurrences, and that such interpretation may serve to mask sexual abuse by females when it does occur. Allen (1991) remarked, "Most importantly, it does not really matter to the victims of female sexual abusers that theirs was a low probability event. What does matter is the possibility that they may experience further stigmatization when professionals disbelieve them" (p. 21).

It should be noted that differences in methodologies and operational definitions among studies concerning the rates at which females commit sexual acts against children make them difficult to compare. Criteria for sexual abuse may be determined in part by age differences between the participants, by relationships between the participants, by the presence or absence of force during the activities, or by the nature of the activities which took place. Such criteria differed between studies. Further, the source of information differed between studies. In some, the information was gathered from known or suspected victims, in some from known or suspected perpetrators, and in some from various samples of the population at large. Additionally, while some studies estimated the rates at which females commit sexual offenses against males by estimating the percentage of female offenders (among all sex offenders against children), others estimated the rates at which females commit sexual offenses by estimating the percentages of individuals who have been molested by a female (as opposed to by a male or as opposed to never having been molested). While exact rates at which females have sexual contact with younger males are difficult to glean from these studies, estimates which have been established by recent researchers increasingly indicate that females are having such contact at rates much higher than was previously suspected.

Effects of Sexual Molestation by a Female

CONSISTENCY OF FINDINGS

Evidence concerning the effects that sexual contact with females has upon children is often contradictory. Within the literature on the subject exist several accounts of children who were greatly disturbed by the molestation, while other accounts do not reveal such negative consequences. On reviewing the literature, Browne and Finkelhor (1986) concluded that sexual molestation by a woman is less disturbing to a victim than is sexual molestation by a man. Finkelhor (1984) for example, described his study in which adult males recounting their sexual experiences before the age of 16 revealed five experiences with older women, only two of which were considered abusive by the males involved. There is some evidence that abuse by a female may, in some cases, be less damaging (or less likely to be damaging) than abuse by a male, particularly when the victim of the female is a male. There is also evidence to support that in some cases, individuals who report sexual molestation by an older females do not perceive the sexual contact to have been harmful. However, there is also a great deal of evidence that sexual abuse by a female has had very negative effects on many individuals.

Particularly where victims are giving a retrospective account of abuse that occurred in childhood, some studies have found that not all males report having been negatively affected by sexual molestation by an older female. A difficulty in assessing the impact of childhood sexual molestation upon males, however, is the suspicion that males are disinclined to reveal emotional vulnerabilities, particularly those resulting from victimization experiences, or in matters concerning their sexuality. Several authors have noted that men are culturally inclined to mask negative reactions to trauma, such as fear, anxiety and depression. Kaufman, Divasto, Jackson, Voorhees and Christy (1980), for example, noted that in cases of men who are raped by men the psychological reaction may be controlled, but the male victims may experience major hidden trauma.

Others have argued that cases of female-perpetrated child sexual molestation in which damage is done to the child are overrepresented in mental health literature. Sexual molestation cases in which little harm is done may not come to the attention of protective or legal authorities, or to the attention of mental health professionals. As such they may be less likely to find their way into available documentation and mental health research. Catanzarite and Combs (1980) raised the point that the reporting and interpretation of mother-son incest may be culturally biased, and more likely to surface when physical or psychological damage has occurred. They noted that this is especially the case in mother-son incest, where physical damage is not likely and for which societal taboos are the strongest. They noted two cases of males whose maternal incest was revealed in encounter groups who were neither "mentally ill or physically or psychologically damaged" (p. 1808).

Landis (1956) reported that college males, in general, report childhood sexual experiences with adults to have been less distressing than do females with similar experiences. The adult offenders reported on by participants in his study were generally males. Boys reporting childhood sexual contact with an adult "deviate" were more likely to report that they were "interested," or "surprised but not frightened" than were the girls. They were less likely than girls to report that they were "frightened," "shocked," or "emotionally upset." It is unclear whether such differences result from true differences in emotional response to sexual abuse, responses of the males to societal expectations of emotional austerity, or differences in the types of sexual contact experienced.

Haugaard and Emery (1989) reported on 101 students reporting sexual abuse, 13 percent of whom were abused by a female. These, however, included seven cases wherein the males reported the experience to have been positive. Analyzed together with three women who reported their molestation by males to have been positive, this group reported less pressure to participate, having felt less guilt at the time and less severe types of impact. In terms of the amount of guilt currently felt and the amount of impact that the experience had on their lives, no differences were found between this group and those who reported that their experiences were not positive. Fritz et al. (1981) similarly found that college males who were molested in childhood, the majority by females, tended to be neutral or even positive about their experiences, and were likely to view the experience as initiation.

Condy et al. (1987) noted that the experience of having been with a female perpetrator was not experienced negatively among all of her subjects, even among those who themselves were imprisoned for a sexual offense. Among the men, the experience was reported to have been "good" by 51 percent of the college men and 66 percent of the imprisoned men. It was recorded as "bad" in 25 percent and 6 percent of cases and "mixed" in 12 percent and 25 percent of cases, again of the college and imprisoned sex offenders, respectively. The fact that the imprisoned sex offenders denied that the experience had a negative impact on them, in spite of the fact that they had gone on to commit sexual offenses, may support the notion that men are less likely to acknowledge sexual abuse as emotionally damaging.

The child molesters in this study were the most likely to have reported that their experience as victims of female-perpetrated abuse was "bad" (9 %) and the least likely to have reported that the experience had been "good" (50%). With the exception of the child molesters and the men who had been molested by an aunt, the men were likely to report that the experience had a good effect on their future sexual contacts; 43 percent of the prison men and 37 percent of the college men felt that the experience had had a good effect on their adult sex life. Men were also likely to have experienced the contact as "bad," in cases where the offender forced the sexual activity upon them, or in cases where the offender was a mother, an aunt, or a sister. The feeling was likely to have been reported as positive at the time if the female was a friend (Condy, 1985). Condy (1985) noted that if the boy was forced, the effect on his adult sex life was unfavorable. Condy also noted a trend for sexual contact at a younger age to be associated with a negative effect on adult sex life, though this trend was not statistically significant.

In cases where the researchers examine subjects who have more recently experienced childhood sexual abuse by a female, there is sometimes evidence of more significant harm to the victim. Ramsey-Klawsnik (1990) reported that, in addition to physical injury and disease, child victims of sexual abuse by a female offender displayed several emotional and behavioral problems. She reported the percentages of children displaying characteristic symptoms for 24 children abused by both a female and a male, and for 19 children abused by only a female. Difficulties noted were as follows: Intense fear reactions (54% both, 58% female abuser only), nightmares and sleep disturbances (21% each category), sexualized behaviors (58% both, 53% female only), regressive behaviors (75% both, 26% female only), hyperactivity (46% both, 5% female only), aggressive behaviors and biting (42% both, 32% female only), disturbed peer interactions (58% both, 21% female only), preoccupation with death (13% both, 32% female only). Males were noted to have displayed more symptomatic behavior than did females.

Shrier and Johnson (1988) noted in their sample of 11 adolescent boys molested by females, that 73 percent reported the immediate effects of such molestation to have been "strong" or "devastating," on a four-point Likert scale (devastating, strong, some effect, not much effect). At the time of reporting, 54 percent reported that the experience continued to have a strong or devastating effect on their lives. Johnson and Shrier (1987), summarizing their observations of the results of sexual abuse on boys (identified as having been sexually abused by either a male or a female perpetrator in the course of questioning during outpatient medical examinations) concluded that, "the vast majority of our study group are functioning well overall and are asymptomatic with the exception of mild to moderate impairments in the areas of sexual identity, sexual functioning, self-esteem, and interpersonal relationships" (p. 652). They also supported the idea that "childhood sexual victimization, whether by male or female molesters, is a high-risk experience that markedly increases the likelihood of acute and future disturbances in important areas of functioning" (p. 652).

Data are not available concerning the consistency with which a child molested by a female will be negatively effected. Some have argued that not all children, and particularly not all male children, will be harmed by such contact. Of course, researchers who find that children are not harmed by sexual contact by a female may not have incorporated all types of "harm," into their studies. Regardless of the consistency with which children are harmed by such sexual contact, several deleterious effects upon child victims of female perpetrators have been noted. These have included a host of emotional and behavioral difficulties, sexual dysfunctions, and sexual acting out. Sexual identity concerns have also been noted among individuals who have had sexual contact with females in childhood. It is uncertain what percentage of victims will suffer ill effects from female-perpetrated sexual molestation. That many undoubtedly do, however, necessitates further study of the female perpetrator of child sexual abuse.

HARM TO MALES FROM FEMALE-PERPETRATED CHILD SEXUAL ABUSE

Emotional difficulties have been described by authors who have treated mental health clients with sexual abuse by a female in their histories. It is likely that such cases are biased, in that mental health professionals see only those cases in which problems have developed as a result of sexual abuse, or in which mental health problems may have preceded the sexual abuse. Nonetheless, case studies serve to point to difficulties which may arise as a result of sexual abuse by a female.

Mayer (1992) stated that the effects of female-perpetrated child sexual abuse on a victim (gender unspecified) are similar to the effect of male-perpetrated child sexual abuse, and may include guilt and self-blame, depression and anxiety. Post-traumatic stress disorder, dissociation, or antisocial behavior may develop. Other difficulties such as suicidality, low self-esteem, ambivalence, and regression may occur. According to Mayer (1992), interpersonal problems may include difficulty with trust, promiscuity and sexual difficulties. In relationships with others, victims may experience confusion about their gender role. They may also victimize others, allow abuse to occur within their families, or be victimized by non-family members.

Hunter (1990) reported that among the effects for male victims following child sexual abuse (regardless of the gender of the perpetrator) are dissociative responses, mistrust of own perceptions, "self-defeating" beliefs, sexual abuse of others, dysthymia, post-traumatic stress, fear, "shutting down" of emotions, guilt, shame, loneliness, anger, behavioral problems, addictive disorders, sexual difficulties, propensity to become involved in abusive relationships, spiritual difficulties, and others.

Maltz and Holman (1987) similarly noted several difficulties experienced by male survivors of incest, with the gender of the perpetrator unspecified. These included low self-esteem, fear, confusion, guilt, and humiliation. Also noted were stress, conflict, depression, rebellion, and drug and alcohol involvement. Sexual problems were noted including hypersexuality and asexuality, as well as gender identity and sexual orientation conflicts. A male survivor of incest with both parents is quoted by these authors as attributing his sexual experiences with other boys, and his "enormous amount of masturbation" to the ambiguous nature of the abuse by his parents. He also reported having "old feelings of violation" in situations of sexual vulnerability. Another male survivor is quoted as attributing his difficulties with impotence to his sexual relationship with his mother.

A host of emotional and behavioral difficulties, as well as sexual identity confusion have been noted by therapists treating individual survivors of female-perpetrated child sexual abuse. In his case study of mother-son incest, Margolis (1984) noted that his patient sexually assaulted his mother and was matricidal; he had no close friends as a teen, and did not live up to his inferred academic potential. As an adult, he beat his first wife and became suicidal and homicidal when she threatened to leave; his second wife threatened to leave him when he acted irresponsibly while drunk. Masters (1963) noted a case of mother-adopted son incest in which the son engaged in homosexual activity, beat a female, and killed his mother.

Wahl (1960) described two case studies of males who had sexual contact with their mothers. In both, psychotic symptoms in adulthood appeared to have been exacerbated by sexual contact with their mothers. In the first case, the son also had sexual contact with his older aunt and neighbor, and had observed his mother in the act of coitus as a teenager. Nightmares, numerous acts of delinquency, sexual contact with his younger brother and other males were a part of his history. As an adult he suffered from social isolation and withdrawal, anxiety and depression, and fear of becoming a homosexual. The second male is noted to have had sexual relations with his brother.

Raphling et al. (1967) noted a case of mother-son incest that occurred in a multi-incestuous family. The son reported having felt depressed and guilty concerning the incident. He later is reported to have forced his wife into abusive sexual relations, and to have had sexual relations with his daughters; he also encouraged his son to have sexual relations with his (the son's) sisters and mother.

 Chasnoff et al. (1986) noted that two of three infants who were molested by their mothers displayed behavioral abnormalities with excessive sexual acting out in their relationships with other children. They concluded that, while a cause and effect relationship could not be concluded, sexual molestation places children at high risk for behavioral abnormalities.

In her 1992 magazine article, Vanderbilt described several cases in which deleterious effects of incest were reported to her. One male, molested by his mother, killed her, stabbed his grandmother, and committed suicide. She also discussed work by Evert in which, of a sample of nine men who had been molested by their mothers, one-fourth had eating disorders. In a much earlier observation, Barry and Johnson (1958) reported that a colleague had seen a case of mother-son incest in which there was no evidence of psychopathology on the part of the son.

Among case studies involving males who have been sexually abused by females, similar problems have been observed. These have included emotional difficulties and problems of low self-worth, drug and alcohol abuse, violence, and the possible exacerbation of psychosis. Several therapists have also observed concerns more specifically related to sexuality. These have included problems with relationships and sexual functioning, sexual identity concerns, and the propensity to sexually abuse others. Several authors have studied the effects of female-perpetrated child sexual abuse on a variety of these sexual concerns in more detail.

Studies Identifying Sexual and Relationship Concerns Among Males Molested by Females

Several authors have commented, in particular, upon dysfunctions in the areas of relationships and sexuality that have been found to be present in males who have had childhood sexual contact with women. Maltz and Holman (1987) noted that when sexual abuse occurs with a female offender, the male may fail to separate emotionally from the mother or mother figure. They noted that such contact may impair the male's ability to establish an emotionally satisfying relationship with a partner, and to take the lead in physically intimate activity. He may become uncomfortable around women, and may become hostile or abusive towards them. They also noted that early sexual contact with older females places the male in the difficult position of having to compete with older males instead of experiencing them as role models. They remarked that incest may impair the ability of the male to learn social skills necessary for intimate relationships.

Some authors have speculated as to the effects that female-perpetrated child sexual abuse may have on a male. Forward and Buck (1978) suggested that mother-son incest can lead to isolation, conditioned impotence, and fear and resentment of women. Justice and Justice (1979) also noted impotence as a possible result of mother-son incest. They also stated that a victim of mother-son incest may become a misogynist, a wife beater, a daughter abuser, a rapist, or a murderer. Renvoize (1982) suggested that homosexuality, fear of women, and an inability to achieve orgasm are all associated with mother-son incest.

Several of these concerns were found among male victims described by mental health practitioners. Maltz and Holman (1987) described the cases of two men who were maternally molested who later experienced impotence and other sexual difficulties. Sarrel and Masters (1982) attributed the sexual dysfunction seen in some of their clients who had been sexually assaulted by females (either as children or as adults) to their sexual abuse, although 10 of the 11 clients had not made this connection.

Shrier and Johnson (1988) noted sexual dysfunction in 21 percent of their sample of adolescent males molested by females. Vanderbilt (1992) discussed findings of researchers whom she interviewed, including those of Evert,[2] whose findings reveal that all of nine men who were molested by their mothers reported sexual problems that they attributed to this abuse. Krug (1989) noted that in 75 percent of the eight cases of sexualized mother-son relationships, the son had multiple concurrent sex partners in adulthood.

The possibility that men who are sexually abused by women may later sexually abuse women has been raised by several authors (Hunter, 1990; Justice & Justice, 1979; Maltz & Holman, 1987; Margolis, 1984; Nasjleti, 1980; Raphling et al., 1967). Groth (1979a) noted that rapists with victimization histories are more likely to have been sexually victimized by females than by males and suggested

---

[2] "Evert" is the *nom de plume* of Bobbie Rosencrans, M.S.W., under which her first book, *When You're Ready* (1987), was published. Her research has since been published by the Safer Society Press as *The Last Secret: Daughters Sexually Abused by Mothers* (1997) under her own name.

that this partially explains their sexual attacks against women. He added that the adult offender's sex crimes may be, in part, a repetition and acting out of the sexual trauma to which he was subjected as a child. High frequencies of molestation by a female have been noted in the histories of incarcerated sex offenders, as previously discussed.

Sexual Identity Concerns Among Males Molested by Women

Several authors have speculated that men who have been sexually abused by women may later develop sexual identity concerns, or may become homosexual as a result of the sexual abuse (Justice & Justice, 1979; Maltz & Holman, 1987; Margolis, 1984; Masters, 1963; Renvoize, 1982; Wahl, 1960). While many authors have made this speculation it is not consistently supported by research.

Thirty-eight percent of the Krug (1989) sample of men sexually abused by their mothers were reported to be homosexual or bisexual. Johnson and Shrier noted that 28 percent of the adolescents molested by females identified as bisexual as opposed to 8 percent of a control group. Boys who were molested by a female were no more likely to report themselves as homosexual, however, than were a control group of unmolested individuals (Johnson & Shrier, 1987).

While evidence suggests that some males who have been sexually abused by a female may have sexual identity concerns, one study provided evidence that homosexual males are not more likely to have been sexually abused by a female. Cameron et al. (1986) found, for example, that greater percentages of heterosexual men had had sexual advances made to them in childhood or adolescence by an adult female, than did bisexual or homosexual men (7% versus 3%); they also had greater amounts of actual sexual contact with adult females before the age of 13 (6% versus 3%). It would appear that while some males who are molested by females may develop sexual identity concerns, sexual molestation by a female is not likely to be a primary cause of homosexuality.

HARM TO FEMALES FROM FEMALE-PERPETRATED CHILD SEXUAL ABUSE

Research related to the effects of female-perpetrated child sexual abuse on female victims began with case studies and speculation. Barry and Johnson (1958) reported that in cases of mother-daughter incest, reactions range from somatic and neurotic symptoms, to psychotic anxiety, to no unusual anxiety whatsoever. Goodwin and DiVasto (1979), in summarizing several cases, reported that mother-daughter incest victims present with symptoms that include encopresis, depression, psychosis, and "migraine headaches with homosexual acting out." Phobic and neurotic complaints were noted in a case of grand-daughter-grandmother incest. They reported on a case of a young woman who had had sexual contact with her mother and who made a self-mutilating suicide attempt during the course of her therapy, and commented based on several case reviews that maternal seductiveness had been implicated in the onset of homosexuality.

Conclusions drawn from studies of larger clinical populations have been similar, although two researchers have noted that women who have a history of having been molested by females tend to have been sexually abused by several other offenders as well (Paiser, 1992; Swink, 1989). Vanderbilt (1992) described a female, molested by her grandmother, who was suicidal as an adult, and who married an abusive man. Vanderbilt also discussed findings of researchers whom she interviewed, including those of Evert (since published in Rosencrans, 1997), who discovered that 80 percent of 93 women who were molested by their mothers had sexual problems that they attributed to this abuse. Almost two-thirds of the women were too frightened of examinations by dentists or by doctors to avail themselves of routine medical treatment. Sixty percent of the women had eating disorders. Self-mutilation was also noted among some of the subjects.

Several authors have made similar findings regarding the emotional difficulties experienced by women in treatment who have experienced sexual abuse by a female. Swink (1989) described at length nine cases of mother-daughter incest and described the effects of such abuse upon the daughters. Denial, repression and minimization were cited as coping mechanisms used by female victims of maternal incest. Dissociation was utilized by all nine of the survivors and was judged to have been more extreme than in cases of victims of other forms of incest. Two of the women were diagnosed as having multiple personalities. Flashbacks were described as being as common in maternally incestuously abused women as in other victims of sexual abuse. Rage was also identified as an issue typically faced by survivors of incest. The nine women studied all suffered a sense of "existential hopelessness," or a lack of a reason to live. They were described as being disillusioned with religion, and subsequently lacking the sense of community provided by organized religions.

Swink (1989) identified several stress- and depression-related concerns among the nine women whom she treated. Tension, anxiety and an inability to relax were common difficulties, as were depression, an external locus of control, and phobias of things or situations associated with the abuse. Stress reactions included headaches (which most of the women experienced), neck tension, a spastic colon, leg weakness, and tunnel vision. Panic attacks were described as being present in five of the nine cases. Though some guilt was noted in the women who survived incest with their mothers, this was observed to be less than for survivors of sexual abuse in general.

Several authors have found compulsive or self-abusive disorders among female survivors of childhood sexual abuse by a female. Among the 10 female victims of female-perpetrated child sexual abuse interviewed by Paiser (1992), five women had engaged in compulsive or self-abusive behaviors, including eating disorders, drug and alcohol addictions, "workaholism," and the inflicting of pain upon themselves. Four of the 10 had experienced suicidal thoughts. Swink (1989) found substance abuse in the history of seven of the nine cases of maternal incest described; two of the nine were overeaters. Swink (1989), in addition, found that eight of the nine female victims of maternal incest had considered suicide with a seriousness judged to be greater than that for the average incest survivor. Two of the individuals had engaged in self-abusive behavior. Dolan (1991) reported overeating, using alcohol, becoming a "super-achiever," and overworking as coping mechanisms; she also indicated that she had used painkillers.

Concerns related to a negative self-concept have been found in female-molested females by several authors. Swink (1989) identified self-concept difficulties, and the sense of having lost their childhoods as common issues faced by incest survivors, including female survivors of maternal incest. Five of nine women were reported to have mild body image distortion, and to judge themselves to be less attractive than they actually were. Dolan (1991) discussed the results of sexual abuse at the hands of her mother, and attributed her subsequent sexual abuse by other individuals in part to the maternal incest. A sense of lifetime shame was described as another result of the incest. Six of the 10 female victims of female-perpetrated child sexual abuse interviewed by Paiser (1992) reported a negative self-image, six reported difficulty preserving a clear sense of self, and seven reported that they felt different from other people. Eight of the participants discussed issues related to their experiencing themselves as lacking safety; four stated that they did not feel safe anywhere in the world.

Several authors have identified concerns related to sexuality among women who were sexually molested by a woman in childhood. Swink (1989) identified sex-role, sexual identity, and sexuality concerns among the nine women that she treated. None of the women had been sexually aroused by the contact. She noted that women molested by their mothers struggled with the issue of sexual identity, and stated that such women take longer to decide upon a comfortable sexual identity than do members of the population at large. Three of the women had periods of promiscuity, six had periods of a lack of desire for sex, one suffered vaginismus.

Among 10 female victims of female-perpetrated child sexual abuse interviewed by Paiser (1992), concerns related to sexuality were also discovered. Most of the participants indicated that the sexual abuse had been quite traumatic for them. Four reported that the most negatively impacted area of life was their sexuality; difficulties attributed to sexual abuse included the need to dissociate during sexual encounters, anxiety during sex, disinterest in sex, and confusion about sexual identity. Paiser (1992) noted that of the sample of 10 females, three were lesbian, three were bisexual, and one was undecided. Mayer (1992) reported that when females are molested by women sexual identity confusion is common, and that homophobia and fear of homosexuality is generated.

Cameron et al. (1986) found larger numbers of homosexual or bisexual females reporting both advances by and sexual contact with an adult female before the age of 13. Eight percent of the bisexual or homosexual females, as opposed to 0.4 percent of heterosexual females reported such advances, and 5 percent of homosexual females, as opposed to 0.1 percent of heterosexual females reported actual sexual contact with an adult female.

Of four lesbians, however, who had sexual contact with a female relative, 75 percent described themselves as having been actively homosexual before the incestuous contact (Simari & Baskin, 1982), suggesting that in some cases of same-gender incest, the homosexuality preceded the incest. It is not clear in this study, however, who initiated this contact; it is possible that the individuals reporting incest may themselves have been the initiators. None of these females reported the incest as negative.

Swink (1989) identified several concerns related to relationships among the nine women whom she treated who had been molested by their mothers. All nine of the women avoided traditional dependent female roles, and strived for equal relationships with their partners. Need for great control, and difficulties with assertiveness in important relationships were noted as common difficulties of daughters abused by their mothers. Lack of trust and intimacy were identified as common issues faced by survivors of any type of incest, including maternal incest. Eight of the nine had been involved in abusive relationships. Among the 10 female victims of female-perpetrated child sexual abuse interviewed by Paiser (1992), six similarly reported a sense of "neediness," that for many resulted in being willing to engage in relationships that were not always in their best interests. Seven reported difficulties with intimacy; trust in interpersonal relationships was reported by all 10 as an issue of great concern.

Concerns about ability to parent have also been discovered among women who were sexually abused by women in childhood. Swink (1989) found that five of nine women treated for sexual abuse by their mothers made deliberate decisions not to have children in order to prevent their abusing them. Four who had children had a history of having physically abused them. Among the 10 female victims of female-perpetrated child sexual abuse interviewed by Paiser (1992) six discussed concerns related to parenting.

While women who have contact of a sexual nature with children are scarcely acknowledged in the literature, in recent years there has been growing evidence that they exist and that they may be seriously harming at least some of the children with whom they have contact. Individuals who have been sexually molested in childhood by a female may experience a variety of concerns. These may include emotional-behavioral concerns, concerns related to sexuality and relationships, and so forth. Very little is known, however, about the backgrounds of these women who molest children, the factors which may have contributed to their having become offenders, or whether there may exist subtypes of female offenders. These issues are of concern for identifying women who may be at risk, treating women who offend against children, and assisting the children who may have been harmed by such contact.

Offenses Committed by Female Offenders

Sex offenses against children by females have been documented by offenders as young as 4 years old (Johnson, 1989), and by women who are grandmothers (Barry & Johnson, 1958; Condy, 1985; Cupoli & Sewell, 1988; Faller,1987; Fromuth, 1983; Goodwin & Divasto, 1979; Petrovich & Templer, 1984; Wulffen, 1934) or great-grandmothers (Ramsey-Klawsnik, 1990). On average female perpetrators are likely to be in their 20s or early 30s (Allen, 1991; Condy, 1985; Faller, 1987; Larson & Maison, 1987; Petrovich & Templer, 1984; Rowan, Rowan & Langelier, 1990; Shrier & Johnson, 1988; Wolfe, 1985). Younger average ages have been found among imprisoned females (19 years in Condy, 1987), and in adolescent and child offender treatment groups (Fehrenbach & Monastery, 1988; Johnson, 1989; Mayer, 1992) (see Appendix A).

Various ages of children against whom the females offend have been reported ranging from as young as one week (Chasnoff et al., 1986) to 16 years (Wolfe, 1985). Differences in the average age of the older female and the average age of the sexually involved child also vary. Both male and female children have been the object of sexual contact with older females.

Sexual activities reported between children and older females represent a wide variety of activities. Intercourse, oral stimulation, fondling and genital penetration, as well as other activities have been documented (Allen, 1991; Condy, 1985; Faller, 1987; Fehrenbach & Monastersky, 1988; Johnson, 1989; Kercher & McShane, 1985; Mayer, 1992; McCarty, 1986; Petrovich & Templer, 1984; Rowan et al., 1990; Russell, 1983; Shrier & Johnson, 1988; Wolfe, 1985; Wulffen, 1934) (see Appendix B).

Females have been reported to be related to the children with whom they have sexual contact in various ways. While some authors have found the majority of female offenders to be unrelated to the children with whom they have contact (Allen, 1991; Condy, 1985; Fehrenbach & Monastersky, 1988; Larson & Maison, 1987; Petrovich & Templer, 1984; Russell, 1983; Shrier & Johnson, 1988), others have found more contact among females and familial children (Fromuth, 1983; Johnson, 1989; Kercher & McShane, 1985; O'Connor, 1987; Rowan et al., 1990; Wolfe, 1985). In part, this difference is accounted for by the population studied. Populations in which subjects have come to the attention of the authorities are more likely to have involved sexual contact within the family. Self-report studies are more likely to reveal greater amounts of sexual contact outside of the family (see Appendix C).

Psychosocial History of the Female Offender

SEXUAL VICTIMIZATION

The suspicion by several authors that women who sexually abuse children have themselves been sexually abused in childhood has been consistently borne out in recent research. Several authors speculated that this was the case prior to such recent research. Justice and Justice (1979), for example, stated early on their belief that mother-son incest offenders who are promiscuous come from "backgrounds of early sexual stimulation, loose standards in the family, or beliefs that a male must be serviced with sex for him to feel affection for a woman or even to have any interest in her" (p. 149). Meiselman (1978) also noted that a mother who molests her son may have incest experiences of her own. Several case studies also revealed that female sex offenders have histories of sexual abuse (Groth, 1979a; Korbin, 1986; Marvasti, 1986; O'Connor, 1987).

Several studies have found a history of sexual abuse among women who were being evaluated or treated for having sexually offended against children. Travin et al. (1990) noted in three of five cases of women who had been referred to them as sex offenders against children, the offender had a history of sexual abuse in childhood. Rowan et al. (1990) stated that three of the nine women evaluated for having sexually molested children had been sexually victimized in childhood. For an additional two females it is not clear whether sexual abuse was part of their histories; one female is said to have been "victimized" (type of victimization unspecified) as an adolescent, and another is said to have believed "that sex with adolescents was normal as this had been her experience." Faller (1988) found that 48 percent of her sample of 40 female sex offenders against children who were in treatment had been sexually abused in childhood. All but one of the 16 female sex offenders assessed and treated by Mathews et al. (1989) had been sexually abused in childhood. Of seventeen mothers in an incest treatment program, and for whom childhood data were available, 76 percent reported childhood victimization (McCarty, 1986). There were strong indications that an additional 12 percent had been incest victims. Wolfe (1985) found that 58 percent of 12 female sex offenders had been sexually abused during childhood, including one woman who offended against an adult female. Another of these females was the victim of stranger. Wolfe speculated that, since 5 of 7 women who offended with males were victims of sexual abuse, their offenses may have been extensions of their childhood victimizations.

Allen (1991) found that 72 percent of female offenders, identified primarily through child protective services records, reported that they had been sexually abused in childhood. Condy et al. (1987) found that the women, primarily from a prison population, who reported having had sexual contact with boys, were themselves likely to have experienced early sexual contact. Of the 16 women reporting contact with boys 81 percent had early contact, as opposed to the 21 percent of the 558 noninvolved women. The mean age of the women at the time of their own contact was 13 years, (R = 3-15 years), and the mean age of the other person was 24 (R = 16-60 years). Larson and Maison (1987) noted that of 15 sex offenders, and an additional woman who had intense sexual fantasies about children, all of whom were treated in a prison setting, 10 had been sexually abused in childhood; seven of these cases involved father-daughter incest.

A history of sexual abuse has also been consistently found among female child and adolescent perpetrators who are in treatment. Scavo (1989) stated that female adolescent sex offenders sometimes have sexual abuse histories of their own which may be the source of their initial referral for treatment. Jackson (1986) reported that 30-40 percent of adolescent sex offenders report having been abused themselves. Fehrenbach and Monastersky (1988) found that 50 percent of 28 adolescent females in a sex offender program had been themselves sexually abused. Two had been both physically and sexually abused. Johnson

(1989) noted that 100 percent of a sample of child female sex offenders had been molested; 85 percent by family members. Of the offenders against the child female offenders, 23 percent had themselves been female. Mayer (1992) presented case illustrations of eight adolescent females who were among 17 adolescents referred for treatment for having been sexually abused, who revealed they themselves had committed sexual offenses. She additionally reported on six cases of 3- to 6-year-old children who acted out sexually against other children and/or animals. All had been severely sexually abused at a very young age.

Knopp and Lackey (1987) collected data from 44 providers of treatment to female perpetrators. They found that most data collection sites reported that 100 percent of the female perpetrators that they treated, across several age groups, had themselves been sexually abused. Of female sex offenders below the age of 11, 100 percent were sexually abused prior to offending. Of those between the ages of 11 and 17, 14 of 16 respondents reported that 100 percent of these offenders had been sexually abused prior to offending; and of adult offenders, 11 of 19 respondents reported that 100 percent of their clients had been sexually abused prior to offending.

Chasnoff et al. (1986) reported on three cases of female-perpetrated sexual abuse that came to their attention in the course of treating substance abusers. They noted that while they had not been sexually abused in childhood, two of these three maternal-neonatal offenders had been raped in adulthood.

One author also noted that it was the perception of the victims of female-perpetrated child sexual abuse that their abuser may also have been sexually abused. Paiser (1992) made the observation that among the 10 female victims of female-perpetrated sexual abuse whom she interviewed, there were several cases in which the victims commented that the woman who sexually abused them may have been similarly abused herself.

Research supports the notion that 50 to 100 percent of all female sex offenders against children who have come to the attention of authorities were themselves sexually abused in childhood. This may be a low estimate in that factors such as embarrassment, repression, and forgetting may interfere with the reporting of such abuse among female offenders. There is also preliminary evidence to support that offenders who do not come to the attention of authorities tend to have been sexually abused in childhood.

PHYSICAL ABUSE

Several authors have noted childhood physical abuse in the backgrounds of female offenders. Groth (1979a) described a 20-year-old single woman who molested her niece as having been a neglected and abused child. McCarty (1986) reported physical abuse in 2 of 17 of cases of mothers who offended against their children, and for whom such data were available. Mayer (1992) described the cases of eight adolescent females who revealed that they had committed sexual offenses against younger children during the course of their treatment for having themselves been sexually abused; of these, two had been physically abused. She also described the case of an adult female perpetrator who had been physically abused in childhood, and of an adult women recounting both physical and sexual abuse at the hands of her mother. Travin et al. (1990) noted a history of childhood physical abuse in three of five cases of females referred to a sex offender program. They noted that a fourth individual had a history of childhood neglect. Regarding an additional four cases of females who committed sex offenses (two cases were of exhibitionism), but who were not convicted of sexual crimes, they commented that all had a history of severe, repeated physical, sexual or psychological abuse, or some combination.

Larson and Maison (1987) reported that of the 16 females treated in a prison setting for sexual offenses against children (15 offenders and one case which involved intense fantasy concerning children without an actual offense), three had been physically abused, seven had been emotionally abused, and one woman had been neglected by her parents. Additionally, one woman had experienced parental abandonment in her childhood. They remarked that all of the women had been physically, and/or sexually, and/or emotionally abused in childhood.

Allen (1991) reported that among reported female sex offenders against children many had experienced abuse by their parents during their adolescent years. He reported that 55 percent had been slapped in adolescence, 45 percent were hit with an object, 42 percent were spanked, 40 percent were pushed, grabbed or shoved. Twenty-two percent reported that in adolescence they had had an object thrown at them, or that they had been kicked, bitten or hit with a fist. Twenty-two percent also reported that they had been beaten up. Three percent had been burned or scalded by their parents in adolescence, 5 percent were threatened with a gun or a knife, and 2 percent had experienced a gun or a knife being used on them by their parents.

Physical abuse has also been found in the histories of female children and adolescents who commit sexual offenses. Of Johnson's 1989 sample of 13 child female sex offenders, 4 had been physically abused. Fehrenbach and Monastersky (1988) found that 21 percent of 28 female adolescent sex offenders had been physically abused. In their examination of these 28 adolescent females, Fehrenbach and Monastersky (1988) found that 20 percent of those who had committed rape (oral, anal, or vaginal intercourse, or penetration of the victim) and 23 percent of those committing indecent physical liberties (touching short of penetration) reported histories of physical abuse.

FAMILY PATHOLOGY IN FAMILIES-OF-ORIGIN

Various types of pathology and family problems have been found in the families-of-origin of females who have sexual relations with children. Groth (1979a) was among the first to have noted an unstable family life in the case of a female perpetrator. Paiser (1992) noted that "The family in which sexual abuse occurs tends to exhibit certain interactional patterns that do not allow the victimized child to grow, separate and move into relationships with the world at large" (p. 31). Masters (1963) noted that incest may occur in families where the mother or sister is promiscuous or is involved in prostitution or where the son is involved in the father's wage earner's role. Poor relationships between the parents of the offenders, generations of abuse, and drug/alcohol problems have all been noted in the backgrounds of these offenders.

In cases where there is sibling incest, or where a minor is involved in a sexual offense, a poor parental relationship and/or an unstable home environment is often found. Justice and Justice (1979) noted that sibling incest occurs in homes in which conditions of the family are chaotic, and in which the parents are passive, preoccupied, or sexually loose. Separation of the parents is commonly found. Sexual abuse among siblings identified in C.P.S. or District Attorney (D.A.) files was found by Kercher and McShane (1985) to have occurred most commonly when the child was living with only one natural parent, and least commonly when the child was living with both natural parents or with neither natural parent. Smith and Israel (1987) found that among 25 families in which there was sibling incest, females were perpetrators against their siblings in 20 percent of the cases; all had mothers who were engaging in extramarital affairs. They also noted that among the 25 cases of sibling incest, family pathology, including distant inaccessible parents, sexually abusive parents or observation of sexual activity between parents by the children, a history of parental sexual abuse at the hands of their own parents, "seductive" or "puritanical" mothers, and family secrets were common. Scavo (1989) also noted that family instability and disharmony is common in the background of adolescent female offenders.

Johnson (1989) noted that 6 of her sample of 13 female child perpetrators were living with their single mothers, three lived with relatives because their parents were unfit, one lived with a mother and step-father, one with a step-mother and father. Only one lived with both biological parents, and in this case, she was being molested by her father.

Johnson (1989) also noted that all of the parents of female child sex offenders had parents with personality deficits. Several additional areas of difficulty were described. The offenders' mothers had series of unsuccessful relationships with men and all but one of these mothers had experienced physical abuse from at least one man. These mothers were depressed and dependent, and had low self-esteem. All but two of the mothers of the child offenders had been sexually molested themselves during childhood, and the remaining two were reluctant to discuss the issue. None of these women had had positive childhoods, themselves. The majority of the child offenders' mothers (at least 54%) had had drug or alcohol problems during their daughters' lifetimes. The author noted that the majority of mothers of offenders had discussed their sexual needs and problems with their daughters, and that there were frequent role reversals that occurred in the interest of meeting the mothers' dependency needs.

Physical and sexual abuse histories were noted among members of the extended families, as well. In 92 percent of these families, one or more parent or grandparent had been a victim of physical abuse, and in 92 percent, at least one parent or grandparent had been sexually abused.

Of the fathers of the female child offenders in this study, five had molested their daughters, one had molested his daughter with his wife, one had left his family during a period when the mother was molesting his daughter, and five had never lived with their daughters for a sustained period of time.

In Johnson's (1989) study, the natural fathers were characterized as

> ... erratic, abrasive, and verbally, emotionally, and/or physically abusive men. They were unable to hold steady jobs and had been involved in illegal activities at least once in their lives. Each had a volatile temper and was emotionally distant from his family-of-origin, and his daughter and her mother ... Most were involved in drug and alcohol abuse. (p. 575)

Similar pathology in the family-of-origin has also been found in the families of female adult offenders. Allen found that of 65 female offenders largely identified through child protective services records, the mothers of 55 percent had only one spouse/partner. Twenty-three percent had two, 17 percent reported three or more, and 5 percent of the offenders did not know how many spouses/partners their mothers had. Of the fathers of these 65 female sex offenders, 51 percent had only one spouse or partner, 26 percent had two partners, and 11 percent had three or more. Nine percent of the female offenders did not know how many partners or spouses their fathers had had.

McCarty (1986) noted multiple caretakers (29%), traumatic breakup of their parents' marriage (41%), and alcoholic parents (29%) in the family histories of offending mothers. In addition, growing up outside of the family home was noted in the background of one offending mother, and having had a mentally ill mother was noted in the background of another. Travin et al. (1990) noted that in five cases of females who were referred to a sex offender treatment program, none had received help from their mothers or other adult caregivers when they themselves were physically, sexually or psychologically abused during childhood. Swink's (1989) description of nine women who were molested by their mothers included one mother who was herself abused by her own father, and physically abused by her mother. After intensive study of female sex offenders, Larson and Maison (1987) hypothesized that the families-of-origin of the offenders helped them to develop the capacity to commit sexual offenses.

Current evidence suggests that female child molesters are raised in unstable families-of-origin. Available evidence, however, consists only of data available for offenders who have been caught or who have come to the attention of mental health professionals. As such, it cannot be ruled out that a history of family pathology may predispose offenders to come to the attention of authorities or mental health professionals. Further research is needed on female offenders who have not necessarily been caught.

PSYCHOLOGICAL DIFFICULTIES OF THE FEMALE OFFENDER

Several authors have speculated that women who commit sexual offenses may be seriously psychologically disturbed; some have commented that such women are likely to be psychotic. Meiselman (1978) noted that mothers who molest their sons may have serious mental disturbances. Mayer (1983) stated that in the case of mother-daughter incest the mother is often "extremely disturbed, manifesting infantile and/or psychotic behavior" (p. 21). Masters (1963) noted that "feeble-mindedness," or a psychotic episode on the part of one of the participants in incest may contribute to the sexual activity's occurrence. Case studies which appeared in the early literature surrounding women who commit sex offenses often described women who were deeply disturbed. Recent literature has described a more heterogeneous population with respect to psychological functioning. While females who commit sexual offenses against children may demonstrate a wide array of disturbances, those who exhibit psychotic symptoms appear to be in the minority. It is likely that earlier case literature described primarily the more deeply disturbed individuals.

Case studies concerning women who molest children revealed a variety of serious mental health problems among these women. In describing mothers involved in mother-son incest, Lukianowicz (1972) reported that one was schizophrenic with limited intelligence, one was depressed, and one was neurotic; of two aunts involved in incest, one is described as hypomanic. Depression and violence on the part of the female offender has been noted in a case study by Shengold (1980). After reviewing several published case studies, Goodwin and Divasto (1979) remarked that in one case of grandmother-granddaughter incest, the grandmother was demented and depressed and was a hypochondriac who abused barbiturates; in a case of maternal incest, the mother was an alcoholic. Korbin (1986) described the case of a female who sexually abused her nephews; she also killed her 8-month-old daughter while using PCP. Marvasti (1986) noted a case in which depression and anxiety existed, as well as drug abuse, and in which the female offender had been diagnosed with borderline personality disorder. Groth (1979a) noted limited intelligence in the case of one female offender, and dependency, depression and rage in the case of a second female perpetrator. Dolan (1991) recalled the mother who had sexual contact with her as being "horribly depressed and trancelike" throughout most of her childhood.

Case studies involving female sex offenders have tended to describe women more severely disturbed than those reported by researchers investigating larger populations of such offenders. Condy et al. (1987) are apparently the only researchers who have reported on female sex offenders who have not necessarily come to the attention of authorities for their sexual offenses. Condy et al. (1987) found that prison women who had been sexually involved with boys and adolescents scored higher on the Schizophrenia and Hypomania Scales of the Minnesota Multiphasic Personality Inventory (MMPI) Mini-Mult, than did non-involved prison women, though by less than one standard deviation. Such women also scored lower on the Lie Scale. She concluded that while elevations on these scales are associated with unconventional lifestyles and socially inappropriate behaviors, the bulk of her evidence did not suggest that psychosis is typical among molesting women (Condy, 1985). Paiser (1992) noted that some of the female perpetrators described by adult female victims might be thought of as emotionally disturbed. One of the 10 victims she studied revealed that the mother who abused her had a multiple personality disorder. Paiser (1992) also noted, however, that other offenders were highly esteemed members of their communities and were quite functional.

Researchers reporting on female sex offenders who have come to the attention of authorities report a variety of mental health concerns. Occasionally an offender is found to be psychotic, or to be intellectually impaired. Various personality disorders are also found among female sex offenders known to authorities. Often the female is found to be depressed. Numerous authors have commented that many female sex offenders have drug or alcohol problems. Several have remarked upon the general dysfunction of these women, for example observing that they achieve below their level of ability, or that they are highly dependent upon others for support.

O'Connor (1987) noted that 48 percent of 25 British women convicted of indecent assault on persons under 16 or gross indecency with children had a history of a psychiatric diagnosis and treatment. Of the 19 offenders who had committed indecent assault against children under the age of 16, the diagnoses were: five cases of depression, one case of schizophrenia, one case of a personality disorder, and one case of a woman for whom the diagnosis was unclear, but who had been taking flupenthixol for three years. Of the six who had committed indecencies with children, one was schizophrenic, one had a schizoaffective disorder, and two had personality disorders. All of these four had been hospitalized for psychiatric treatment.

Rowan et al. (1990) commented that among nine cases of females evaluated for sexual offenses against children, one was diagnosed as schizophrenic, eight had Axis II diagnoses, one was mildly retarded and five were of borderline intelligence. In three of the nine cases, the woman had a history of drug or alcohol abuse, or was using alcohol at the time of the offense. Ramsey-Klawsnik (1990) observed that in 75% of offender-victim pairings, the child was both physically and sexually abused by the female offender.

Wolfe (1985) found that only one of 12 female sex offenders was mentally ill, suffering from schizophrenia. Five of these women were substance abusers. These six women all offended against children. Swink (1989) described the cases of nine women sexually abused by their mothers. One of these maternal offenders had a psychotic break, one saw a psychiatrist for depression, one saw a psychiatrist and made suicide attempts, and one suffered agoraphobia, and was under psychiatric care. In addition, five of these women were alcoholic or abused drugs, eight were physically abusive and all were described as psychologically abusive and particularly critical. Faller (1987) found that 48 percent of the female child molesters in her study had mental difficulties; of these, 33 percent were mentally retarded or brain damaged, and 18 percent had suffered at some time from psychosis. Substance abuse was reported for 55 percent of these women; alcohol was abused in 13 cases, drugs in six cases, and both in three cases.

In evaluating four individuals who were referred for psychiatric difficulties, Travin et al. (1990) discovered they had acted out sexually (in one case physically against an unspecified child, in one case physically against several younger relatives, and in two cases via exhibitionism). One individual was diagnosed with a borderline personality disorder, one with severe bipolar disorder, one with paranoid schizophrenia, and one with schizoaffective disorder. All had histories of chronic mixed substance abuse. Among five additional women who were referred after having molested children, one was described as depressed, anxious and dependent; one as passive, withdrawn and inadequate; one as suffering from depersonalization disorder, and one as withdrawn with an extensive history of alcohol abuse.

In McCarty's (1986) sample of of 26 mothers who offended against their children, 11 offended only against female children. Seven offenders against female children acted alone; of these, five suffered serious emotional disturbances, as documented by either psychological testing or by a history of psychiatric hospitalization. Four offenders against female children acted as a co-offender; of these only one was considered disturbed, and was thought to be a psychopath by her victim's therapist. Of the eight offenders against males only, two were considered to be disturbed; one had suffered a "nervous breakdown," and one was noted to have a sexual pathology. Of the two cases in which a female molested both a male and a female child, one was considered to be mildly disturbed, and one to have impaired reality testing and some emotional disturbance. McCarty (1986) noted dependency as an issue among co-offending mothers and female accomplices to sex crimes. She additionally noted that two women had had brain surgery in their childhoods, resulting in epilepsy.

Mayer (1992) discussed eight adolescent offenders who represented typical cases in a group of 17 female adolescent offenders, all of whom had originally been referred for having been sexually abused. Of these eight cases, two were diagnosed with conduct disorder, one with histrionic personality disorder "with dissociative features," five were diagnosed as either having or developing borderline personality disorder; of these five, two were also learning disabled and one was also diagnosed as having attention-deficit disorder. In the same publication, Mayer also described cases of adult female offenders: one had been diagnosed as psychotic, one as being depressed and having a low IQ, and one as having borderline personality disorder. In addition, the daughter of one of these offenders, who was abused by her mother, and was herself an offender, was diagnosed as having a borderline personality disorder.

Several authors have remarked upon the general limitations in functioning exhibited by female sex offenders against children. Mayer (1992) described briefly cases involving adult female offenders. Among them were a female who received Supplemental Security Income because she was unable to support herself due to her emotional difficulties, another who received Aid to Families with Dependent Children because she did not have paid employment. Allen (1991) noted that 43 percent of 65 female offenders reported that they were unemployed. Several of the offenders had no fixed place of residence and moved between several places over the course of weeks. The mean annual income for the female offenders was $7250, with over 75 percent earning less than $10,000. Ten percent of the offenders were professionals. Forty percent of the offenders were high school graduates, while educational levels ranged from the seventh grade to the Masters level. Most of those employed at paying jobs were employed in traditional women's occupations.

Allen (1991) found only small evidence of juvenile delinquency in the histories of 65 female sex offenders. The mean level of thefts during adolescence for the female offenders was 2.6, and the mean numbers of times arrested or appearing in juvenile court was 0.5. The average number of times that the females ran away was 1.8, with 43 percent of the female offenders reporting that they ran away from home. Given, however, that Allen found large amounts of physical and sexual abuse in the childhood homes of these perpetrators, the running away may have constituted adaptive rather than antisocial behavior. Allen (1991) also found that 15 percent of the female offenders had received money for sexual activity and that 80 percent of these offenders had been paid by two or more people; it is not noted whether this may have occurred in the context of a sexually abusive relationship, however.

Grayson (1989) commented that researchers Larson and Maison found low educational levels, "lives of chaos and disorganization," and sometimes a history of other crimes among imprisoned female sex offenders. Also noted was the fact that women who coped by denial had more normal psychological profiles as measured by several psychological testing instruments. Those who admitted to their offenses were likely to be in more distress, to have lower self-concepts, to show more confusion in thinking, and to be less well adjusted.

Larson and Maison (1987) discussed the difficulties seen among 14 imprisoned female sex offenders whom they saw in group therapy, together with a woman who turned herself in for the sexual abuse of a male adolescent, but who was not charged with a crime, and a woman who had intense fantasies about sexual behavior with children, but who did not act on her feelings. They found these women experiencing several difficulties, including an external locus of control; dichotomous thinking, with victim or perpetrator roles being primary personality configurations; global shame, rather than behavior-specific guilt; "emotional anesthesia" and emotional isolation; psychosexual immaturity, which often approximated that of their victims; poor capacity to form relationships; and a poor understanding of human sexuality. Among these women, Larson and Maison found that 6 of the 16 had chemical dependency problems, and that 6 of the 16 were more than 40 pounds overweight. They observed that women who sexually abuse children are likely to have low self-esteem. Two of the women had been placed in a psychiatric hospital, one for observation, and one for a short period of treatment.

Larson and Maison (1987) further found that the mean educational attainment of female sex offenders was 11 years, with a range of 8 to 16 years and a mode of 12 years. Low IQs were not noted among this population, in contrast with other studies; the average IQ was 108, with a range of 92-117. Overall, it was noted, the women held service or factory jobs, with the exception of one woman, who was a teacher. They noted that without assistance, the work histories and job skills of most of the clients were such that most could not survive economically on their own.

Several rigid defense mechanisms were also noted among the women, generally as a result of having grown up in dysfunctional or abusive homes. Larson and Maison (1987) observed that the women suffered from a sense of "fluid reality," a form of cognitive distortion of reality akin to magical thinking. Blocking memories, dichotomous thinking, minimizing intelligence and behaving dependently were noted as defenses, as were "fogging," distorting reality by "adding in" pieces, and becoming fluid in a way that lessened their boundaries and minimized their impact within their families-of-origin.

Johnson (1989) noted academic and social problems in all 13 of her sample of female child offenders; two had IQs in the mentally retarded range. All were depressed and anxious. Additionally, some engaged in stealing, fire-setting, and running away. Scavo (1989) noted that among female adolescent offenders, common difficulties were a poor self-concept, intense anger, feelings of helplessness, and social isolation. Behavior problems were also noted as common reasons for initial referral into therapy.

Several of the authors referred to have remarked upon the existence of substance abuse in the histories of female sex offenders (Goodwin & DiVasto, 1979; Korbin, 1986; Marvasti, 1986; Rowan et al., 1990; Swink, 1989; Travin et al., 1990; Wolfe, 1985) With some consistency, substance abuse has been found to exist in the backgrounds of many female sex offenders against children. This has been documented in several case studies. Masters (1963) noted that narcotics addiction or alcoholism may be factors in incest. Weinberg (1955) described a case of mother-son incest in which the mother was described as a chronic alcoholic. In one of the case studies examined by Wahl (1960), the mother of a son reporting incestuous relations was reported to be an alcoholic. Margolis (1984) noted a case in which mother-son incest occurred after the mother had been drinking. Sugar (1983) described heavy alcohol use and occasional drug use in the case of a mother who attempted sexual contact with her daughter, and described drug abuse in the case of a female who molested her younger female cousin. Maltz and Holman (1987) quoted a male survivor of incest with his mother who noted that he began having sex with her after she began drinking heavily. O'Connor (1987) noted sedative and alcohol abuse in one of the cases of convicted female sex offenders. Chasnoff et al. (1986) noted that three of 25 women in a substance abuse program had sexually abused their infants.

Others have researched the frequency of drug and alcohol problems among known female sex offenders. McCarty (1986) noted serious drug abuse in 46 percent of independently offending mothers, and in 22 percent of co-offenders, and 20 percent of accomplices. Condy (1985) reported that 19 percent of college men and 20 percent of imprisoned men who were molested by females recalled the women having drug and alcohol problems. Such was the case for 11 percent of the rapists, 26 percent of the child molesters, and 23 percent of the nonsex offenders. However, she found no differences in rates of drug/alcohol abuse between prison women who had sexual contact with boys, versus those who did not. Twelve percent of college men who were molested, and 6 percent of the male prisoners who had been molested indicated that the molesting female had had mental or emotional problems; such was the case for 5 percent of the rapists, 9 percent of the child molesters, and 4 percent of the nonsex offenders. Of 65 female sex offenders in Allen's (1991) sample, 17 percent identified themselves as alcoholics; 26 percent indicated that they had used drugs.

HUSBANDS AND MATES

What literature is available concerning female child sexual molesters suggests that they often have less than exemplary relationships with those whom they choose as spouses or mates. Often the women do not have a primary or love relationship with an adult at the time of their involvements with children and in some cases are using the children or adolescents as primary partners. In cases where the female offender has a mate, the relationship is often tumultuous. In many cases the partner has a drug or alcohol problem, or is physically or sexually abusive toward the woman or her children. In some cases, women fearing such brutality become sexually involved with their children as a result of having been coerced by their partners. Larson and Maison (1987) remarked that female sex offenders have difficulties with their relationships in general, and particularly those with men; they noted that female perpetrators repeatedly engage in harmful relationships, often because of their use of denial as a primary coping mechanism.

That female perpetrators have difficulties with their marriages or romantic relationships has been noted in the discussions of several cases of female offenders.

Some female perpetrators are reported to be experiencing difficulties or abuse in their primary love or marital relationship (Groth, 1979a; Lukianowicz, 1972; Margolis, 1984; Marvasti, 1986; Travin et al., 1990; Wahl, 1960; Weinberg, 1955); or they divorce (Maltz & Holman, 1987) at the time of their perpetrations. Masters (1963) cited rejection by a marriage partner as a possible contributor to incestuous relations. Some female sexual abusers are reported to be living without a mate, or with a physically or psychologically absent mate (Dolan, 1991; Groth, 1979a; Justice & Justice, 1979; Lukianowicz, 1972; Margolis, 1984; Marvasti, 1986; Mayer, 1983; Meiselman, 1978; Shengold, 1980; Swink, 1989; Weinberg, 1955); they may use an adolescent or male child to fulfill the role of husband or mate. Some female perpetrators commit their offenses with their mates (Larson & Maison, 1987; McCarty, 1986; Rowan et al., 1990; Wolfe, 1985). Some female offenders are reported to be generally promiscuous (Groth 1979a; Lukianowicz, 1972; Wahl, 1960; Weinberg, 1955), or to have a history of several marriages (McCarty, 1986; Wahl, 1960; Weinberg, 1955). Many authors who have examined female sex offenders against children have found an absence of positive primary love relationships; either mates are often absent or primary love relationships are highly dysfunctional.

McCarty (1986) noted such unstable relationships among a sample of mothers who were female offenders, observing that 85 percent of her sample of offending mothers had married in their teens, with 31 percent married at age 15 or younger. She noted that eight independent offenders were experiencing a crisis in their marriages at the time of their offenses, and that co-offending mothers usually were in their second or third marriage. She notes that 42 percent of the independent offenders and 56 percent of the co-offenders had histories of "sexual indiscretions" with men. Two co-offenders and one independent offender had a history of prostitution.

Kercher and Mc Shane (1985) found that many of the female offenders in their sample were unmarried. They found that the majority of female offenders identified through C.P.S. and D.A. records were single: 37 percent of the females were single, 26 percent were separated or divorced, 26 percent were married, and one (3%) was in a common law marriage; the marital status of the others was unknown. Of the females who abused females, 48 percent were single and 31 percent were separated or divorced. Females who abused males were slightly more likely to be married (56%) than not.

Wolfe (1985) similarly noted that three of twelve female sex offenders were divorced, three were single, and six were married. Three offenders against children and one offender against an adult indicated that they committed their offenses in compliance with the desires of a male on whom they depended for survival. In one case, an offender's husband threatened to kill her infant unless she committed her offenses; in another case, the female offender's resistance to taking part in sexual abuse was met with severe abuse by her husband. Half of the offenders had not completed high school, only three were employed at intake, and nine were socially isolated, suggesting possible dependency on their spouses among those who were married.

Rowan et al. (1990) noted one case of a female who assisted a male in raping a 13-year-old girl out of fear that this alcoholic boyfriend would beat her if she refused. They noted that in six of nine cases of sexual abuse of children by women, the female had acted in the company of a dominant male. In two other cases the woman was living alone with her child at the time of the incident, and in one case the woman was married to a man who was physically ill.

Larson and Maison (1987) reported that of 16 women treated in a prison setting (15 for sexual abuse of children or adolescents, one for intense sexual fantasies involving children), two were divorced, three were never married, for one there was no information, and 10 were married. Eight of the women abused the children in concert with their husbands; one abused with her married lover; two women were involved in assisting in the gang rapes of two adolescents who had made advances towards their boyfriends; one helped a pimp rape an adolescent girl. The women were often victims of physical and sexual abuse within their marriages or relationships. Grayson (1989) noted that some female offenders had been sexually abused within relationships with men. She quoted researcher Larson as saying, "For some of these women, sex with a child was the nicest and only non-violent sex they had known" (p. 10).

Among another sample of convicted female sex offenders against children, motivations cited for the offenses also included factors related to chaotic love relationships. O'Connor (1987) noted fear of being beaten by a boyfriend, boredom following a broken marriage (complicated by drug and alcohol abuse), and revenge against an unfaithful husband as motives listed by convicted female sex offenders against children. He noted two cases of female offenders whose husbands were both physically and sexually violent towards them, and who were additionally alcohol and/or drug abusers. One case is noted of an offender who was married to a man who beat her and who became a chronic mental patient.

Allen (1991) noted extremely abusive relationships between female sex offenders and their spouses or live-in partners. Fifty-four percent of female offenders had been pushed, shoved or grabbed by the spouse, 23 percent had been beaten up by the spouse, 15 percent had been threatened with a gun or knife, 28 percent had been kicked, bitten or hit with a fist, 28 percent reported that a spouse had thrown something at them, 18 percent had been hit with something, 5 percent had been burned or scalded, and 3 percent had had a gun or a knife used on them by a spouse or partner. The female offenders had also abused their spouses. Thirty-eight percent had thrown something at their spouses or partners, 20 percent had hit them with an object, 16 percent had kicked, bitten or hit their spouses, 8 percent had beaten up a spouse or partner, 6 percent had threatened their spouse/partner with a knife or gun, 2 percent had burned or scalded their partners, and 2 percent had used a gun or a knife on their partners. However, 82 percent of the offenders reported being moderately to extremely satisfied with their sexual relationship with their spouse or partner, while only 9 percent reported being moderately to extremely dissatisfied. Allen asked female offenders how satisfied in general they were with their martial or live-in relationships, and how satisfied they were with their children. On a 7-point Likert scale, with the highest score being 3 (very satisfied), the lowest being 0 (very dissatisfied), and 1.5 indicating neutral or indifferent, the mean satisfaction score with respect to partners was 1.8, and with children was 2.5.

Allen (1991) also found that 26 percent of female child molesters had only one sexual partner (not including the victims) during the previous 5 years, while 9 percent had had more than 10 partners. The mean number of partners was 3.6. The mean number of spouses or live-in relationships reported by the female offenders was 2, with a range from 0-7.

Swink (1989) described several cases of females who were molested by their mothers; some gave retrospective information related to their mothers' relationships with men. Among nine cases of women molested by their mothers were two cases in which the mothers' husbands left the family, and four cases in which the husbands were alcoholics. Additionally, one of these mothers had a boyfriend who physically and sexually abused her children, one had a husband who had sexual affairs with men, women, and their children's friends, one of the husbands physically and sexually abused the children and had affairs, one of the husbands was physically abusive towards the children, and one of the husbands sexually abused the children. Further alluding to the extent of pathology in the families chosen by the female perpetrators are similar findings by Paiser (1992) that 10 female *victims* of female perpetrators (the majority of whom were mothers or relatives) had all experienced other forms of abuse — in addition to sexual abuse — while growing up. Such abuse included physical (eight cases), emotional (six cases), verbal (six cases), satanic/ritual abuse (two cases), and observing the abuse of others (four cases).

Available data would suggest that female child molesters have great difficulty in their primary love relationships. They are often without a primary love relationship. They may also be emotionally disenfranchised from their current partners or spouses. At times a crisis in a relationship with a mate may precipitate the sexual offense. In cases where female offenders have a primary love relationship it is often highly dysfunctional. Commonly found among the mates of female sex offenders are men who are physically or sexually abusive towards the woman or her children, or men with alcohol or drug problems. In that the female sex offender may also have these, or similar problems, the relationship difficulties may often be compounded. The female offender may also have several marriages or sexual partners.

Conclusions such as these, it must be noted, have been based upon findings from populations of offenders who have come to the attention of authorities or mental health practitioners. As such they may not be representative of women who offend against children but whose crimes do not come to the attention of the authorities. It may be the case that women who exist in highly dysfunctional environments are more likely to be investigated when a charge of sexual abuse is made against them. Little is known about the relationships of female sex offenders who have not come to the attention of authorities.

Data have just begun to be collected on females who have sexual contact with children. Existing information is largely based upon case impressions from clinical and criminal populations. Further research is necessary to replicate current findings, and to begin to examine those individuals who have engaged in sexual acts with children but who have not come to the attention of legal authorities for their actions. A childhood history of sexual and physical abuse, as well as various types of pathology in families-of-origin has been associated with later molestation of children by females. It has yet to be shown whether such forms of childhood trauma are predictive of later propensity to have sexual contact with children. The finding of a correlation between these psychosocial variables and later sexual contact with children would prove useful in the identification and treatment of the female sex offender.

Subtypes of Female Offenders

DESCRIPTIONS OF SUBTYPES FROM THE LITERATURE

Various researchers have attempted to classify into subtypes the kinds of females who sexually abuse children. Such categorization has generally been made on the bases of small and biased samples, without statistical confirmation of clinical impressions. Subtypes have been developed by differentiating the perpetrators by their relationships to victims, the dynamics of the assaults, and the psychosocial histories of the female offenders.

There is a sparsity of data in the literature where these subtypes are concerned. Studies by Faller (1988), Larson and Maison (1987), Mathews et al. (1989), McCarty (1986), Sarrel and Masters (1982), and Swink (1989) have made investigations into subtypes of female perpetrators. Prior to these studies, authors on the topic alluded to subtypes of female-perpetrated incest. Several authors attempted to categorize and describe incest in which the mother was the perpetrator. Descriptions of "typical" cases and subtypes of maternal incest in the literature are inconsistent and at times contradictory.

Justice and Justice (1979) in commenting on mother-son incest reported that the mother

> ... may deeply love her son and rationalize incest as the highest expression of such love, she may consider she is providing him with sex education, she may be seclusive, shut off from the world with her son and turn to him for human contact, or she may be promiscuous and shares sex with her son along with a number of other males. Finally, she may simply be psychotic. (p. 102)

They noted that incestuous mothers may be widowed or divorced and project unsettled Oedipal wishes onto a son, who assumes a position as "man of the house." Others, they noted, become totally preoccupied with their sons, believing that a male child makes their lives complete, and slide into incest from sex play. The mothers who are promiscuous "come from backgrounds of early sexual stimulation, loose standards in the family, or beliefs that a male must be serviced with sex for him to feel affection for a woman or even to have any interest in her" (p. 149). This promiscuity may extend to a son.

Finkelhor (1984) characterized the maternal offender as being poor and black, and prone to physical abuse. He commented that she has a tendency to choose the oldest child, though at a very young age. The ethnicity of the female offender has not been confirmed by other studies, however. Others have not found most offenders to be black (Allen, 1991; Larson & Maison, 1987). Paiser (1992) found that all of 10 victims in her study, the majority of whom discussed sexual abuse by a female relative, most commonly a mother, were Caucasian.

Mayer (1983) stated that mother-son incest most often occurs when the father is absent or is out of the home. She added that in cases of mother-daughter incest the mother is often extremely disturbed, and may effect a role reversal in her relationship with her daughter. Weinberg (1955) also commented that mother-son incest occurs when the father is absent or very subordinate, and remarked that it occurs in families in which the sexual culture is loose; where the mother initiates the relationship, it is described as being ambivalent — intimate but hostile.

Forward and Buck (1978) stated their belief that mother-son incest is necessarily based on tenderness, because the son must sustain an erection. This notion was disputed by Sarrel and Masters (1982) who found that men who were assaulted under the most traumatic and violent of circumstances could sustain an erection. Wulffen (1934) also recorded the case of a male who was raped by a female with the assistance of several male and female individuals, and who sustained an erection. Forward and Buck (1978) estimated that in 95 percent of cases the father is no longer a part of the nuclear family, or is no longer in the home. They described the mother as generally a highly dependent woman who needs a man. They described the mother-son relationship as being characterized by strong love and guilt on the part of the mother.

Forward and Buck (1978) described three types of mother-son incest. In the first, there may be no sexual contact, but the two may undress, bathe, or sleep together. The son assumes the father's role and may fantasize about sexual contact with the mother. The second form involves sexual contact short of intercourse. The third type involves actual intercourse between the mother and son. They described a case in which such incest began after a request for divorce which devastated the mother, and in which the son took on the social role of man of the house and husband.

In contrast to the notion that mother-son incest generally occurs when the father is outside the home, Nielsen (1983), reported that a mother is most likely to be involved in sexual activity with her children "in conjunction with the father, step-father, or boyfriend" (p. 140).

Other researchers have attempted to categorize other forms of female-initiated child sexual abuse. Allen (1991) noted a particular subtype of female offenders that identifies victims as "boyfriends." He noted that the ages of the boys involved fell between 13 and 16.

Faller (1988) found that the female sex offenders in treatment who were the subjects for her study fell into five categories. The five categories she described were polyincestuous abusers, single parent abusers, psychotic abusers, adolescent perpetrators, and noncustodial abusers.

Twenty-nine of her sample of 40 (73%) were classified as abusing in *polyincestuous* family situations. In such cases, there were at least two perpetrators, and usually two or more victims; such families were characterized by multiple sexually abusive relationships and group sex with children of both sexes. Faller stated that in these cases sex abuse may be traceable through several generations in a family, with offenders and victims also being located outside of the family. She observed that it is typical for males to initiate the sexual abuse in polyincestuous cases. Mothers typically perpetrated "fewer and less intrusive" sexual acts than the males, and in some cases were following the instructions of the males, apparently against their will.

Of Faller's 40 cases, six (15%) involved a mother who was a *single parent*. These mothers did not have ongoing relationships with men. In only two cases was the offender married to the father of her children, and if there was more than one child, the children tended to have more than one father. The oldest children in these cases were described as having surrogate partner responsibilities and adult roles.

Three of Faller's (1987) 40 female perpetrators were categorized as *psychotic* (7.5%). Faller described the psychotic offender as having out-of-control libidinal impulses and developing a delusional system as a justification for sexually abusive behavior. The three women had abused their daughters, and one of the three had additionally abused a niece.

Three of Faller's 40 subjects were *adolescents* (8%). These females are described as having poor peer relationships and as lacking alternative sexual outlets. They had access to children, or else chose them as playmates or as children to babysit, or the like. Sexual activities were noted to have been designed to please the perpetrator rather than the victim.

Only one of Faller's 40 perpetrators was a *noncustodial abuser,* who was recently divorced and who abused her children during visitations. Faller noted that a sexually abusive divorced parent has usually resisted the breakup, and, devastated by the loss, uses the child sexually for both emotional gratification, and as a means of expressing anger at the spouse. She noted that sexual attraction to the children may be present before the divorce, and that the lack of structure and supervision during visitation may play a role in the occurrence of sexual abuse.

Sarrel and Masters (1982) examined 11 cases in which a male had been molested by a female, and found four categories of female perpetrator. All of the men had been seen for treatment. Six had been seen at the Yale Human Sexuality program for a wide variety of problems. Five had requested treatment for sexual dysfunction or disorders from the Masters and Johnson Institute. The authors interviewed all 11 males.

Four categories of female sex perpetrator emerged from their work; three were categories of women molesting children, one involved females assaulting adult males. The categories which emerged were as follows: *forced assault* (three adult males, one teen), characterized by the use of physical restraints, believable threats of violence, or both; *"babysitter" abuse* (two cases), characterized by the seduction of a young boy by an older female who is not a relative, and which may involve direct or implied threats if the incident is reported to the parents; *incestuous abuse* (two cases), in which a male minor is seduced by an older female relative, and *dominant woman abuse* (two adult males, one teen), in which an adult male is intimidated or terrified by an aggressive sexual approach that does not involve direct physical force.

Mathews et al. (1989) conducted interviews with 16 female sexual offenders and found that three categories of offender emerged: *Teacher/Lover, Predisposed,* and *Male-Coerced.* These categories were differentiated based on "the crimes the women committed, their perceptions of the victims, the involvement of co-offenders, and psychological similarities and differences" (p. 3).

According to Mathews and her colleagues, the *Teacher/Lover* is generally involved with prepubescent and adolescent males. She relates to them as a peer, and seeks to "teach" them about sexuality. They found that only one female sexual offender in their sample fit this profile. This woman was a victim of emotional, verbal, and physical abuse as a child. Her first sexual experiences were described as abusive and coercive, and her relationships with men were described as traumatic and chaotic, including physical and sexual assault by her lovers, gang rape on several occasions, forced prostitution, involvement with drug dealers, and marriage to a convicted sex offender. It is reported that she feared older men and, as such, fell in love with an adolescent male, whom she met through her two sons. She also played sexual games and had sexual contact with other adolescents of both genders.

The *Predisposed* offenders are described as having been victims of severe sexual abuse, usually by more than one family member, that was initiated at a young age, and persisted over a long period of time. Most were later "promiscuous" although they did not enjoy sex. The authors reported strong indications that sexual abuse has been in the families of these offenders for years. Victims of such offenders are their family members, and were their own children in all but two cases. The goals of the interaction included the establishment of emotional intimacy. These women reported "lashing out and hurting those around them, even as children." Seven such cases are described. In each of these cases the woman acted independently. Five of the seven women abused chemicals; two compulsively overate. All reported that they would do anything to keep men around, and had a history of "unhealthy and dangerous relationships." Only two of the seven women had been able to hold jobs.

Eight cases were described in which the offender fit the *Male-Coerced* category. Women in this category were described as very dependent and nonassertive women who initially engaged in sexually abusive activity with a male who has previously abused children. Some of the offenders later initiated the abuse themselves. They were reported to be passive, and to feel powerless in inter-personal relationships, and to endorse a traditional lifestyle as a homemaker. All mentioned a fear that they could not attract a husband, and a subsequent need to maintain an abusive relationship. All were subjected to verbal abuse by their husbands, and some were physically abused. All were reported to be "totally dominated" by their husbands. Their victims were children both within and out-side of their families.

This sample of sixteen was drawn from a nonprofit corrections agency in Minne-apolis, Minnesota. One portion of this agency served women referred from the District Court and Probation, the other served women referred from Juvenile Probation and Child Protective Services. In 1984, this agency began an outpa-tient treatment program for female sex offenders. Apparently offenders were involved with the other agency programs in many cases.

McCarty (1986) differentiated 26 mothers from an incest treatment program into two types of incest offenders, based upon whether they had acted independent-ly or with a male in committing their offenses. She found that the *independent offenders* had troubled childhoods in which they were sexually abused, usually by a brother. They were of average intelligence and able to hold a job and live independently. They tended to have had only one marriage which occurred in teenage years. Roughly half of these offenders abused drugs or were emotional-ly disturbed. The victim in these cases was usually a daughter.

The *co-offending mothers* also had troubled childhoods in which they were sex-ually abused, usually by an adult caretaker. Married as teenagers, these offend-ers were usually on their second or third marriage, and had a strong need to be taken care of. About half were of borderline intelligence, and roughly three-fourths did not work outside the home. About half had a history of "sexual indis-cretion." The victims were likely to be a son or daughter.

Also included as a category were *accomplices*. These mothers' roles in enabling the sexual abuse were extensive enough to compel law enforcement officials to prosecute them as offenders. These women tended to be of average intelligence and to be employed outside of the home. They tended to be married as teenagers and to have a strong need to be taken care of. The victim tended to be a female child.

Swink (1989) described similar categories in her review of nine cases of mother-daughter incest. The three categories described by Swink were co-victims, indi-rect abusers, and direct abusers.

Co-victim offenders were described as being controlled by someone who was abusive to them, and who used them to perpetrate abuse on their daughters.

The mothers were afraid and powerless, and were passive, unwilling participants in the abuse. One such case was described in her review of nine cases.

Indirect abusers were described as abusive women who did not have actual sexual contact with their daughters. Rather, they offered their daughters to other individuals to be sexually abused. They sometimes received reward or payment in exchange. Swink described three such cases, one of which involved a woman who also had direct sexual contact with her daughter.

Direct abusers included those women who had direct sexual contact with their daughters. Six such cases are described.

Larson and Maison (1987) differentiated female offenders by their motivations for committing the abuse. They derived their categories from studying 15 sex offenders with whom they worked in a prison setting, and an additional woman who was treated for intense sexual fantasies concerning children. Some of the women had more than one motivation for their offenses against their victims. They noted that motivations for three of the women stemmed from *being dependent on the husband.* The motivation in these cases was not sexual or affectional, but rather a means of pleasing the husband and reducing their fears of abandonment. The husbands took the lead in these cases.

Three women were identified who reported having been *in love with their victims.* The attachment to the child was reported to be intense, as was the fear of abandonment. All of these women had a history of abandonment and an extended history of feeling lost and unloved.

Seven women appeared to have been motivated primarily by *anger.* These women are reported to have had a great deal of free-floating anger that was displaced onto the victims. These women tended to offend in concert with other individuals.

One of the women was motivated by *revenge against her husband.* Apparently this woman had sex with her 11-year-old son to get back at her husband for having been attracted to their daughter.

Larson and Maison (1987) also noted that women can be motivated to sexually abuse a child by being a *psychosocial peer* of the child; they noted one such case.

Three women were motivated by *being "pansexual,"* or in a situation where sexual meaning is attached to every day interaction patterns among family members. They also noted that women can be motivated by a combination of dependency and pansexuality.

VARIABLES EMERGING FROM SUBTYPE CATEGORIES

From these attempts at typing female sex offenders, several factors have emerged which have been combined in order to create subcategories of female offenders. *Whether or not the female co-offended with a male,* generally with one upon whom she was dependent, is thought by some to be a factor which might discriminate among female offenders (Faller, 1987; Larson & Maison, 1987; Mathews et al., 1989; McCarty, 1986). While not seen as a separate type of offender, a female co-offending with males against a 17-year-old was also noted by Sarrel and Masters (1982). The *number of marriages* was thought to differentiate the "independent" from the "co-offender," with the "co-offender" having more marriages (McCarty, 1986). *Dependency* was also seen by McCarty (1986) as differentiating these two types of offenders, with the co-offender being the more dependent; Mathews et al. (1989) also noted this characteristic. Larson and Maison (1987) also noted dependency upon a male initiator as a type of motivation for sexually abusing a child. McCarty (1986) noted that a *higher IQ* and better *ability to hold a job* differentiated the "independent" from "co-offending" female.

The *extent of sexual abuse in the history of the offender* was identified by both Faller (1987) ("polyincestuous") and Mathews et al. (1989) ("predisposed") as a factor which might differentiate between subtypes of female perpetrator. In a similar way, Larson and Maison (1987) noted "pansexual behavior" as a type of motivator.

The lack of a current adult partner, and subsequent placement of the victim into the role of an adult lover or spouse was seen by Mathews et al. (1989) ("teacher/lover"), and by Faller (1987) ("single parent" and "noncustodial abuser") as a factor which may differentiate among female offenders. Larson and Maison (1987) also noted this in identifying "being in love," and being a "psychosocial peer" as motivations for sexual contact with children and adolescents. Sarrel and Masters (1982), noted one case which fit this criteria, though they did not utilize this factor in differentiating among female perpetrators. Faller (1987) noted that *a recent crisis with a partner* ("noncustodial") was a factor assisting in the differentiation of subtypes of perpetrators. Mathews et al. (1989) also noted that the *goal of intimacy in the sexual offense* is a factor which may discriminate "predisposed" offenders from others.

Other possible differentiating factors include whether the offender was psychotic, as described in a category by Faller (1987), and as described in one of the cases illustrated by Sarrel and Masters (1982); whether the offender was an *adolescent* (Faller, 1987), or a *babysitter* (Sarrel & Masters, 1982).

Whether or not the offense is incestuous is a factor thought by Sarrel and Masters (1982) to discriminate among perpetrators. Mathews et al. (1989) also included incest as a factor which assists in discriminating the predisposed offender from other categories. McCarty (1986) also included the *relationship of the female to her own perpetrator and to her victims* as factors that differentiated between "independent" and "co-offending" mothers.

Sarrel and Masters (1982) included the *type of coercion* used by the female as a factor differentiating between types of perpetrator.

Substance abuse was noted to be present in the "predisposed" category by Mathews et al. (1989), and in the "independent offender" category by McCarty (1986).

Revenge at a mate or anger were noted by Faller (1987) ("noncustodial abuser") and by Larson and Maison (1987) as motivators in some cases of sexual abuse of a child by a female.

The categories based on these variables are in need of further research. Different researchers have combined these variables in different ways based on clinical impressions of their subjects, and have come up with different categories. Research is needed to determine which of these factors combine to form "types" of female offenders when subjected to statistical analysis. Research is also needed which gathers data from unreported female offenders, to rule out the possibilities that females who have been reported are biased because of character traits or histories that caused them to be admitted into the system, that are unrelated to their offenses.

Variables Contributing to a Severe Outcome Following Sexual Abuse

RELATIONSHIP OF ELEMENTS OF SEXUAL ABUSE TO NEGATIVE OUTCOMES

Consistently, a number of authors have noted sexual abuse in the histories of female perpetrators. Several authors have noticed that various factors related to sexual abuse are associated with a more negative outcome for the female victim. While authors have yet to examine whether these factors directly correlate with the propensity to engage in sexual relationships with children, literature suggests that women with a more severe history of molestation may be more damaged by these experiences. Total number and severity of molestation experiences, as measured by frequency or duration of contact, have been shown in some studies to be related to a more negative outcome for the female victim of child sexual abuse, as has the number of perpetrators. It is yet unexamined whether the increased likelihood of offending against children is among the untoward effects that increase with these factors.

Severity of Act

Several studies have examined the severity of childhood sexual abuse as it relates to untoward effects for the victim. Hunt and Baird (1990) noted that the nature of the sexual abuse, among other variables, affects the degree of trauma that the child experiences. Two studies examined children who had recently been sexually abused. Friedrich, Urquiza and Beilke (1986) found that more severe sexual abuse was among factors related to higher internalizing behavior for sexually abused girls, as measured by the Achenbach Child Behavior Checklist. Conte and Schuerman (1987) found that the number of types of child sexual abuse was among variables that contributed to a worse impact. They measured impact by examining a symptom checklist completed by parents of children who had been sexually abused, the majority within six months prior to the study.

Landis (1956) also found more severe outcomes among more severely victimized women. Among college students, 20 percent of the women who had been exposed to exhibitionists in childhood indicated temporary or permanent emotional damage, while 47 percent of those exposed to coitus, and 80 percent of those subjected to attempted rape indicated the same. Eighty percent of the girls who had been threatened with rape and 50 percent of those who had been approached for intercourse felt that they had acquired temporary or permanent adverse ideas about sex, while 23 percent of those exposed to exhibitionists and 28 percent who had been fondled felt the same. Haugaard and Emery (1989) found that sexually abused college students did not differ from nonabused college students, except for a subcategory who had experienced the more severe types of abuse. Among those who had experienced oral, anal or vaginal intercourse, the victim group gave lower ratings of their peer and sexual relationships, and showed lower levels of trust, emotional stability and self-perceived social skills. The Comrey Personality Scales and the Texas Social Behavior Inventory were used as measures.

Browne and Finkelhor (1986) reviewed several studies that found that less serious sexual abuse was associated with less trauma. They also reviewed work by Russell which was in press, in which it was found that among adult women, 59 percent of women reporting intercourse, anal intercourse or oral sex as a form of childhood sexual abuse also reported having been "extremely traumatized," as opposed to 36 percent of those reporting fondling of unclothed breasts or genitals, and 22 percent reporting unwanted kissing or touching of clothed parts of the body.

It is not yet known to what extent more severe types of sexual abuse contributes to the likelihood of females engaging in sexual activity with children. Further research is needed to examine whether the propensity to engage in sexual acts with children is related to more severe sexual molestation in childhood.

Number of Contacts: Duration and Frequency

Several studies suggest the possibility that an increased number of incidents of sexual abuse in childhood may correspond to a more negative outcome. Hunt and Baird (1990) for example, noted the duration of abuse among the factors which affect the degree of trauma experienced by the sexually abused child. No study presently exists, however, which examines whether women who have been sexually abused a greater number of times have a greater propensity to sexually abuse others.

Finkelhor (1986) reviewed 11 studies that examined the duration and frequency of sexual abuse as it relates to aspects of adult functioning. He treated duration and frequency synonymously, as he noted that they tend to be highly correlated. He noted that six of the 11 studies associated duration of childhood with greater trauma, three found no relationship, and two found that longer duration is associated with less trauma.

Russell's (1986) study was among those reviewed by Finkelhor. In her survey of adult women, 73 percent of those whose abuse lasted for five years rated the experience as extremely traumatic, as compared to 62 percent of those whose abuse lasted one week to five years, and 46 percent of those who were abused only once. Tsai, Feldman-Summers, and Edgar (1979) reported that a longer duration of incest had more adverse effects on adult functioning, as measured by the MMPI and a problems checklist, than did incest of shorter duration in a group of adult sexual abuse victims. Finkelhor (1986) also reviewed a study that showed duration to be related to a worse outcome on similar measures in a community study.

Bagley and Ramsey (cited in Finkelhor, 1986) found that the general mental health of adult victims as measured by a composite of indicators concerning depression, psychoneurosis, suicidal ideation, psychiatric consultation, and self-concept was worse for longer lasting experiences. In Briere and Runtz's student sample (cited in Finkelhor, 1986), duration was the variable most consistently related to higher symptom scores on a variety of Hopkins Symptom Checklist Scales.

Friedrich, Urquiza and Beilke (1986) stated that a high frequency of abuse is among factors related to a higher internalizing behavior for sexually abused girls, as measured by the Achenbach Child Behavior Checklist. Additionally, a higher frequency of sexual abuse (as well as a greater number of perpetrators) was associated with more sexual acting out, as measured by the Achenbach Child Behavior Checklist, for both the female and male children.

Others have not found such a relationship, however. Langmade (1983) found that duration of incestuous relationships falling above the median of reported experiences did not bear a relationship to sex anxiety, sex guilt, sexual satisfaction or sexual activity among 34 women seeking treatment.

Tufts' New England Medical Center (cited in Finkelhor, 1986) found no association between duration of abuse and measures of distress as measured by the Louisville Behavior Checklist and the Purdue Self-Concept Scale, as well as other measures. Finkelhor (1979) himself found no association among college students between duration of sexual abuse and their self-rating of how negative the experience was. Seidner and Calhoun (cited in Finkelhor, 1986) reported that a high frequency of abuse was associated with a higher self-acceptance, but lower social maturity scores on the California Psychological Inventory for college students.

Courtois (1979) did not find duration or frequency of incest to be correlated with subjects' rating of short- or long-term impact on any of eight life spheres: social, psychological, physical, sexual, familial, sense of self, relation to men or relation to women. Her sample of 31 subjects were solicited from the newspaper, and were women 18 or older who had experienced incest.

Feinauer (1989) found that the number of incidents of sexual abuse in childhood did not make a significant impact upon subjects' Derogatis Symptom Checklist-Revised Edition (SCL-90R) scores at the time of their entering therapy as adults in any area except for depression. Those individuals who were victims of only one incident of sexual abuse scored as more depressed than did other women who had been sexually abused more often.

Johnson (1989) noted a long duration of sexual abuse among child female sex offenders. Four had been molested two or more years, five for a year, and three 2 to 5 times. Johnson (1989) also noted a high frequency of sexual abuse among child female sex offenders.

Number of Offenders

Hunt and Baird (1990) noted that the greater the number of offenders, the more emotional and social trauma is experienced by the child victim of sexual abuse, because of the greater invalidation of trust in adult-child relationships. Friedrich et al. (1986) reported that sexual acting out in children seen clinically for child sexual abuse, as measured by the Achenbach Child Behavior Checklist, was related to the number of perpetrators, among other factors.

Browne and Finkelhor (1986) reviewed three unpublished studies related to the effect of the number of offenders on the results of child sexual abuse. One study found that the number of contact incidents involving different perpetrators was the most important single contributor to a multivariate analysis predicting outcome on a composite measure that included depression and substance abuse. Another study found that chronic depression and anxiety, measured by the Hopkins Symptom Checklist, were significantly higher among students with multiple perpetrators. A third study is reported by Finkelhor to have confirmed these findings in a community sample.

It has not yet been shown whether being victimized by a higher number of sexual perpetrators in childhood might correlate with a higher propensity to sexually abuse children as an adult female. That a higher number of perpetrators is related to sexual acting out in girls, and to the depression and substance abuse often described in cases of female child molesters, suggests that this may be a possibility.

Females whose sexual abuse is more severe tend to be found to be suffering from more adverse effects, in general. Severity has been measured in several different ways, including the total incidents of abuse (or frequency/duration), severity of the sexual acts, and the total number of perpetrators. It has yet to be determined whether greater severity of sexual abuse in childhood might lead to a greater propensity to molest children in later years.

Summary and Hypotheses

The literature to date has documented several psychosocial history variables common to the backgrounds of female sex offenders. It has yet to show that these variables more frequently occur among female sex offenders than among control groups of females, however, or that such variables predict the severity of female child molesters' assaults against children. Such information would be useful in the identification and treatment of female offenders, and possibly in the understanding of the development of females into child molesters. The literature to date has also suggested several subcategories of female child molesters. The categories are based primarily on clinical impression, and have yet to be confirmed by statistical analysis.

Little is presently known about the female sex offender. Studies which have been conducted on this population have primarily reported upon known sex offenders, who have been seen for psychological treatment or assessment. Apparently, no study has yet been completed on this population for which federal protection of the confidentiality of client data has been obtained. Further study of this population is needed. While there is growing awareness that populations of female child molesters exist, they remain largely underresearched.

The purpose of this study was to collect data on female child molesters, including those who had not previously come to the attention of legal authorities for their sexual activities with children. The study provided federal protection of the information provided by the participants to encourage subjects' participation, and to protect the identity of subjects. This study compared psychosocial history variables of female offenders with those of a matched control group of nonoffenders, to examine whether the female offenders might have had greater pathology in their backgrounds. It was hypothesized that female child molesters would have a more severe history of childhood sexual abuse, greater psychosocial trauma related to their families-of-origin, more male sexual partners, more self-reported dependency, and a history of lower incomes than would a matched control group.

Additionally, it was hypothesized that psychosocial trauma variables related to sexual abuse history and family-of-origin pathology would significantly predict the severity of the child molesters' sexual activities with children. An exploratory factor analysis also examined the hypothesis that there is statistical evidence to support classification of female child molesters into subgroups, as previously described in the literature.

A further purpose of this study was to collect descriptive data on female child molesters, as they are a largely unstudied population. Data were collected on the female offenders' psychosocial histories, sexual abuse histories, and histories of sexual contacts with children.

CHAPTER 3

Method

Data Collection Sites

Subjects were recruited from various populations suspected of having large numbers of sexual offenders. These included seven prisons, three drug treatment facilities, and three treatment centers for concerns related to sexual abuse. Five surveys from female child molesters, in total, were collected from the three sexual abuse treatment facilities; 15 surveys, in all (child molesters and nonmolesters), were collected from these three sexual abuse treatment facilities. One survey from a female child molester was collected from the three drug and alcohol rehabilitation centers; 27 surveys in all were collected from the three drug and alcohol treatment facilities. Thirty-seven surveys, in total, were collected from female child molesters in the seven prisons; 470 surveys in all were collected from prison subjects. Because of the nature of the programs in the different facilities, and the varying availability of staff, the method of obtaining subjects varied slightly at each institution. A description of the data collection sites and the means of obtaining subjects at each follows.

SEXUAL ABUSE TREATMENT FACILITIES

DATA COLLECTION SITE A was a children's mental health agency, located in a rural setting in a Southwestern state, which has as a component a treatment team that specializes in the treatment of incestuous families. Subjects were members of a group for adults who were molested as children. While the size of the group varied, it had a capacity of up to 12 members. Data were collected twice from this group. Initially, the group mailed the surveys independently. When this yielded few returned surveys, however, the group opted to complete the surveys at home and return them as a group.

DATA COLLECTION SITE B was an outpatient, community-based treatment program that treated child sexual abuse victims and their families located in an urban setting in a Southwestern state. Surveys were collected from two different types of therapy groups, ranging in size from 8-10 members each. The first was an adult orientation group for adult survivors of sexual abuse, nonrelated offenders, and nonoffending parents. Adult survivors had received 6-18 months of prior treatment before entering the group, which was designed to assist them in their treatment, as well as to assist the offending and nonoffending parents of child victims in the understanding of the effects of sexual abuse on a child. The second type of group was the adult survivor group, consisting of individuals who had been sexually molested in childhood. Surveys were returned both individually by mail, and as a group via a staff member.

DATA COLLECTION SITE C was a private practice in an urban setting specializing in the treatment of sex offenders, who were most commonly referred by family services or probation/parole departments in several states in the Midwest. The females in treatment were alleged offenders who did not deny their child molestation offenses, but who had not necessarily been convicted. Available adult members of two therapy groups for female offenders were asked to take part in the survey; one group consisted of offenders aged 17-19, and one consisted of older adults. The women were given the surveys to complete and mail on their own.

DRUG AND ALCOHOL TREATMENT FACILITIES

DATA COLLECTION SITE D was a 38-bed, residential, long term drug and alcohol treatment facility located in an urban setting in a Southwestern state. The women in this facility were gathered into a group and the purpose of the survey was explained to them. Data were collected two times at this facility at six-month intervals. Surveys were completed as a group, and returned by mail by a staff member.

DATA COLLECTION SITE E was a 156-bed, residential, long-term drug and alcohol treatment facility serving men and women in an urban setting in a Southwestern state. The women in this facility were gathered into a group and surveys were collected from interested participants by a staff member. Data were collected twice at this facility at six-month intervals.

DATA COLLECTION SITE F was a 48-bed, 28-day inpatient drug and alcohol treatment program. It was located in an Eastern urban setting. Volunteers were solicited following an evening women's group; interested participants returned their surveys directly to the researcher as a group.

PRISONS

DATA COLLECTION SITE G was a Southeastern state prison that housed up to 660 female inmates of minimum, medium and maximum security. Data were collected over a number of days at this facility. The primary method of data collection involved the researcher visiting the women's home wards accompanied by a member of the psychological treatment staff. In most cases, the women completed the surveys as a group and returned them directly to the researcher. In some wards, where time was sparse due to programming, women were also given the option of placing their sealed surveys in interdepartmental mail for return to the examiner by way of the assistant director's secretary, who had been briefed on confidentiality concerns. A small number of surveys were also given to residents by their ward counselors for return in this manner.

DATA COLLECTION SITE H was a Western state prison that housed up to 87 females of minimum, medium and maximum security. Data at this facility were collected twice, at roughly six-month intervals. A contact person at this facility served as a research assistant. Surveys were given to interested women, collected in sealed envelopes the following day by a prison official, and mailed to the examiner.

DATA COLLECTION SITE I was a Midwestern medium and minimum security state facility for females. It had a capacity of 650 women. Inmates from this facility were called in large groups, in roughly alphabetical order, to a large room where a prison official and the researcher explained the survey. Data were collected in one day. Women willing to take part in the survey completed a consent form both from the researcher and from the prison, prior to beginning; those who were not interested returned to their wards. Women who were not readily available because of their participation in a work program, and those who were judged by the prison staff member to be too disruptive to be conveniently summoned to take part, were excluded.

DATA COLLECTION SITE J was a Midwestern state women's prison housing up to 860 women of all levels of security. Data were collected from this facility on one day.

The researcher visited several of the prison wards with a prison-provided escort. Interested women on each ward met as a group to receive a brief description of the survey. Those who were interested completed and returned the surveys.

DATA COLLECTION SITE K was a Midwestern state women's prison, housing 150 inmates, of all levels of security. Two specific groups were targeted at this facility: women who were convicted sex offenders, and women who were in treatment for having been sexually abused. A prison official collected surveys in these groups and returned them by mail.

DATA COLLECTION SITE L was a women's prison in a Southwestern state which typically housed 3500-3600 inmates, of all levels of security. Due to limited availability of staff, only convicted female child molesters were solicited from this facility. The 10 convicted offenders at this institution were spoken to as a group by a prison staff member. Interested subjects returned the study independently, by mail.

DATA COLLECTION SITE M was a state prison for all levels of security in a Southwestern state, housing about 770 women. Due to limited availability of staff, only convicted female child molesters were solicited from this facility. The women were called individually to a staff member's office and spoken to about the survey. Surveys were returned as a group.

Sample Description

Forty-three women were included in the sample of female offenders. Thirteen were convicted child molesters who had been identified by prison officials as possible participants. The remaining 30 were identified only by their descriptions on their surveys of sexual activities that they had engaged in with children who were under the age of 15, when the respondents were either 5 or more years older, or where they forced the child to participate in the sexual activities. For the purposes of this study, these 43 subjects are referred to as female child molesters, perpetrators, or offenders. These terms are used interchangeably in this study. They are not meant to reflect the various legal meanings of these words, which may differ depending on locality.

Thirty-five of the 43 women provided information concerning their sexual activities with children. These thirty-five included four of the 13 women who were convicted of child molestation. Nine of the 13 convicted sex offenders provided information about their backgrounds and their own sexual abuse histories, but did not provide information about their sex crimes.

All of the 43 women except one provided their ages. At the time of completing the survey, the women ranged in age from 18 to 48 years, with an average age of 34. Of the 43 women, nearly all were Caucasian. Thirty-five women (81%) identified themselves as being Euro-American or White, five women (12%) identified themselves as being African American or Black, and two women (5%) identified themselves as being Native American. One respondent (2%) left the space blank.

The majority of the 43 female child molesters (27 or 63%) had at least a high school education. Seventeen of the women in the sample had finished high school, but had not attended college, with three of these specifying that they had received a G.E.D. (after finishing either the eighth or the ninth grade). Ten women (23% of the sample of 43 women) indicated that they had attended college. Of these, six had completed 2 or more years, and one had completed her Bachelors degree.

Sixteen of the 43 female child molesters (37%) had not completed high school. They had completed a 9th-grade education (4 women), a 10th-grade education (4 women), or an 11th-grade education (6 women). Of those who had completed the 10th grade, one was working on a General Equivalency Diploma and another had attended a community college for one year.

The women, by and large, did not earn large incomes. They were asked to estimate their hourly wages at their highest paying job during the last year that they were employed. Five (12%) of the women listed a wage that was under $4 per hour. Sixteen (37%) of the women listed an amount that was between $4 and $5.99 an hour, five (12%) listed an amount between $6 and $7.99, and four (9%) listed an amount between $8 and $10. Only three women (7%) listed an hourly wage that was over $10 an hour; in two cases between $10 and $13, and in one case $30 per hour.

In four cases (9%), the women indicated that the question was not applicable, and in three cases (7%) no amount was given. In three cases (7%) the response was idiosyncratic. One woman listed $400, without a decimal point, and it is unclear what amount she wished to indicate, one woman wrote "250+ room and board," and it is unclear if she was listing an hourly wage, and one woman wrote, "don't remember."

For the 35 women who provided data concerning their sexual activities with children, comparisons were made between the oldest age at which they acknowledged having had such sexual contact, and their present age, in order to approximate the amount of time that had passed since their most recent offense. The amount of time varied widely, and ranged from under a year to 32 years. The average estimated amount of difference between the reported age during the last offense and their age at the time of the survey was 10 years.

Originally, it was hoped that 60 female child molesters would be surveyed. This hope, however, proved unrealistic, and the solicitation of subjects was ceased after questionnaires were collected from 43 child molesters in the 13 data collection sites.

Procedure

The means of examination consisted of a three-page self-report survey. As no such survey currently exists in the literature, this survey was developed on the basis of a review of the literature on women who have had sexual contacts with children.

DEFINITIONS

Researchers have defined "sexual abuse" in various ways. As this study was among the first to examine females who sexually offend against children, it was decided to utilize a relatively liberal definition of abuse rather than a restrictive definition. The definition of sexual abuse used in this study was limited to activities that included direct sexual contact, in order to exclude activity that might not be considered overtly sexual in nature (hugging, kissing, viewing a nude older female, and the like). However, the age of the victim at the time of the sexual activity, and the minimum difference in ages between the perpetrator and victim was kept fairly liberal, in comparison with other studies, in order to over-include, rather than under-include, "borderline" cases where actual sexual contact had taken place.

Fromuth and Burkhart (1987) have reviewed various ways in which sexual abuse has been defined within the literature, showing the effects on prevalence rates that result from various definitions. The definition chosen for this study was similar to the more liberal definitions identified, where the age of the victim and the differences in ages between the offender and victim are concerned. It is more restrictive, however, than many definitions in defining actual sexual contact.

A relatively inclusive age range for defining victims was chosen. Victims were defined as those subjects with whom the offender had sexual contact when the victim was age 15 or younger at the time of the first sexual contact, and where at least one of two additional criteria was met: either a minimal age difference between the victim and the perpetrator of 5 years existed, or the perpetrator forced the sexual activity on the victim. No stipulations were made about the relationship between victims.

The definition chosen was expected to over-include some cases that may be considered "borderline" abuse cases because of the minimal age difference requirements between participants, and because of the relatively older ages of children that could be included as victims. It was hoped that these cases would contribute to the study by showing trends in sexual contact between older females and younger individuals, and would have the effect of preventing the discarding of those cases where the sexual contact between the older female and the younger individual may have been experienced as abusive by the younger individual, in spite of minimal age differences. It was expected that the inclusion of only those cases where actual physical sexual contact occurred had the effect of minimizing undue over-inclusion of cases in which the sexual contact was not abusive in nature.

DEPENDENCY SELF-REPORT

A component of the survey used for this study estimated comparative amounts of dependency among the subjects. A self-report of dependency characteristics based on the *Diagnostic and Statistical Manual of Mental Disorders (Third Edition-Revised) (DSM III-R)* criteria for Dependent Personality Disorder was used. The *DSM III-R* is a standard means by which Dependent Personality Disorder is diagnosed. In order to make the criteria suitable for self-report, and to make some of the criteria understandable to the subject, minor substitutions were made in the wording of some criteria. In order to fully detect differences among subjects, a 5-point Likert scale was used for each criterion. Subjects were asked to rate how closely each of the *DSM III-R* criteria described them. The total of the Likert scale points was used as an estimate of dependency for comparison of this trait among subjects. The range of the scale was 9 points, indicating strong agreement with dependency criteria, to 45 points, indicating strong disagreement with the dependency criteria.

Because of the anticipated small numbers of women who would meet criteria as a child molester, and the anticipated difficulties in gaining their cooperation, reliability and validity data were not collected on the instrument, including the dependency scale, prior to its use.

CONFIDENTIALITY AND CONSENT

Federal protection of the identity of the subjects in this study was sought prior to beginning this research, through section 303(a) of the Public Health Services

Act as amended by Public Law 93-282 (42 U.S.C. 242a (a)). A Confidentiality Certificate was obtained for this survey, protecting participants from each of the data collection sites used for the study. The Certificate prevented prosecution of subjects who inadvertently identified themselves on the self-report questionnaires for the information they revealed. Additionally, the Confidentiality Certificate prevented the researcher from revealing the identity of subjects, and prevented the researcher from being compelled to reveal the identity of subjects in any federal, state, or local civil, criminal, administrative, legislative, or other proceeding. Possible conflicts between the legal duty to report child abuse cases to proper authorities and the duty to safe-guard the well-being of research subjects were thereby avoided. It was believed that the benefit of the information gained by this study justified the protection of these subjects, as to date there is very little available literature concerning females who have had sexual contact with children.

After they reviewed and signed a consent form, subjects were given a three-page self-report questionnaire that reviewed basic demographic information, brief psychosocial history information, and information concerning the sexual abuse history of subjects both as possible victims, and as possible offenders (see Appendix D).

To protect the privacy of the subjects, individuals completing the questionnaires were given a blank sheet of heavy, colored paper to be used in covering their responses. They were also given individual letter-sized envelopes for sealing their surveys prior to returning them. Wherever possible (and in most cases) the sealed questionnaires and signed consent forms were collected separately, in separate large brown envelopes, to ensure that names were not included with the questionnaires. In some settings, individuals opted to return the surveys themselves, by mail, rather than return them to the researcher or to a staff member. In some cases, subjects elected to first turn in their consent forms to the researcher or to the proper contact person at their facility, and in some cases they opted to mail both the survey and the consent form together. Postage was provided to several subjects who chose to mail their own surveys. In cases where the subject returned her consent form and survey in the same envelope, they were separated by the researcher upon their receipt.

The consent form used in the survey described the nature of the study, highlighted protections afforded by the Confidentiality Certificate obtained for this study, and suggested steps that the subjects might take to further insure their privacy. The consent form also emphasized the subjects' right to discontinue the survey at any time without penalty, listed a mailing address for the researcher, and provided brief instructions (see Appendix E).

DATA COLLECTION

Wherever possible, the researcher collected data in person at the data collection sites. Where this was not possible, an assistant was appointed by the director, or by the appropriate individual at each site. Individuals at the institutions who agreed to collect data for the researcher also were given a letter, highlighting the federal protection of confidentiality for the subjects, reviewing other subject rights, and providing instructions for administering the survey (see Appendix F).

At data collection sites that had sufficient staff support, all willing females were allowed to participate, in order to survey women who were not necessarily known to have committed acts of child molestation. Nonoffenders, that is, women who did not report sexual contact with children and who were not known to be convicted child molesters, served as a matched control subject pool. At three data collection sites, only known child molesters were asked to take part in the survey.

Women in the control group were matched for age (within ten years of the matched female offender), education (less than high school, graduated high school, some college, and college graduate were used as matching categories), race, and type of data collection site (prison, drug and alcohol treatment facility, or sexual abuse treatment center). Where possible, female sex offenders were randomly matched with controls from the same site from which their surveys were obtained. Where this was not possible, they were matched with individuals from a similar type of data collection site. One of the prisons (data site K), was excluded as a matched control pool because it was known to contain several convicted child molesters who did not acknowledge their offenses (and whose surveys were collected along with other subjects' surveys, and unidentifiable as those of known offenders).

In a few cases, data were missing, and the following guidelines were used to match such individuals. Where data regarding education were not available (1 case), the individual was matched with a subject whose education fell at the mean for the entire sample. Where subjects did not list their age (1 case) or race (1 case), they were not matched for these criteria. Data collection site C was unique among the three sites that were treatment centers for child sexual abuse, in that the subjects were all in treatment for having molested a child. Because the women in this population were predominantly African American, few had matched controls available in the pool of subjects from sexual abuse treatment facilities. Because these women were previously known to have committed a crime and to have come to the attention of the authorities, they were matched with subjects from the prison population.

CHAPTER 4

Results

Differences in Psychosocial Histories

Females reporting sexual contact with children were randomly matched with respect to age, race, education, and source of data to a control group. Because the severity of childhood sexual abuse is a variable most commonly thought to differentiate between the female child molesters and nonoffenders, this hypothesis was tested with a t test at the .05 level of significance. It was hypothesized that the offenders would have comparatively more sexual abuse in their histories. Sexual abuse was defined in such a way as to allow for the combining of two considerations often thought to be related to the severity of sexual abuse history: the number of times that sexual contact with offenders occurred, and the types of activities which took place. The number of times that a subject was sexually abused was computed by adding together each of the subject's estimates of the number of times that she had had sexual contact with each of the people who sexually abused her.

For each of the people by whom the subjects reported having been sexually abused, another question was asked concerning the types of sexual contact that occurred. Thirteen types of possible sexual contact were listed and the subject circled those that applied.

Generally, the more intrusive the sexual contact, the more types of contact were circled (for example, if sexual intercourse was indicated to have occurred, various types of fondling were also generally indicated to have occurred). Thus, the number of types of sexual contact reported for each perpetrator was a rough estimate of the severity of the nature of the sexual contact. The total number of types of sexual contact that the subject reported for each of the people who abused her added together served as a measure of the intrusiveness of the sexual contact that she had experienced. This measure of severity was increased by the number of different acts experienced by the (female offenders as) victims, and/or by the number of perpetrators offending against them.

These two estimates of severity of childhood sexual abuse — the total number of incidents of sexual contact with all offenders and the total number of types of sexual contact experienced with all offenders — were combined into one variable that estimated severity of childhood sexual abuse history. This was done by adding the z scores for both variables, which were computed using data supplied by the offenders and their matched control group.

Z scores describe how far above or below average with respect to the standard deviation the variables are, with positive z scores indicating scores that are above the mean and negative z scores indicating scores that are below the mean. Once the z scores were computed for each subject with regard to the total number of incidents of childhood sexual abuse that she had experienced, and the number of types of sexual contact that she had experienced, the two z scores could be meaningfully added together. The resulting estimate of abuse severity took into account both the number of sexual abuse incidents *and* the number of different kinds of acts that an individual had experienced, and gave an indication of how they compared to the rest of the sample of 43 perpetrators and their matched controls.

The variable used to compare childhood sexual abuse histories then was an estimate of how far above or below the average for this sample the individual subjects were in terms of the number of times they had been sexually abused in childhood, and the number of types of abusive sexual contact that they had experienced.

While the comparative severity of the female child molesters' history as victims of childhood sexual abuse was somewhat greater than that of the matched controls, it was not significantly greater. Both groups had severe sexual abuse histories. There was some tendency for the female child molesters to report a sexual abuse history that was more severe than average with regard to the criteria selected, while their matched control group reported a history that was somewhat less severe than average for the two groups (see Table 1).

Table 1

T Test Differences Between Female Child Molesters and a Matched Control Group on *Z* Scores Related to a Sexual Abuse History Variable*

N	MEAN	SD	POOLED T VALUE	VARIANCE DF	ESTIMATE 2-TAIL PROBABILITY
OFFENDERS					
40	.27	1.33	1.72	76	.09
CONTROL					
38	– .28	1.46			

* This variable was an estimate of the comparative severity of sexual abuse history between the offenders and the matched control group. It took into account the number of estimated sexual contacts a subject had with all of her offenders and the number of different types of sexual contact that she experienced with all of the individuals who sexually abused her.

A multivariate analysis of variance was also completed, comparing the female perpetrators and their matched control group at the .05 level of significance. A multivariate analysis of variance test was used to test the hypotheses that the women who had had sexual contact with children would report more dependency, a greater number of male sexual partners with whom they had intercourse, more frequent monthly incidents of family-of-origin pathology, and less income than would a matched control group.

The number of male sex partners with whom they had experienced intercourse was estimated by the women on their surveys. Their income was estimated in response to a question asking about their hourly wage at their highest paying job during the last year that they were employed.

The number of usual monthly incidents of family-of-origin pathology was estimated by adding numbers supplied by the subjects in response to three questions related to types of family pathology commonly described in the families-of-origin of female child molesters. The subjects answered three screening questions related to the number of times in a typical month while growing up that they had received an injury from an adult, that they had seen their mothers injured, or that someone in their home had use drugs or alcohol to the extent of experiencing a temporary change in behavior. The estimates provided in response to these three questions were added together as an estimate of the number of incidents of family pathology occurring in a typical month. This number could range from zero to 93.

Dependency was measured by a Likert scale scoring of the *DSM III-R* criteria for dependent personality disorder. The total score was used as an estimate of dependency. The dependency score could range from 9, indicating strong agreement that the dependent personality disorder criteria reflected their own experience, to 45, indicating strong disagreement that these criteria described their own experience (see Table 2).

Table 2
Analysis of Variance Univariate *F* Tests with (1,49) D.F.

	F	SIGNIFICANCE OF F
# MONTHLY INCIDENTS OF FAMILY-OF-ORIGIN PATHOLOGY		
	.49	.488
DEPENDENCY		
	9.54	.003*
HOURLY WAGE		
	.012	.92
# MALE SEX PARTNERS		
	1.60	.211

* Significant

If two or more of these variables in the multivariate analysis of variance were found to be significantly different between the research and control groups, the differences were to be analyzed using a Fisher's Least Significant Difference test, which is more liberal in detecting differences than other similar tests (Huck, Cormier & Bounds, 1974). Because this research is among the first of its kind to be conducted on women who commit sexual offenses against children, a liberal test was chosen in order to reveal trends in the findings.

As predicted, the female offenders reported a significantly greater amount of dependency (significance less than .05) than did the matched control sample.

The significance level was .003; however, when several variables are compared on the same sample, it increases the chances that any single variable will be significant by chance. To allow for this, a Bonferoni adjustment was made. Allowing for the actual number of variables in this multivariate analysis of variance (MANOVA), the actual significance is .009. Forty-one of the offenders fully completed the Likert Scale. Their mean score on this scale was 28.32 with a standard deviation of 9.32. The mean score for dependency for the nonoffenders was 32.24, with a standard deviation of 7.6, with 41 subjects fully completing the Likert Scale. Lower scores on this scale indicated greater agreement with dependency criteria.

Although female child molesters reported slightly more incidents of family-of-origin pathology in a typical month (the number of times that someone in their home drank or used drugs so that they had a temporary change in behavior added to the number of times in a typical month that they saw their mother injured and the number of times that they themselves received an injury), the reported frequency of such incidents was not significantly greater than that reported by the matched control group. The mean number of monthly such incidents reported by offenders was 13.6, with a standard deviation of 18, with 41 subjects providing information concerning this variable. The mean number of incidents reported by nonoffenders was 9.49 with a standard deviation of 14.73, and with 35 subjects providing information for this variable.

The average incomes reported by the offenders and their control group also did not significantly differ. The offenders reported a highest average hourly wage of $7.14 during the last year worked, with a standard deviation of 5.33, with 32 subjects providing information. The nonoffenders reported an hourly wage of $6.43 (standard deviation 2.84), with 37 subjects reporting this information.

The average number of male partners with whom the subjects had experienced sexual intercourse also did not significantly differ between the groups, although the average was slightly higher for the offenders. The 37 nonoffenders responding to this question reported an average of 25 partners, with a standard deviation of 29. The 37 child molesters providing information on this question reported an average of 33.94 male sexual partner, with a standard deviation of 39.

CHILDHOOD VARIABLES AS PREDICTORS OF SEVERITY OF SEXUAL PERPETRATIONS IN ADULTHOOD

A step-wise analysis of regression was performed at the .05 level of significance to test the hypothesis that the severity of sexual abuse in childhood, as modified by family-of-origin pathology, would be predictive of the propensity for female offenders to perpetrate more severe forms of child sexual abuse (see Table 3). Two variables related to severity of sexual abuse history in childhood, and one variable related to family-of-origin pathology were used as independent variables to predict the severity of the perpetration offenses for the female child molesters.

Table 3

Correlations Between Measures of Childhood Psychopathology and Severity of Sexual Offenses Against Children Among Female Child Molesters

	NUMBER OF VICTIMS	TOTAL NUMBER SEXUAL CONTACTS OCCURRING (WITH ALL CHILDREN)	TOTAL NUMBER TYPES OF SEXUAL ACTIVITIES REPORTED WITH ALL CHILDREN LISTED
TOTAL NUMBER OF PEOPLE REPORTED WHO MOLESTED FEMALE CHILD MOLESTER IN CHILDHOOD			
	r = .11 p value = .23	r = – .09 p value = .28	r = .06 p value = .35
SEVERITY OF MOLESTATION IN CHILDHOOD REPORTED BY FEMALE CHILD MOLESTER			
	r = .05 p value = .36	r = – .11 p value = .24	r = .04 p value = .4
TYPICAL MONTHLY FREQUENCY OF FAMILY-OF-ORIGIN PATHOLOGICAL INCIDENTS REPORTED BY FEMALE MOLESTER			
	r = – .05 p value = .39	r = – .17 p value = .17	r = – .06 p value = .38

The following were used as independent variables. The first variable was the total number of usual monthly incidents of family-of-origin pathology experienced by the subject while growing up (as defined by the number of times in a usual month that the subject was injured by an adult plus the number of times in a usual month that the subject saw her mother receiving an injury plus the number of times in a usual month that a person living in the subject's home used drugs or alcohol to the extent that it induced behavioral change). The second independent variable was the total number of people that the subject reported to have sexually abused her in childhood. The third independent variable estimated the severity of the female sex offender's sexual abuse in childhood relative to the other 43 offenders (z score of number of sexually abusive incidents in childhood plus the z score of the number of types of sexual contacts). These three independent variables were expected to combine to predict the severity of the perpetration of sexual offenses against children on the part of the female offenders.

Three dependent variables were used to measure the severity of the female offenders' reported sexual contact with children. The first was the total number of children that each perpetrator abused. The second was total number of times that sexual contact occurred for all of the victims listed by the perpetrator. The third was the total number of types of sexual contacts reported to have occurred with children. This last variable increased both with the total number of sexual acts reported to have occurred with a given child, and the number of children reported to have been sexually abused. Each of the acts reported to have occurred between a perpetrator and a child was added.

It was anticipated that the severity of psychosocial pathology (particularly of sexual abuse) in the childhoods of the female child molesters would lead to more severe sexual acting out against children. However, none of these independent variables regarding a background of childhood psychosocial pathology significantly correlated with the severity of the offenders' sexual acting out. Neither were there "trends" in the direction of significant correlation. Offenders tended to have large numbers of sexual abusers, a history of sexual abuse that was severe in frequency and the number of types of abuse experienced, and childhood histories that involved apparent psychosocial pathology. However, among the female offenders, it was not the case that as the reported severity of these variables increased the reported severity of their sexual acting out also increased. There was no correlation between any of the independent and dependent variables, and as such a step-wise multiple regression analysis (which further analyzes the variables that significantly correlate) could not be completed.

SUBTYPES OF FEMALE OFFENDERS

Analysis of the data was completed using an exploratory rotated varimax factor analysis, set at the .05 level of significance, with factors with eigenvalues greater than one examined. This statistical analysis tested the hypothesis that there exists statistical support for the classification of female perpetrators into sub-types, based on commonly observed differentiating variables (see Table 4).

Ten variables were entered into the factor analysis. The first was education, which was entered as 1 through 4, indicating less than a high school education, high school graduation, some college, or college graduation, respectively. The second variable entered was the total Likert scale measure of dependency which ranged from 9 (indicating more dependency) to 45 (indicating less dependency).

The third variable entered was a psychiatric history variable, which ranged from 0-2: a score of two indicated that the subject had both received psychiatric medication and been placed in a psychiatric hospital; a score of 1 indicated that the subject reported one or the other; and a score of zero indicated that the subject reported neither. The fourth variable entered was the measure of the comparative severity of child sexual abuse history among the offenders (the z score of the number of times a subject had been sexually abused added to the z score of the number of types of sexual contact she had experienced, in comparison to the sample of 43 offenders).

The fifth variable was the number of victims with whom the offender reported that she was forced to have sexual contact. The sixth variable was a measure of income, and was defined by the reported highest hourly wage during the last year of employment. The seventh variable entered was the number of children with whom a subject reported having had group sex.

The eighth variable was the mean age of the subject's victims at the time of the first offense against each victim. The ninth variable was the average age of the offender at the time of her first offenses against against each victim. The tenth variable was the number of victims that were listed by an offender to whom she was related; immediate and extended family relationships were included, as were "step-" and "foster-" child relationships. It was thought that three categories of female perpetrator would emerge.

It was thought that the first factor, describing the "co-offending" or "forced" offender, would describe a subtype of offender who tended to report a greater number of victims with whom the offender was forced to have sexual contact, a greater number of children with whom the offender had group sex, a lower income and education, and a lower Likert scale score on the *DSM III-R* criteria for dependent personality disorder (indicating greater congruence with dependency criteria) than that of other offenders.

Second, a factor describing a "girlfriend" or an "immature" offender was thought to be possible that would describe a subtype of offender for which the average age of victims was greater, and for which fewer of the victims would tend to be relatives.

Third, a factor describing an "adolescent" offender was thought to exist that would describe a subtype of offender tending to report a younger average age at first offense, and a less severe history of sexual abuse.

Table 4
Factor Analysis of Subtypes of Female Child Molesters

Factor	1	2	3	4
Eigenvalue	2.7	1.63	1.26	1.0
EDUCATION				
Correlation	.05	– .60*	.28	.25
DEPENDENCY				
Correlation	– .20	– .39	– .03	.50
PSYCHIATRIC HISTORY				
Correlation	.70*	.07	.26	.09
COMPARATIVE SEVERITY OF SEXUAL ABUSE HISTORY				
Correlation	.04	.76*	.05	.06
TOTAL NUMBER OF VICTIMS OFFENDER WAS FORCED TO HAVE CONTACT WITH				
Correlation	.48	.28	.60*	– .31
INCOME				
Correlation	.00	.01	– .05	.90*
TOTAL NUMBER OF VICTIMS WITH WHOM PERPETRATOR HAD GROUP SEX				
Correlation	.26	.71*	.25	– .08
MEAN AGE OF VICTIMS AT FIRST SEXUAL CONTACT WITH PERPETRATOR				
Correlation	.59*	– .11	– .62*	– .15
MEAN AGE OF PERPETRATOR AT FIRST SEXUAL CONTACT WITH HER VICTIMS				
Correlation	.85*	.18	– .12	– .17
NUMBER OF RELATED VICTIMS				
Correlation	.06	– .06	.84*	– .05

*Correlated

While severity of childhood sexual abuse and various descriptions of mental health problems have been included in previous categories of subtypes of female offenders, they have tended to have been grouped in different ways. It was thought that the variables related to these issues would not load on any of the above factors.

Factors with an eigenvalue of over 1 in the factor analysis were examined in order to assess the extent to which these factors supported previous descriptions of subtypes of offenders reported in the literature. Four such factors emerged, lending statistical support for three subtypes of offenders. Loading on this first factor were variables related to extent of psychiatric treatment, age at first offense, and average age of victims at the time of first contact. The first factor suggested a subtype of child molester who tended to be somewhat older than the other offenders at the time of her first offenses against victims, was more likely than the other child molesters to have had a history of having been treated in a psychiatric hospital or of having been placed on psychiatric medication, and who tended to have somewhat older victims.

Loading on the second factor were variables related to severity of the offenders' sexual abuse history, the number of victims with whom the offenders reported having had group sex, and the amount of education reported by the offender. The second factor suggested a subtype of child molester who had less education, reported a severe history of sexual abuse when compared to the other offenders, and who was likely to have involved more victims in group sex.

Loading on the the third factor were variables related to the number of relative victims, the average age of victims at the time of first victimization, and the number of victims with whom the offender reported having had been forced into sexual contact. This factor suggested a subtype of offender who was likely to have more relative victims, younger victims, and more victims with whom the offender was forced to have sexual contact.

A fourth factor also emerged with an eigenvalue of one; however, the only variable loading on it was income. This raises the possibility that there exists a subtype of offender with a greater income, for which none of the previous variables are related to offenses. However such an offender has not been previously described in the literature.

PSYCHOSOCIAL HISTORY

Mental Health

Information provided by the offenders regarding their history of psychiatric hospitalizations and of psychiatric medications suggested a more serious history of psychological pathology among these offenders than was supposed at the onset of the study. Of the 43 offenders providing background data, 21 (49%) had a history of having received psychiatric medication. Twenty-two (51%) had a history of having been treated in a psychiatric hospital. Seventeen of the women (40%) had been both hospitalized and placed on medication at some point in their histories. Likewise 17 of the women (40%) had neither been hospitalized nor placed on psychiatric medication.

As a means of obtaining an estimate of the comparative amount of dependency among the women, a self-report 5-point Likert scale based on the *DSM III-R* criteria for Dependent Personality Disorder was used. The scale was used primarily for comparative rather than diagnostic purposes. However, where the offender indicated that she either "strongly agreed" or "agreed" with 5 of the requisite criteria, by self-report she met the criteria for a diagnosis of Dependent Personality Disorder. In 16 of the 43 cases (37%), the offenders met the criteria for a diagnosis of Dependent Personality Disorder.

Responses that offenders gave to a question asking about drug and alcohol use also suggested that many of the offenders may have had an alcohol or substance abuse problem (see Table 5). Subjects were asked to estimate the number of times in a usual month that they preferred to use enough drugs or alcohol so that they had a temporary change in behavior. This question was originally

Table 5
Self-Reported Preferences of Female Child Molesters for Monthly Drug/Alcohol Intake

	RESPONSE	FREQUENCY	
QUESTION: HOW MANY TIMES IN A USUAL MONTH DO YOU PREFER TO USE ENOUGH ALCOHOL OR DRUGS SO THAT YOU HAVE A TEMPORARY CHANGE IN BEHAVIOR?	25–30	11	(26%)
	15–20	4	(9%)
	2–3	2	(5%)
	0	24	(56%)*
	Descriptive responses	2	(5%)**

*Two women qualified their responses by noting in the margin that they used to drink daily, and one woman noted in the margin that before prison she used "it to do the sexual things that people wanted."

**One woman wrote "used to be a lot," and one woman briefly described a history of experimentation as a teen and some drinking as an adult.

intended for use as a screening question to compare whether female offenders might report higher rates of use of these substances than would a matched control group. After reviewing the subject responses, however, it became apparent that many of the women wrote "zero" because they had newly entered treatment for an alcohol or substance abuse problem. Given these responses, the question was dropped for comparison purposes.

Nonetheless, the responses of the women raised the possibility that some may have experienced alcohol or substance abuse problems. While the screening question used is not intended as a diagnostic measure, the responses of several of the female offenders to this question were noteworthy.

Family-of-origin

The women in this study were asked several questions concerning their families of origin. Several of the questions screened for family pathology.

The women were asked how many times in a usual month, while growing up, they had seen someone who lived in their home use enough drugs or alcohol so that they saw a temporary change in his or her behavior. The question was designed primarily to be used for comparison purposes, and for use in correlational statistics, rather than as a definitive measure of substance abuse in the home. However, subject responses to this question suggested that for many, substance abuse in the home may have been a problem. Ten of the women (23%) gave responses indicating that use of drugs or alcohol was a daily or near daily occurrence. Fifteen women (35%) gave a response of zero.

Some of the women gave responses to this question in written form, rather than as a numerical estimate. Five women's written responses suggested that substance abuse was a frequent occurrence: "frequently," "several," "many," "most of my childhood." One wrote that when she was between the ages of 16 and 17 there was a man in her home who was drunk every day. One additional woman wrote "12 years." Three women (7%) gave responses suggesting that substance abuse was infrequent: "seldom," "occasionally," "3 (summer months)." Additional responses are recorded on Table 6.

The women were asked a screening question about physical injuries that had been inflicted upon them in childhood. The question was primarily for use in comparing their responses to those of a matched control group and other correlational analyses, and was not primarily for use in determining whether child abuse had occurred. The women were asked to estimate the number of times in a usual month that an adult had given them an injury that was "as bad as a cut, a bruise, swollen skin, or worse," during the time that they were growing up.

Table 6
Family-of-Origin Pathology

	RESPONSE	FREQUENCY (% to nearest whole number)	
QUESTION: WHEN YOU WERE GROWING UP, HOW MANY TIMES IN A USUAL MONTH DID YOU SEE SOMEONE WHO LIVED IN YOUR HOME DRINK ENOUGH OR USE ENOUGH DRUGS SO THAT YOU SAW A TEMPORARY CHANGE IN HIS OR HER BEHAVIOR?	25–31 (or "daily")	10	(23%)
	20	1	(2%)
	Written response indicating frequent occurrence	5	(12%)
	1–6	7	(16%)
	0	15	(35%)
	Written response indicating infrequent occurrence	3	(7%)
QUESTION WHEN YOU WERE GROWING UP, HOW MANY TIMES IN A USUAL MONTH DID AN ADULT GIVE YOU AN INJURY THAT WAS AS BAD AS A CUT, A BRUISE, SWOLLEN SKIN, OR WORSE?	10–30 (10, 15, 20 & 30)	4	(9%)
	Written response indicating frequent occurrence	5	(12%)
	2–5	5	(12%)
	0	24	(56%)
	Written response indicating infrequent occurrence	3	(7%)
	Blank	2	(5%)
QUESTION: WHEN YOU WERE GROWING UP, HOW MANY TIMES IN A USUAL MONTH DID YOU SEE YOUR MOTHER GET AN INJURY THAT WAS AS BAD AS A CUT, A BRUISE, SWOLLEN SKIN, OR WORSE?	10–20	3	(7%)
	Written response indicating frequent occurrence	3	(7%)
	1–5	5	(12%)
	0	26	(60%)
	Written response indicating infrequent occurrence	3	(7%)
	Doesn't apply (mother left family when respondent was 4 or 5)	1	(2%)
	Blank	2	(5%)

The women's responses indicated that several were likely to have been subjected to frequent childhood physical abuse. Five women (12%) reported that they had received such injuries 2-5 times per month. One woman each (9% total), gave responses of 10, 15, 20, and 30 times per month (see Table 6).

Eight women did not give numbers, but wrote in a descriptive response. Three of these women (7%) indicated that such injuries happened occasionally ("occasionally," "occasionally — maybe once every few months," and "4 times per year"). Five of the women (12%) indicated that such abuse happened with frequency ("everyday ages 4-11," "usually quite a few times in a month," "a lot," "most of my childhood," and "real often") (see Table 6).

The women were also asked to estimate the number of times in a usual month that they had seen their mothers receiving a similar injury. Twenty-six women wrote zero (60%). However, several gave responses suggesting that they had witnessed the injury of their mothers on a regular basis. Their responses are also recorded on Table 6.

Some women responded with descriptive statements, rather than numerical estimates. Three (7%) gave written responses suggesting that such was a frequent occurrence: "a lot when I was young," "many," "years." Three (7%) wrote in responses to indicate that such activity occurred, though on less than a monthly basis: "once only," "very seldom — maybe 1-2 times in several years," "1-2 times per year."

The women were asked how many times their fathers and mothers had been married or had lived with a lover, as a general measure of family stability. For fathers, the most common response (55% of cases) was that they had been married or lived with someone only once. Asked the same questions about their mothers, the respondents indicated that their mothers had one spouse or partner in only 16 cases (37%) (see Table 7).

Love and Sexual Relationships

The women were asked several questions concerning their sexual histories, including: how many times they themselves had been married or had had a live-in lover; with how many adult males, and with how many adult females they had had sexual contact; and about their sexual preference, on a five-point Likert scale. The sexual preference five-point Likert scale included the choices "prefer men," "prefer men but have had some contact with females," "prefer both males and females equally," "prefer females, but have had some contact with males," and "prefer females." The responses that the women gave did not necessarily correspond to the sexual behavior that was reported on separate questions.

Table 7

Parents' History of Marriage and "Live-In" Relationships

	RESPONSE	FREQUENCY *(% to nearest whole number)*	
QUESTION: HOW MANY TIMES HAS YOUR FATHER BEEN MARRIED OR LIVED WITH A LOVER?	Once	22	(55%)
	Twice	7	(16%)
	Three times	4	(9%)
	Five times	2	(5%)
	Six times	1	(2%)
	Seven times	1	(2%)
	Many	1	(2%)
	Don't know	5	(12%)
QUESTION: HOW MANY TIMES HAS YOU MOTHER BEEN MARRIED OR LIVE WITH A LOVER?	Once	16	(37%)
	Twice	13	(30%)
	Three times	7	(16%)
	Four times	2	(5%)
	Five times	2	(5%)
	None	1	(2%)
	Blank	2	(5%)

Large numbers of female perpetrators reported having had sexual contact with adult females (see Table 8).

All of the women except for one (who was among the younger participants) indicated that they had been married or had had a live-in lover. Only five women reported having had only one marital/live-in partner (see Table 8).

The subjects were asked to estimate the number of adult male sexual partners that they had had. The numbers estimated varied widely, from 0 (in the case of

Table 8
Adult Relationships of 43 Female Child Molesters

	RESPONSE	FREQUENCY (% to nearest whole number)	
QUESTION: HOW MANY TIMES HAVE YOU BEEN MARRIED OR LIVED WITH A LOVER?	Zero	1	(2%)
	One	5	(12%)
	Two	13	(30%)
	Three	11	(26%)
	Four	6	(14%)
	Five	3	(7%)
	Six	1	(2%)
	Seven	1	(2%)
	15–20	2	(5%)
QUESTION: WHICH OF THE FOLLOWING BEST DESCRIBES YOUR SEXUAL PREFERENCE?	I prefer males	28	(65%)*
	I prefer males but have had some contact with females	8	(19%)
	I prefer both males and females equally	2	(5%)
	I prefer females but have had some contact with males	2	(5%)
	I prefer females	1	(2%)**
	"Neither one"	1	(2%)***
	Blank	1	(2%)****

* 10 of the 28 also reported having had sexual contact with at least 1 adult female

** This individual reported having had sexual intercourse with men

*** Responses to previous questions indicated this individual had had sexual contact with both genders

**** This young respondent did not report sexual intercourse with adult males or sexual contact with adult females

a very young adult participant who had been sexually active as a teen in her age group) to over 100. It appears that some of the women had few sexual partners, while others had been very sexually active.

Some of the women gave descriptive rather than numerical estimates of their sexual contacts with males. Four women (9%) wrote words suggesting large numbers: "uncountable," "several," "many," "can't remember — too many." One gave a response indicating that she had had 3-4 adult male partners "in the past 10 years," and one indicated that she had been married once, but it was not clear that she had understood the question. One woman, as indicated, who was among the younger participants, wrote zero, but indicated elsewhere on the survey that she had had sexual contact with same-age partners in her mid to late teens. The respondents were also asked to estimate the number of women with whom they had had sexual contact. Twenty-four (56%) of the female offenders had had sexual contact with at least one adult female. All of these women had also had sexual intercourse with men.

Sexual Abuse Histories of Female Offenders

Of the 43 female offenders, 32 women (74%) reported having a history of sexual activity before the age of 15 that met this study's criteria for sexual abuse. Although the responses of several additional women were not tabulated because they did not meet this study's specific criteria (victim younger than 15, and either at least 5 years' age difference between victim and offender or force used to enact sexual contact), they spontaneously reported incidents in which they were victims of sexual abuse or potential abuse such as incest, rape, other early sexual experiences and spousal rape.

The average age at which the female sexual offenders in this study first experienced sexual contact with their own childhood sexual abuser was 7.57, with a range of 1-14 years. The average difference between the youngest and oldest ages at which each female offender had sexual contact with a sexually abusive individual was 7.7 years. That is, an average of 7.7 years passed between the female perpetrators' first sexually abusive experience in childhood, and her last reported sexual contact with any of the people who began sexually molesting her in childhood.

SEXUAL OFFENDERS AGAINST FEMALE CHILD MOLESTERS

Among the study's respondents, female offenders with a sexual abuse history, as a rule, had experienced sexual contact either with multiple offenders, or with a closely related offender, or both. Of the 32 (75%) female child molesters reporting a history of their own childhood sexual abuse, 25 (58% of the total sample of 43 female offenders) had as a perpetrator at least one relative or step-relative. Twelve of the women who reported sexual abuse experiences (28% of the total sample) had only one offender; however, in 10 of these 12 cases the offender was a relative or step-relative.

Table 9
Sexual Contacts of 43 Female Child Molesters with Adults

	RESPONSE	FREQUENCY (% to nearest whole number)	
QUESTION: WITH HOW MANY ADULT MALE PARTNERS HAVE YOU HAD SEXUAL INTERCOURSE?	1–5	6	(14%)
	6–10	12	(28%)
	11–15	2	(5%)
	16–20	2	(5%)
	21–25	1	(2%)
	26–30	3	(7%)
	46–50	2	(5%)
	51–60	1	(2%)
	100+	7	(16%)
	Written response indicating a very large number	4	(9%)
	Other	3	(6%)
QUESTION: WITH HOW MANY ADULT FEMALE PARTNERS HAVE YOU HAD SEXUAL CONTACT?*	1	6	(14%))
	2–5	13	(30%)
	6–9	3	(7%)
	18	1	(2%)
	"Several"	1	(2%)
	"0 in past 20 years"	1	(2%)

* Percentage of total 43 female perpetrators does not equal 100%, because fewer than 100% reported homosexual contact

Twenty of the women (47% of the total sample) had multiple offenders. The number of multiple offenders for any single woman ranged from 2 to 7. One woman, in addition to describing three offenders, noted in the margin that she had roughly 20 boyfriends aged 19 to 25 when she was 14 and 15; these boyfriends might have met criteria as sexual abusers and would have then increased the range of abusers reported by the female offenders if more information had been provided (see Table 9).

For the 32 female child molesters reporting their own history of childhood sexual abuse, a total of 74 abusive relationships were described. The 74 offenders against the female perpetrators in childhood were for the most part males; only two of the 74 offenders were females. The average difference in age between the female offender and the person(s) who abused her in childhood was 18.49 years, with a range of 1-59 years; this average was based on the 72 of 74 victim/offender pairings for which an estimate of the perpetrator's age was given. Relationships of the female offenders to their own victimizers are shown in Table 10.

While the "boyfriend" category may appear to be a relatively benign category of sexual abuse, such was not necessarily the case. Five of the 11 such pairings included sexual contact that occurred against the will of the female, in addition to meeting or exceeding the age difference criteria; three of these five cases also included sexual contact that was retrospectively viewed by the woman reporting it as abusive or bad.

DYNAMICS OF THE FEMALE OFFENDER'S EXPERIENCE OF SEXUAL ASSAULT IN CHILDHOOD

Female child molesters often reported a history childhood sexual victimization that involved sexual contact with a relative or with multiple offenders. In addition, the sexual contact was often reported to have been bad or abusive, and against the will of the female. Of the childhood sexual abuse experiences reported in the histories of the female offenders, most included sexual contact that was against the will of the female involved. In 53 of these 74 pairings (72%), the sexual contact with a specific perpetrator included contact that was against the will of the female involved, and only in 16 cases (22%) did it *not* include such contact. In 2 cases the space was left blank, and in 2 cases the woman circled both yes and no in response to the question asking whether the sexual contact had ever occurred against her will. Most of the pairings were also retrospectively viewed as having been abusive or bad. Of the 74 pairings, 57 (77%) were viewed as abusive or bad, while only 15 (20%) were not. In two cases the space was left blank.

In five of the cases, the woman reported the sexual contact with an offender had included contact that was against her will, but did not view the sexual contact as

Table 10
Relationships of 32 Female
Child Molesters to the 74 People
Who Abused Them

RELATIONSHIP	NUMBER OF VICTIM/OFFENDER PAIRINGS	RELATIONSHIP	NUMBER OF VICTIM/OFFENDER PAIRINGS
BOYFRIEND		CLASSMATE	
	11		1
BROTHER		SCHOOL JANITOR	
	11		1
UNCLE		FRIEND OF SISTER	
	7		1
GRANDFATHER OR STEPFATHER		MOTHER'S FRIEND	
	6		1
FATHER OR STEPFATHER		MOTHER'S BOYFRIEND	
	6		1
COUSIN OR ADOPTIVE COUSIN		SISTER'S BOYFRIEND	
	5		1
STRANGER		FRIEND'S FATHER	
	5		1
NEIGHBOR		FEMALE FOSTER PARENT	
	4		1
FAMILY FRIEND		"MAN I MET"	
	3		1
BABYSITTER (1 FEMALE)		AUNT'S BOYFRIEND	
	2		1
FRIEND		FRIEND'S FATHER	
	2		1
ACQUAINTANCE		UNKNOWN (LEFT BLANK)	
	1		1

abusive or bad. In six cases, the reverse occurred; although the contact was not against her will, the woman retrospectively viewed the relationship as abusive or bad.

Sexually Abusive Activities Directed Towards Female Perpetrators During Childhood

For the most part, the sexual contacts experienced by the female offenders in their own childhoods were severe in nature. All of the 32 woman who reported a history of sexual abuse had experienced genital stimulation. Twenty-one of these women had experienced some form of oral sex as a part of their abuse histories, 26 had experienced intercourse, 10 had experienced some form of anal penetration, and 6 of the women had been involved in group sex as a part of their victimization experiences.

The 32 female offenders reported a total of 74 perpetrators who had sexual contact with them when they were children. Only two of the 74 victim-offender pairings (3%) involved only breast stimulation, and in both of these cases the offender was not the only sexual perpetrator listed for that respondent. In one of the cases involving only breast stimulation, the victim was manually stimulated by the offender. In the second case, the victim stimulated the breasts of her female offender with her mouth and hands, and group sex was listed as an additional form of sexual contact with this offender (see Table 11).

For fifteen of the 74 victim-offender pairings (20%), manual genital stimulation either toward the victim or offender occurred (without intercourse, oral sex or anal penetration). In seven of the 74 pairings (9%), oral sex (without intercourse or anal penetration) was involved in the sexual contact.

For the majority female offenders, childhood sexual contact with their offenders included intercourse. Of the 74 victim-offender pairings, 48 (65%) involved sexual intercourse. In 24 of the 48 cases involving intercourse, oral sex (but not anal penetration) was also involved; in five such cases (three of which involved the same victim), group sex was also involved.

In 10 of the 48 cases involving intercourse, both anal penetration and oral sex were also involved. In seven of these cases, anal intercourse occurred, and in three of these cases the anal penetration involved a finger or object. In the seven cases involving anal intercourse (as well as intercourse and oral sex) mutual anal penetration with an object or finger also occurred in four cases. In two of these four cases, group sex was also involved (a different victim was involved in each of the two cases).

Table 11
Childhood Sexual Victimization Experiences of 32 Female Offenders

TYPE OF ACTIVITY	FREQUENCY OF VICTIM/OFFENDER PAIRINGS (% of 74 pairings to nearest whole number)	
BREAST STIMULATION ONLY		
1 CASE INVOLVED GROUP SEX	2	3%
MANUAL GENITAL STIMULATION		
MAY INCLUDE BREAST STIMULATION, BUT NOT INTERCOURSE, ORAL SEX, OR ANAL SEX	15	20%
6 – Of victim		
4 – Of abuser		
5 – Of both		
ORAL STIMULATION OF GENITALS		
MAY INCLUDE BREAST OR MANUAL GENITAL STIMULATION, BUT NOT INTERCOURSE OR ANAL STIMULATION	7	9%
4 – Of victim		
2 – Of abuser		
1 – Of both		
SEXUAL INTERCOURSE		
MAY INCLUDE BREAST OR MANUAL GENITAL STIMULATION	48	65%
14 – Without additional oral sex or anal penetration		
24 – With additional oral stimulation		
11 – *Of victim (2 cases also involved group sex)*		
5 – *Of abuser*		
8 – *Of both (3 cases also involved group sex)*		
10 – With additional oral sex and anal penetration		
7* – *Anal intercourse (mutual anal penetration in 4 cases)*		
(1 – + oral stimulation of victim)		
(3 – + oral stimulation of abuser)		
(3 – + oral stimulation of both)		
3 – *Anal penetration (not anal intercourse)*		
(0 – + oral stimulation of victim		
(1 – + oral stimuation of offender		
(2 – + oral stimulation of both)		
MISCELLANEOUS		
TOTAL MISCELLANEOUS	2	3%
1 – Anal penetration of offender, no oral sex, anal sex, or intercourse		
1 – Data describing type of sexual contact missing		

* Among these 7 cases were two in which group sex was involved, in addition to intercourse, anal intercourse, mutual anal penetration, and mutual oral intercourse

In the three cases involving anal penetration with a finger or object, but not anal intercourse (in addition to intercourse and oral sex), one involved anal penetration of the perpetrator, and two involved anal penetration of the victim.

Female Offenders' Sexual Contacts with Children

VICTIMIZATION PRECEDING PERPETRATION

Not all of the female offenders reported having experienced childhood sexual abuse. Among the offenders who did, however, none began offending at an age younger than that of her own first experience of having been sexually abused. Twenty-six offenders provided information concerning both a history of having been sexually abused, and descriptions of their sexual activities with children. The amount of time between having first been victimized and having first engaged in victimization ranged tremendously, from less than 1 year to 39 years. The average difference between the age listed at the first victimization, and the age listed at the first offense was approximately 13 years. Eight female offenders reported engaging in sexual offenses against others before the last sexual contact with their own sexual abusers had occurred.

AGES OF PARTICIPANTS AND GENDERS OF VICTIMS

Thirty-four of the 43 perpetrators acknowledged and described their sexual offenses. An additional woman, a convicted child molester, described the offense for which she was convicted, but wrote that she had been raped by her alleged victim.

These 35 offenders described offenses against a total of 56 victims. Most of the offenders reported having offended against only one child. Eleven of the offenders reported having had either 2 or 3 victims. One offender reported having had seven victims. Of the 56 victims, 35 were male, 18 were female, and the gender for 3 could not be discerned from the stated relationship. Of the 35 female offenders, 19 had exclusively male victims, 8 victimized females only, 5 victimized children of both genders, and again, the genders of 3 victims were not discernable.

Ages of the offenders at the time of their first offenses ranged from 8 to 42. The average age of the offender at the time of her first offense against her first

Table 12
Ages Female Child Molesters
Reported Having Sexual Contact
with Victims

		FREQUENCY *(% to nearest whole number)*	
AGE OF OFFENDER			
	Below 20	12	(34%)
	20–29	13	(37%)
	30–39	7	(20%)
	40–49	1	(3%)
OTHER			
	1 offense in 20's, later offenses in 30's	1	(3%)
	1 offense at age 8, later offenses in 30's	1	(3%)

Table 13
Ages of Victims of
Female Child Molesters

		FREQUENCY *(% to nearest whole number)*	
AGE OF VICTIMS			
	1–2 years	6	(11%)
	3–5 years	12	(21%)
	6–8 years	9	(16%)
	9–11 years	10	(18%)
	12–15 years	19	(34%)

Table 14
Female Offender/Victim Age Differences in 56 Pairings

		FREQUENCY (% to nearest whole number)	
OFFENDER/VICTIM AGE DIFFERENCES			
	30 or more years	4	(7%)
	20–29 years	6	(11%)
	10–19 years	15	(27%)
	5–9 years	24	(43%)
	0–5 years	7	(13%)
	Offender younger than victim by 2 years	1	(2%)

victim was 21.12. The average age of the offender at the first of each her victim/offender pairings was 21.

Most of the perpetrators began all of their offenses at about the same age (see Table 12). There were four exceptions. One woman began her offenses against 3 children two and four years apart. One woman's first offenses against different victims were separated by 10 years. One woman committed an offense at the age of 8, and then later offenses at about the same time during her 30's. One woman had offenses at the ages of 12 and 19.

Many of the women acknowledged offenses that occurred before they were aged 16. For thirteen of the 43 offenders at least one offense occurred when the female offender was 15 or younger. Of the 56 victim/female-offender pairings 25 involved a female offender who was 15 or younger, generally an adolescent. One woman molested seven children when she was between the ages of 13 and 14.

The average age of the children molested was 8.76 (see Table 13). The average difference in age between the female offender and her victim was 11.91 years (see Table 14). One of the offenders was 2 years younger than the victim at the time of her offense, but reported the sexual contact took place even though the victim did not want the sexual contact.

DURATION OF OFFENSES

Offenders were asked to list their age at the first and last sexual contact with each victim. These ages were used to estimate the duration of the sexual contacts with each victim. In 34 of the 56 victim/offender pairings (61%), the contact reportedly lasted for less than a year. In 19 of the pairings (34%) the contact lasted between 1 and 5 years. In three pairings (5%), it lasted 7-11 years.

The difference between youngest age at the time of a first sexual contact with a victim, and the oldest age at the time of the last sexual contact with a victim was tabulated for each perpetrator, as a means of roughly estimating the number of years that the perpetrator was offending. The difference ranged between less than a year and 22 years. The average difference in ages of the perpetrator between the first and last acknowledged offenses was 7 years.

NUMBER OF SEXUAL CONTACTS WITH VICTIMS

Most commonly, the offender reported having had sexual contact only once with each victim, with such reported to have been the case with 23 (41%) of the 56 victims involved. It was also quite common for the offender to report only a few contacts with the victim; in 25 (45%) of the 56 cases, the offenders reported having contact with a victim between 2-20 times. A larger reported number of sexual contacts with each victim was uncommon. Six offenders (11%) reported having sexual contact with victims between 30-50 times, and one woman (2%) reported 200 contacts with a victim.

RELATIONSHIPS BETWEEN FEMALE OFFENDERS AND VICTIMS

At least 30 of the 56 victims who were described by the perpetrators (54%) were related to their offenders. Relationships in these cases were as follows: cousin (7), son or step-son (9), daughter (7), brother or foster-brother (3), sister or foster-sister (3), and nephew (1).

Twenty-five (45%) of the victims were not related to the female offender. Six of the victims were molested when the offenders were baby-sitting them. Six of the victims were listed as "friends" or as "friends of the family." Two victims were listed as either a boyfriend or as the partner in an affair. Four victims were simply listed as children. The remaining victims included a friend's cousin, a friend's son, a brother's friend, and a runaway.

In one case, the relationship to the victim was left blank. The remaining case was that of an unrelated male who the female offender said raped her.

TYPES OF SEXUAL CONTACTS BETWEEN
FEMALE OFFENDERS AND VICTIMS

As Table 15 shows, in three of the 56 offender/victim pairings (5%), the sexual contact involved stimulation of the breasts, only; in one of these cases, group sex was listed as an additional source of sexual contact. In eleven of the 56 cases (20%), manual stimulation of genitals was the primary source of sexual contact, irrespective of whether breast stimulation was also involved. One such case also involved genital-to-genital contact (not intercourse), which the offender spontaneously described in the margin.

Thirteen of the fifty-six offender/victim pairings (23%) included oral sex, without intercourse. Cases involving oral sex were tabulated irrespective of whether manual fondling or breast stimulation was also involved. Twenty-three of the 56 cases (41%) involved sexual intercourse. Eight of the 23 cases involving intercourse additionally involved oral sex.

In two of the cases where sexual intercourse and oral sex were involved, the victims were listed as females; it is not clear what accounts for the fact that the female victims were listed as having had sexual intercourse with the female offender. It is possible that the activity engaged in more closely resembled intercourse than other forced choice options (for example, digital or object penetration, or frotteurism). Alternately, as the offender indicated that she was forced into the activities, it is possible that the second person engaged in the intercourse, but that the activity was not perceived to have been group sex.

In two cases (4%), the primary form of sexual contact was written in the margin. In one case involving a female, the offender manually stimulated the female child, and also wrote that her husband had required the girl to wear a dildo and to use it on the offender. In another case involving a young male child, the offender indicated that she had held the child and "rubbed him on me," in a way that she now considers sexually abusive or bad.

In three cases the (same) female left the spaces describing the sexual contact blank, and in one case, the convicted molester who stated that she had been raped by her victim, simply wrote, "rape," in the space (see Table 15).

ABUSE CRITERIA/PERCEPTIONS OF ABUSE BY THE OFFENDER

Either of two criteria was utilized for defining a female sex offender against a child who was 15 or younger. The first was an age difference of five years, with

Table 15
Types of Sexual Contact with Victims
Engaged in by 32 Female Offenders

TYPE OF ACTIVITY	FREQUENCY OF VICTIM/OFFENDER PAIRINGS *(% of 56 pairings to nearest whole number)*	
BREAST STIMULATION ONLY		
EXCLUDES BREAST STIMULATION ACCOMPANIED BY OTHER SEXUAL ACTIVITY	3	5%
1 – Oral stimulation of offender by female child 1 – Manual stimulation of offender by male child 1 – Mutual oral and manual stimulation with female child (also included group sex)		
MANUAL GENITAL STIMULATION		
MAY INCLUDE BREAST STIMULATION, BUT NOT INTERCOURSE, ORAL SEX, OR ANAL SEX	11	20%
4 – Of female child 3 – Of male child (1 case non-intercourse genital-genital contact) 0 – Of offender by female child 1 – Of offender by male child 0 – Of both offender and female child 3 – Of both offender and male child		
ORAL STIMULATION OF GENITALS		
MAY INCLUDE BREAST OR GENTIAL STIMULATION, BUT NOT INTERCOURSE OR ANAL STIMULATION	13	23%

10 – Without additional anal penetration
     2 – *Of female child*
        (both involved in group sex)
     4 – *Of male child*
        (1 involved in group sex)
     0 – *Of offender by female child*
     1 – *Of offender by male child*
     3 – *Of both offender and female child*
        (1 case group sex)
     0 – *Of both offender and male child*
3 – With additional anal penetration
     2 – *Mutual oral sex and anal penetration of of female child (1 case group sex)*
     1 – *Mutual oral sex and anal penetration of offender by female child (group sex)*		

Table 15
(Continued)

TYPE OF ACTIVITY	FREQUENCY OF VICTIM/OFFENDER PAIRINGS *(% of 56 pairings to nearest whole number)*	
SEXUAL INTERCOURSE		
MAY INCLUDE BREAST STIMULATION OR MANUAL GENITAL STIMULATION	23	41%
15 – Without additional oral sex or anal penetration		
8 – With additional oral stimulation		
2 – Of male child (1 case group sex)		
1 – Of offender by male child		
2 – Of both offender and female child		
2 – Of both offender and male child		
1 – Of both offender and child, gender unknown		
MISCELLANEOUS		
TOTAL MISCELLANEOUS	3	5%
1 – Forced simulated intercourse by female child wearing strapped-on dildo		
1 – Male child held by and "rubbed on" by offender, later perceived by offender as abusive or bad		
1 – Offender reports she was raped by victim		
OTHER		
DATA NOT SUPPLED	3	5%

the perpetrator as the older individual. Most of the 56 victim/female offender pairings (51 pairings) met this criteria. Women were also asked to describe cases where they had forced the child to have sexual contact with them, regardless of their own age at the time. To confirm that force was used, only those cases were included as meeting this criteria where the subject answered "no" to the question, "did the other person want the sexual contact with you?" Only 5 of the victim/offender pairings were defined by this "force" criteria alone. In 4 of these 5 cases the offender was older than the victims but by less than 5 years. One offender was 13 and offended against a 9- and a 10-year-old.

In one case the offender was younger than the victim, a 12-year-old offending against a 14-year-old. At age 19, this offender had sexual contact with a 14-year-old adolescent.

In most of the 56 female offender/victim pairings, the offender indicated that she now believed her behavior to have been abusive or bad (see Table 16). Of the 10 cases where the abuse was not thought to have been abusive or bad, seven involved adolescent victims between the ages of 13 and 15, who were perceived to have wanted the sexual contact. However, one of the cases involved a 15-year-old offender who had sexual contact with a 4-year-old child who was perceived to have wanted the sexual contact. Another case involved a 42-year-old woman who had incestuous sexual contact with 10- and 11-year-old girls who were perceived to have not wanted the sexual contact. Most of the sexual contacts were viewed by the female offenders as unwanted on the children's part.

Twelve of the offenders had more than one victim. Of these 12, 6 (50%) believed that none of their victims wanted the sexual contact, 2 (16%) believed that some of their victims wanted it while others did not, 1 (8%) believed that all of her victims wanted the contact, and 3 (25%) gave consistently undecided responses ("both," "yes and no" or "?") for all of their victims.

When combined with offenders who had only one reported victim, 14 of the 35 offenders (40%) believed that none of their victims wanted the sexual contact, 15 (43%) believed that all of their victims wanted the sexual contact, 2 (6%) gave different answers for different victims, and four (11%) gave consistently undecided responses.

OFFENDERS' ADULT RELATIONSHIPS AS THEY PERTAIN TO SEXUAL OFFENSES

Most of the female offenders did not indicate that they had been forced into the sexual contacts. Of the 56 victim/offender pairings, only 10 (18%) involved cases where the offender said that she was forced into having the sexual contact, including the one case where the convicted offender maintained that her apparent victim had actually raped her. In 33 of the 56 cases (58%) the offender stated that she was not forced; for 11 victims (20%), offenders left the question blank. In an additional 2 of the pairings (4%), the offender (the same woman in both cases) wrote she had been drugged by her husband and encouraged to participate.

Six of the 35 offenders who described their offenses (17%) said they were forced to participate during at least one of their offenses, one convicted child molester

Table 16

Perceptions of 35 Female Child Molesters Related to Offenses Against 56 Victims

	RESPONSE	FREQUENCY *(% to nearest whole number)*	
QUESTION: DID THE OTHER PERSON WANT SEXUAL CONTACT WITH YOU?	Yes	19	(34%)
	No	29	(52%)
	Other *("Blank", "yes and no", "both")*	8	(14%)
QUESTION: DO YOU NOW CONSIDER SEXUAL CONTACT WITH THIS PERSON TO HAVE BEEN ABUSIVE OR BAD?	Yes	45	(80%)
	No	10	(18%)*
	Other *(Offender says she was raped)*	1	(2%)

* 7 of the 10 pairings involved victims ages 13–15 perceived to have wanted the sexual contact

(3%) indicated that she had been raped by her victim, 20 (57%) were not forced in any of their offenses, and in eight of the cases (23%) it is not clear whether or not the offender was forced, generally because the response was left blank.

All of the offenders were asked to answer a forced-choice question asking them to describe the typical state of their love-lives with adults during the times of their offenses against children. Only 3 of the 35 women (9%) indicated that they were involved in a good relationship. Bad relationships were indicated by 12 women (34%) as the typical state of their love life at the time of their offenses. The typical state for 4 women (11%) involved having just ended a relationship, and 3 (9%) indicated that the typical state was not to have been involved in an adult or same-age love relationship in over a year. Eight of the women (23%) left the question blank; two of the women who left the question blank indicated that they committed the sexual offenses in conjunction with their husbands.

Five additional women (14%) answered the question idiosyncratically. Two checked both that they were involved in a bad relationship and also checked that they had just ended a relationship. One indicated both that she had just ended a relationship and that she was in a good relationship. One indicated that while not in a relationship, she often had sexual encounters, and one woman wrote that the question "does not apply."

CHILD PROTECTIVE SERVICE OR POLICE INVOLVEMENT

Asked if child protective services or the police had ever questioned them about their sexual contacts with younger children, the most common response of the perpetrators (16 of 35, or 46%) was to leave the question blank. Of those who answered the question, 8 (23%) indicated that they had been questioned, while 10 (29%) indicated that they had not. While she did not answer the question, an additional woman wrote in the margin that she had been sent to prison for the child molestation offense. Of the 8 who stated that they had been questioned, 4 were known to be convicted, imprisoned sex offenders; two were from a sample known to contain a large percentage of convicted sex offenders; and the remaining two were from a prison sample, where it was unknown if they were serving time for child molestation.

CHAPTER 5

Discussion

Psychosocial Histories

SEXUAL ABUSE HISTORIES

The female offenders in this sample, by and large, experienced childhood sexual abuse that was severe by any definition. In each category of severity, the majority had experienced severe forms of sexual abuse. Most commonly, the subjects had experienced sexual contact with a relative or a person who was known to them, and had been abused by more than one offender. Most had experienced sexual intercourse, and sexual contact involving oral sex or anal penetration and/or intercourse was not uncommon. The average offender was first abused at a young age, and there were several years separating her first and last sexual contact with an abuser, indicating lengthy duration. Contact with most offenders (and the female child molesters when they were child victims) involved sexual activity that was against the will of the victim, and that contact was retrospectively viewed as having been abusive or bad.

The sexual abuse history of the female child molesters was not comparatively more severe than the sexual abuse history of their matched control group, to a significant degree. The control subjects also had a history of severe childhood sexual abuse. That there was a trend towards the female child molesters having a more severe sexual abuse history, however, suggests that with a larger group of subjects significance in this area might be found. The control group was not composed of a random sample of the population at large; its members were likely to have had a more severe history of sexual abuse than would members of a more random sample. Future research might compare the severity of the history of child sexual abuse among female child molesters with that of a sample of women in the population at large. In that most of the control group was selected from a prison sample, a history of severe child sexual abuse would appear to be common not only to female child molesters, but to women with other antisocial behavioral problems. This connection warrants further research.

FAMILY HISTORIES

Data supplied by the offenders suggested that many had experienced unstable and possibly chaotic family-of-origin home lives. Many provided data suggesting that they or their mothers had been the recipients of frequent physical abuse during the time that they were growing up. Many of the questions concerning childhood psychosocial trauma were designed for comparison purposes only, and were not designed to definitively detect all forms of the types of trauma screened for. Where data were provided concerning the responses of participants to these screening questions, this should be kept in mind.

The screening question for physical abuse directed towards the offender as a child, for example, addressed only abuse that occurred on at least a monthly basis and which left injuries. Other forms of physical abuse (blocking air supply, beatings short of leaving injuries, locking in an enclosed space, and so forth) would not have been captured by this question, nor would serious abuse that occurred on less than a monthly basis. Similarly, the screening question concerning possible physical abuse of the respondent's mother excluded injuries which might have occurred when the subject was not present or physical abuse that did not leave injuries. It also excluded such injuries which happened on less than a monthly basis. Some of the women spontaneously recorded that they had seen their mothers receive injuries, or had themselves been the recipients of injuries that occurred fewer than one time per month.

In addition to violence in the home, many of the women had experienced other forms of childhood instability. Many of the female offenders had witnessed frequent drinking or drug use in their family homes while growing up. Many of the women indicated that their parents had had multiple marriages or live-in partners. It is unlikely that many of the women experienced positive upbringings. Given that most of the women were severely sexually abused, it is possible that a factor contributing to their potential to become perpetrators was the lack of a support network sufficient to assist them in successfully managing the resulting trauma from their sexual abuse. In many cases, it would appear that the family environment was such that it may have compounded rather than reduced the effects of such abuse.

The control group also had a large amount of family-of-origin pathology as measured by the screening questions. The child molesters in this sample reported slightly but not significantly more frequent incidents of monthly family-of-origin pathology (their own physical injury by an adult, the witnessing of the injury of their mother, the use of drugs or alcohol to the extent that it induced behavior change by a member of the household) while growing up than did their control group, who also reported these occurrences to be frequent. It may be the case that with other variables included as family pathology, the trend for there to be differences in the family histories would be significant. It would appear likely that female child molesters and their control groups (largely from prisons) have more family-of-origin pathology than do members of the population at large, and this may be an area for future research for both groups.

MALE SEX PARTNERS

Both the control group and the female child molesters reported large numbers of male sex partners, on average. The female child molesters reported slightly more male sex partners, but the differences did not reach statistical significance. Some subjects noted either on their surveys or in comments made while taking the surveys that they had worked as prostitutes. It is not known how the participants decided whether or not to include their sexual customers in their responses, or how this may have affected the results of this study.

LOVE RELATIONSHIPS

The female child molesters provided data suggesting possible problems in their own primary love relationships. Most of the offenders indicated that the typical state of their love-lives during the time of their offenses was to be in a bad relationship. Further research is needed to understand how these relationships relate to sex offenses. Potentially, they may contribute to stress somehow relieved through the sexual offenses against children, or perhaps the partners in some way contribute to the notion of sexual contact with an adult as something which is threatening or degrading. Possibly the bad relationships during the times of the offending are explained by the female offender having had poor abilities to relate with others, and poor judgement regarding the choice of partners at that particular period in her life. The bad relationship may have been with a male child molester with whom she co-offended. For the women who were forced to have sexual contact with children, it is likely that being involved in a bad relationship had a direct impact on their offense behaviors. They may have been forced into sexual contact with children by the person with whom they reported being in a bad relationship.

Women with comparatively more severe abuse histories and less education tended to be more likely to be involved in group sex with children. It is unclear if such group sex involved another adult; however, it seems likely that these women would be easy targets for coercion from another child molester into sexual activities with children. These women may have also been influenced to have sexual contact with children in the context of a negative relationship with another adult.

The factor analysis in this study also suggested the possibility that while some women are overtly forced into sexual activity with children, others who are less well educated and who have the more severe histories of sexual abuse (even when compared to other female child molesters) may be more vulnerable to coercion in which force is not necessary. Future research is required to examine the dynamics of the love relationships which involve a female child molester, and the means by which such women are convinced by others to have sexual contact with children.

ECONOMIC ACHIEVEMENT OF OFFENDERS

The offenders in this sample, by and large, earned low wages. Lack of achievement may be a treatment concern for female child molesters. Given the chaotic and abusive families-of-origin typically described by these offenders, the messages that these women received concerning their ability to achieve may be worthy of further exploration. The lack of achievement may be symptomatic of additional problems, such as low self-esteem, possible learning disabilities, or mental health problems, which warrant further study. The reported low wages together with the large amount of dependency found among the female offenders may serve to place them at a high risk for difficulty in extracting themselves from unfavorable relationships with individuals who financially support them. Where such individuals are co-offenders, a lack of economic achievement may place female offenders at risk for further offending.

There were no significant differences found between the reported wages earned by the offenders and those earned by the control group. The wages were low for both groups. However, given the greater self-reported dependency of the offenders, they may perceive themselves as less able to provide for themselves, or may prefer to have others provide for them. Given that many of the offenders were in prison at the time of their participation in the survey, it may be that the sources of their wages when they were working were illegal (drug dealing, prostitution, gambling, theft, etc). The wording of the question concerning hourly wages is likely to have minimized the likelihood that such was the case. However, some offenders may have concerns for being able to legally support themselves. It should also be noted that incomes for offenders in this sample may not be representative of those of female offenders in general. As this was largely a prison sample, it is possible that lower income women were more likely to have come to the attention of the authorities for child molestation or for other crimes and may be overrepresented.

DEPENDENCY

The offenders in this study were significantly more likely to agree that symptoms of dependency described them than were the subjects in the matched control group. Given that the control group was drawn from prisoners, substance abusers, and individuals seeking treatment for concerns related to sexual abuse, it might be expected that the control group was more dependent than the population at large. The sense of dependency experienced by female child molesters is likely to be great, and to well exceed that experienced by individuals in the population at large.

MENTAL HEALTH CONCERNS

This study found that a large number of female child molesters had been psychiatrically hospitalized, or had received psychiatric medication. Further research is necessary to determine the exact nature of the mental health problems that brought them to the hospital and caused them to have been medicated. It is possible that in addition to mental illness, these women may have received care for suicidal or homicidal ideation. Most had psychosocial backgrounds compatible with possible depression and suicidal ideation, and many subjects were in prison, where it is assumed that they were placed for acting out behavior, which for some may have included forms of violence. Given their history of psychiatric interventions, it is noteworthy that the subjects, who were largely drawn from prison populations, had presumably not been found not guilty by reason of insanity. This raises the possibility that affective disturbances, suicidal and/or homicidal ideation, or personality disorders may have accounted for the hospitalizations and medication rather than psychotic disorders which might more readily be accepted as grounds for an insanity plea.

About a third of the women met the criteria for Dependent Personality Disorder by their self-report of symptoms. Others reported symptoms of dependency falling short of this disorder but may have met the criteria if evaluated by an outside assessor, or if the questions had required dichotomous responses, as might be required in a diagnostic evaluation; many agreed that several criteria applied to them and were neutral with respect to other criteria.

Many of the women in this study also indicated a preference for frequent drinking or drug use. While such results do not definitively point to substance abuse disorders, they are consistent with the results of other studies that have found large amount of substance abuse disorders among female sex offenders. Some women in this survey indicated that they preferred not to drink or use drugs at all. For some such women, this may represent a long term preference for not using drugs or alcohol. For others, it may represent a recent change in preference or a recent involvement in a treatment program that involves abstinence. For others it may represent a preference to be free from a current alcohol or drug problem. For still others the preference may be a temporary result of being incarcerated, with restricted access to alcohol and drugs.

The frequent drug and alcohol use, history of potential sexual identity concerns, difficulties in love relationships, dependency, and history of psychiatric medication and hospitalizations common to many offenders in this study, suggest the diagnosis of Borderline Personality Disorder as a potentially common disorder among this population. Further research is needed to explore the mental health diagnoses of the female child molester population. This study found evidence of mental health problems among the majority of the female child molesters, and further research concerning the exact nature of these problems is needed.

Relationship Between Sexual Abuse History and Sexual Abuse Perpetration

Further research is needed to examine the relationship between having been sexually abused and becoming abusive, where female child molesters are concerned. Several contributing relationships may be speculated, that require further research. It is intuitive that the world view developed by individuals who have been subjected to severe forms of sexual abuse might include distorted perceptions of human sexuality, and less firmly established sexual boundaries. Sexual abuse perhaps hinders the ability of some offenders to appropriately discern wanted from unwanted sexual contact both in herself and in her victims. Defense mechanisms for coping with abuse, such as dissociation, denial, or minimization, once learned, may interfere with the capacity of the offender to develop empathy which might lessen the likelihood of an offense. Lack of self-worth or lack of self-protection skills resulting from severe abuse may also reduce the effectiveness with which a female is able to remove herself from a relationship with a co-offender.

That none of the offenders began their sexual victimization of children at an age younger than that of their first experience of sexual abuse strongly implicates a history of sexual abuse as a contributing factor in the development of a woman into a child molester. However, while most of the female child molesters reported a severe history of sexual abuse, some reported sexual abuse that did not meet criteria for the study. Further, that there was no significant difference between the severity of sexual abuse histories between the offenders and nonoffenders suggests that although childhood sexual abuse history is common to female child molesters, it is inadequate as a complete explanation for their later offending behaviors. The exact nature of the contribution of a childhood sexual abuse history in the development of a woman into a child molester is not well understood.

This study was unable to show a correlation between the comparative severity of the child sexual abuse histories among female child molesters (or a variable screening for family pathology), and the severity of their own sexual abuse against children. In large part this may be due to the reluctance of the offenders to provide details of their sexual offending. Several convicted offenders did not describe their offenses, and it is likely that other offenders minimized them. This is probably the primary factor accounting for the complete lack of relationship found between the severity of offenders' childhood sexual abuse histories and degree of family-of-origin pathology, and the severity of the offenders' sexual abusing of children. Several other factors such as the "fluid reality" of the offenders and their memories and defense mechanisms may have also distorted the accuracy of some of the information reported, reducing further any possible correlational relationships.

This study examined the relationship between severity of sexual abuse victimization and sexual abuse perpetration among child molesters, most of whom had very severe sexual abuse histories. A correlation between severity of sexual abuse victimization history and sexual abuse perpetration history might be shown in a sample with greater variation in these areas, such as might occur with a very large sample of offenders, or in a sample of females that included nonoffenders. This may be an area for future research.

Alternatively, it may be the case that no such relationships exists. A history of sexual victimization was found to typically precede the sexual perpetration. However the severity of the sexual abuse (or of other family-of-origin pathology) may not have been a primary factor influencing the severity of the sexual acting out.

Other factors related to psychological variables of the individual or other social history variables may interact with the history of psychosocial trauma to increase or reduce the effects of severe sexual abuse and other trauma on the offending behavior of the female child molester. It may be that factors such as the reaction of the first or subsequent victims, or the reaction of the offender to sexual contact with a child, influences the likelihood of the first sexual contact with a child being repeated, being extended to more victims, or coming to involve more forms of sexual contact. Where women sexually abuse children in conjunction with others who have coerced or forced them to participate, their ability to remove themselves from the relationship with their co-offenders may influence the progression of their sexual abuse against children more than other elements of their psychosocial histories. Given the large number of subjects reporting a history of psychiatric treatment, psychological problems may also largely contribute to offense behaviors. Further research is needed to explore possible influences related to the severity of female offenders' perpetration of sexual abuse against children.

Subtypes of Female Offenders

The factor analysis in this study provided preliminary statistical support for the existence of some of the subtypes of female offenders previously noted in the literature, and raised the possibility that there may be two types of offenders who offend in groups. The factor analysis was somewhat limited by the use of a large number of variables selected with respect to the number of subjects, and by the small number of variables selected with respect to the large number which have been observed to cluster into subtypes in the literature on female offenders.

The number of variables utilized in the factor analysis was large, given the relatively small number of subjects. A large number of variables used in a factor analysis increases the likelihood that factors (in this case subtypes of offenders) will emerge by chance, and this should be borne in mind. For other purposes requiring greater statistical certainty, the number of variables selected might have been more conservative. However, given the limited amount of research on the subject of female child molesters, it was the purpose of this study to use more liberal statistics in order to identify trends, and to examine whether there is preliminary statistical support for clinically held observations related to subtypes of female child molesters. For this purpose the less stringent ratio of variables to subjects was thought reasonable.

The relatively small number of subjects prevented a larger number of variables from being entered into the analysis. Several other variables thought to differentiate female offenders into sub-groups could not be included. The factor analysis was preliminary, and included only some of the variables more commonly observed to cluster to form subtypes of female child molesters. It was by no means inclusive of all of the variables observed to have clustered into subtypes by other researchers.

These limitations in mind, there appeared to be three primary factors which emerged from the analysis, supporting clinical observations which have described different types of female child molester. The first factor appeared to describe a subtype of offender who tends to be somewhat older, to have somewhat older victims, and to be more likely to have a history that includes having been placed in a psychiatric hospital or having received psychiatric medication.

The types of psychiatric medication used by these offenders and the reasons for the psychiatric hospitalizations were not specified by the screening questions. Psychotic female child molesters are only infrequently described in the literature outside of case studies. Some individuals reporting a history of psychiatric hospitalizations or medication may have had a history of major mental illnesses or psychosis; however, this may not have been the case for many such offenders. Given the difficult psychosocial histories of the female offenders, many may have been hospitalized or given medication for suicidal or homicidal ideation, or for childhood or adolescent behavioral problems. It is possible that the subtype of offender suggested by the first factor had a more prolonged history of psychological or psychiatric disturbance prior to offending, given the higher average age at the time of first offenses that tended to be reported.

The second subtype of offender suggested by the factor analysis tended to have a history of more severe sexual abuse and less education than did the other offenders, and a likelihood of reporting more victims with whom group sex had occurred. This factor suggested a subtype of offender who may have grown up with a limited sense of sexual boundaries, having experienced sexual abuse that happened on more occasions and/or which involved more types of sexual activity than was the case for other offenders. It also suggests a subtype of offender who may have had less intelligence or less confidence to achieve an education. This subtype of offender may tend to have had fewer intellectual or emotional resources for developing views of the world in which sexual acts between adults and children did not occur. That members of this subtype tended to report more victims with whom group sex had occurred raises the possibility of the offenses having occurred in conjunction with a person who coerced the offender; this subtype of female offender would appear to be an easy target for such an individual. However, it is also possible that a member of this subtype of offenders may involve more than one child in sexual activity at a time. This subtype closely resembles that described by Faller (1988) as "polyincestuous offenders," and may also be similar to the "Male-coerced" category described by Mathews et al. (1989).

The third factor suggested a subtype of offender that was more likely to have reported more victims with whom the offender was forced to have sexual contact. This type of offender was also likely to have reported younger victims, and more victims who were related to her. Where victims are young and related to the female offender, it may be that force is required in order for her to have sexual contact with the children. Conversely it may sometimes be the case that force might be felt a necessary justification for the behavior after it has occurred, and be more likely to be perceived retrospectively.

Similar categories, in which the female child molester tends to have been forced into sexual contact with children have been described by Mathews et al. (1989) (Male-coerced), McCarty (1986) (co-offending mothers), and Faller (1987) (polyincestuous). However, this factor analysis raises the possibility of two dynamics being involved in situations where a female offends with another person. In one, the female may be forced to participate in sexually abusive behaviors with children, while in another it may be the case that the female has been an easy target for coercion that did not require force. These hypotheses require further research.

It was expected that women who reported more victims with whom they were forced to have sexual contact would also report more victims with whom group sex occurred, and that these two variables would group onto the same factor. It was expected that this would occur because women had been forced by another offender to take part in group sex. However, that a subtype was found in which female offenders participated in group sex independent of force, raises the question of whether the group sex may have resulted from coercion from another adult who also participated in sexual contact with a child or children, or whether the group sex occurred as a result of the women independently involving more than one child in sexual activity. It cannot be ruled out that the subtype which was more likely to be involved in group sex resulted because the female child molester coerced or forced another adult to participate in the sexual activity with children, although previous literature would suggest that this is unlikely.

No support was found, in examining the ten variables which comprised this factor analysis, that would suggest a subtype of offender that begins offending in her childhood or teenage years. Because of the limitations of this factor analysis in terms of number of variables entered, and because of the small number of women in this sample who began offending as children or teenagers, no firm conclusions can be drawn about the variables which such offenders have in common that differentiate them from adult offenders. However, in many ways their psychosocial histories appeared to be similar to those of adult offenders.

The factor analysis suggested the possibility of three separate primary contributors related to sexual offense behavior towards children on the part of females. A prolonged and serious history of mental health problems may be a factor related to some female offenders' sexual acting out. A lack of sexual boundaries, resulting from extremely severe sexual abuse in childhood and a lack of education and possibly intelligence with which to develop boundaries against sexual contact with children may be another. Finally, some women may be forced into sexual contact, and this may be a primary factor related to their offending. Given the limitations of this preliminary factor analysis, these contributors warrant further research.

Population Studied

This study had some advantages over previously conducted research. The use of the Confidentiality Certificate in gathering information from female sex offenders was apparently unique to this research. The Confidentiality Certificate insured that women who reported sexual contact with children would not suffer negative legal consequences as a result of having revealed such information. While it is likely that not all of the participants or potential participants were reassured by this Certificate, it is also probable that many were encouraged to participate, and to provide more accurate data concerning their sexual activities with children than would otherwise be the case.

The provision of this protection for female sex offenders had some advantages over previously used methods of obtaining data from female child molesters. In most previous studies, data were collected from women in therapy, or from women who had been involved with protective services or criminal proceedings. In such cases, women were not protected from adverse consequences for providing data concerning their offenses; on the contrary adverse consequences were highly likely, given the obligation of mental health therapists, protective services workers, and those involved in criminal proceedings to protect children who may have been sexually abused. The participants in this study may have more readily divulged information concerning their sexual involvement with children, as well as the more deviant aspects of their psychosocial histories than has been the case in previous studies.

A large portion of the women in this study were not known to have previously come to the attention of authorities, and as such may be more closely representative of female child molesters who have not been detected than those in previous studies. Most previous studies of female perpetrators have relied only on the report of known or convicted offenders who were presently in therapy, or involved with protective services or criminal courts. The exception to this is the study by Condy (1985), which examined sexual contacts that prison women had with younger males.

Women in previous studies who participated in therapy as a consequence of adversarial court proceedings or out of fear of losing their children through child protection proceedings may have been more guarded about revealing personal information about themselves, particularly information concerning a pathological psychosocial history. This may also have been the case for women who were involved with protective services or the courts. It is likely that the women who willingly took part in this study and who were honest to the extent that they openly acknowledged illegal sexual offenses may have also more openly described their psychosocial histories. This would be consistent with the findings of the study by Condy et al. (1987), in which it was found that women who acknowledged sexual contact with male children and adolescents had lower Lie Scales on the MMPI Mini-Mult than did other prison women.

It is thought that the portion of the survey requiring descriptions of perpetration of child molestation was the most risky portion for the offender to complete. This information, when supplied, was generally an admission of having engaged in illegal activities. It is therefore likely that where information about perpetration against children was supplied accurately, the additional information which did not involve illegal activities may have also been accurately supplied. A subject who acknowledged and described in writing sexual offenses against a child may also have been more likely to have acknowledged additional uncomfortable aspects of her psychosocial history. It is likely that she relied less heavily on denial, minimization, and repression as defenses, and that she withheld less information due to lack of trust concerning how the information will be used.

AGES OF PARTICIPANTS

None of the participants in this study was over the age of 48 at the time of survey completion. It is not clear what accounted for the lack of older participants, who might have been expected to have engaged in greater numbers of sexual offenses, given that they had a greater number of years in which to offend, and given that their cohorts had less access to treatment for childhood sexual victimization. It is possible that the young ages of the women may have represented a cohort effect in terms of willingness to report issues concerned with human sexuality. Women whose values concerning human sexuality were formulated prior to the "sexual revolution" of the 1960s and 70s may have been less likely to self-report deviant sexual activity. They may also have been less likely to have acted on their sexual feelings towards children, given the sexual mores present during their early adult years. It is possible that the memories of the older female child molesters functioned less well due to aging, or the more solidified use of denial or repression. Additionally, older subjects, particularly those in the prison samples, may have had more time in which to develop mistrust of risky self-revelation. Given the poor survival skills, high rates of drug and alcohol abuse, depression and suicidal ideation, and abusive relationships commonly found among female sex offenders, they may also have a high mortality rate, which might have decreased the pool of available older female sex offenders among the populations surveyed.

Nor did any of the subjects report having engaged in an offense against a child beyond the age of 42. This was partly a reflection of the relatively young ages of the subjects. It is also likely to have reflected the fact that a large number of the subjects were incarcerated, and at the age of their incarcerations were likely to have lost access to potential victims. To a lesser extent, the younger ages at the time of offending may reflect a tendency for female child molesters to have sexual contacts with victims in their younger years.

SEXUAL ACTIVITY AMONG FEMALE SEX OFFENDERS

A large number of the female offenders in this study reported having engaged in homosexual activity with adult females, in addition to having engaged in sexual activity with children and with adult males. This finding is confounded by the fact that the majority of the participants in the study were imprisoned women for whom heterosexual contacts may not have been readily available. All of the women who reported homosexual contact were in prison. Nonetheless, the finding warrants further study among non-prison samples of female sex offenders. It raised the possibility that female offenders against children may be, in a sense, "omnisexual," unable to easily establish or enforce their sexual identities or boundaries. However, it was unclear in what context the sexual contact with adult women reported by the female offenders occurred. For example, while it may have occurred in a consensual adult sexual relationship, it could have occurred as sexual abuse against the female offender in childhood, as coercive or forced sexual activity experienced as an adult or in mutually coercive sexual contact with children.

A general lack of sexual boundaries among some offenders was also suggested by their commonly reported sexual contacts with large numbers of adult males. For several of the offenders it was further suggested by the lack of consistency in their stated sexual preferences and their reported sexual behaviors. Research further documenting a general lack of sexual boundaries in female offenders or sexual identity confusion would be useful in helping to understand the dynamics of sexual offenses of women against children.

For some offenders, it is possible that while they may prefer sexual contact with adult males, they may view this contact as more threatening than sexual contact with females or children. Because most of the female offenders had experienced severe forms of sexual abuse at the hands of males, sexual contact with men may be perceived as dangerous or as threatening. Sexual contact with females and children may be viewed as less so.

Rosencrans (1993) has also raised the hypothesis that female offenders against female children may be acting on societally repressed homosexual urges. She suggested that homosexual women who feel that approaching other adult females for sexual contact is unacceptable or threatening may turn to their own daughters for sexual gratification. While only a small number of the offenders in this sample offended exclusively against female children, such concerns may have been a factor in their offenses. This may account for the discrepancy between the statements of these individuals that they prefer males and their sexual behavior descriptions that included sexual contacts with adult females.

SEXUAL CONTACTS WITH VICTIMS

Most of the women reported only a few sexual contacts with their victims. It is not clear whether this represents an accurate recounting of the offenders' histories. It is possible that the women may have underestimated the number of contacts with their victims. The majority of the offenders began offending against all reported victims at about the same age. There were exceptions to this, however. Notably, two individuals had an offense in childhood, and later offended as adults. In the majority of cases, the offenders were related to their victims. In no case was a victim described as a stranger, although a small number of participants simply listed the victim as a child, rather than specifying the relationship.

In the majority of victim/offender pairings, the women indicated that the sexual contact with their victims had been abusive or bad, and for just over half of the offender/victim pairings, they viewed it as unwanted on the part of their victims. It is possible that these responses represented a lack of denial which may contribute to their desire for treatment.

The majority of cases that were not viewed as abusive or bad involved young adolescent participants. Several authors have commented upon the societal expectations that adolescents enjoy sexual initiation with an older female as a factor which has served to conceal abuse against this age group. Nonetheless, given that previous research has indicated that some adolescents do not experience such sexual contact as abusive, and given that some of the adult females in the present study did not believe that such experiences were abusive, the possibility must remain open that in some cases, the dynamics of sexual exchange between an adolescent and an older female are not experienced as abusive by the younger participant. Such cases would appear among the more difficult for which to formulate legal and treatment recommendations. On one hand, sexually abusive incidents where the victim has experienced trauma have been documented, and require therapeutic and legal intervention. However, needlessly involving the court or therapists in the early sexual experiences of adolescents who have not been traumatized might be arguably unduly intrusive.

FEMALE OFFENDERS' SELF-REPORTS OF DETECTION

Most of the female offenders left blank the question concerning whether or not they had been questioned about any of their offenses by CPS or police. It is not clear why. They may have missed the question, which was uniquely positioned on the page, or they may have been threatened by the question, fearing that they would be questioned about their behaviors if they had not previously been. A large number of those who indicated that they had been questioned about their sexual behaviors with children were among the pool of known convicted child molesters. Among the rest of the sample, it was rare for the women who answered the question to indicate that they had been questioned by police, suggesting that child sexual molestation by a female offender may often go undetected.

TREATMENT CONSIDERATIONS FOR FEMALE SEX OFFENDERS

Several treatment considerations, as well as possible motivations for treatment on the part of the female child molester were suggested by this research. Most offenders described psychosocial histories that would suggest that they had experienced psychosocial trauma, that they may be motivated to address. Many believed that they had been abusive or had behaved badly towards the child or children with whom they had sexual contact, suggesting that pervasive denial in this area may not be a therapeutic problem. Many expressed a preference to be drug and alcohol free in a usual month, suggesting a possible motivation for therapy.

Consistent with what has been found in other studies, this research suggested several issues which may be of concern to female child molesters who seek therapy. Many had been in psychiatric hospitals and/or had received psychiatric medication. Details surrounding these events may be of use to the individual clinician treating the offender. Many of the offenders reported symptoms of dependency, and many met the criteria for a diagnosis of Dependent Personality Disorder. Many also reported a preference for the frequent use of drugs and alcohol.

The psychosocial histories of the offenders were frequently traumatic and unstable. Most offenders had histories of childhood sexual abuse. Many grew up in homes where frequent drug or alcohol use took place, many received frequent injuries from adults, and many witnessed the frequent injury of their mothers. Many had parents who had been married more than once.

Relationships with other adults were also likely to have been problematic. The offenders themselves tended to report that they were in bad love relationships at the time of their sexual contact with children. Many had sexual contacts with many males, and some with many females. Some had several marriages. For several, sexual identity confusion was suggested by the inconsistency of their report of their sexual preferences and their actual sexual behaviors.

Study Limitations

DATA COLLECTION SITES

Because female offenders are thought to be few in number in the population at large, women were solicited from populations thought to be at high risk. Because Condy (1985) found a relatively large number of female perpetrators in prison, several prisons were solicited to take part in this study. Because large numbers of female perpetrators have been noted to have drug and alcohol problems (Allen, 1991; Condy, 1985; McCarty, 1986), and because large numbers of female perpetrators have been noted to have sexual abuse histories themselves (Allen, 1991; Condy et al., 1987; Faller, 1988; Fehrenbach & Monastersky, 1988; Johnson, 1989; Knopp & Lackey, 1987; Larson & Maison, 1987; Mathews et al., 1989; Mayer, 1992; McCarty, 1986; Paiser, 1992; Rowan et al., 1990; Wolfe, 1985), individuals were also solicited in drug and alcohol treatment facilities, and in sexual abuse treatment facilities.

The latter two data sources might have been expected to artificially inflate the number of women reporting drug and alcohol abuse and sexual abuse problems.

However, the results do not appear to have been largely influenced by this factor. While she, in fact, reported that she preferred the daily use of drugs or alcohol, only one female offender in the sample (2% of the offenders) was drawn from a drug and alcohol program. Five (12%) of the women were drawn from sexual abuse treatment groups for sexual abuse survivors, treatment groups for parents of molested children, and sex offender treatment groups; three of these women (60%) had sexual abuse histories while two did not; this rate is actually slightly lower than was the case for the population of offenders at large (74%).

The facilities taking part in this study were themselves not a random sampling of the population of similar facilities at large. Data collection sites were solicited with several factors in mind: convenience for data collection, size of the facility, likelihood that the facility would be interested in participating on the basis of their location or their previously conducted research, or their acquaintance with the researcher. The data collection sites that agreed to take part in this study appeared as a rule to have directors and staff who were more interested in research in general, and more familiar with the literature related to child sexual abuse.

Wherever possible, facilities that declined to participate were questioned about their reasons. The most common reason given was that there were not sufficient staff members or resources available to provide for the study. A few short-term drug and alcohol treatment facilities declined on the basis that a survey of a sensitive nature would jeopardize the tenuous sobriety of their clients. (Such an effect was not noted, however, by those drug and alcohol treatment centers that participated in this study). A similar concern regarding jeopardy to the stability of clients was also expressed at an inpatient psychiatric hospital that specialized in the treatment of severely disturbed individuals with a history of sexual abuse. Other reasons for refusal were more idiosyncratic. One center director expressed concerns about the lengthy approval process at his facility and a conviction that since the drug and alcohol population was of upper socioeconomic status, there would be no female offenders. One treatment director felt that it would "dilute" therapy at her inpatient treatment facility. One prison official also expressed a conviction that there were no female sex offenders in her facility. One expressed concerns that the clients would not be able to read. One Midwestern state prison system declined to participate simply indicating that a study on female sex offenders was not "appropriate."

SELF-REPORT DATA

This study relied upon self-report data, which is limited by the participants' ability and willingness to divulge information. While the range varied substantially, subjects in this study were reporting on offenses that were estimated to have happened an average of 10 years ago. The length of time that had passed may have affected the accuracy of the subjects' recollections.

With the population studied, other factors may have limited this self-report data. The defenses of repression, minimization and denial on the part of the sexual abuse victims or child molesters may also have reduced the accuracy of the subjects' recollection. Larson and Maison (1987) have also observed a "fluid reality" among female sex offenders, with offenders' descriptions of their lives described as unclear and frequently changing. These factors may have reduced the accuracy with which subjects were able to describe their offenses or psychosocial histories. Additionally, a lack of trust is thought to have played a strong role in reducing the number of female perpetrators who were willing to participate in this study. Difficulty with trust was likely to have been a particular concern in the prison population, where the women had previously experienced the negative consequence of incarceration when their deviant behaviors were discovered by others.

Difficulties with trust or memory, as well as defense mechanisms, may have served to reduce the amount of childhood trauma that was reported by the offenders. It is unknown whether there might also exist factors which could cause a female child molester to overreport such trauma. For example, it is unknown if a history of trauma might be viewed by female offenders as justification for sexual offenses, and if so, whether this might influence the reporting of their psychosocial histories.

The women who revealed themselves as having had sexual contact with children on this written questionnaire are not likely to be a random sampling of the female child molesters at large. They are likely to be comparatively more trusting, better readers, and less likely to be currently utilizing the defenses of denial, minimization or repression when contrasted with other female child molesters. They may also have better memories. It is possible that they are also better educated and more intelligent than those offenders who chose not to participate in the written survey. They may also be more interested in having others benefit from their participation in research.

It is thought that the number of female child molesters identified in this study is a gross underestimate of the actual number of offenders in the populations surveyed. In one prison for example, ten women who were convicted child molesters agreed to take part in this study. Their surveys were combined with those of additional women in the same prison who were in a group for adult survivors of sexual molestation. In spite of this, a total of only three returned surveys included descriptions of sexual offenses against children. Similarly, in two prisons, data were collected only from convicted female child molesters. In one such prison nine convicted offenders agreed to complete the survey, however, only five of these provided information concerning their offenses, and one of these five maintained that she had been raped by her victim. In another prison, data were collected from four convicted child molesters, and none provided data concerning her sex offenses. It is possible that having had the negative experience of being imprisoned when their offenses were previously revealed, convicted women were more reticent than was the general population of female child molesters to provide information concerning their offenses. Nonetheless, the very low rate at which known offenders were willing to supply information concerning their offenses, even without any threat of prosecution, strongly suggests that nonconvicted offenders may also have been likely to underreport their offenses.

Women who supplied information concerning their psychosocial histories, but who did not describe sexual offenses against children were used as a matched control group for several psychosocial history variable comparisons. Given the demonstrated reluctance of the known child molesters to report their offenses, it is possible that this matched control group contained women who were actually unacknowledged child molesters. To some extent, this may have influenced those statistics in which a matched control group of female offenders and nonoffenders was used. This would have the effect of minimizing any differences in psychosocial history variables between the known offenders, and the supposed nonoffenders.

The control group used for comparing psychosocial history variables was chosen from the same types of facilities from which the female offenders were selected. This was to reduce the effects of differences related to idiosyncrasies of the specific populations. The control group selected allowed for the fact that among the populations surveyed (prisoners, substance abusers, and individuals in treatment for concerns related to sexual abuse) there might be greater amounts of unusual self-report material not specific to child molesters. It prevented the self-report material specific to the populations surveyed from being attributed to the population of female sex offenders. However, a limitation of this approach was that it did not allow for comparisons of offenders with a more "normal" control group. Thus, while it was not found that there were significant differences between the offenders and their control group in the areas of family pathology, severity of sexual abuse history, number of male sex partners or income, it remains for future research to determine whether offenders differ from members of the population at large in these areas. The information provided by the offenders would suggest that this is a distinct possibility.

SURVEY INSTRUMENT

There are presently no known surveys or inventories for the population of female child molesters for which reliability and validity data are available. Literature on female sex offenders suggests that they are prone to dissociation, have difficulties with trust, and experience reality in a fluid manner. As such, it is suspected that the reliability of test and survey instruments used in their research would be unique to this population, and less than would generally be obtained for a given instrument on a more stable population. Given the small number of female sex offenders who have availed themselves to research, and given their reluctance to identify themselves, it will likely be some time before reliability data become available for survey instruments for this population. The instrument used in the present study similarly lacks such reliability data, and the results must be interpreted with this in mind. The responses to the questions on this survey should be viewed as a sample of the results that female child molesters are capable of producing, rather than the only results that they might produce over time.

In a similar fashion, the results of this study must be interpreted with the fact in mind that the survey used has not been validated. In particular, several of the questions regarding psychosocial history were screening questions, used primarily for comparison purposes, and were not expected to definitively identify the problems for which they screened. For example, the questions which screened for childhood physical abuse, family alcoholism or drug abuse, maternal abuse, and the subject's own substance abuse fall into this category.

The measure used for assessing dependency was similarly not validated before use. While it is based upon standard criteria for assessing Dependent Personality Disorder described in the *DSM-III-R*, it involved the use of a Likert scale for assessing these criteria which has not previously been used. The large number of women who appeared to have met criteria for the disorder, however, points to their formal evaluation for this disorder as an area for further research.

In a similar fashion, the means of gathering information on the childhood sexual victimization, and the sexual offenses committed by female offenders was not validated. Comments of staff members who assisted with this study suggested that some of the subjects had difficulty understanding the grids used in gathering information in these areas, and no female perpetrator with less than a ninth-grade education completed this survey. A contact person at one prison facility commented upon the learning disabilities of the female sex offenders as one difficulty which interfered with their completion of the survey. These factors may have reduced the potential validity of the survey.

It is possible that not all potential subjects were able to read the survey. Some of the female sex offenders who were excluded from the survey because of illiteracy or difficulties reading may have had a lower IQ than was the case for the sample obtained. In addition, some may have had greater psychosocial stress in childhood that interfered with their capacity to concentrate and to learn in school. Others may have had additional problems such as mental illness, personality disorders, or drug and alcohol problems which interfered with their ability to learn. It is thought that many potential subjects excluded from this survey because of illiteracy or reading difficulty may have been more disturbed, in general, than those for whom data were obtained.

Likewise, some female child molesters who were excluded from this survey because of difficulties in reading the survey may have had a more extensive history of offending against children. Some of the problems and coping deficits that contributed to reading difficulties, such as lower IQ, learning disabilities, poor motivation, mental health difficulties and psychosocial stress, may also have been factors which reduced the ability of women who experienced sexual urges towards children to develop coping strategies alternative to acting upon such urges.

OPERATIONAL DEFINITIONS

Operational definitions chosen for this study, by necessity, limited the results. Sexual abuse takes many forms. The sexual abuse (both experienced and perpetrated) documented in this survey, while extensive, was not all-inclusive. Other forms of sexual abuse important to the understanding of the female child molester may not have been uncovered by this study.

For the purposes of this study, sexual abuse was limited to sexual activity which involved actual physical contact and which was more overtly sexual than hugging and kissing. The study did not examine forms of sexual abuse that involved non-contact activities, such as harassment, being made to view pornography, exhibition or voyeurism, attempted but not completed sexual acts, and so on. Further, the forced choice options for describing sexual contact in this study, while allowing for the description of a wide range of sexual contacts, were not all-inclusive and may not have captured all forms of sexual contact which took place. One woman, for example, who was not a female perpetrator of sexual abuse, wrote to the examiner that touching a man's chest is a sexual experience which should have been included in the list of possible sexual experiences. She also wrote that she had been sexually abused as a child, but that the abuse had consisted of an adult male rubbing his penis against her buttocks, which was not included as a form of abuse on the questionnaire. Some perpetrators spontaneously described in the margin other forms of sexual contact that they had had with children, including simulated intercourse with a dildo, and stimulation of their own genitals with parts of the child's body other than with his or her mouth or hands. Where these types of sexual contact were noted by perpetrators, they were described in the results section. However, not all of those individuals who experienced such contacts are likely to have noted them.

The age criteria for defining child sexual abuse in this study were fairly inclusive, requiring a five-year age difference between the offender and victim and no minimum age difference for the perpetrator. These criteria allowed for the inclusion of cases that involved actual sexual contact, but which, because of the young age of participants or the minimal age differences between participants might not universally be viewed as abusive. These inclusive criteria intentionally included cases which might be viewed as "borderline," in terms of the certainty that the sexual contact that occurred was abusive. Given the limited research in the area of female child molesters, it was thought more appropriate to overinclude, rather than overexclude such cases. However, these criteria allowed for the inclusion of individuals who were adolescents or children at the time of their offenses, as well as individuals for whom the age differences between themselves and their victims were minimal, and such should be kept in mind when generalizing findings.

In addition to the age difference criterion, sexual abuse was included if it involved force. The women were asked to describe cases involving force where the victims (herself or her own victims) were under the age of 15, regardless of the age of the perpetrator. In cases that did not meet the age-difference criterion, a screening question was used to ensure that the "force" criterion had been understood. In descriptions of her own abuse, sexual contact was included as abuse if the offender (describing her experiences as a victim) answered "yes" in response the question, "was the sexual contact ever against your will?" In descriptions of sexual contacts between the subjects and children, sexual contact was included as abusive if subjects answered "no" to the question, "did the other person want the sexual contact with you?" This criterion to some extent left open the type of force used to gain the compliance of an unwilling victim. While in some cases physical force may have been used, in other cases the force may have involved other forms of coercion.

This study defined as victims only those individuals who were forced to have sexual contact, or who had sexual contact with an individual at least 5 years their senior, when they were 15 or younger at the time of the sexual contact. Many women however, spontaneously described sexual abuse that did not meet the criteria for this study. For example, one female perpetrator included the experience of having been raped several times when she was 17. Some women described incestuous experiences that did not meet age difference or force criteria, but which arguably could have been classified as abusive, given the violation of societally held dictates for sexual contact. Additionally, some women described sexual contacts that did not meet age difference or force criteria, but which were now believed to have been abusive or bad. Other forms of child sexual abuse than those operationally defined for the purposes of the study clearly exist, and are areas for continued research.

There is no universally accepted definition of child sexual abuse. The definitions of victims and of perpetrators of child sexual abuse used for this study are unique to this study and this must be kept in mind in generalizing the findings. The definitions used for this study included only cases involving actual sexual contact, and only victims who were 15 and younger. It did not use a minimum age for offenders, and set a minimal age difference criterion in defining offenders. It combined both an age difference criterion and a "force" criterion.

Directions for Future Research

Research on female child molesters is in its infancy. Further study of this population is necessary in order to facilitate the identification and treatment of this population and its victims.

This study found that most offenders had sexual abuse histories that were severe by any criteria. Yet, while no offender (with a history of sexual abuse) began sexually abusing victims at an age younger than that of her own first sexual victimization experience, no relationship could be demonstrated between the severity of the offenders' self-reported victimization experiences and the severity of their own victimizing behaviors. Further, the female sex offenders did not report sexual abuse experiences that were comparatively more severe than those of their matched control groups, who were largely female prisoners. Further research is necessary to explore the relationship between a sexual victimization history and a sexual abuse perpetration history among females.

A severe sexual abuse history appeared to be the norm among the control groups for this study, which were largely comprised of females who had engaged in other forms of antisocial behavior. The study of the relationship between sexual victimization and later antisocial behavior may prove useful to the understanding of female sex offenders. A severe sexual abuse history seems to not only precede sexual abuse perpetration, but other forms of acting out behavior as well.

Potentially, a history of sexual abuse may suggest several more specific risk factors for antisocial behavior. Resulting anger, lack of confidence in adult social and sexual situations, lack of ability to enforce sexual boundaries, lack of sense of self-worth, and so on may contribute to the development of a sexual abuse victim into a perpetrator of many sorts of antisocial behavior, including sexual abuse against children. A sexual victimization history may also suggest exposure to individuals who model behavior that is impulsive, interpersonally exploitive, and lacking in empathy. Further research into the relationship between sexual victimization and sexual offending is necessary. Previous research and results from this factor analysis suggest that the dynamics of females' sexual contact with children differ among females offenders.

Further research is also needed in order to identify factors other than sexual abuse which contribute to the likelihood that a female will become an offender, and the relationships that these antecedents have to later sex offenses. This study suggested that dependency in some way contributes to the development of a female into a sex offender. A history of family-of-origin pathology, a general lack of sexual boundaries, drug or alcohol abuse, and a history of psychiatric disturbances also appear to be risk factors that warrant further exploration. Further research is needed to explore the relationship that these variables have to childhood sexual abuse.

REFERENCES

References

Allen, C. (1991). Women and men who sexually abuse children: A comparative analysis. Orwell, VT: *The Safer Society Press.*

Apfelberg, B., Sugar, C., & Pfeffer, A. (1944). A psychiatric study of 250 sex offenders. *American Journal of Psychiatry, 100,* 762-770.

Banning, A. (1989). Mother-son incest: Confronting a prejudice. *Child Abuse and Neglect, 13,* 563-570.

Barry, M., & Johnson, A. (1958). The incest barrier. *Psychoanalytic Quarterly, 27,* 485-500.

Bender, L., & Blau, A. (1937). The reaction of children to sexual relations with adults. *American Journal of Orthopsychiatry, 7,* 500-518.

Benward, J., & Densen-Gerber, J. (1979). Incest as a causative factor in antisocial behavior: An exploratory study. *Contemporary Drug Problems, 4(3),* 303-339.

Browne, A., & Finkelhor, D. (1986). Impact of child sexual abuse: A review of the research. *Psychological Bulletin, 99*(1), 66-77.

Butler, S. (1978). *Conspiracy of silence: The trauma of incest.* Volcano, CA: Volcano Press.

Cameron, P., Coburn, W., Larson, H., Proctor, K., Forde, N., & Cameron, K. (1986). *Child molestation and homosexuality.* Psychological Reports, 58, 327-337.

Catanzarite, V., & Combs, S. (1980). Mother-son incest. *JAMA, 243*(18), 1807-1808.

Chasnoff, I., Burns, W., Schnoll, S., Burns, K., Chissum, G., & Kyle-Spore, L. (1986). Maternal-neonatal incest. *American Journal of Orthopsychiatry, 56*(4), 577-580.

Chideckel, M. (1935). *Female sex perversions: The sexually aberrated woman as she is.* New York: Eugenics.

Condy, S. (1985). *Parameters of heterosexual molestation of boys.* Unpublished doctoral dissertation, California School of Professional Psychology — Fresno, Fresno, CA.

Condy, S., Templer, D., Brown, R., & Veaco, L. (1987). Parameters of sexual contact of boys with women. *Archives of Sexual Behavior, 16*(5), 379-394.

Conte, J., & Schuerman, J. (1987). Factors associated with an increased impact of child sexual abuse. *Child Abuse and Neglect, 11*, 201-211.

Courtois, C. (1979). The incest experience and its aftermath. *Victimology: An International Journal, 4*, 337-347.

Cupoli, J., & Sewell, P. (1988). One thousand fifty-nine children with a chief complaint of sexual abuse. *Child Abuse and Neglect, 12*, 151-162.

De Jong, A., Hervada, A., & Emmett, G. (1983). Epidemiological variations in childhood sexual abuse. *Child Abuse and Neglect, 7*, 155-162.

De Francis, V. (1969). *Protecting the victim of sex crimes committed by adults.* Denver: American Humane Association.

Dolan, B. (1991, October 7). My own story. *Time Magazine*, p. 47.

Evert. K., & Bijkerk, I. (1987). *When you're ready: A woman's healing from childhood physical and sexual abuse by her mother.* Walnut Creek, CA: Launch Press.

Faller, K. (1987). Women who sexually abuse children. *Violence and Victims, 2*(4), 263-276.

Faller, K. (1988). The spectrum of sexual abuse in daycare: An exploratory study. *Journal of Family Violence, 3*(4), 283-298.

Faller, K. (1989). Characteristics of a clinical sample of sexually abused children: How boy and girl victims differ. *Child Abuse and Neglect, 13*, 281-291.

Fehrenbach, P., & Monastersky. (1988). Characteristics of female adolescent sexual offenders. *American Journal of Orthopsychiatry, 58*(1), 148-151.

Feinauer, L. (1989). Comparison of long-term effects of child abuse by type of abuse and by relationship of the offender to the victim. *The American Journal of Family Therapy, 17*(1), 48-56.

Finkelhor, D. (1979). *Sexually victimized children.* New York: The Free Press.

Finkelhor, D. (1984). *Child sexual abuse: New theory and research.* New York: The Free Press.

Finkelhor, D. (1986). *A sourcebook on child sexual abuse.* Beverly Hills: Sage.

Finkelhor, D., Hotaling, G., Lewis, I., & Smith, C. (1990). Sexual abuse in a national survey of adult men and women: Prevalence, characteristics, and risk factors. *Child Abuse and Neglect, 14,* 19-28.

Forward, S., & Buck, C. (1978). *Betrayal of Innocence.* New York: Penguin Books.

Friedrich, W., Urquiza, A., & Beilke, R. (1986). Behavior problems in sexually abused young children. *Journal of Pediatric Psychology, 11*(1), 47-57.

Fritz, G., Stoll, K., & Wagner, N. (1981, Spring). A comparison of males and females who were sexually molested as children. *Journal of Sex and Marital Therapy, 7*(1), 54-59.

Fromuth, M. (1983). The long term psychological impact of childhood sexual abuse. Unpublished doctoral dissertation, Auburn University, Auburn, Alabama.

Fromuth, M., & Burkhart, B. (1987). Childhood sexual victimization among college men: Definitional and methodological issues. *Violence and Victims, 2*(4), 241-253.

Gebhard, P., Gagnon, J., Pomeroy, W., & Christenson, C. (1965). *Sex offenders: An analysis of types.* New York: Harper & Row.

Gomes-Schwartz, B., Horowitz, J., & Cardeelli, A. (1990). *Child sexual abuse: The initial effects.* Newbury Park, CA: Sage.

Goodwin, J., & DiVasto, P. (1979). Mother-daughter incest. *Child Abuse and Neglect, 3,* 953-957.

Grayson, J. (1989, Summer). Female sex offenders. *Virginia Child Protection Newsletter,* pp. 5-7, 11-13.

Groth, N. (1979a). Men who rape: *The psychology of the offender.* New York: Plenum.

Groth, N. (1979b). Sexual trauma in the life histories of rapists and child molesters. *Victimology: An International Journal, 4*(1), 10-16.

Groth, N., & Burgess, A. (1980). Male rape: Offenders and victims. *American Journal of. Psychiatry, 137*(7), 806-810.

Groth, N., & Loredo, C. (1981). Juvenile sexual offenders: Guidelines for assessment. *International Journal of Offender Therapy and Comparative Criminolgy, 25*(1), 31-39.

Haugaard, J., & Emery, R. (1989). Methodological issues in child sexual abuse research. *Child Abuse and Neglect, 13,* 89-100.

Huck, S., Cormier, W., & Bounds, W. (1974). *Reading statistics and research.* New York: Harper & Row.

Hunt, P., & Baird, M. (1990). Children of sex rings. *Child Welfare, 69*(3), 195-207.

Hunter, M. (1990). *Abused boys: The neglected victims of sexual abuse.* Lexington, MA: Lexington Books.

Jackson, M. (1986, September 3). PHASE extends to female sex abusers. *Ramsey County Review,* p. 1.

Johnson, R., & Shrier D., (1987) Past sexual victimization by females of male patients in an adolescent medicine clinic population. *American Journal of Psychiatry, 144*(5), 650-652.

Johnson, T. (1989). Female child perpetrators: Children who molest other children. *Child Abuse and Neglect, 13*(4), 571-585.

Justice, B., & Justice, R., (1979). *The broken taboo: Sex in the family.* New York: Human Sciences Press.

Kaufman, A., Divasto, P., Jackson, R., Voorhees, D., & Christy, J. (1980). Male rape victims: Noninstitutionalized assault. *American Journal of Psychiatry, 137*(2), 221-223.

Kendall-Tackett, K. & Simon (1987). Perpetrators and their acts: Data from 365 adults molested as children. *Child Abuse and Neglect, 11,* 237-245.

Kercher, G., & McShane, M. (1985). Characterizing child sexual abuse on the basis of a multi-agency sample. *Victimology: An International Journal, 9*(3-4), 364-382.

Kinsey, A., Pomeroy, W., & Martin, C. (1948). *Sexual behavior in the human male.* Philadelphia: W. B. Saunders.

Knopp, F., & Lackey, L. (1987). *Female sexual abusers: A summary of data from 44 treatment providers.* Orwell, VT: Safer Society Press.

Korbin, J. (1986). Childhood histories of women imprisoned for fatal child maltreatment. *Child Abuse and Neglect, 10,* 331-338.

Krug, R. (1989). Adult male report of childhood sexual abuse by mothers: Case descriptions, motivations and long-term consequences. *Child Abuse and Neglect, 13,* 111-119.

Landis, J. (1956). Experiences of 500 children with adult sexual deviation. *Psychiatric Quarterly Supplement, 30,* 91-109.

Langmade, C. (1983). *The impact of pre- and postpubertal onset of incest experiences in adult women as measured by sex anxiety, sex guilt, sexual satisfaction and sexual behavior.* Unpublished Doctoral Dissertation, Rosemead School of Psychology, Biola University, La Mirada, CA.

Larson, N., & Maison, S. (1987). *Psychosexual treatment program for female sex offenders: Minnesota Correctional Facility-Shakopee.* St Paul, MN: Meta Resources.

Lidz, R., & Lidz, T. (1969). Homosexual tendencies in mothers of schizophrenic women. *The Journal of Nervous and Mental Disease, 149(2),* 229-235.

Lukianowicz, N. (1972). Other types of incest. *British Journal of Psychiatry, 120,* 308-313.

Maltz, W., & Holman, B. (1987). *Incest and sexuality: A guide to understanding and healing.* Lexington, MA: Lexington Books.

Margolis, M. (1977). A preliminary report of a case of consummated mother-son incest. *Annual Psychoanal, 5,* 267-293.

Margolis, M. (1984). A case of mother-adolescent son incest: A follow-up study. *Psychoanalytic Quarterly, 53,* 355-385.

Marvasti, J. (1986). Incestuous mothers. *American Journal of Forensic Psychiatry,* 7(4), 63-69.

Masters, R. (1963). *Patterns of incest.* New York: Julian Press.

Mathews, R., Matthews, J., & Speltz, K. (1989). *Female sexual offenders: An exploratory study.* Orwell, VT: Safer Society Press.

Mayer, A. (1983). *Incest: A treatment manual for therapy with victims, spouses and offenders.* Holmes Beach, FL: Learning Publications.

Mayer, A. (1992). *Women sex offenders: Treatment and dynamics.* Holmes Beach, FL: Learning Publications.

McCarty, L. (1986). Mother-child incest: Characteristics of the offender. *Child Welfare, 65(5),* 447-458.

Meiselman, K. (1978). *Incest: A psychological study of causes and effects with treatment recommendations.* San Francisco: Jossey- Bass.

Nasjleti, M. (1980). Suffering in silence: The male incest victim. *Child Welfare,* 59(5), 269-275.

Nielsen, T. (1983, November). Sexual abuse of boys: Current perspectives. *The Personnel and Guidance Journal,* p. 139-142.

O'Connor, A. (1987). Female sex offenders. *British Journal of Psychiatry, 150,* 615-620.

Paiser, P. (1992). *Relational experiences of women survivors of female-perpetrated childhood sexual abuse.* Unpublished doctoral dissertation. Massachusetts School of Professional Psychology, Boston, MA.

Petrovich, M., & Templer, D. (1984). *Heterosexual molestation of children who later become rapists.* Psychological Reports, 54(3), 810.

Pierce, L., & Pierce, R. (1987). *Incestuous victimization by juvenile sex offenders. Journal of Family Violence, 2*(4), 351-364.

Plummer, K. (1981). Pedophilia: Constructing a sociological baseline. In Cook, M., & Howells (Eds.), *Adult sexual interest in children* (pp. 225-250). New York: Academic Press.

Raphling, D., Carpenter, B., & Davis, A. (1967). Incest: A genealogical study. *Archives of General Psychiatry, 16,* 505-511.

Ramsey-Klawsnik, H. (1990, April). *Sexual abuse by female perpetrators: Impact on children.* Paper presented at the 1990 National Symposium on Child Victimization, "Keepers of the children," Atlanta, GA.

Reinhart, M. (1987). Sexually abused boys. *Child Abuse and Neglect, 11,* 229-235.

Renvoize, J. (1982). *Incest: A family pattern.* London: Routledge & Kegan Paul.

Risin, L., & Koss, M. (1987). The sexual abuse of boys: Prevalence and descriptive characteristics of childhood victimizations. *Journal of Interpersonal Violence, 2*(3), 309-323.

Rist, K. (1979). Incest: Theoretical and clinical views. *American Journal of Orthopsychiatry, 49*(4), 680-691.

Rosencrans, B. (1993, June 25-26). Unpublished comments. National Institute of Mental Health Working Conference on Female Sex Offenders.

Rowan, E., Rowan, J., & Langelier, P. (1990). Women who molest children. *Bulletin of the American Academy of Psychiatry and the Law, 18*(1), 79-83.

Russell, D. (1983). The incidence and prevalence of intrafamilial and extrafamilial sexual abuse of female children. *Child Abuse and Neglect. 7*, 133-146.

Russell, D. (1986). *The secret trauma: Incest in the lives of girls and women.* New York: Basic Books.

Sarrel, P., & Masters, W. (1982). Sexual molestation of men by women. *Archives of Sexual Behavior, 11*(2), 117-131.

Scavo, R. (1989). Female adolescent offenders: A neglected treatment group. *Social Casework, 70*(2), 114-117.

Schultz, L., & Jones, P. (1983). Sexual abuse of children: Issues for social service and health professionals. *Child Welfare, 62*(2), 99-108.

Sheldon, V., & Sheldon, R. (1989). Sexual abuse of males by females: The problem, treatment modality, and case example. *Family Therapy, 16*(3), 249-258.

Shengold, L. (1980). Some reflections on a case of mother/adolescent son incest. *International Journal of Psychoanalysis, 61*, 461-476.

Simari, C., & Baskin, D. (1982). Incestuous experiences within homosexual populations: A preliminary study. *Archives of Sexual Behavior, 11*(4), 329-344.

Shrier, D., & Johnson, R. (1988). Sexual victimization of boys: An ongoing study of an adolescent medicine clinic population. *Journal of the National Medical Association, 80*(11), 1189-1193.

Smith, H., & Israel, E. (1987). Sibling incest: A study of the dynamics of 25 cases. *Child Abuse and Neglect, 11*, 101-108.

Spencer, M., & Dunklee, P. (1986). Sexual abuse of boys. *Pediatrics, 78*(1), 133-138.

Sugar, M. (1983). Sexual abuse of children and adolescents. *Adolescent Psychiatry, 11*, 199-211.

Swink, K. (1989, March). *Therapeutic issues for women survivors of maternal incest.* Presented at the Association for Women in Psychology, National Conference, Newport, Rhode Island.

Travin, S., Cullen, K., & Protter, B. (1990). Female sex offenders: Severe victims and victimizers. *Journal of Forensic Sciences, 35*(1), 140-150.

Tsai, M., Feldman-Summers, S., & Edgar, M. (1979). Childhood molestation: Variables related to differential impact of psychosexual functioning in adult women. *Journal of Abnormal Psychology, 88*, 407-417.

Vanderbilt, H. (1992, February). Incest: A chilling report. *Lear's,* pp. 49-77.

Wahl, C. (1960). The psychodynamics of consummated maternal incest: A report of two cases. *Archives of General Psychiatry, 3,* 188-193.

Weinberg, S. (1955). *Incest behavior.* Secaucus, NJ: Citadel Press.

Williams, L., & Farrell, R. (1990). Legal response to child sexual abuse in day-care. Criminal *Justice and Behavior, 17*(3), 284-302.

Wolfe, F. (1985, March). *Twelve female sexual offenders.* Paper presented at "Next steps in research on the assessment and treatment of sexually aggressive persons (Paraphiliacs)", St Louis, MO.

Wulffen, E. (1934). *Woman as sexual criminal.* New York: American Ethnological Press.

Yorukoglu, A., & Kemph, J. (1966). Children not severely damaged by incest with a parent. *Journal of the American Academy of Child Psychiatry, 5*(1), 111-125.

APPENDICES

Appendix A

Ages of Children and Female Perpetrators Described in Previous Literature and Gender of Children*

	ALLEN (1991)	CONDY (1987)	CONDY (1987)	CONDY (1987)	CONDY (1987)	FALLER (1987)
N	65	57	97	3	13	40
SAMPLE	Self-report of sex offenders identified through CPS and attorney general's office records, a sex offender's treatment program and a prison	College men	Incarcerated males	College females reporting contact with younger males	Imprisoned females reporting contact with younger males	Female perpetrators in treatment
AVERAGE AGE OF OLDER FEMALE	33	23	25	26	19	26
RANGE	18–62	16–46	16–61	19–39	18–32	13–47
AVERAGE AGE OF CHILD		13	13	15	14	6 (males) 6 (females)
RANGE	6–15	6–15	3–15	14–15	13–15	
GENDER OF CHILD	11 females 25 males	Males	Males	Males	Males	37% males 64% females

*Age to nearest whole number

	FEHRENBACH & MONASTERSKY (1988)	JOHNSON (1989)	KERCHER & McSHANE (1989)	KNOPP & LACKEY (1987)	LARSON & MAISON (1987)
N	28	13	35	476	16
SAMPLE	Female adolescent sex offenders in treatment	Female child offenders in treatment	Female sex offenders identified through CPS and DA files	Female perpetrators as described by treatment providers	14 females imprisoned for sexual offenses + 1 un-charged offender +1 woman who experienced fantasies only
AVERAGE AGE OF OLDER FEMALE	14	7 (at 1st offense)			26
RANGE	10–18	4–9 (at 1st offense)			22–54
AVERAGE AGE OF CHILD	5 (excludes 1 adult victim)	5			10 (males) 12 (females)
RANGE	(sd=2)	1–11			2–16
GENDER OF CHILD	36% males 57% females 7% both	Both	9 males (26%) 26 females (74%)	317 females 329 males	Both

Appendix A

	MAYER (1992)	McCARTY (1986)	O'CONNOR (1987)	PAISER (1992)	PETROVICH & TEMPLER (1984)
N	8	21	25	10	49
SAMPLE	Sample of adolescent females in therapy for sexual abuse, reporting experiences in which they victimized children	Mother offenders in treatment	Convicted British female sex offenders against children in childhood by women	Individuals responding to a request for interviews with women molested	Incarcerated rapists reporting contact with older females
AVERAGE AGE OF OLDER FEMALE	12				27 (sd=10)
RANGE	11–14				16–54
AVERAGE AGE OF CHILD	6	10 (males) 6 (females)		(Estimated age at onset of abuse) 6 cases < 4 years 3 cases between 5 and 9 years 1 case unsure	11 (sd=5) (24% below age 12)
RANGE	6 months–9 years	4–17 (males) 2–15 (females)			4–16
GENDER OF CHILD	5 males 7 females	8 males 11 females 2 both	9 males 11 females 1 case both	Females	Males

289

	RAMSEY-KLAWSNIK (1990)	ROWAN, ROWAN & LANGLIER (1990)	SHRIER & JOHNSON (1988)	SIMARI & BASKIN (1982)	WOLFE (1985)
N	47	9	11	4	11
SAMPLE	Children referred for evaluation of complaints of sexual abuse, found to have been sexually abused by a female	Sex offenders identified during evaluations done for the judicial system and social services agencies	Male medical patients	Lesbians reporting incest	Female sex offenders against children, referred for assessment of sexual deviance
AVERAGE AGE OF OLDER FEMALE		33	26		31
RANGE		20–65	16–36		23–37
AVERAGE AGE OF CHILD	5 years, 8 months	7 (males) 7 (females)	12	8	12 (males) 10 (females)
RANGE	11 months–12 years	2–10 (males) 5–13 (females)	5–17	5–10	2–16 (males) 7–13 (females)
GENDER OF CHILD	27 males (23% of all cases of males having been abused) 16 females (35% of all cases of females having been sexually abused)	6 males 7 females	Males	Females	3 cases, 8 total females 6 cases, 8 total males 2 cases both

Appendix B

Ages of Children and Female Perpetrators Described in Previous Literature and Gender of Children*

	ALLEN (1991)	CONDY (1987)	CONDY (1987)	CONDY (1987)	CONDY (1987)
SAMPLE	65 Female sex offenders, 34% of whom admitted to sexual activities	57 college men reporting contact with older female	97 prison men reporting contact with older female	3 college females reporting contact with younger males	13 prison females reporting contact with younger males
INTERCOURSE	30% (vaginal or anal)	68%	82%	100%	85%
ORAL SEX		53%	62%	0%	85%
FONDLING		84%	81%	67%	100%
FORCE?		14%	11%	0%	15%
OTHER	42% touching, fondling, or oral sex 28% exhibitionism or voyeurism (of penetration)				
MALE CO-OFFENDER?					

* Percentages to the nearest whole number

291

	FALLER (1987)	FEHRENBACH & MONASTERSKY (1988)	JOHNSON (1989)	KERCHER & McSHANE (1985)
SAMPLE	40 female perpetrators in treatment	28 female adolescent sex offenders in treatment	13 female child sex offenders in treatment	35 female sex offenders identified through CPS and DA files
INTERCOURSE	20% of perpetrators, 14% of victims		1 case	6% (heterosexual penetration)
ORAL SEX	28 % of perpetrators, 32% of victims		12 cases	44% of cases involving a female perpetrator and a boy, 8% of cases involving a female perpetrator and a girl
FONDLING	38% of perpetrators, 38% of victims		13 cases	21%
FORCE?			38%	
OTHER	Digital intercourse – 25% perpetrators, 25 % victims	Rape (oral, anal, vaginal intercourse, or penetration with a finger or foreign object) – 54%	Vaginal penetration with finger – 6 cases	Make female give sexual performance – 9%
	Group sex – 55% perpetrators, 44% victims	Indecent liberties (sexual touching short of penetration) – 46%	Vaginal penetration with an object – 6 cases	Prostitute a female – 19%
	Allowing others to use victim – 8% perpetrators, 16% victims		Anal penetration with a finger – 8 cases	Homosexual penetration – 20%
	Photos – 13% perpetrators, 10% victims		Simulating intercourse – 11 cases	Distribute erotic material –
	Making kids engage in sexual activity – 15% perpetrators, 14% victims		Genital contact with no penetration – 13 cases	
	Misc. – 33% perpetrators, 27% victims		French kissing – 1 case	
MALE CO-OFFENDER?	24 cases, others possible			

292

	KISIN & ROSS (1987)	KNOPP & LACKEY (1987)	LARSON & MAISON (1987)	MAYER (1992)	McCARTY (1986)
SAMPLE	101 college males reporting sexual abuse by a female in childhood	911 female offenders as described by treatment providers	14 convicted female sex offenders in prison therapy group and 1 unconvicted sex offender	8 adolescent victims in therapy for sexual abuse, recounting experiences of themselves victimizing children	26 mother sex offenders in treatment
INTERCOURSE	51% (penetration)			1 – perpetrator	
ORAL SEX				7 – perpetrators	
FONDLING	39%				
FORCE?	10% force or threats of physical harm				
OTHER	51% exhibition	Child molestation – 569 cases Rape – 77 cases		1 digital vaginal penetration and vaginal penetration with an object 1 anal penetration with an object	
MALE CO-OFFENDER?	9%	15% of 646 hands-on offenses had co-perpetrators 83% co-offenders were male / 17% female	6 cases – husbands 1 case – husband and adult children 1 case – married lover 1 case – pimp 2 cases – gang rapists		9 co-offenders 12 independent offenders 5 accomplices

	PAISER (1992)	PETROVICH & TEMPLER (1984)	RAMSEY-KLAWSNIK (1990)
SAMPLE	10 female subjects reporting sexual abuse in childhood by a female	49 incarcerated rapists	45 female offender-victim combinations involving 32 female offenders and 43 child victims, reported by children referred for evaluation of sexual abuse and judged to have been abused
ORAL SEX	3 – victims	73 cases Fellatio and cunnilingus + intercourse – 34 cases Cunnilingus + intercourse – 1 case Fellatio + intercourse – 3 cases Fellatio and cunnilingus – 2 cases Fellatio – 1 case Cunnilingus – 5 cases	29% 60%
FONDLING	6 – victims	Female to male – 4 cases Mutual - 1 case	
FORCE?			80% overpowering 58% threats 75% additional physical abuse
OTHER	5 – voyeurism 2 – exhibitionism 1 – "seduction" 4 – medical / cleaning rituals 3 – penetration 2 – enemas 2 – sexual talk 2 – forced to witness sex		87% sexualized kissing or fondling 62% child forced to kiss, touch, or stimulate offender 51% anal or vaginal digital penetration 27% rape with objects 56% sadistic sexual activity 16% child pornography 11% made child have sex with other children 11% ritualized or cult activity
MALE CO-OFFENDER?			34% of offenders abused with others 19% of offenders undetermined

	REINHART (1987)	RUSSELL (1984)	SHRIER & JOHNSON (1988)	WOLFE (1985)
SAMPLE	8 male children seen in a medical clinic for suspected abuse and 8 age and race matched females	25 female offenders identified through randomly dialed female victims	11 male medical patients	11 female perpetrators being assessed for sexual deviance
INTERCOURSE				5 cases
ORAL SEX				Cunnilingus – 2 cases, 2 victims
FONDLING				(Indecent liberties) 1 case, 2 victims
FORCE?			1 case in 11	2 cases, 3 victims
OTHER		Very serious (oral, anal. vaginal sex) – 2 cases Serious (fondling, digital penetration, simulated intercourse) – 18 cases Least serious – 5 cases		Rape – 1 case, 2 victims Menage à trois – 2 cases, 3 victims
MALE CO-OFFENDER?	Half of abusers of boys had male co-offender, 3 of 4 abusers of females had a co-offender			Half 1 case male coerced 5 cases male accompanied

Appendix C

Relationships of Female Offenders to Victims as Described in Previous Literature*

SUBJECTS	ALLEN (1991) — 22 female sex offenders' self-report of relationship between self and 11 female victims	ALLEN (1991) — 47 female sex offenders' self-report of the relationship to them of their own 7 female sex offenders in childhood	ALLEN (1991) — 22 female sex offenders' self-report of relationship between self and 25 male victims
MOTHER	6 cases, 2 cases adoptive mother	3 cases	13 cases / Also, 1 foster mother
AUNT		1 case	1 case
COUSIN	1 case		1 case
SISTER	2 cases		1 case
GRANDMOTHER			
FRIEND/ACQUAINTANCE			3 cases boyfriend
NEIGHBOR		1 case	1 case
TEACHER			
BABY-SITTER			
STRANGER			
OTHER		1 case step-niece / 1 case teacher's wife	1 case girlfriend of victim's brother / 3 cases friend of brother

* Percentages to nearest whole number

	ALLEN (1991)	CAMERON ET AL. (1986)	CAMERON ET AL. (1986)
SUBJECTS	27 male sex offenders' (as victims) self-report of relationship between self and 30 female offenders in childhood	2734 randomly selected women reporting sexual contact with 15 female caretakers	1606 randomly selected men reporting sexual contact with 123 female caretakers
MOTHER	3 cases	2 cases stepmother	2 cases / Also, 4 cases stepmother
AUNT	1 case		
COUSIN	5 cases		
SISTER	6 cases / Also, 2 cases half-sister / Also, 1 case step-sister	3 cases	15 cases / Also, 6 cases step-sister
GRANDMOTHER			
FRIEND/ ACQUAINTANCE			Yes/scouts, 3 cases
NEIGHBOR	3 cases		
TEACHER		3 cases secondary teacher	2 cases elementary / 15 cases secondary / 1 case private teacher
BABY-SITTER	1 case		
STRANGER	6 cases		
OTHER	2 cases prostitute	6 cases other relatives / 1 case "for whom baby-sat"	60 cases other relatives / 15 cases "for whom baby-sat"

SUBJECTS	CONDY, TEMPLER, BROWN, & VEACO (1987) — 57 college men reporting sexual contact with 93 older females in childhood/adolescence	CONDY, TEMPLER, BROWN, & VEACO (1987) — 97 prison men reporting sexual contact with 190 older females in childhood/adolescence	CONDY, TEMPLER, BROWN, & VEACO (1987) — 3 college females reporting sexual contact with 3 adolescent or younger males	CONDY, TEMPLER, BROWN, & VEACO (1987) — 13 prison females reporting sexual contact with 19 adolescent or younger males	CUPOLI & SEWELL (1988) — 1059 children receiving medical evaluations for sexual abuse reporting 26 female offenders
MOTHER	3 cases	3 cases			5 cases
AUNT	6 cases	5 cases			
COUSIN	1 case	18 cases		1 case	
SISTER	1 case	4 cases			
GRANDMOTHER	2 cases	2 cases			1 case
FRIEND/ ACQUAINTANCE	29 cases	63 cases	2 cases	10 cases friend	18 cases (known to victim but not to family)
NEIGHBOR	21 cases	40 cases	1 case	6 cases	
TEACHER	4 cases	12 cases			
BABY-SITTER	14 cases	23 cases			
STRANGER	12 cases	20 cases		2 cases	2 cases
OTHER					

	FALLER (1987)	FEHRENBACH & MONASTERSKY (1988)	FROMOUTH (1983)
SUBJECTS	40 female perpetrators in treatment who sexually abused 63 children	28 female adolescent sex offenders in treatment	482 college students reporting child sexual abuse experiences with 7 female offenders
MOTHER	12 cases mother to some of victims *(2 cases step-mother as well as mother)* 22 cases mother to all victims		3 cases
AUNT	3 cases *(these also mother to some victims)*		
COUSIN			1 case
SISTER	1 case sister only 1 case sister as well as neighbor	3 cases sister to victim 1 case step-sister to victim 4 cases foster sister to victim	1 case
GRANDMOTHER	4 cases, total *(1 case grandmother only, 2 cases mothers as well as grandmothers, 1 case both mother and neighbor as well as grandmother)*		
FRIEND/ ACQUAINTANCE		16 cases acquaintance to victim	
NEIGHBOR	5 cases neighbor or family friend *(3 of these also mothers, 1 of these also both grandmother and mother, 1 case also sister)*		
TEACHER			
BABY-SITTER	1 case	Regardless of other relationships, 19 offenses (68%) took place while offender was babysitting	
STRANGER			1 case
OTHER	4 cases total *(2 cases girlfriend to father, 2 cases mothers as well as girlfriends to father)*	4 cases otherwise related to victim	

	JOHNSON (1987)	KENDALL-TACKETT & SIMON (1987)	KERCHER & MCSHANE (1985)	LARSON & MAISON (1987)
SUBJECTS	13 female child offenders (relationship to 1st victim only)	365 adults molested as children, seeking treatment, reporting 12 females as primary victimizers	35 female sex offenders identified through CPS and DA files	15 convicted female sex offenders in treatment for sex offenses; reported relationship to some or all of victims
MOTHER		9 cases	17 cases; 2 cases stepmother	5 cases mothers (1 also grandmother); 1 case stepmother (also listed as unrelated)
AUNT			1 case	2 cases
COUSIN	3 cases		1 case	
SISTER	7 cases		1 case sister; 1 case stepsister	
GRANDMOTHER				1 case (listed previously as grandmother)
FRIEND/ACQUAINTANCE		3 cases friend of family	15 cases	
NEIGHBOR				
TEACHER				
BABY-SITTER				
STRANGER			2 cases	
OTHER	3 cases outside family		5 cases relationship unknown	2 cases relationship unknown; 7 cases unrelated (1 of these was also a mother; 1 was also a stepmother)

	MAYER (1992)	PAISER (1992)	PETROVICH & TEMPLER (1984)	RAMSEY-KLAWSNIK (1990)
SUBJECTS	8 adolescent females in therapy for sexual abuse, reporting 12 victims	10 women responding to a request for subjects molested by a female during childhood reporting female offenders	49 incarcerated rapists reporting sexual contact with 73 older females	Relationship of 32 female offenders to 43 children determined to be their victims
MOTHERS		7 cases Also, 1 foster mother	2 cases Also, 1 foster mother	47% 2% foster mothers
AUNT		2 cases (live-in aunts)	5 cases	
COUSIN				
SISTER	3 foster sisters to 4 victims 3 half-sisters to 5 victims (1 also sister's girlfriend)		1 case	12% (biological, adopted, and foster siblings)
GRANDMOTHER		1 case	2 cases	12% grandmothers 2% great-grandmothers
FRIEND/ACQUAINTANCE	(1 case girlfriend's sister) (Also half-sister to victim)	2 cases family friend	22 cases friend of family	
NEIGHBOR	1 case		23 cases	
TEACHER		1 case	4 cases	
BABY-SITTER	1 case	1 case	7 cases	
STRANGER		2 cases male and female stranger perpetrators reported together	4 cases	
OTHER			1 case probation officer 1 case co-worker	25% surrogate caretakers (daycare, babysitters teachers, etc.)

	ROWAN, ROWAN & LANGELIER (1990)	RUSSELL (1983)	SIMARI & BASKIN (1983)	WOLFE (1985)
SUBJECTS	9 females undergoing sex offender evaluations for social service agency/ the judicial system	25 female perpetrators reported by random dial survey of 930 women	4 lesbian subjects reporting incest in childhood (relationship to subject reported)	11 female child molesters and 1 accomplice to rape assessed in a treatment program
MOTHER	7 cases mothers (1 of these was a mother to some of victims and the girlfriend to some victims' father) 1 case foster mother	1 case		5 cases mothers 2 cases step-mothers
AUNT			1 case	
COUSIN		2 cases	3 cases	
SISTER		3 cases		
GRANDMOTHER				
FRIEND/ ACQUAINTANCE		7 cases friend 2 cases friend of family 8 cases acquaintance		2 cases
NEIGHBOR				
TEACHER				
BABY-SITTER				
STRANGER				3 cases
OTHER	1 unspecified (1 mother also girlfriend to children's father)	2 cases other relatives		

Appendix D

Consent Form

Dear Participant:

Thank you for agreeing to take part in this study. This research is being done in order to develop a better understanding of the types of sexual experiences that young people have. This questionnaire will ask questions about you, and about sexual experiences that you may have had when you were young, and about any sexual experiences that you may have had with young people. If you are uncomfortable with this subject matter, you may refuse to take part in this survey. If you become uncomfortable with the subject matter, or for any reason decide that you do not wish to continue, you may also stop at any time. There is no penalty for choosing not to take part in this study.

Because of the sensitive nature of the information that you are providing, special steps have been taken to protect your privacy. A Confidentiality Certificate has been obtained for this study through the Department of Health and Human Services in order to ensure that any information that you provide on this questionnaire will be kept private. This Certificate is not an endorsement of this study by the Secretary. This Certificate protects you by ensuring that the people doing this research cannot be compelled to identify research subjects in any civil, criminal, administrative, legislative, or other proceedings whether Federal, State or local. In other words, the researchers cannot share your answers with anyone, and no one can force them to do so. This does not prevent you from sharing your answers with others, if you choose to do so, after you have taken part in the study. It also does not prevent you from requesting that your answers be given to a third party, if you choose. NO INFORMATION THAT YOU SUPPLY MAY BE GIVEN TO ANYONE BY THE RESEARCHERS WITHOUT YOUR WRITTEN CONSENT

Please do not put your name on the questionnaire, and do not talk to other people while you are completing this survey, or show other people your answers. This will further ensure your privacy. Please answer all of the questions as best as you can. If a question does not apply to you, you will find a place to indicate that it does not apply. It is important to our research that all questions be answered, and that they be answered honestly. You may take as much time as you need to finish the questionnaire. You may ask for help if you do not understand the meaning of a word, but again, please do not discuss your answers with others, or show other people your answers.

Please sign below to show that you understand these instructions, and that you have willingly agreed to complete this questionnaire. Do not turn in this consent form with your questionnaire; it is to be collected separately. Thank you again for your participation in this research. A brief summary of the results from this research will be mailed to the organization where you are completing this questionnaire, following this study's completion. Questions, or requests for copies of the results of this study may be sent to me care of the California School of Professional Psychology-Fresno, 1350 M St., Fresno, CA, 93721

Sincerely,
Julia Hislop, MA

I have read and understood the directions above, and agree to take part in this research.

_____ _____ *(Please sign and date.)*

Appendix E

Questionnaire

1. How old are you ?____

2. What was the last year of school that you finished? (check one)

    8th or below____ 9th____ 10th
    11th____ 12th____
    13 Some college____
    14 Associate's degree or 2 years of college____
    15 More than 2 years of college____
    16 Bachelor's degree____
    17 Some graduate school____
    18 Master's degree____
    19 More than a Master's degree____

3. Which of the following best describes your ethnicity?

    African American/Black____
    Asian____
    Euro-American/White____
    Hispanic____
    Native American/American Indian____
    Other (specify)_____

4. During the last year that you were employed, what did you make per hour at your highest paying job?____

5. How many times have you been married or lived with a lover?____

6. How many times has your mother been married or lived with a lover?____

7. How many times has your father been married or lived with a lover?____

8. When you were growing up, how many times in a usual month did you see someone who lived in your home drink enough or use enough drugs so that you saw a temporary change in his or her behavior?____

9. When you were growing up, how often in a usual month did an adult give you an injury that was as bad as a cut, a bruise, swollen skin, or worse?____

10. When you were growing up, how many times in a usual month, did you see your mother get an injury that was as bad as a cut, a bruise, swollen skin, or worse?____

11. Have you ever been placed on psychiatric medication? (Circle one)   Yes / No

12. Have you ever been treated in a psychiatric hospital? (Circle one)   Yes / No

13. For each of the following statements, circle the number that best describes how closely you agree

    1=strongly agree
    2=agree
    3=neutral
    4=disagree
    5=strongly disagree

A) I am unable to make everyday decisions without a lot of advice or reassurance from other people

    1   2   3   4   5

B) I allow others to make most of my important decisions, like where to live, or what job to take

    1   2   3   4   5

C) I agree with people, even when I believe they are wrong, because I'm afraid of being rejected

    1   2   3   4   5

D) I have difficulty starting projects or doing things on my own

    1   2   3   4   5

E) I volunteer to do things that are unpleasant or demeaning in order to get other people to like me

    1   2   3   4   5

F) I feel uncomfortable or helpless when I am alone,
and will go to great lengths to avoid being alone

    1   2   3   4   5

G) I feel devastated and helpless when close
relationships end

    1   2   3   4   5

H) I am frequently preoccupied with fears of being
abandoned

    1   2   3   4   5

I) I am easily hurt by criticism or disapproval

    1   2   3   4   5

14. With how many adult male partners have you
had sexual intercourse?____

15. With how many adult females have you had
sexual contact?____

16. Which of the following best describes your
preference when it comes to choosing a sexual
partner? (Circle one)

    A) I prefer males

    B) I prefer males, but have had some
       contact with females

    C) I prefer both males and females
       equally

    D) I prefer females, but have had some
       contact with males

    E) I prefer females

17. How many times in a usual month do you prefer
to use enough alcohol or drugs so that you have a
temporary change in behavior?____

(Questionnaire, page 2)

This page of the questionnaire asks questions about sexual contacts that you may have had when YOU were 15 or younger. Specifically, it asks about sexual contacts that you may have had at this age with people who either forced you to have sexual contact with them or who were 5 or more years older than you were. (Please do not include any people who were 5 or more years older but who only had sexual contact with you when you forced them.) Sexual contact means any kind of sexual touching that is more than hugging or kissing. Please answer all of the questions. If they do not apply to you, please check "does not apply." If you are not sure about an answer, put in your best estimate or guess. There are 2 made up examples to show you how to fill in the chart. The list on the bottom of the page will help you to answer the question about the kinds of sexual contacts that you may have had.

	How many times did you have sexual contact with this person?	How old were you the first time that you had sexual contact with this person?	How old was this person the first time you had sexual contact with him or her?	How old were you the last time that you had sexual contact with him or her?	Was the sexual contact ever against your will?	Do you now consider sexual contact with this person to have been abusive or bad?	How was this person related to you?	What kinds of sexual contact did you have? (Use the list below to help you answer.) Circle all that apply.	Was this person male or female?
Example 1	20	15	20	16	Yes / (No)	Yes / (No)	boyfriend	(1)(2)(3) 4 5 6(7)(8)(9)(10)(11) 12 13	(M)/ F
Example 2	50	7	35	14	(Yes)/ No	(Yes)/ No	neighbor	1(2)(3)(4)(5) 6 7(8)(9) 10 11 12(13)	M /(F)
PERSON 1					Yes / No	Yes / No		1 2 3 4 5 6 7 8 9 10 11 12 13	M / F
PERSON 2					Yes / No	Yes / No		1 2 3 4 5 6 7 8 9 10 11 12 13	M / F
PERSON 3					Yes / No	Yes / No		1 2 3 4 5 6 7 8 9 10 11 12 13	M / F
PERSON 4					Yes / No	Yes / No		1 2 3 4 5 6 7 8 9 10 11 12 13	M / F
PERSON 5					Yes / No	Yes / No		1 2 3 4 5 6 7 8 9 10 11 12 13	M / F
PERSON 6					Yes / No	Yes / No		1 2 3 4 5 6 7 8 9 10 11 12 13	M / F
PERSON 7					Yes / No	Yes / No		1 2 3 4 5 6 7 8 9 10 11 12 13	M / F

(Continue on the back of this page if necessary)

Use this list to answer the question above about the kinds of sexual contacts that you had:

With any of these people, did you ...

1 Touch the person's genitals with a hand
2 Touch the person's genitals with a mouth
3 Touch the person's breasts (if female) with a hand
4 Touch the person's breasts (if female) with a mouth
5 Put a finger or object in the person's anus (butt)
6 Have sexual intercourse

Did any of these people ...

7 Touch your genitals with a hand
8 Touch your genitals with a mouth
9 Touch your breasts with a hand
10 Touch your breasts with a mouth
11 Put a finger or object in your anus (butt)
12 Put a penis in your anus (butt)
13 Involve you in group sex

_____ **"Does not apply"** *(Check here if none of the questions on this page applies to you)*

(Questionnaire, page 3)

This page of the questionnaire asks questions about sexual contacts that you may have had with people when THEY were 15 or younger. Specifically, it asks about sexual contacts that you may have had with people of this age when you were either 5 or more years older or you forced the other people to have sexual contact with you. (Please do not include any people who were 5 or more years younger but who only had sexual contact with you when they forced you.) Sexual contact means any kind of sexual touching that is more than hugging or kissing. Please answer all of the questions. If they do not apply to you, please check "does not apply." If you are not sure about an answer, put in your best estimate or guess. There are 2 made up examples to show you how to fill in the chart. The list below will help you to answer the question about the kinds of sexual contacts that you may have had.

	How many times did you have sexual contact with this person?	How old were you the first time that you had sexual contact with this person?	How old was this person the first time you had sexual contact with him or her?	How old were you the last time that you had sexual contact with him or her?	Did the other person want the sexual contact with you?	Do you now consider sexual contact with this person to have been abusive or bad?	How was this person related to you?	What kinds of sexual contact did you have? (Use the list below to help you answer.) Circle all that apply.	Was this person male or female?	Were you ever forced by somebody else to have sexual contact with this person?
Example 1	2	15	10	16	**Yes** / No	Yes / **No**	I was her babysitter	**1** 2 3 4 5 6 7 8 9 10 11 12 **13**	M / **F**	Yes / **No**
Example 2	10	20	15	21	**Yes** / No	Yes / **No**	boyfriend	1 2 **3** 4 5 **6** 7 8 9 **10 11 12** 13	**M** / F	Yes / **No**
PERSON 1					Yes / No	Yes / No		1 2 3 4 5 6 7 8 9 10 11 12 13	M / F	Yes / No
PERSON 2					Yes / No	Yes / No		1 2 3 4 5 6 7 8 9 10 11 12 13	M / F	Yes / No
PERSON 3					Yes / No	Yes / No		1 2 3 4 5 6 7 8 9 10 11 12 13	M / F	Yes / No
PERSON 4					Yes / No	Yes / No		1 2 3 4 5 6 7 8 9 10 11 12 13	M / F	Yes / No
PERSON 5					Yes / No	Yes / No		1 2 3 4 5 6 7 8 9 10 11 12 13	M / F	Yes / No
PERSON 6					Yes / No	Yes / No		1 2 3 4 5 6 7 8 9 10 11 12 13	M / F	Yes / No
PERSON 7					Yes / No	Yes / No		1 2 3 4 5 6 7 8 9 10 11 12 13	M / F	Yes / No

(Continue on the back of this page if necessary)

Use this list to answer the question above about the kinds of sexual contacts that you had:

With any of these people, did you ...

1 Touch the person's genitals with a hand
2 Touch the person's genitals with a mouth
3 Touch the person's breasts (if female) with a hand
4 Touch the person's breasts (if female) with a mouth
5 Put a finger or object in the person's anus (butt)
6 Have sexual intercourse

Did any of these people ...

7 Touch your genitals with a hand
8 Touch your genitals with a mouth
9 Touch your breasts with a hand
10 Touch your breasts with a mouth
11 Put a finger or object in your anus (butt)
12 Put a penis in your anus (butt)
13 Have group sex with you

Have you ever been questioned about any of the behaviors listed above by the police or by a child protection agency?   Yes / No

Which of the following best describes the typical state of your love life during the times in your life when you were having sexual contact with someone who was 15 years or younger?

I had just ended a relationship with an adult or same-age lover or husband within the past year

I had a good relationship with an adult or same-age lover or husband

I had a bad relationship with an adult or same-age lover or husband

I had not been involved with an adult or same-age lover or husband in more than a year

_____ **"Does not apply"** *(Check here if none of the questions on this page applies to you)*

Appendix F

Letter to Examiners

Dear Administrator:

Thank you very much for agreeing to provide subjects for this research project concerning women who have had sexual contact with minors. The following are guidelines for administration of the questionnaire.

The survey may be administered either in a group setting, or to individuals. The group setting is preferable, to ensure that the larger numbers of questionnaires are returned. If the questionnaires are given to groups, ample space should be provided, so that subjects have the guarantee of privacy in recording their answers.

Subjects may read the directions on their own, or the directions may be read to them, depending on your judgment of the reading level of the participants. Subjects may have the meanings of words explained to them, but should not be told how to answer questions. Once subjects understand the meaning of the words in the questionnaire, they should be asked to interpret the meaning of questions on their own.

A Confidentiality Certificate has been issued for this research to legally protect the identities of the subject. THE CERTIFICATE PROHIBITS INDIVIDUALS OTHER THAN THE RESEARCHERS FROM VIEWING THE ANSWERS OF THE SUBJECTS. It is important that no one is allowed to have access to the information that the subjects provide, including any staff members who may collect the data. This will be particularly important to keep in mind when answering questions that subjects may have while they are completing questionnaires. Subjects should not put their names on questionnaires, nor should they discuss their answers while they are completing the study. Consent forms for participation in this study should be collected separately from the questionnaires. Subjects should turn in their questionnaires in a sealed envelope, or mail them on their own, in the envelope provided.

Subjects should be allowed to refuse to participate in this study or to change their minds about taking part in the research at any point while they are completing the questionnaire without penalty of any sort. Participation in this study may prove to be stressful for some subjects; all subjects should be made aware of any available counseling resources prior to their completing the questionnaires.

Thank you again for agreeing to provide subjects for this research. Should you have questions regarding this survey, I can be reached by telephone at the following number: (555) 555-5555. A brief summary of results will be mailed to you, following this study's completion.

Sincerely,
Julia Hislop, MA

PART THREE

Women Who Sexually Molest Female Children

TERESA DUNBAR

CONTENTS

ABSTRACT

Research indicates that an estimated 23% of the female population in the United States have been sexually abused in childhood, and that 5%, or 1.5 million, were molested by women (Allen, 1990; Finkelhor, 1984; Russell, 1986). A comparative analysis was made of six studies of women who sexually molested prepubertal female children. Findings were supported by individual case studies from various authors. The organization of male and female etiologies for sexual abuse suggests that both genders share characteristic similarities, yet have gender-circumstantial differences that influence the development of adult molesting behavior. The etiologies for male sexual abuse were presented using Finkelhor and Araji's (1986) four-factor model on pedophilia (emotional congruence, sexual arousal, blockage, and inhibition). The etiologies of female sexual abuse were organized using Travin, Cullen, and Protter's (1990) classifications of biological, learned/behavioral, and psychodynamic factors. A theoretical discussion was designed using reported learned/behavioral and psychodynamic case study observations of female molesting behavior. Examination of the findings emphasizes the importance of primary mother-daughter attachment, early female identity formation, and female socialization as influences on later female molesting behavior. Analysis of the six core studies also suggests that social recognition of female sex offenders was hampered by the criminal justice system's use of a double standard in convicting male and female abusers. The sentencing of such female sex offenders appears to be derive from the cultural role that women are stereotyped to play. The overall findings contribute to the understanding of women who sexually molest female children.

CHAPTER 1

Introduction

Empirical findings concerning the sexual abuse of female children have been oriented to the study of male sex offenders, usually against prepubertal female minors. Results of empirical studies on males who molest children suggest that the causes of such sex offenses are varied, and that etiologies are based on the circumstances of the offense, the age of the victim, and the psychodynamics of the offender. Current empirical studies are presented that reveal sexual abuse of children by women who are primarily lower and middle-class Caucasians with no designated ethnic classification. Finkelhor and Russell (1984) estimate that women abuse 5% of the female victims whose cases are "reported" to the authorities. These and other researchers indicate that within the reviewed research, women sex offenders have more frequently chosen same-sex victims than male sex offenders (Faller, 1987; Mathews, Matthews, & Speltz, 1989; McCarty, 1986). Goodwin and DiVasto (1979) state that mother-daughter incest is more common than "rare," and is likely to increase as mothers increasingly take on the single parenting of daughters.

Most case studies of women who sexually molest children indicate that there are social and legal complexities in reporting molesting females. For many professionals in the field of child abuse, the biological composition of a woman's body seemingly does not lend itself to causing sexual trauma to a female minor. The possession of a penis in most cases appears to be the essential factor needed for confirmation of child sexual abuse. This belief is influenced by Western social attitudes, which have historically dismissed female sexual abuse because "it is of little significance," and "not very exciting" (Mathis, 1972, pp. 53-54). Society in general has not accepted the idea that females have sexual impulses and drives, causing them to be seen as sexually harmless.

Because Western social systems are established on behavioral norms of male dominance and importance, confirmed case studies of female sex offending have attributed its causes as similar to that of male molesting behavior. The seemingly limited incidence of child sexual molestation by women has created neither the need nor interest among professionals to consider developmental aspects of the offender's gender in the study of female molesting behavior. Such failure to distinguish etiological specifics concerning female and male sexual behavior reinforces cultural attitudes about male significance and female oppression, and points to the need for further research on the topic.

CHAPTER 2

Review of the Literature

Similarities and Differences: Male and Female Sex Offenders

Female sex offenders against female children share similarities with, yet are also distinct from, male offenders. Women sex offenders have engaged in sexual activities that include voyeurism, kissing, fondling, oral sex, digital penetration, sex games, and mutual masturbation (Allen, 1990; Faller, 1987; Finkelhor, Williams, & Burns, 1988; Goodwin & DiVasto, 1989; Lidz & Lidz, 1969; Mathews et al., 1989; McCarty, 1986; Wolfe, 1985). Some studies report mothers who have chosen to sleep with a female child as a means to be more sexually active and close with the victim (Lidz & Lidz, 1969; Sugar, 1983).

Case studies have identified the frequently unmonitored bathing activity between a mother and child as an opportunity to sexually fondle the victim (Mathews, et al., 1989; McCarty, 1986). Russell (1986) noted cases of child breast sucking, a maternal nurturant interaction, used as a means for self-stimulation with an age-inappropriate child. Lidz and Lidz (1969) revealed studies of incestuous mothers who directed their daughters to undress and be subjected to critical speculations. Some of these mothers became involved in their daughters' bowel movements and gave enemas to themselves while directing the child to watch. Additional case investigations of women sex offenders include mothers who simultaneously physically and sexually abused their daughters (Goodwin & DiVasto, 1979), victims who were directed to masturbate their mothers to receive nurturance (Lidz & Lidz, 1969), and mothers who sexually stimulated their daughters for sensual pleasure (Forward & Buck, 1978).

Studies also reveal that women engaged in pornographic picture-taking of children, forced female and male victims to watch the abuser and others have sex, and coerced children into having sex with other children and adults (Faller, 1987; Finkelhor et al., 1988; Mathews et al., 1989; Wolfe, 1985). The study by Finkelhor et al. (1988) of day care abuse indicates that more women than men committed multiple sexual abuse and acts involving sexual penetration, and were more likely to force children to sexually abuse others and more frequently participate in ritualistic mass abuse.

Importance of the Study

The National Center on Child Abuse and Neglect (1988) indicates that female children are more susceptible to being sexually abused and are more likely than male children to experience injury and impairment. Prevalence studies show that of the total population of females in the United States, an estimate of 29 million have been sexually abused. Allen (1990) indicates that when this estimate is multiplied by 5% — the rate of sexually abused female children molested by women (Finkelhor & Russell, 1984) — the results show that 1.5 million female children have been sexually abused by women.

The sexual molestation of female children is rarely associated with women. Research shows that women both molest independently and are frequently coerced to assist males in abuse. Unfortunately, most of the literature on the etiology of molestation concerns male eroticism and sexuality. Male molesting behavior is termed "pedophilia," a label that has never been applied to female sex offenders because of their inability to "fit" the diagnostic characteristics. The investigation of case studies on female sex offenders indicates the irrelevance of labeling their behavior as an erotic-sexual experience as this is never included in their reported reasons for molesting. Some female sex offenders admit being orgasmic while molesting female children (Mathews, et al., 1989), but none state that they initiated sex primarily for erotic stimulation.

Current theories about female sex offenders have speculated that the adult chooses her victims to fulfill specific emotional needs (Faller, 1987). The woman expresses or acts out an emotional bond with the victim which is not primarily directed at coitus or orgasm. The woman's sexual feelings are directed more towards intimacy and physical closeness (Sax & Deckwitz, 1992). Women who sexually molest male children do so because they feel a sense of rejection, lone-liness and isolation from a male adult figure, and a desire for the child to act as a protector and confidant (Lloyd, 1987). Molestation of male children by women is relatively socially tolerated because of the culturally stereotyped expectation and acceptance of boys "making it" with girls and women. The sexual initiation of boys by women is seen as a non-threatening act that helps the child prepare for manhood. Adult males who experienced sex with women in childhood often indicate that they did not feel "victimized" or "abused" (Condy, Templer, Brown, & Veaco, 1987; Fromuth & Burkhart, 1987; Risin & Koss, 1987).

There is less social approval of sexual relations between women and girls, per-haps because of the prejudice against lesbianism. Unlike men, women who experienced such childhood molestation developed significant identity distur-bance and confusion (Russell, 1986), and acquired a variety of emotional/physi-ological symptoms including encopresis, depression, psychosis, and migraine headaches (Goodwin & DiVasto, 1989).

Women who sexually molest female children have great needs for attention and affection, and desire emotional nurturance from the child (Lloyd, 1987). Some women sex offenders indicate that they had been deprived of early nurturance and caretaking by their maternal and familial sources. They feel no sense of attachment or belonging and are confused about their gender or identity (Litz & Litz, 1969; Mathews, et al., 1989). The causation of some female molesting behavior suggests arrested development of the abuser.

Social attitudes concerning women sex offenders — especially those who molest female children — limit recognition, investigation, and treatment of such offend-ers. Given the estimated number of females molested by women, and the diverse professional opinions concerning the significance of female molesting behavior, this research seeks to enhance awareness and understanding of women who molest female children. The study compares women's sexual abuse of children with male offender-related research on the topic and identifies developmental, psychological, and psychosocial factors related to female sexual behavior. Research findings suggest that women sex offenders have differing develop-mental, familial, and cultural experiences than male sex offenders do that influ-ence them to molest female children.

Focus of the Research

This study's purpose was exploratory and theoretical. The main objectives of the research were: 1) to present case study etiologies of male and female molesting behavior; 2) to explore characteristics of female molesting behavior; 3) to identify circumstantial differences between male and female offenders; 4) to recognize similarities among women sex offenders against female children; 5) to create a basis for the theoretical analysis of female molesting behavior for further research; and 6) to investigate the criminal justice system's actions concerning women who molest. More specifically, the following questions guided the research:

- What characteristic and etiological similarities and differences exist between female and male sex offenders?

- Is the distortion of early female identity formation important to the causation of adult molesting behavior?

- Can a woman's molesting behavior be theoretically associated with learned/behavioral and psychodynamic influences?

- Does gender-related stereotyping encourage female abuse toward other females?

- How does the criminal justice system view female offenders, and how does this influence the conviction and treatment of such abusers?

CHAPTER 3

Method

Organizing the Data

This study investigated case study observations of women and men (18 years of age and older) who sexually molested prepubertal (13 years of age and younger) female children, and identified developmental, sociological, and psychological factors that elicited adult molesting behavior. The basis of the research was organized from the findings of six group studies (Allen, 1990; Faller, 1987; Finkelhor et al., 1988; Mathews et al., 1989; McCarty, 1986; Wolfe, 1985), whose conclusions were supported by additional case study observations from various authors. The classification of biological, learned/behavioral, and psychodynamic determinants of female molesting behavior helped to compare and organize gender-related etiologies (Travin, Cullen, & Protter, 1990). Finkelhor and Araji's (1986) "four-factor model" was used to explain male pedophilia, and related findings from several sources were incorporated. A computer search was used for both molesting genders using the following keywords: sexual child abuse, female sex offender, psychosexual behavior, and female deviant behavior.

The organization of the above research material assisted in isolating an etiological hypothesis of female molesting that included the investigation of learned/behavioral and psychodynamic factors. The findings suggested that unfulfilled childhood nurturing needs and disrupted or insufficient maternal attachment formation affect a female's sense of identity and belonging, in turn creating a need that is fulfilled by sexual abuse.

Familial influences and cultural stereotyping contributed to the female's inability to establish a sense of identity and created feelings of dependency. The female's early and continued emotional deprivation establishes a life-long desire to feel connected to others and in control of herself. The following psychosocial factors are found to be significant among women who molest female children:

- *Early mother-daughter attachment* explores the complexity of same-sex maternal nurturing.

- *Female identity formation* considers the significance of self-development.

- *Female socialization* recognizes narcissistic parenting, cultural standards of female development and the effects of emotional dependence on female reasoning. A computer search was conducted using the following keywords: feminist theory, gender, sex-role identity, female development, and social power.

Studies of female sex offenders indicate that only the most overt acts of sexual abuse by women are likely to come to the attention of the criminal justice system (Travin et al., 1990). Case studies indicate that the justice system's stereotyped patriarchal orientation contributes to the protection and underreporting of women sex offenders. Criminal evaluations of the female offenders in the six core studies suggest three areas of investigation that included 1) legal perspectives concerning female criminals, 2) legal response to such women, and 3) treatment effectiveness regarding female sex offenders. A computer search was conducted using the following keywords: female sex offender, criminal justice, offending women, sexism and crime.

Limitations of the Study

Research has not substantiated what female behavior designates "sexual abuse." Such a limitation enables women to engage in molestation without it being identified as such.

Related studies do not consistently differentiate between the terms "sex offender" (convicted felon) and "child molester" (not convicted). Both terms are, therefore, interchangeable in the study.

Research sources are not informationally and statistically consistent in the organization and presentation of case variables. In addition, the validity of the investigative research is limited to self-reports and interviews with women sex offenders and their female victims.

The research data is based on samples of convicted offenders, molesters referred for psychiatric or psychological evaluation by a court, and offenders engaged in hospitalized treatments. It is probable that the characteristics of such groups are seriously skewed by judicial biases and reporting.

A substantial proportion of female molesting behavior is never communicated to the authorities. Reported incidents are likely to be a nonrandom sample of the total population. The findings derived from such incidents may be biased by this selection.

Authors of the six core studies were personally contacted, but were unable to release further case study information because of continuing investigation of the data, unavailability of statistics, or participant confidentiality (Allen, 1990; Faller, 1987; Finkelhor et al., 1988; Mathews et al., 1989). Two authors did not respond (McCarty, 1986; Wolfe, 1985).

Terminology

CHILD MOLESTER: An adult who has sexual contact with a prepubertal child.

FIXATED CHILD MOLESTER: A person who is persistently sexually attracted to children, regardless of other sexual experiences of the abuser (Groth, 1978).

INCEST: Adult sexual acts performed on children who are related to the abuser.

PATRIARCHY: A set of male social relations that has a material base and hierarchical relations. Such a bonding creates solidarity among its members that enables them to control women. Patriarchy is the system of male oppression of women (Hartmann, cited in Westkott, 1978).

PEDOPHILIA: The enduring characteristic of an adult's sexual attraction to children (Bolton, Morris, & MacEachron, 1989). The various professional definitions of this term describe male sexual behavior. Research on female sex offenders rejects the use of the term because of its irrelevance to female sexuality.

SEX OFFENDER: An individual who has been legally convicted of a criminal sexual act.

SEXUAL ABUSE: A sexual act perpetrated against an individual without her or his consent.

SITUATIONAL CHILD MOLESTER: Child molesting behavior that begins in adulthood after the abuser has established primary sexual attraction towards adults (Groth, 1978).

Case Study Observations

Reducing an individual's behavior to one diagnostic cause avoids understanding the complexity of human development. A multi-dimensional approach is essential to understanding male and female molesting behavior. Different offender characteristics and etiologies indicate the various emotional needs of an adult.

Case study findings on male sex offenders provide a basis for analyzing the behavior of female sex offenders. Research varies on male and female abuser typology and on the offender's reasons for molesting prepubertal females. Studies of male and female molesters indicate differing developmental expectations, circumstantial experiences, and social role orientations that suggest reasons for molesting. This study recommends distinctive categories and perceptions of male and female offenders.

Researchers are investigating the possibility that some individuals, perhaps at a critical life phase, are more vulnerable than others to becoming adult sex offenders (Finkelhor & Araji, 1986; Money, 1990). The characteristics of sex offenders suggest that this orientation could begin at infancy. However, studies continue to explore the types of "pedogenic" processing that lead to a specific kind of adult sex offending behavior (Finkelhor & Araji, 1986).

Male Sex Offenders

The average male child molester is shy, passive, unassertive, and introverted (Langevin, Paitich, Freeman, Mann, & Handy, 1978; Wilson & Cox, 1983). He is usually moralistic and guilt-ridden (Quinsey, 1977), with poor social skills contributing to difficulty in developing heterosexual relationships (Pawlak, Boulet, & Bradford, 1991). Typically, the male offender experienced substance abuse and violence in his childhood home, lacked a close relationship with his father, had parents who abandoned him or were separated or divorced, and was subjected to physical and/or sexual abuse and neglect. The absence of childhood nurturance, physical affection, and modeling of healthy sexuality are also found (Tingle, Barnard, Robbins, Newman, & Hutchinson, 1986).

Male sex offenders' developmental profiles are connected with the etiologies of their sexual abuse. Characteristics of the abuser's sexual crime provides insight to the male's reasons for molestation. Analysis of the molesting behavior also includes noting the victim's age and type of sexual behavior exhibited, as well as determining if the behavior were molestation or incest, fixated or situational, violent or non-violent. Levin and Stava (1987) indicate that the nonforceful child molester has low self-concept, inhibited aggression, and a strong need for approval, and the violent child assaulter (sociopathic offender) is a hostile, socially alienated, and self-centered person who has poor control over his impulses (Quinsey, 1977).

ETIOLOGIES OF MALE SEX OFFENDING BEHAVIOR

Table 1 uses Finkelhor and Araji's (1986) four factors to summarize the past 40 years of research on the causes of male molesting behavior. No one theoretical concept has been unquestionably accepted by researchers as the main cause of male molesting behavior. Current literature indicates that neuropsychological impairment, childhood psychodynamic development, and cultural influences may all contribute to males sexually molesting female minors (Bierker, 1989; Hendricks, Fitzpatrick, Hartmann, Quaife, Stratbucker, & Graber, 1988; Howells, 1981; Hucker, Langevin, Wortzman, Bain, Handy, Chambers, & Wright, 1986; Money, 1990). Finkelhor and Araji (1986) have consolidated these hypothetical findings in a four-factor model to organize the causes of "pedophilic" behavior. Males molest for reasons of emotional congruence, sexual arousal, blockage, or disinhibition. The model is presented in this study as a basis to understand male molesting behavior.

Emotional Congruence

Theories of emotional congruence see male molesting behavior as a result of arrested psychological development in which emotional needs are satisfied by a child. Fraser (1976) calls this male behavior "narcissistic inversion." The deprivation of maternal love and acceptable male role modeling in childhood forces the abuser to resolve his emotional pain by narcissistically remaining in love with his child image. In doing so, he projects his love onto other children similar in age to him at the time of his childhood pain. These children then become "love objects" for him and are a form of self-recognition.

Gaddini (1983) also sees male molesting behavior as a result of distorted early maturational processing during empathy development (attachment) with the maternal caretaker. The male's deprivation of maternal sensory experiences, in which feelings and thinking evolve, significantly interferes with the formation of a sense of self, intrinsic ego-development, and stage of differentiation. Deprived

Table 1
Etiologies of Male Molesting Behavior

THEORY	CONTRIBUTING SOURCES
EMOTIONAL CONGRUENCE — Arrested psychological development in which emotional needs are satisfied by a child	
Developmental deprivation of maternal love and acceptable male role modeling	Fraser, 1976
Deprivation of early maternal sensory experiences	Gaddini, 1983
A cognitive defense against childhood psychological traumas which produced feelings of anxiety, low self-esteem, and isolation	Gillespie, 1956; Lambert, 1976;Langevin et al., 1985; Socarides, 1959; Stoller, 1975
The need to overcome shame, humiliation, and powerlessness experiences in childhood	Rosen, 1979
A response to male socialization values on being dominant, powerful, and initiator of sexual relationships	Hite, 1981; Russell, 1982
Acts on the social norm of male dominance, which implies ownership over wife and children	Faller, 1988; Herman, 1981; Rush, 1981; Sommers-Flanagan & Walters, 1987
SEXUAL AROUSAL — Factors that elevate inappropriate sexual behavior	
Childhood sexual experiences facilitate early conditioning/imprinting	de Young 1982; Gebhard et al., 1965; Groth & Burgess, 1977; Howells, 1981; Marshall & Christie, 1981; Money, 1981; Wenet, Clark & Hunner, 1981
Biological factors, including hormonal levels, chromosomal abnormalities, and neurological impairment	Berlin, 1982; Bernard et al., 1989; Bradford, 1985; Flor-Henry et al., 1991; Freund et al., 1991; Gaffney & Berlin, 1984; Goy & McEwan, 1977; Hendricks et al., 1988; Hucker et al., 1986; Hutchinson & Hutchinson, 1990; Langevin, Wortzman, Wright, & Handy, 1989; Lilly et al., 1983; Miller et al., 1986; Money, 1961
Socialization through child pornography and advertising	Dworkin, 1983; Russell, 1982

Table 1
(Continued)

BLOCKAGE — Factors that inhibit emotionally fulfilling heterosexual relationships

Unable to resolve childhood anger with early maternal caretaker	Bierker, 1989; Faller, 1988
A need to receive nurturance and protection that was not experienced in childhood	Bierker, 1989; Faller, 1988
Dysfunctional marital/adult relationships	de Young, 1982; Gebhard et al., 1967; Meiselman, 1978; Mohr et al., 1964; Peters, 1976
Females are experienced as being subservient to males	Alexander and Lupfer, 1987

INHIBITIONS — Overcome conventional restraints against having sex with children

Psychopathic tendencies, senility, neurologically impaired, psychotic involved in substance abuse	Barnard et al., 1989; Bierker, 1989; Cushing, 1950; Flor-Henry et al., 1991; Hendricks et al., 1988; Karpman, 1954; Marshall & Christie, 1981,
Situational stress	Barnard et al., 1989
Influence of patriarchal norms	Armstrong, 1983; McIntyre, 1981; Nelson, 1982; Rush, 1980

of this maternal act that gives him "psychological birth," the male will seek it by maintenance of a permanent state of emotional fusion with another.

Stoller (1975) labeled male molesting behavior as a "perversion" in which unresolved problems in libidinal and family development are reenacted through sexual fantasies. The fantasies are seen as cognitive defenses against childhood-induced psychological traumas (physical and/or sexual), which produce feelings of anxiety, low self-esteem, and isolation (Lambert, 1976; Langevin, Hucker, Ben-Aron, Purins, & Hook, 1985). In acting on such fantasies, the offender expresses a symbolic mastery and anger over the past trauma (Stoller, 1975) and experiences an escape from reality (Socarides, 1959). Such a theoretical approach identifies superego and moral conscience impairment which is also a precondition for an individual who sexually abuses children (Gillespie, 1956).

Rosen (1979) similarly discusses the functional nature of male sexual perversions, which he sees as "regulators of self-esteem." He interprets the sexual acting out of perversions as precipitated by traumatic and stressful external life events that have an impact on self-concept. The male's sexual relationship with female minors helps him to overcome a sense of shame, humiliation, or powerlessness that he experienced with adults in childhood.

Cultural theories related to male development include feminist theories about male molesting behavior. These theories involve male socialization that encourages children to be "appropriate" or "emotionally congruent" objects for sexual interest by adults (Hite, 1981; Russell, 1982). Primary among such theories is that male socialization gives value to men who are dominant, powerful, and initiators of sexual relationships. When a male operates in this cultural message, he will prefer to relate to "partners" who are younger, smaller, and weaker than himself. Children fit such a male need, more so than many women.

The social value of male power is also seen in the implied ownership that a man is held to have over wife and children. Sommers-Flanagan and Walters (1987) state that such a cultural norm has two messages: that the owned are different (possibly less important) than the owners; and that society promotes, and pressures males into, individuality and achievement. This norm gives priority to their psychological and material needs. A society that encourages male dominance gives permission for men to abuse children sexually (Herman, 1981; Rush, 1980) and provides the rationalization for doing so (Faller, 1988).

Sexual Arousal

Research in this area investigates factors that elevate inappropriate sexual arousal. A prevalent theory is that childhood sexual experiences cause some adults to find children arousing (Money, 1981; Wenet, Clark, & Hunner, 1981). Research indicates that many male molesters were sexually victimized in childhood and hypothesizes that the traumatic ordeal facilitates an imprinting or conditioning process (Gebhard, Gagnon, Pomeroy, & Christenson, 1965; Groth & Burgess, 1977; de Young, 1982). As the child victim grows into adulthood, he may be unable to differentiate erotic arousal from parental, protective, affectionate love, which contributes to him having sex with children (Howells, 1981; Marshall & Christie, 1981). The male's childhood victimization, therefore, becomes a social learning process, in which the molesting adult models the experienced sexual stimulation that children have on him (Howells, 1981; Wenet, et al., 1981).

Biological factors such as hormone level (Gaffney & Berlin, 1984), chromosomal abnormalities (Berlin, 1982; Bradford, 1985; Goy & McEwen, 1977; Money, 1961), and neurological impairment (Bernard, Fuller, Robbins, & Shaw, 1989; Freund, Watson, Dickey, & Rienzo, 1991; Hendricks et al., 1988; Hucker, et al., 1986; Hutchison & Hutchison, 1990; Lilly, Cummings, Benson, & Frankel, 1983; Miller, Cummings, McIntyre, Ebers, & Grode, 1986) have also been suggested as contributing to male sexual arousal in relation to control, fantasy, and ability. Researchers who explore the biological determinants of male molesting behavior indicate that such information is more valid for diagnoses because it is not based on observation or self-reports. Future investigations are necessary to substantiate the association between biological influences and male molesting behavior.

Sexual arousal is also seen as a social learning process that encourages adult interest in children. Dworkin (1995) and Russell (1982) believe that child pornography and advertising are a form of social learning that teaches sexual arousal with children to males who would not otherwise have become involved in it. Child pornography often includes themes of sex with adults. The adult who masturbates with the use of such material learns that children are sexually arousing and reinforces that learning with the powerful reward/stimulus of orgasm.

Blockage

Theories about blockage include explanations of why some males fail to have their sexual and emotional needs met in adult heterosexual relationships. Related research suggests that normal development or normal gender/age tendencies are blocked, causing the male to become sexually interested in children. Such blockage is divided into two types: developmental blockages involving Oedipal conflicts in which the male is prevented from moving into the adult heterosexual stage of development; and situational blockages where a male with apparent adult heterosexual interests is blocked from normal sexual outlets because of the loss of a relationship or other transitory crisis.

The male sex offender with a developmental blockage is described as having intense conflicts about his mother, or "castration anxieties," that make it difficult or impossible for him to relate to adult women. Faller (1988) and Bierker (1989) characterize the male's attempts to sexually interact with women as impeded by a need to express the anger he feels toward his mother and/or a need to receive the nurturance and protection he did not get as a child. The woman/wife disappoints the male in his emotional impasse, and he turns toward a child to receive and express such feelings.

Theories describing the male with a situational block consider the family dynamics model of incest in which the individual's marital relationship has broken down. The wife has become alienated for reasons of emotional or physical illness, social commitments, or employment, and the husband is too inhibited or moralistic to find sexual satisfaction outside the family (de Young, 1982; Gebhard et al., 1965; Meiselman, 1978). In such families, the male turns to the daughters as substitutes to meet sexual needs (Mohr, Turner, & Jerry, 1964; Peters, 1976).

A theory involving situational blockage is that offered by Alexander and Lupfer (1987), whose study of family characteristics and sexual abuse shows that father-daughter incest is associated with very traditional family values. In such families, children are seen as subservient to adults, and females are seen as subservient to males. The themes of power and ownership seem to be more socially significant than engaging in adult heterosexual relationships. Such an attitude encourages the sexual molestation of female children.

Disinhibition

This area includes theories about how adults overcome conventional restraints against sexual activity with female minors. In such situations, ordinary controls on male sexual behavior are overridden, creating a level of acceptability for the adult-child sexual relationship. Male sex offenders with disinhibition are described as senile (Cushing, 1950; Karpman, 1954), neurologically impaired (Flor-Henry et al., 1991; Hendricks et al., 1988), psychotic (Barnard, Fuller, Robbins, & Shaw, 1989), involved in substance abuse (Marshall & Christie, 1981), and having psychopathic tendencies (Bierker, 1989).

Situational factors used to explain disinhibition include stress that is usually related to unemployment, loss of love, or death of a significant person. Males who sexually molest daughters and step-daughters have shown reduced inhibitions after separation or divorce from their wives. The male whose children do not live with him will feel an abatement of normal parental responsibilities, which reduces his inhibition to sexually molest the child.

Feminist researchers present cultural disinhibition arguments. Their studies indicate that 1) the seduction of children has been sanctioned by religion and law throughout history (Rush, 1980), 2) the legal system is reluctant to prosecute offenders (Armstrong, 1983), and 3) there is a tendency for the public and investigating professionals to blame the victims for the molestation (McIntyre, 1981; Nelson, 1982). Patriarchal views continue to significantly influence current social attitudes. Sexual abuse is a stereotyped behavior for males, yet children and women continue to be thought of as less important than, and subservient to, men. Men are also led to believe that they have more intense erotic needs, and they are considered to be more masculine when they act to satisfy such urges. The "Catch-22" of patriarchal social rule in convicting male sex offenders is that the patriarchy is forced to turn "against its own" as it prioritizes male omnipotence.

Female Sex Offenders

Current research indicates that the average female sex offender has feelings of inferiority, dependency, and isolation, with emotional needs for acceptance, attention, and closeness (Faller, 1987; Mathews, et al., 1989; McCarty, 1986). Sex offending women often live in violent relationships with other adults and wish to fulfill the others' needs (Mathews et al., 1989; Wolfe, 1985). Such females have experienced failed or emotionally empty sexual relationships with other adults and exhibit psychological difficulties in childhood development, sex-role identity, and socialization (Allen, 1990; Chasnoff, Burns, W., Schnoll, Burns, K., Chisum, & Kyle-Spore, 1986; Faller, 1987; Finkelhor, et al., 1988; Goodwin & DiVasto, 1989; James & Nasjleti, 1983; Mathews et al., 1989). Women involved in individual and co-offending molestation act on feelings of powerlessness and lack of control and behaviorally respond to others with blind obedience, passivity, and subordination, with no concept of a self-identity (Finkelhor et al., 1988; Mathews et al., 1989).

The characteristics and behavior of female sex offenders differ according to situational needs, developmental experiences, and emotional maturity. Mathews et al. (1989) have categorized female offenders into three typologies: "teacher-lover" in which the woman denies or minimizes the negative impact of her abuse and believes that her sexual behavior with children (males) is positive and desired by the child; "predisposed" in which the woman has had an extensive history of abuse and is extremely needy for love and attention; and "male-coerced" in which the woman's own childhood abuse and feelings of low self-esteem, passivity, and powerlessness in interpersonal relationships cause her to be controlled by another's desire to molest.

ETIOLOGIES OF FEMALE SEX OFFENDING BEHAVIOR

Six studies of female sex offender characteristics formulated the basis to understand molesting behavior by women (Table 2).

Additional research from other sources confirmed and added to the findings suggested by the core studies. Some authors (Rowan, Rowan, & Langelier, 1990) have integrated the causes of female molestation with those presented by Finkelhor and Araji's (1986) four-factor model. However, this appears to be a hasty hypothetical presumption that has not been fully explored given developmental and cultural gender differentiations, as well as the limited research on female sex offenders.

Women sex offenders share some similar characteristics with male offenders. However, women experience developmental and social circumstances that are different from those of males, reinforced through familial and cultural influences. These differences, along with the genders' biological makeups, create a diversity in formulating etiologies and treatment for both types of offenders.

Travin, Cullen, and Protter (1990) state that the major determinants of molesting by females consist of biological, learned/behavioral, and psychodynamic factors. Formulating the findings of the six core studies and other related research helps to organize the research on the etiology of female abuse (Table 3). Researchers state the political and social complexity of studying female sex offenders as compared to male offenders. Results indicate that female sex offenders have been randomly investigated in the past 20 years, with little professional interest given to the findings.

Biological Determinants

In comparison to research on male offenders whose biological makeup suggests causation for deviant sexual behavior, limited studies exist that integrate similar observations with females. Several sources have noted that limited or borderline intelligence, as well as mental conditions that affect judgment or impulse control, are often found among female sex offenders (Faller, 1987; Finkelhor & Araji, 1986; McCarty, 1986; O'Connor, 1987; Rowan et al., 1990). Other case studies have observed that the chronic illness of the offender or her adult partner is a significant factor in a woman's desire to be sexually comforted by a female child (Lidz & Lidz, 1969; Goodwin & DiVasto, 1979).

Few researchers have investigated the biological makeup of a female as influential in promoting a pattern of molesting behavior. Mellor, Farid and Craig's (1988) study of female hypersexuality involved a 40-year-old woman who began having intercourse at age 12 and continuously struggled with being sexually assaultive with adults and children. The female was treated with cyproterone acetate, which blocked androgen receptors and inhibited androgen production responsible for the hypersexuality. The subject's uncontrollable sexual behavior ceased with drug treatment. Similar experiments with female hypersexuality have been reported by Sarel and Masters (1982).

Research into female sex offender arousal patterns suggests that a relationship exists between androgens and physical and sexual aggression. Cooper, Swaminath, Baxter, & Poulin's (1990) psychologic, physiologic, and endocrine case study involved a 20-year-old female who had repeatedly slapped, engaged in oral sex with, and inserted objects into the vaginas of two prepubertal sisters over several months. The subject was born prematurely, lacked appropriate parental care, experienced many family moves, had an extensive history of sexual abuse since age three, grew up socially isolated, experienced strong sexual cravings at 12, and complained of frequent depression with suicidal ideation since early adolescence. At age 20, she was preoccupied with violent sexual fantasies involving adults and children of both sexes and experienced continual sexual tension with compulsive masturbation.

Cooper et al. (1990) found developmental, psychological, and physiological similarities between their subject and male sex offenders. They report that in most sex offender cases, kinetic elements including genetic, experiential, CNS (epilepsy, mental retardation, dementia), hormonal (androgens), and psychiatric (mania), significant in identifying behavioral etiologies, are likely to overlap. Their subject's physiological sexual arousal pattern (as measured by vaginal photoplethysmography) showed similarities to the penile plethysmography in 40% of male sex offenders. Cooper et al. indicated that vaginal photoplethysmography has rarely been used in assessments of female sex offenders and encouraged its use, as the physiological arousal mechanism is homologous for both sexes.

Adams, Gold, and Burt (1978) indicate that some women initiate sexual behavior most frequently during the ovulatory period (days 12-17) of the menstrual cycle. At that time in the cycle, the level of androgenic hormone androstenedione peaks. When estrogen and progesterone were given in the form of contraceptive pills, the ovulatory peak of female-initiated sexual behavior was

Table 2
Case Study Characteristics of Women Sex Offenders

	WOLFE 1985	McCARTHY 1986	FALLER 1987	FINKELHOR, WILLIAMS, BURNS 1988	MATHEWS, MATHEWS, SPELTZ 1989	ALLEN 1990
# OF FEMALE SEX OFFENDERS	12-6-F/F[a]	26-11-F/F	40[a]	147[a] In-depth study on 22	15-14-F/F	65[a]
AGE	18-38 years Mean – 29.5		13-47 years Mean – 26.1	16-77 years Mean – 35	17-42 years Majority early 30's	18-49 years Mean – 32.8
RACE	100% caucasian		95% white[a]	68% white[a]	86.5% caucasian	92% white, non-Hispanic[a]
FEMALE VICTIM[b] RELATIONSHIP	5-S 4-D	Most often daughters[a]	40-D, R, N	236 female children in child care	20-D 5-R 3-N	3-D 2-AD 2-S 1-R
VICTIM AGE	Mean – 10.2	Mean – 6.4	Mean – 6.1	Mean – 2.1	Mean – 7.4[a]	Mean[a] – "minor"
ABUSE[c]	C, M, RA, PP FS, OP		GS, F, C, DP, EX, WS, PP	K, F, M, DP, AP, OP, C, RL, forced C-C sex	SG, M, K, F, WS, C. DP	EP, F, C
USED FORCE	25%		–[a]	44-54%		20%
COERCED OR WITH OTHERS	50%	58%	72.5%	76%	73%	
ORGASMIC WHEN ABUSING	5				9	
USED FANTASY	8				6	

Table 2
(Continued)

DURATION	1 x to 18 months+[a]		1 x to 21 months+[a]		1 x to 6½ years	
ABUSED IN CHILDHOOD	7 – sexually	13 – sexually		19 – sexually	All – sexually	Majority – physical/sexual abuse
SUBSTANCE ABUSE	42%	82% of the 11 F/F abusers	Yes[a]	55%	Yes[a]	17% – alcoholics 26% – other drugs
EDUCATIONAL LEVEL[d]	2 – C 9 – HS	Average and borderline	HS, C[a]	26 – 12th grade and below 12 – HS 5 – HS+	Unknown	7th grade to master's degree
MARITAL STATUS[e]	50% – M 25% – NM 25% – D	85% – M or D[a]	63% – M 21% – NM[a]	—[a]	—[a]	
EMPLOYEE	25 %	75%	90%	—[a]	27%	45%
SOCIALLY ISOLATED	9	Yes[a]	No[a]	Yes[a]	9	Yes[a]
DEPENDENT	4	Yes[a]	Yes[a]	Yes[a]	Yes[a]	Yes[a]
MENTAL DIFFICULTIES	5[a]		Yes[a]	19	Yes[a]	Yes[a]
PSYCHOTIC	1			3		

[a]Indicates acknowledgement of variable but undetermined number, or lack of informational clarity.

[b]Victim: D=daughter; AD=adopted daughter; R=relative; N=neighbor; S=stranger

[c]Abuse: K=kissing; F=fondling; M=masturbation; C=cunnilingus; AP=anal penetration; DP=digital penetration; OP=object penetration; GS=group sex; FS=forced sex; EX=exploration EP=exposing; PP=pornographic pictures; WS=watched sex; RL=ritualistic abuse; SG=sex games; RA=rape

[d]Educational Level: HS=high school; C=college

[e]Marital Status: M=married; NM=never married; D=divorced

Table 3
Etiologies of Female Molesting Behavior

THEORY	CONTRIBUTING SOURCES
BIOLOGICAL	
Chronic illness	Goodwin & DiVasto, 1979; Lidz & Lidz, 1969
Heightened sexual behavior during the female's monthly ovulatory vertex	Adams, et al., 1978
Arrested development through limited intelligence	Finkelhor & Araji, 1986; O'Connor, 1987
Borderline intelligence	McCarty, 1986; Rowan et al., 1990
Mental conditions (brain damage/mental retardation) affect judgment and impulse control	Faller, 1987
Inhibited androgen production caused by hypersexuality	Mellor et al., 1988
Relationship between androgens and physical/sexual aggression	Cooper et al., 1990
LEARNED/BEHAVIORAL	
Basic dependence	Groth, 1982; Lidz et al, 1965; Lidz & Lidz, 1969; Lloyd, 1987; James & Nasjleti, 1983; Mathews et al., 1989; McCarty, 1986
Limited social skills, social isolation	Chasnoff et al., 1986; Lidz & Lidz, 1969; Lloyd, 1987; Mathews et al., 1989; O'Connor, 1987; Wolfe, 1985
Seductive behavior in mothers is more socially tolerated	Goodwin & DiVasto, 1979
Substance abuse	Chasnoff et al., 1986; Faller, 1987; Groth, 1982; James & Nasjleti, 1983; Mathews, et al., 1989; McCarty, 1986; O'Connor, 1987; Wolfe, 1985
Coerced and/or accompanied by a male or others; behavior was approved by a dominant male	Faller, 1987; Mathews et al., 1989; McCarty, 1986
Sexually abused in childhood	O'Connor, 1987; Rowan et al., 1990; Wolfe, 1985
Cultural or familial conditioning to sexual activity with children	Chasnoff et al., 1986; Faller, 1987; Mathews et al., 1989; McCarty, 1986; O'Connor, 1987

Table 3
(Continued)

Commercially motivated	Finkelhor & Araji, 1986; Rowan et al., 1990
Result of early imprinting, imitation, and shaping	Mathews et al., 1989; Travin et al, 1990

PSYCHODYNAMIC

Experienced emotional neglect and oppression in childhood	Lidz et al., 1965
Psychotic; personality disorder; desire to experience wholeness; attempt to prevent further psychic disintegration	Chasnoff et al., 1986; Faller, 1987; Lidz & Lidz, 1969; Rowan et al., 1990; Travin et al., 1990; Wolfe, 1985
Loss of a significant relationship (that had an internal representation)	Chasnoff et al., 1986; Goodwin & DiVasto, 1979; Green et al., 1974; James & Nasjleti, 1983; Lidz & Lidz, 1969; Mathews et al., 1989; O'Connor, 1987; Wakefield et al., 1990
Mother was absent during formative years; lack of empathy; lack of early maternal attachment	Groth, 1982; Lidz & Lidz, 1969; Lloyd, 1987; Wilking, 1990
Experienced confused gender identities or self-identity	Foreward and Buck, 1978; Lidz and Lidz, 1969; Mathews, et al., 1989; Rowan, et al., 1990
Abuse was a form of aggression expressing early childhood experiences; an inability to channel rage; lack of impulse control	Finkelhor & Araji, 1986; Galdston, 1981; Mathews et al., 1989; Stoller, 1975
Need for nurturance; desire to be loved; no sense of intimate attachment or belonging; unfulfilled emotional needs; need for attention and affection; overwhelming dependency	Bierker, 1989; Faller, 1986; Foreward & Buck, 1978; Goodwin & DiVasto, 1979; Groth, 1978, 1982; Justice & Justice, 1979; Lloyd, 1987; Mathews et al., 1989; McCarty, 1986; Renvoize, 1982
Infantile and needy and desiring "emotional feeding" from daughter; serious emotional disturbance	Foreward & Buck, 1978; Mayer, 1983; McCarty, 1986
Emotional development complications/early traumatizations; retarded psychosocial development	McCarty, 1986; O'Connor, 1987; Wolfe, 1985
Sexual preoccupations/compulsions	Finkelhor & Araji, 1986; Wolfe, 1985

suppressed. Research on female sex offenders has not investigated the time dur-ing the menstrual cycle that abusers have molested, or if they were taking hor-monal medication. Possibly some women may be prevented from molesting by regulation of the ovulatory vertex.

Learned/Behavioral

Some theorists and researchers suggest that sexual behavior in humans is large-ly determined by processes of social learning. Such studies emphasize the importance of childhood conditioning experiences. Ford and Beach (1951) state that an individual's sexuality is affected by previous experience in two ways: 1) the kind of stimulation and the types of situations capable of evoking sexual excitement; and 2) the overt behavior through which this excitement is expressed. Kinsey, Pomeroy, Martin, & Gebhard (1953) similarly indicate that learning and conditioning, in connection with human sexual behavior, involve the same processes as learning and conditioning other behavior. The individ-ual's development of molesting behavior is, therefore, likely to involve operant and observational modeling (Howells, 1981).

Determinants of a female's early sexual behavioral development include the processes of imprinting, imitation, and shaping by means of parental direction. Freud (1933) was the primary theorist who believed that 1) parents had the greatest influence on the child's development, 2) the child created psychic struc-tures in response to parental behavior, 3) adult sexual behavior can be traced to effects of parental behavior in infancy, and 4) sexual desire and gratification had origins in infancy long before their obvious upsurge at puberty. The six core studies for this theory indicate that the offending woman has experienced early parental and familial sexual and/or physical abuse that led her to engage in sub-stance abuse (mostly alcohol) and co-offending molestation. Such behavioral outcomes of childhood molestation are presented as familially learned determi-nants of adult sexual abuse.

THE EFFECTS OF CHILDHOOD ABUSE. In 1983, Russell reported that over one-third of the United States female population has experienced sexual abuse by a father, stepfather, or uncle prior to 18 years of age. Studies indicate that women sexu-ally abused in childhood are more likely to display depression, sexually dys-functional conduct, low self-esteem, anxiety, self-mutilation, poor interpersonal relationships, and substance abuse (Murphy, Kilpatrick, Amick-McMullan, Veronen, Paduhovich, Best, 1988). Owens (1984) states that such females usual-ly experience emotions of denial, nonacceptance, aggression, and an inability to feel needed. They also have lower levels of social conformity that cause them to resist adaptation to socially established norms. As adults, these women may be unable to ask for nurturance and will limit physical touching to times when they are sexually exploiting because of their inability to distinguish healthy caring from promiscuous sexual behavior (Maltz & Holman, 1987).

Sexual abuse research indicates that of female children who are sexually victimized, the majority are sexually offended during their prepubertal years (Finkelhor, 1984; Russell, 1986). The effects of sexual molestation in childhood can disrupt the developmental learning stages of trust, autonomy, initiative, and productivity (Lindberg & Disted, 1985), and create more symptoms of psychological disturbance in later years (Murphy et al., 1988). Early sexual victimization disturbs the female child's maturation process and thereby restricts her natural ego development (Kendall-Tackett & Simon, 1987; Nadelson & Notman, 1984). The disruption of this natural process has the potential to cause distortions in the female's instinctual urges (Stein, 1973). Females who are sexually abused before their own childhood sexual identity is fully developed will experience more sex-role confusion and patterns of disorientation in their adult sexual behavior (Simari & Baskin, 1982).

Many sexually abused women activate the emotional effects of childhood abuse in every relationship that offers the possibility of intimacy (Stein, 1973). If the early molestation trauma remains undisclosed and psychologically unresolved and untreated, the female will experience difficulty in separating sex from feelings of love and affection, a situation that encourage the development of her own molesting behavior (Forward & Buck, 1978). Her behavior of "sexual loving," stimulates her desire to control the childhood experience of being sexually used by another, which promotes feelings of powerlessness (Maltz & Holman, 1987).

SUBSTANCE ABUSE. Several sources indicate that a significant percentage of women substance abusers also had histories of childhood sexual abuse (Miller, Downs, Gondoli, & Keil, 1987; Rohsenow, Corbett, & Devine, 1986). The six core studies, as well as others, indicate that alcohol abuse is a common factor in over one third of molestation cases (Faller, 1987; Mathews et al., 1989; Miller et al., 1986; McCarty, 1986; Wolfe, 1985). Although the connection between alcoholism and sexual abuse continues to be studied, there is a professional consensus that alcohol abuse in women is a response to underlying emotional pathology (Beckman, 1976; Light, 1988; Wilsnack, 1976; Wood & Duffy, 1966).

Clinical reports of alcohol abuse in women indicate that it is a complex problem involving the interaction of several variables: biochemical, psychological, and sociocultural. Biochemical predispositions to alcohol abuse through inheritance of personality or psychiatric disorders and pharmacogenetic mechanisms continues to be explored. However, it cannot be assumed that genetic factors, which can possibly contribute to alcohol dependency, also influence the woman's likelihood to commit crime while inebriated. Rather, the study of alcohol abuse and female behavior through polygenic models suggest that there are different degrees of multiple genetic factors affected by strong environmental influences (Cloninger, Christiansen, Reich, & Gottesman, 1978; Light, 1988).

Psychodynamic characteristics of substance abusing women have also been identified in female sex offenders. The psychological factors associated with both types of women include: 1) a high frequency of early traumatic life experiences and/or stressful factors that encourage behavioral isolation and loneliness; 2) an unusually ambivalent relationship to the father who was typically alcoholic, psychotic, or absent from home, accompanied by an estranged relationship with the mother; 3) identity and sex-role confusion that emphasized the social feminine behavior of passivity, dependence, and desire to be cared for; 4) strong feelings of self-deprecation, inferiority, and insecurity with intense needs for love and acceptance by others (Beckman, 1976; Light, 1988; Mathews et al., 1989; McCarty, 1986).

A significant emotional conflict considered to be the major contributing factor to alcohol abuse among females, and which is equally evident in female sex offenders, is the woman's struggle with dependency behaviorally characterized by narcissism, attention-seeking, passivity, and attachment (Mathews et al., 1989; Zimberg,1983). The dependency needs of the abusing female are repressed when she is intoxicated, and she experiences artificial feelings of power, control, and enhanced self-esteem that cannot be otherwise achieved. When sober, the abusing woman experiences profound feelings of worthlessness and inadequacy, which lead to unconscious needs for nurturance. The issue of female dependency significant to the study of female molesting behavior is theoretically discussed later in this study.

Sociocultural factors also enable women to depend on alcohol, and include experiences with unfulfilling interpersonal relationships and/or cultural stereotypical messages that enhance feelings of inadequacy and acceptability. When a woman drinks excessively, she releases the anger and hostility connected to social feelings of inferiority and worthlessness (Beckman, 1976; Wilsnack, 1984; Wood & Duffy, 1966). The cultural messages that communicate the women's unimportance are later presented in the theoretical orientation and criminal law sections of this study. Current sociocultural factors limit female development and prolong the substance abusing female's psychological confusion and learned dysfunctional behavior.

The reliance on alcohol, which subsequently leads to abuse of other addictive chemicals (Light, 1988), suggests that the woman is projecting uncontrollable, disturbed feelings that reenact learned childhood conceptions of dysfunctional familial patterns reinforced by current circumstances. Light (1988) states that a woman's negative or unfulfilling childhood experiences disrupts her emotional development, and encourages the evolution of depersonalization, schizoid tendencies, avoidant/borderline personality traits, and identity sex-role confusion.

COERCED FEMALES. Significant to the findings on women sex offenders is their co-offending role in the molestation of female children. Early studies of women molesters did not find their co-offending participation as harmful the male's behavior. Women were believed to be non-directive and assume a more observant role (Faller, 1987; Finkelhor, 1984; Zuelzer & Reposa, 1983).

Current studies recognize that women are frequently persuaded into sexually abusing children by adults of both genders (Faller, 1987; Finkelhor et al., 1988; Mathews et al., 1989; McCarty, 1986), and indicate that women frequently have a more active/initiatory role in group molesting situations (Finkelhor et al., 1988; Mathews et al., 1989).

Co-offending females are characteristically socially isolated, emotionally and economically dependent, and lacking in impulse control. The female's fear of abandonment forces her to yearn for someone to protect and take care of her (Mathews et al., 1989). She is easily influenced by more powerful individuals who often have deviant social histories (Finkelhor et al., 1988). Faller (1987) indicates that coerced females have an innate desire and expectation of nurturance by other adult(s). McCarty (1986) believes that the involved adults are seeking maternal nurturance denied them in childhood that they hope to obtain through the female victim.

Finkelhor et al. (1988) note that most female "followers" learn to sexually abuse children even when no other adults are involved. The once-submissive female has been taught to project her hostility, anger, and helplessness onto others by molesting children and other adults to experience power and control. Female initiators are sometimes reported to be "commercially" motivated, making money through the pornography and prostitution of children (Faller, 1987; Finkelhor et al., 1988; Mathews et al., 1989). Case studies involving such lone female molesters are more likely to be unreported or unsubstantiated, and, therefore, less likely to be included in research reports (Finkelhor et al., 1988).

Psychodynamic Determinants

Several studies indicate that some female sex offenders endure psychological difficulties exhibited in sexual behavior. Such psychic impasses have been diagnosed in some female sex offenders as indications of psychoses (Faller, 1987; Finkelhor et al., 1988; Wolfe, 1985), emotional developmental complications or traumatization (Allen, 1990; McCarty, 1986; O'Connor, 1987; Rowan et al., 1990;

Wolfe, 1985), and sexual preoccupations or compulsions (Finkelhor et al., 1988; Wolfe, 1985). Psychotic etiologies of female molesting behavior also include the woman treating the female child as "the bad self" (Galdston, 1965), the mother's misperception of the child at the time of the abuse (Bishop, 1978), and the woman's inability to channel rage and aggression into acceptable directions (Galdston, 1981; Mathews et al., 1989).

Some studies indicate that the loss of significant relationships having strong internal representations is a motive for female sex offending behavior (Goodwin & DiVasto, 1979; Green, Gaines & Sandgrund, 1974; Lidz & Lidz, 1969; Mathews et al., 1991; O'Connor, 1987). This observation is supported by Wahl (1960) who suggests that some female offenders experienced an abnormal pre-Oedipal period that lacked the essential key relationship of maternal attachment. Other sources indicate that female sex offenders had unsatisfying adult experiences and were either separated, divorced, or involved in an unsatisfying relationship with another adult at the time of the abuse (Table 2).

Emotional role reversal in caretaking responsibilities is also detected in female sex offenders. In such situations, the adult female has great needs for nurturance and relies on a child to provide the necessary emotional comfort (Lloyd, 1987). Earlier research by Groth (1978) supports this finding; he saw women who had incestuous relationships with their daughters as lonely, isolated, insecure, dependent, needing intimacy and warmth, and feeling inadequate to carry out adult role expectations. He states that such women have no feelings of emotional attachment, belonging, or relatedness to others, and notes that when the adult female was an independent offender, she had a strong need for nurturance and control. Such feelings most likely originate from the woman's childhood in which her own mother was either physically or emotionally absent during her formative years (Groth, 1982; Lidz & Lidz, 1969).

Similar observations concerning adult female nurturing needs are also noted by Lidz, Fleck and Cornelison (1964), who studied four cases of homosexual tendencies in mothers whose daughters developed schizophrenia. Their investigations revealed that the mothers had experienced emotional neglect and oppression in their own childhood, and had married husbands who continued to undermine their self-esteem, which increased their dependency. The mothers indicated difficulties in forming warm, close relationships with spouses and in properly catharting from their daughters. Each case showed the mother's highly eroticized interest in her daughters' body, including sensuous physical intimacies. None of the mothers had been able to provide good nurturant care during the daughter's childhood, and each did not establish clear physical boundaries between herself and the child, and between her needs and those of the daughter. Female children who experience such maternal behavior are left with feelings of being emotional and physical adjuncts to their mothers, burdened by the need to support the caretakers from whom they have insufficient differentiation. Daughters who have not developed a sense of separation and individuation from their own mothers will likely not perceive their own daughters' need for individuation and will continue the process of experiencing the female child as a continuation of themselves.

Women who experience insufficient psychic childhood development in nurturance, identity, and autonomous behavior will continue to function with noticeable behavioral abnormalities as adults. Psychologically, a woman sex offender experiences the female minor as an extension of her personal self-image, or as a magical symbol of satisfying unfulfilled childhood needs (Forward & Buck, 1978; McCarty, 1986). Women in this category are unable to give up the hope of obtaining the mothering and protection that they missed as children, and will attempt to satisfy their needs for tenderness, attention, and support through sexual behavior with female children (Justice & Justice, 1979).

Table 2 organizes case study etiologies of female molesting behavior using the biological, learned/behavioral and psychodynamic categories. The comparison of male and female etiologies for sexual molestation indicates the influence of biological makeup, psychological development, familial conditioning, and cultural norms for both genders. Specific etiologies recorded for female sex offenders that were not significant among male offenders included: an incomplete or confused self-identity; a dependence on others for self- fulfillment; vulnerability to being coerced into molesting; feelings of oppression and neglect; and lack of emotional attachment to any significant individual or group. Particular etiologies found among male sex offenders that were not evident in female offenders included: response to social norms that encouraged dominance, power, and initiation of sexual behavior; acting on social norms that projected male ownership of children and women; the reliance on children and child pornography as a means to fulfill erotic needs; and the belief that masculinity is measured by the ability to satisfy sexual urges.

CHAPTER 4

Discussion

Influencing Factors

The theoretical orientation of this study is based on learned/behavioral and psychodynamic factors that influence women to sexually molest female children. Research on female sex offenders indicates that such women had no self-definition (Mathews et al., 1989), often overidentified with the child (Wilking, 1990), and attempted to experience "wholeness" through female victimization (Morgenthaler, 1988). Some women see their female victims more as "extensions of themselves," than as separate individuals (Forward & Buck, 1978; McCarty, 1986). Case study findings also imply that female sex offenders have unfulfilled emotional and physical developmental needs that cause limited and distorted identity formation (Levine, Risen, & Althof, 1990; Lidz & Lidz, 1969; Mathews et al., 1989). Female sex offenders reported that they molested because they were extremely dependent, in need of nurturance, and feeling lonely, isolated, and insecure. Such women expressed helplessness in carrying out female social role expectations (Groth, 1978, 1982; Goodwin & DiVasto, 1979; Mathews et al., 1989; Renvoize, 1982; Wolfe, 1985).

Related research on female sex offenders suggests that deficiencies in maternal attachment from birth to 3 years of age may contribute to a woman's intentions to act out unfulfilled maturational needs during adult developmental stages

(Groth, 1982; Wilking, 1990). However, this early lack of effective maternal care-taking is not the sole contributor to the behavioral motivation of women who become sexually involved with female children. The female offender's familial and cultural influences must also be assessed. Studies suggest that the physical or emotional absence and/or abuse by a male caretaker or partner during the female offender's early development, as well as the narcissistic neediness of the primary caretaker(s), may create the emotional dysfunction that female sex offenders characteristically display (Mathews et al., 1989; Miller, 1981; Rose, 1991). Such parental caretakers construct a "family system" that denies the emotional well-being and growth of the female child, causing her to seek alternate ways to achieve psychological fulfillment in later years. Cultural messages reinforce denial of a female's psychological growth by effectively communicating a status of powerlessness and insignificance to women. Such messages may encourage women who have limited self-development to rely on others to define their identity.

The maternal, familial, and cultural factors considered significant in understanding the development of same-sex molesting behavior in women include the following: 1) primary mother-daughter attachment, 2) early female identity formation, and 3) female socialization. An investigation of developmental deficiencies in these maturation processes indicates that the female can experience enhanced emotions of loss (of self to the maternal love object), fear (of being isolated from others), and anger (over being subservient and culturally oppressed). In later growth stages, the woman seeks to control and satisfy unmet psychosocial needs by emotionally enmeshing herself with typical nurturing female children more needy than herself.

PRIMARY MOTHER-DAUGHTER ATTACHMENT

"Every mother contains her daughter within herself, and every daughter her mother ... Every woman extends backwards into her mother and forwards into her daughter" (Jung & Kereyi, 1969, p. 162).

The female child's first few years of life are the primary period in her personality formation. Dinnerstein (1976) emphasizes the unacknowledged role that a mother emotionally represents to her newborn female child. The maternal caretaker's role is crucial during the child's pre-Oedipal stages of development (Gardiner, 1987), and the child's successful progress through them is dependent on the appropriateness of the mother's behavior. The mother is the infant's first experience of humanness, love, and environment, as well as the child's primary experience of nurturance, stimulation, and social intercourse.

The female's emotional relationship to her mother is the means by which her most fundamental feelings will be formed and expressed. This is where she first learns the necessity for submission, in which she is forced to subordinate her own will in her attempts to please and satisfy her necessary source of continued existence. During this time, the mother may experience the female child as a narcissistic mirror, a supplier of nurturance, the fulfillment of her incomplete self, a phallic extension of her person, a projected part of her body, an ego graft, a psychic drain, or a sadistic reminder of her own inadequacy (Offerman-Zuckerberg, 1988). Whatever the child's symbolism to the mother is, the female's psychological growth will correspond to the mother's own history of self-definition. The mother will pass on to her daughter that which she herself has experienced. If the mother has not successfully accomplished the childhood stages of symbiosis and separation/individuation with her own mother, then she reinforces emotions of continuance, dependency, and limited self-identification in her daughter.

Research on the developmental histories of women sex offenders frequently finds poor maternal attachment during the pre-Oedipal phase of the molesters' development. Wilking (1990) states that a woman's early social and emotional learning, and her mother's, are just as important as the female child's biological characteristics. The success of the mother-daughter attachment during the infant's symbiotic and separation/individuation stages (Mahler, 1968) influences the child's capacity to free herself from instinctive dependency (Call, 1984). Maturational inadequacies during this period can substantiate the females' lack of certainty and direction to achieve a sense of personal independence from their primary love object — Mother. This puts the female child in an emotional bind of always seeking nurturance from others. In reality, this developmental deficit in itself does not create a women's sexual offending behavior, but it appears to be a risk factor that contributes to the emotional instability of women who molest.

Symbiosis

Mahler (1968) long ago theorized that disruption of, or deprivation in, the mother-child relationship during the symbiotic and separation/individuation phases can cause the child, in adulthood, to exhibit behavioral manifestations of developmental tasks that were disturbed or not completed. Seemingly, difficulties in the mother-daughter early bonding relationship may cause some women to search longingly for the feelings and expectations that they believed were denied them by their primary caretakers.

According to Mahler (1975), infants experience early life in a state of "symbiosis." In this phase (0-5 months), the child functions and behaves as though she and the mother are a dual omnipotent system. Mahler indicates that the essential feature of symbiosis is the child's powerful illusionary fusion with the image and common boundary of the mother. Ego boundaries (a sense of personal psychological division) between mother and daughter are less easily formed and defined (unlike that of mother and son), and both share a sense of sameness and continuity (Chodorow, 1978a).

Friday (1977) indicates that the mother's first emotion toward her daughter is self-love, in which the daughter is maternally viewed as a narcissistic extension. The female child, once biologically within the mother, is now an extension or double of the mother herself. During this emotional connection, the mother and daughter reflect or mirror to one another what they are seeing in the other. The mother affirms and communicates the infant's capabilities, laying the groundwork for self-esteem and self-worth, and the female child begins to identify herself through the mother's mirrored image. Each confirms the other's existence. "When I look I am seen and so I exist" (Winnicott, 1971, p. 114).

Self-love, or narcissism, is believed by several object- relation theorists to be a normal stage of early child development (Kohut & Wolf, 1978; Mahler et al., 1975; Miller, 1981). Narcissism that has extended beyond the normal developmental stage can cause a deficit in the structure of the female self and reflects unfinished, archaic, self-seeking fulfillment of infantile needs. Kohut (1971) states that some females become narcissistic adults because of an unempathetic maternal caretaker who failed to help the child achieve a cohesive self by appropriately mirroring the child's accomplishments. Without positive maternal mirroring, it is likely that the female infant will develop a ceaseless dependency and longing to connect herself to a nurturing source that promotes self-love. She will always be in search of someone to affirm and support her existence. The infant's unfulfillment or fixation in the symbiosis stage will distort the developmental process of separating from the primary caretaker and cause future self-identifying experiences and behaviors to become increasingly inappropriate and pathological as she matures. Kohut and Wolf (1978) indicate that an adult who has grown up in this dilemma will experience depression and will try to cover up such emotions and stimulate self-fulfillment through promiscuous sex or other compulsive activity.

Several theorists explain an adult's sexual interaction with children as dependent on narcissism — a love for the child that the adult once was (Fraser, 1976; Gordon, 1976; Kraemer, 1976). A mother can work out her unresolved association with her own mother in her relationship with her daughter (Chodorow, 1978a). The woman who sexually molests female children expresses an absent or limited maternal-infant self-identification and self-love. The adult female remains in a state of mirroring her desire for nurturance and self-love toward someone who closely represents her own image and feelings of helplessness: a female child.

If a female has a favorable experience of the symbiotic union with the mother, then she can make a smooth psychological differentiation from the mother to a further psychological expansion of femininity beyond the symbiotic state. Equally so, if she has an negative relationship with her primary caretaker, then further complications related to her identity and self-worth will evolve.

Separation/Individuation

Mahler, Pine, and Bergman (1975) define "separation" as the child's psychological differentiation, distancing and disengagement from the mother. "Individuation" is seen as the child's evolving intrapsychic autonomy from the maternal source. The female child (5 months to 3 years of age) successfully achieves a sense of separation and individuation through maternal behavior that encourages identity formation. The child's increased awareness of the separation between herself and her mother stimulates her sense of an outside world, and the evolution of her own ego.

During this period in the female child's development, the mother's emotional availability and her willingness to let go of the child are very important. The frustration of this process, which is connected to the feminine Oedipus complex, in which the female child turns her attachment from her mother to her father, will prolong the stage of symbiosis and lack of separation/individuation even into adulthood (Chodorow, 1978b). The mother's absence during this stage, or her refusal to allow the female child to individuate from her, will foster life-long fears of separation and limit ego development, which are characteristics of women sex offenders (Groth, 1982; Mathews et al., 1989).

Winnicott (1962) termed the "good enough mother" as one who adapts and changes according to the needs of her daughter, and who gradually decreases the growing child's dependence on her. The ability of the child to move away from the mother, physically and emotionally, is crucial in her formation of the psychic representation of the "I," or ego. Lerner (1985) speculates that conflicts often arise between a daughter's sense of a separate "I" and her perception of a collective "we," and attributes this conflict to a lack of psychological distance and unclear boundaries in the mother-daughter dyad. By keeping the daughter close to her, the mother keeps her daughter's ego confounded with her own. As a consequence, the daughter never develops an individualized sense of self, which may be characterized as a clear sense of where her mother stops and where she begins. Such an ego boundary weakness results in the female's need to enmesh herself with others in order to have a sense of who she is (Westkott, 1978). The non-existence of the female's sense of "I-ness" will subject her to a life-long struggle to attempt to separate from her mother to define herself (Fischer, 1983). Additional aspects of female individuation will be explored in the "Female Identity Formation" section of this study.

Rich (1976) states that possibly there is no other human relationship similar or equal to the cathexis between mothers and daughters, and that the loss of the daughter to the mother, and the mother to the daughter is the fundamental female tragedy: a loss of self. Although every woman participates in the mother-daughter experience, a severely diffused relationship involving conflict and ambivalence concerning intradyadic separation, individuation, autonomy, and nurturance will evolve into a form of emotional disturbance (Boyd, 1985; Flax, 1981; Greenspan, 1983; Litwin, 1986), and possibly be the basis for promoting sexually perversive behavior by the female adult.

FEMALE IDENTITY FORMATION

"The most important developmental task facing women today is the formation of identity ... it is in the realm of identity that a woman bases her sense of herself as well as her vision of the structure of her life" (Josselson, 1987, p. 3). The process of identity formation takes place throughout the female's lifetime and is shaped by her many personal aspects and social experiences. Josselson (1987) states that some of these include natural talents, intelligence, social class, physical attractiveness, genetic aspects of temperament, physical limitations, early deprivation, and traumatic experiences. She indicates that "identity" is a person's unconscious act of integrating parts of the personality with the realities of the social world through choices and decision-making, allowing the female to shape her idea of who she is. As a consequence, the female experiences both a sense of internal coherence and a meaningful relatedness to her world.

Aries and Olver (1985) state that although there is presently no clear empirical evidence regarding women having more difficulty than men in developing an identity, there is sufficient clinical evidence that supports differences in male and female self-development. Women tend to identify or define themselves through their relationships and emotional responses with others; men tend to recognize their self-definition by separating and creating more distinct boundaries between themselves and those outside themselves (Bardwick, 1971; Chodorow, 1978a; Gilligan, 1977; Hoffman, 1972).

Eichenbaum and Orbach (1983) state that the female child's identification process does not fully separate the child from its maternal source. Rather, a female's sense of herself is seen as circularly related and integrated with the identity of her own mother. The authors indicate three major activities that shape this mother-daughter relationship. First, the mother identifies with her infant's gender because, in reality, she has reproduced herself. Second, the mother projects feelings she has about herself onto the daughter, lacking the ability to differentiate herself from her child. Third, the mother unconsciously behaves toward her daughter as she internally acts toward the "daughter" part of herself. Similar observations by Hammer (1976) and Chodorow (1974) suggest that a mother relives her own childhood, as well as her own mother's identity, through her daughter. The mother's intense emotional identification process with her daughter causes her to experience herself as her own mother, and to sense her own childhood feelings that she has towards her own mother.

A female child's experience of a separate sense of self begins in infancy. The mother's self-concept, how she feels about herself, and how she sees herself as a person is passed on to the daughter (Hollender, 1973). Chodorow (1978a) reports that daughters internalize many of the mother's behaviors, values, and thoughts. The daughter becomes "like her mother" because she is reinforced to do so (Weitzman, 1984).

The result of early mother-daughter emotional rapport causes the female to experience herself as continuous with mother, and later with others, experiencing fewer established barriers of differentiation and separateness than males. The early experience of relational dynamics in female identity formation encourages the child to define herself through interpersonal relationships and environmental interactions. Such a basis of dependent identity formation causes females to experience difficulty in knowing what they genuinely want or feel apart from what others expect or approve of (Wolowitz, 1972), and "sets them up" to experience an intense fear of being stranded or isolated from others (Gilligan, 1982).

The fear of isolation is primarily established when the pre-Oedipal female encounters a developmental separation from her significant source of nurturance — which is most often the mother. Developmental separation from the nurturing figure can create aloneness, helplessness, and anxiety, as well as competence and freedom. The female who pursues individuation from her primary caregiver may be indicating that she is ready to take responsibility for who she is and what she does, rather than to attribute such growth to another. The female who engages in establishing a self-worth that is not entirely other-oriented is more capable of organizing her personality and identity so that it is coherent and meaningful to her world.

Marcia (1966) states that for an individual to establish an identity, she must experience some crisis regarding her childhood perception of herself. Such a crisis causes the female to weigh personal and situational possibilities and to experiment with self-related choices. She then makes a commitment as to what to believe, what to do, and what to become. Those females who successfully transcend crisis and make such commitments can be assumed to have achieved a "stage-specific identity." Those who are denied or avoid the process, neither experiencing identity crisis nor forming commitments, remain in a state of identity diffusion. In this position, the female does not establish a sense of who she is or know what she wants, and reacts to impulses, memories, and personal traits in a manner that reflects an incoherent connection with her core self (Josselson, 1987).

The female who is reinforced to maintain an attachment to others because of the mother's own inability to reinforce individuation is one who experiences a sense of not knowing who she is. Her dysfunctional relational identity formation with her maternal source causes her to interpret loss relationships or isolation as a deprivation of psychological stabilizers that help to structure and ensure her self-worth. Her inability to initiate self-direction causes her to become fearful and dependent.

Research on female sex offenders indicates that these women are unable to identify themselves. They characterize themselves as subordinate and emotionally enmeshed with others for the purpose of psychological security. Mathews et al. (1989) report that such women have no identity of their own, are restricted in understanding their self-concept, and have no self-definition or positive idea of who they are. This limitation in self-development inhibits such women from understanding the personal boundaries between themselves and others and prevents them from seeing the wrongness of their molesting behavior.

Because identity is a configuration of aspects of the female's personality, the qualitative differences among females and the various ways in which their female identity is formed are important. Josselson (1987) emphasizes the importance of understanding "the different pathways to development as a woman, and the different roads a girl may travel on the way to womanhood" (p. 5). She indicates that knowing a woman's identity formation process can explain her personality makeup and life-course differences. Such information is significant to understand the crucial dimensions of female development and even creates a basis for understanding women who molest female children. Josselson (1987) indicates that professionals should consider the differences in female identity formation and recognize women who have attained a solid and reliable sense of identity as compared with those whose identities are more precarious.

FEMALE SOCIALIZATION

"Females who are denied the childhood right to express a full range of personal emotions and to feel authentic cannot differentiate or mature. The female will remain emotionally fused with her behavior, and will be unaware as to any inappropriateness to molesting" (Mathews et al., 1989, p. 90).

Research on female sex offenders indicates that they have feelings of extreme anger and describe themselves as nobodies, with few rights and little value (Finkelhor et al., 1988; Galdston, 1981; Mathews et al., 1989). The women stated that they were hungry for love and attention, yet lived their lives fulfilling the needs of other people (Groth, 1978; Lloyd, 1987; Mathews et al., 1989; O'Connor, 1987).

Understanding the dynamics that cause some women to molest female children requires an investigation of the abuser's childhood development regarding her experience of empowerment and oppression. A female who has been subjected to abuse and submissiveness in childhood is unaware as an adult of how these behaviors influence future abuse or that she has the power to stop abuse (Rose, 1991). Unfortunately, the female frequently responds to her own experience of past or current feelings of powerlessness and oppression by abusing others. The adult behavior is associated with the individual's childhood knowledge of her self-definition and self-worth.

Investigations of the female sex offender's complications in self-definition and behavioral submissiveness shows that such problems originate during early childhood and are continually shaped by maternal example, parental control, and cultural gender-role expectations, which ultimately enhance female dependency and affect reasoning abilities. While exploring the influence of family and culture in the lives of women who sexually molest female children, it is evident that such women are not criminally oriented to abusing, but are acting from and expressing developmental inhibitions perpetuated by these two sources.

PARENTAL INFLUENCES

Case studies on female sex offenders indicate that they were sexually, physically, and/or emotionally abused by parental caretakers during childhood (Table 2). In actuality, the abusive act itself perhaps does not cause the female victim to abuse others as an adult, but, more significantly, what was developmentally denied her as a child by "loving" parents can contribute to the origins of abusive behavior. Female sex offenders describe themselves as feeling unloved, and having great needs for attention and affection (Faller, 1987; Mathews et al., 1989;

McCarty, 1986). They had no sense of attachment or belonging and felt unaffiliated with any significant group or other (Groth, 1978, 1982; Lidz & Lidz, 1969; Travin et al., 1990).

Belief in the myth that all parents love their children is a main determinant in undermining family behavior and can perpetuate later abusive behavior in individuals. The idealization of parents is what Miller (1983) terms an aspect of "poisonous pedagogy" that prevents the consequences of familial child abuse from being examined more fully. The love the child is "supposed" to have for the parent ensures the concealment of familial abuse. Miller (1983) reports that the child's belief that parents are always right and that every act of cruelty, whether intentional or unintentional, is an expression of love is often an assumed culturally influenced concept.

The traumatic effects of many socially accepted aspects of "parenting" indicate that abusing caretakers have themselves been deprived of the childhood nurturing and individuation needs necessary to guide the development of their own children. Miller's (1981) work with narcissistic parents reveals that their feelings of self-love and self-alienation originated in childhood, in which their need for respect, echoing, and understanding had not been adequately met. Such adults lacked a mirroring parent or other empathic adult who could accept and reflect their childhood emotional range of feelings. This central aspect of the adult's childhood self was repressed, and she or he learned early to present an idealized, conforming "false self" to retain the parent's "love" on which her or his survival depended. For the female sex offender parented as a child by such needy individuals, the assumed "loving" parent-child relationship is actually one in which the child provides the adults with the attention, approval, and respect that they had not experienced in their own childhood. Because the female child in such a family system is denied her own needs of nurturance and self-development, she, like her parents, attempts to satisfy such emotional needs with children when she herself is an adult.

The female child's role as a narcissistic extension of the parents' idealized selves may cause her to feel that her entire existence is to fulfill her parents' expectations. Such a focus prevents the child from realizing her own rights and individuality (Horney, 1942). The child's response to this familial oppression pattern is one of fear (of lack of control) and anger (toward her abusive parents). Such feelings may become repressed because of her dependency and lack of self-worth and may later be recognized as reasons for molesting children (Mathews et al., 1989).

In focusing on parental influence, it is significant to comprehend the parental power as it relates to female sex-role stereotyping and the consequences of the child's powerlessness. The parallel between the parents' lack of emotional nurturance and the female child's suppressed feelings of self-worth is enhanced by adult expectations of how the female child should act. Females are "supposed" to develop traits of empathy and caring that reinforce the manifestation of a "false self," an aspect that Miller (1981) earlier identified in narcissistic parents. A female child's "unfeminine" feelings (anger, resentment, envy, aggression) become unacceptable to such parents and are split off or repressed in the female personality. Miller (1984) states that many women suffer from a narcissistic disturbance resulting from parental misuse of the child's emotional responsiveness. Unless a woman is allowed to express her unconscious anger and rebellion at being forced to satisfy her parents' unmet emotional needs at the sacrifice of her own self-realization, she will expect others to fulfill her unsatisfied narcissistic needs for approval. She will desire to find an understanding, empathic "mother," most likely a female child who is expected to develop such characteristics. Miller (1981) indicates that change and growth in the adult female cannot occur unless feelings associated with the childhood "lost self" are acknowledged and integrated.

The current research on female sex offenders indicates that these women have conflicts with revenge, power, and control (Mathews et al., 1989), and they desire to hurt children in much the same way that they had been hurt. The female victims were often used by the adult female abusers to satisfy emotional needs that were not met by the adults in their own childhoods. Such women were divorced or separated from husbands/boyfriends, had no significant "other" in their lives, or had an unstable sexual relationship with another adult. Schwartz (1984) considers the makeup of the nuclear family as a primary factor in women desiring sexual attention from children. The woman who is frequently deprived of attention, power, or sources that enhance self-esteem in childhood will seek to satisfy such needs with adult partners later in life. However, the more absent or disappointing her male relationships or partner, the more she will look to children as a substitute and/or for vicarious satisfaction.

Related research also suggests that women who sexually interact with female children are not acting out of sexual desire for the child, but instead are projecting suppressed feelings of the early denial of self-realization by parental needs. Miller (1983) argues that crime represents a reenactment of childhood experiences influenced by parental and social factors. The process by which a female child is shaped by familial adult power shares similarities with how she is made to conform to social expectations. The female child's early survival requires that she develop psychological characteristics pleasing to these two dominant group influences, which directs her emotionality and creates characteristics of vulnerability, weakness, and cooperation. The female child who assumes these characteristics is considered well-adjusted. The female who questions the basis for such behavioral and emotional orientations creates conflict and risks rejection. Either way, the female is limited by environmental expectations and gender-role status.

CULTURAL EXPECTATIONS OF FEMALE NURTURANCE

Researchers in Western society have perceived sexual molestation of children by women as rare, as well as less serious and traumatic than abuse by male offenders (Bernard et al., 1989). Some studies suggest that the reality of professional underreporting of female sex offenders may exemplify the inconceivable nature of their behavior, but report the difficulty in identifying such actions when the female gender role is that of nurturer and caretaker (Finkelhor, 1984; Groth, 1982; Russell, 1986). Plummer (1981) presents his cultural observations concerning the "sociology of pedophilia." He states that in Western culture men are viewed as needing more direct sexual gratification or release than women. Women are seen as being less sexual and more emotional, maternal, and nurturing.

The cultural stereotyping of female emotions reinforces the patriarchal concept that females are socially expected to nurture men, not vice versa. From infancy, women's psychic orientation is organized around the principle that they exist to serve others' needs. Their sense of powerlessness and lack of choices have been passed on to them by their own mothers, who were also subjected to social and psychological oppression (Chodorow, 1974). The social message concerning female responsibility assumes that men do not have the psychological capacity to nurture (because they have been raised and nurtured primarily or exclusively by women and receive little, if any, nurturing from men), but continuously deserve, need and are entitled to a female's care and attention. As a result of this male limitation and expectation, a female's focus is on what she can do for another, and not on what she can do for herself (Miller, 1976). The message communicated is that the female's psychological needs are less valuable than the gender's nurturing responsibilities. Realistically, because women are judged and formed by male standards, it is not inconceivable that females will behaviorally share similar nurturing orientations that will satisfy their desire for care and attention. It is, therefore, understandable why women turn to female children for caretaking when this dynamic has been socially ingrained and encouraged.

The cultural restraints on females not only encourage women to obtain nurturing from other females, but assist in perpetuating the cycle of women sexually abusing female children for purposes of seeking nurturance. A woman who seeks female minors for personal closeness has more likely held back from or been denied her own need for childhood nurturance. As a "good girl," she attempted to emotionally provide for her mother's or another adult's desires in an effort to gain love, and as a means of survival. In adulthood, her own unful-filled childhood nurturing needs cause her to turn to her own daughter or other female minors in hopes of emotional satisfaction (Caplan, 1981).

Westkott (1986) states that the cultural assumption of female nurturance does not necessarily encourage an emotionally needy mother to keep her daughter in an extended pre-Oedipal state, but does give the mother permission to devalue the daughter's needs by imposing her own needs of nurturance onto the child. A mother's identification with her daughter as a female is important to the extent that she has internalized the cultural assumptions that 1) daughters are of less value than sons, 2) their needs are less important, and 3) they exist to serve the needs of others, including those of mother (Caplan, 1981).

The cultural demand for female care, which is supported by a family hierarchy that assumes male superiority, is the social foundation of women's powerless-ness through nurturing responsibilities. Daughters, who have the least power and the lowest status, are automatically burdened with the caretaking of others, a status that is readily reinforced by mothers whose experiences are similar. The devaluation of females is unfortunately a "normal" gender assumption, because of its historical basis and because it exists from the beginning of the female's life (Horney, 1926). It is, therefore, not difficult to comprehend the female sex offender's mentality of not knowing that obtaining nurturance from female minors is wrong or inappropriate. Unfortunately, the women who sexually molest female children are participants in the cultural and psychological oppression of their own gender.

THE INFLUENCE OF DEPENDENCY ON FEMALE REASONING

Western culture's stereotype of passive, dependent females and strong, inde-pendent males not only mirror the desires of a male-oriented social system, but also formulates acceptable female and male development. Trask (1986) indicates that Western culture's support of a patriarchal view of the sexes visualizes males as the ego or "Self" of the hierarchical power system, and females are consid-ered extensions of the male and often termed "the Other." This cultural defini-tion of the feminine self was noted earlier by deBeauvoir (1952) who described the female gender as "beings who are distinguished by their absence of choice" (p. 24).

To be an object, rather than a subject, means that the female is denied alterna-tives, intention, and the freedom to change her situation. With no independent basis for judgment or action, females are held at the mercy of the patriarchal order. Bartkey (1990) states that the female's state of helplessness and dependency is culturally intentional, and is for the purpose of making the female incapable of understanding or changing her situation. This allows males to maintain superiority without resorting to violence and denies females the opportunity or choice of autonomy as it relates to separation and individuation.

This condition of female inferiority is maintained through two cultural processes: gender stereotyping and sexual objectification. The cultural stereotyping of females describes who females are without understanding the gender's needs or formulating a respect for the gender's rights. Stereotyping defeats any orientation of women experiencing autonomy. Females who do achieve individualization and independence threaten the predetermined gender image and are commonly ostracized by the patriarchal system. Women cannot assume masculine behavioral traits (separation and individuation) and still be socially accepted.

The culturally posited female inferiority by means of sexual objectification reduces a woman to an identity as a dependent instrument that serves a purpose for others. She is perceived not as a significant human being, but is judged for beauty and sexual comfort. The cultural focus on sexualized behavior as a means of pleasure and a form of acceptance encourages women who sexually interact with female children to mirror parental and cultural messages of their oppressed status, affirming their participation in the belief that females are less humanly significant than males. Such oppression of females is a "psychic alienation" of the gender that separates women from the essential attributes of social identity (Fernon, 1983).

Although the expectation of "humanness" includes that of cognitively understanding what is morally "right and wrong," the insignificance of female development — reinforced through maternal, familial, and cultural communications — inhibits women from confirming and articulating their own moral beliefs. In other words, a woman who is deprived of her rights and value as a person becomes limited in her capacity to judge or formulate moral statements. Female sex offenders consistently mention their dependent and inferior status as significant factors for their sexualized behavior with children (Table 2). It is important to identify how this dependency limits female's initiative to formulate a separate identity and to independently evaluate her actions. Women who are not expected to develop autonomous behavior perceive themselves as having no choices, and correspondingly excuse themselves from the consequences and responsibilities of their behavior.

The female's early parental and later cultural experiences of psychological oppression and inferiority make it difficult for her to formulate an identity and to develop self-esteem. Women with significant dependency needs fear abandonment and desire only to please, to be loved, and to be cared for in return. In Western culture, women are encouraged to depend on male acceptance, attachment, and judgment as their guidelines for personal decision-making. Their concept of self-worth is based on the males' opinions. Because women are discouraged from forming their own identity and decision-making standards, the male version of experiencing life becomes the female's norm for learning as well.

If females in general are subjected to environmental depersonalization, which encourages dependence and affects their ability to establish moral reasoning, what is to discourage women from projecting their reality of insignificance onto similar powerless individuals? Sayers (1987) states that often women fail to recognize the anger and rage caused by such social subordination. Rather than consciously experience the feelings of frustration and rage over their social helplessness, dependent individuals will most likely project such feelings onto others who have less status than they do, such as children. A woman's offending behavior can therefore be interpreted as an expression of repressed emotional pain. According to Hockmeyer (1988), such a response reinforces the woman's social oppression and submission to the patriarchal status quo.

The female sex offender seeks to liberate herself from social "alienation" by emotionally returning to the gender that gave her life. In doing so, she seeks the nurturance and comfort that she believes (and which is culturally reinforced) only another female can understand and provide. Such behavior is not seen by the woman as abusive, but as a progressive step in obtaining that which she had never experienced: acceptance.

The presented theoretical concept suggests that the majority of adult female sex abusers of female children have dysfunctional developmental experiences relating to maternal attachment, identity formation, and socialization (Figure 1). The disruption of early female maturation processes can encourage certain characteristics to evolve in the form of sexual behavior with female children. The theory suggests that women sex offenders should be respectfully understood and receive treatment congruent with their needs.

Figure 1:
Development of the Female Sex Offender of Female Children

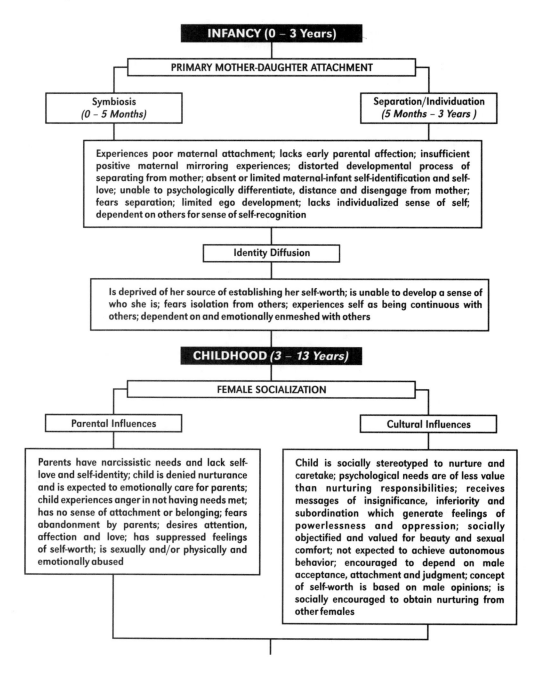

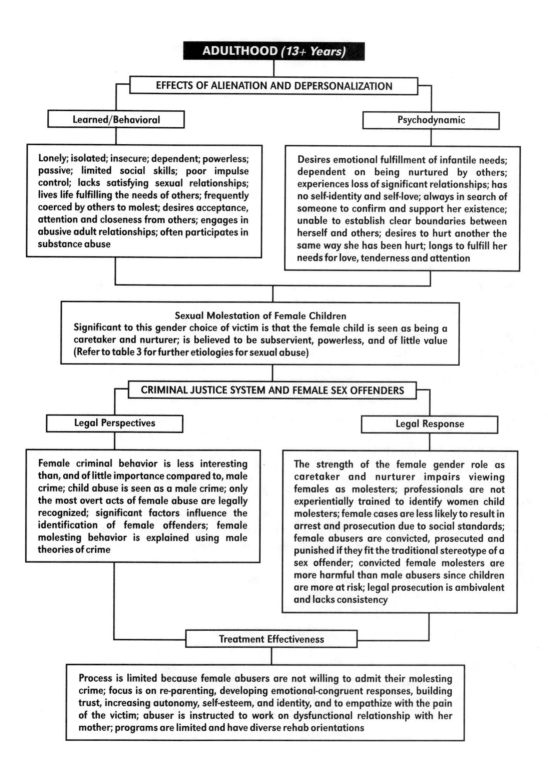

ADULTHOOD (13+ Years)

EFFECTS OF ALIENATION AND DEPERSONALIZATION

Learned/Behavioral

Lonely; isolated; insecure; dependent; powerless; passive; limited social skills; poor impulse control; lacks satisfying sexual relationships; lives life fulfilling the needs of others; frequently coerced by others to molest; desires acceptance, attention and closeness from others; engages in abusive adult relationships; often participates in substance abuse

Psychodynamic

Desires emotional fulfillment of infantile needs; dependent on being nurtured by others; experiences loss of significant relationships; has no self-identity and self-love; always in search of someone to confirm and support her existence; unable to establish clear boundaries between herself and others; desires to hurt another the same way she has been hurt; longs to fulfill her needs for love, tenderness and attention

Sexual Molestation of Female Children
Significant to this gender choice of victim is that the female child is seen as being a caretaker and nurturer; is believed to be subservient, powerless, and of little value (Refer to table 3 for further etiologies for sexual abuse)

CRIMINAL JUSTICE SYSTEM AND FEMALE SEX OFFENDERS

Legal Perspectives

Female criminal behavior is less interesting than, and of little importance compared to, male crime; child abuse is seen as a male crime; only the most overt acts of female abuse are legally recognized; significant factors influence the identification of female offenders; female molesting behavior is explained using male theories of crime

Legal Response

The strength of the female gender role as caretaker and nurturer impairs viewing females as molesters; professionals are not experientially trained to identify women child molesters; female cases are less likely to result in arrest and prosecution due to social standards; female abusers are convicted, prosecuted and punished if they fit the traditional stereotype of a sex offender; convicted female molesters are more harmful than male abusers since children are more at risk; legal prosecution is ambivalent and lacks consistency

Treatment Effectiveness

Process is limited because female abusers are not willing to admit their molesting crime; focus is on re-parenting, developing emotional-congruent responses, building trust, increasing autonomy, self-esteem, and identity, and to empathize with the pain of the victim; abuser is instructed to work on dysfunctional relationship with her mother; programs are limited and have diverse rehab orientations

Criminal Law and Female Sex Offenders

Given the limited studies of female sex offenders and the various state laws concerning child abuse, it is difficult to determine how women sex offenders are legally recognized and prosecuted. Although a comprehensive analysis of the criminal justice system regarding this population is beyond the scope of this research, an investigation of this factor in the six studies that formed the basis of this study suggests limited legal recognition, convictions, and treatment of molesting females (Table 4). This section briefly reviews the core studies' current legal perspectives on female sex offenders, the legal response to such offenders, and the orientation and effectiveness of treatment programs.

LEGAL PERSPECTIVES ON FEMALE SEX OFFENDERS

Generally, female sexual abusers are seldom acknowledged in the literature on child abuse and are more likely not to be reported or included in public statistics. Known cases are considered rare and frequently presented as psychoanalytic case studies of offenders and/or victims (Lidz & Lidz, 1969; Wahl, 1960) because women frequently disclose their molesting behavior during treatment in psychotherapy (Allen, 1990; Marvasti, 1987). The belief that sexual abuse of children by women occurs "in only a fraction" of the child abuse cases (Finkelhor, 1984; Russell, 1986) causes these women to be virtually ignored or totally discounted, obscuring the existence of such offenders (Allen, 1990). However, for some researchers, there is no doubt that the number of females arrested for sexual offenses against children has increased and is greater than that reported (Travin et al., 1990).

The cultural norm is that sexual abuse of children has always been a male crime and a male problem. In analyzing female criminality, Pollock-Byrne (1990) indicates that women have always been socially viewed as an "interesting anomaly to the reality of maleness" (p. 9). Females were considered to be less important than males, and their illegal behavior was seen as uninteresting and of little importance (Allen, 1990). Such cultural views have not changed considerably, causing theories on female crime to be frequently sexist and lacking in empirical support (Bierker, 1989; Rowan et al., 1990) As a result, limited analysis of female sexual abuse allows for only the most overt acts of molestation to be legally recognized. Travin et al. (1990) state that these offenses are frequently characterized by the bizarre nature of the sexual act and the level of violence directed against the victim. As one theorist put it, the act in general has to be lewd, grossly scandalous, disgusting, offensive, and an outrage to public decency for it to be legally recognized (O'Connor, 1987).

Table 4
Legal Consequences for Female Sex Offenders

	WOLFE 1985	MCCARTHY 1986	FALLER 1987	FINKELHOR, WILLIAMS, BURNS 1988	MATHEWS, MATHEW, SPELTZ 1989	ALLEN 1990
# OF FEMALE OFFENDERS	12 6 – F/FC[a]	26 11 – F/FC	40[a]	147[a] In-depth study on 22	16 15 – F/FC	65[a]
BELIEF IN WRONGNESS OF MOLEST[b]	3 F/MC – No 1 F/FC – No 8 – Yes		17 – Yes	83% – No, blamed others[c]	6 IO – Yes 7 CO – PR 3 NCO	27% – Yes
PREVIOUS ARREST RECORD[d]	1 – PAR 1 – JR 1 – CPS 9 – No			16% – Yes[c]	12 – No	4% – Yes
POLYGRAPH SUBSTANTIATION	8 – Yes 4 – No					
CONVICTED FOR MOLEST	2 – Yes[a] 2 – No	4 – Yes		17 – Yes 5 – No[c]	7 – No	54% – CHR 85% – CNV
SENTENCE FOR MOLEST[f]	1 – 3 months in hospital 3 – PRO 3 – PPD	1 – 99 years prison		12% – P 12% – 1 to 2 years 18% – 3 to 5 years 18% – 6 to 10 years 12% – 10 to 20 years 30% – 25+[c]	9 – P, 2 to 15 years+T 5 – P, 2 months to one year	30% – P 27% – PRO 32% – &/or T

[a]Indicates lack of informational clarity

[b]Wrongfulness: F/MC= female, male child abuse; F/FC=female/female child abuse; IO=individual offender; CO=coerced; PR=partially responsible; NCO=not coerced

[c]Indicated that the study icluded 36 male sex offenders but the author did not clarify which gender received which conviction

[d]Record: PAR=prior arrest record; JR=juvenile record; CPS=children's protective services

[e]Conviction: UNK=unknown; CHR=charged; CNV= convicted

[f]Sentence: PRO =probation; PPD=pre-prosecution diversion opportunity; T=treatment; P=prison

The FBI Uniform Crime Reports (Grayson, 1989), and The Study of National Incidence and Prevalence of Child Abuse and Neglect (1988) depend on the criminal substantiation of professionals and agencies to estimate the types of abuse and offenders for their nationwide reports. Unfortunately, these sources have indicated limitations in calculating sexual abuse cases involving women for the following reasons: 1) states vary in their classification or definition of child abuse (Vanderbilt, 1992), 2) cultural norms and ethnicity permit or require adult females to have close contact with children as nurturers and caretakers, 3) female victims need emotional and psychological support and will not reveal the abuser's identity for fear of not having these needs met, 4) certain crimes will receive more attention or are more obvious than those involving female child molesters (Spurlock & Robinowitz, 1990), 5) political agencies may find female child molesting crimes socially shocking and may choose not to expose them (Bierker, 1989), and 6) law enforcement personnel are not trained to detect such individuals and to substantiate this behavior (Finkelhor et al., 1988; Goodwin & DiVasto, 1979).

Current theories about female criminality indicate that "opportunity" and "socialization" are the two significant factors that explain female deviant behavior (Pollock-Byrne, 1990). Case studies of sexual abuse by women in day care facilities by Finkelhor et al. (1988) support this hypothesis and indicate that the abusers did not have a specific, conscious, preexisting sexual preference for day-care-age children, but rather most of the abuse seemed to be opportunistic. The children in the day care facilities were not sexually attractive, but more vulnerable and available. These authors propose that the female abusers may not have molested at all if they had not been so physically near children.

Different gender-role expectations, socialization patterns, and opportunities to commit particular offenses affect the recognition of criminal females. From a legal perspective, women are seen as more likely to engage in criminal behavior most appropriate to their social role and in behavior that is more closely related to how they are viewed by themselves and others (Naffin, 1981; Pollock-Byrne, 1990). The historical social expectations of women must be revised as a necessary step in recognizing and treating female criminally abusive behavior.

LEGAL RESPONSE TO FEMALE SEX OFFENDERS

Analysis of the six core studies indicates that there is inconsistency in legally prosecuting the discovered female molester. Finkelhor et al. (1988) theorize that society is more likely to respond strongly to sexual acts of rape and involuntary sexual intercourse committed on children by males than to those committed by women. Men arrested for rape are less likely to find their cases dropped because the men are seen as a threat to community safety. The social response to women who commit similar acts is ambivalent. These authors state that cases involving women are less likely to result in arrest or prosecution. However, they have also discovered that if a woman is convicted of a sexual offense, she is just as likely as a male offender to receive a lengthy prison sentence. Their findings show that the criminal justice system is more likely to prosecute, convict, and punish females who "fit" the stereotyped image of sex offender than women (or men) who do not. Women, or groups of adults who provide child care services and who are suspected of molesting, are less likely to be legally prosecuted. Such people do not represent the "typical" offender, and legal action against child care workers may possibly reflect a feeling of social threat (Williams & Farrell, 1990).

Allen (1990) agrees that male and female sex offenders in the criminal justice system are treated differently. He states that women are socially expected to be nurturing caretakers and reasons that the stereotypical expectations of the female gender-role preclude viewing females as capable of behavior that conflicts with this cultural ideal. Allen's (1990) case study reports that female sex offenders were the least likely to be criminally charged and were regarded as being "out of place" in the criminal justice system.

The biases of the legal system in criminal substantiation and treatment of female child molesters are enhanced by several factors:

1. Child protective services personnel are not normally perceptually and experientially trained to anticipate women who molest children. The lack of education concerning such abusers leads to biased reporting and a higher probability of false case substantiations in investigations (Finkelhor et al., 1988; Mathews et al., 1989).

2. Finkelhor et al. (1988) indicate that very few of their female child care abuse cases were verified because of insufficient evidence. Incidents involving only one or two older children, one molester, no weapons or physical force, and no sexual intercourse or fellatio were less likely to move to trial, suggesting that these cases may have lacked corroborative evidence, may not have been treated seriously, or may not have been allocated sufficient priority by prosecutors' offices. The lack of awareness about women sex offenders leads people to report only the most traumatizing abuse by females. In contrast, sexual abuse by males is more likely to be disclosed, even when it is less serious and less likely to be substantiated.

3. The different legal treatment of female offenders is influenced by the victims and the nature of the abuse (Allen, 1990; Finkelhor et al., 1988; Mathews et al., 1989). Investigations have shown that prepubertal children may not be competent to testify. They may be seriously emotionally disturbed as a result of the abuse, or corroborating evidence may be absent due to the nonviolent nature of the sexual molestation characteristic of female molesters (Mathews et al., 1989).

4. Female offenders are more reluctant than male offenders to admit that they have molested a child, making it difficult for prosecutors to determine the extent of the sexual crime. Allen (1990) states that females may have a "higher recognition threshold" for sexual abuse than males, and thereby have an awareness of the social deviance of molesting behavior. The extensive denial that female sex offenders exhibit may relate to guilt and anger at having been caught.

5. The legal system's biases concerning male and female sex offenders may derive from the belief that female molesters are even more deviant and harmful than male abusers (Allen, 1990). As previously mentioned, male abusers might be considered a threat to the security and safety of the community, but children are seen as more at risk with a sexually abusive mother or female caretaker. Allen's (1990) research shows that while similar numbers of female and male offenders were legally charged, more female than male offenders were put in jail. Allen found two significant sentencing differences between the two groups: 58% of the female offenders had their children removed from their homes and custody as compared to 21% of the male offenders; and 14% of the female offenders were placed on medication, as compared to only 3% of the male offenders. Female offenders are seen as more psychosomatically vulnerable than male offenders, and, therefore, more in need of medication.

Sentencing variation of female sex offenders in the six core studies suggests that the legal system has more difficulty substantiating female sexual abuse than male abuse. Some researchers indicate that it is difficult to understand why most female molesting charges are dropped and few abusers are legally prosecuted (Allen, 1990; Finkelhor et al., 1988; Mathews et al., 1989). Some researchers suspect that investigators have different ideas about which cases to drop, and list several factors as influencing prosecuting women sex offenders: legal technicalities, insufficient evidence, incompetent witnesses, limited resources of both staff and time in prosecutors' offices, withdrawal of parental or victim cooperation, and concern about trauma to child witnesses (Finkelhor et al., 1988). Because much is still unknown about female molesters, the sentencing patterns, norms, and guidelines these abusers remain ambiguous.

TREATMENT EFFECTIVENESS FOR FEMALE SEX OFFENDERS

Consideration of the etiological motives of women who sexually molested female children (Table 3) raises the question whether such offenders should be prosecuted and/or treated. Adler (1988) indicates that a caring, therapeutic approach would be more effective than a punitive one to control child sexual abuse, and emphasis should be placed more on understanding than on blame. He states that although prosecution does punish offenders, it does little to solve offenders' problems. Of the six investigated studies, only one evaluated the effects of a treatment program on female offenders.

Mathews et al.'s (1989) research on 16 female sex offenders indicated that ten of the offenders saw treatment as a positive and long overdue intervention that helped them change negative behavior patterns. The program focused on re-parenting, developed congruent emotional responses, built trust, increased autonomy, and helped the women to understand development of self-esteem and identity. Participants indicated that it was the first time anyone had taken them seriously, helping them to define problems and formulate a plan for behavioral change. The treatment focus emphasized self-awareness and helped the women to feel like "whole persons." As they gained emotional insight, the women reported a clearer sense of self and a comprehension of the effects of their molesting behavior. The offenders indicated that the most important aspect of their treatment was the caring, supportive, and non-judgmental atmosphere in which they felt respected as human beings.

Mathews et al.'s (1989) treatment program also focused on developing the female offender's ability to empathize with the victim's pain. The offender's refusal to acknowledge such feelings helped to deny memories of her own childhood victimization. Travin et al., (1990) emphasize that treatment orientations for the female offender include seeing her as victim as well as victimizer. Allen (1990) similarly indicates that women in general are socialized to be sexual abuse victims, not molesters.

When the female explores her own issues of childhood victimization, she can empathize with the pain that she has created in children whom she has molested. Female offenders who find it difficult to recognize their own victimization report that they had very dysfunctional family relationships, especially with their mothers. An important part of some treatment programs, therefore, is to have the offender improve her relationship with her mother. Deficient mother-daughter bonding is believed to make the achievement of adequate parenting impossible (VCPN, 1989).

Studies show that treatment programs will not be effective for all sex offenders. Mathews et al. (1989) state that some female offenders saw treatment as frightening, restrictive, and too burdensome, and refused to participate. Comparison of female and male sex offenders in Allen's (1990) research indicated that 20% of the females and 10% of the males felt that changing their molesting behavior was unlikely. Sixty percent of the females and 71% of the males reported behavioral change to be likely or somewhat likely. Allen's (1990) study suggests that female offenders may be more skeptical of the effectiveness of treatment than male offenders. Perhaps some of the skepticism may be related to the females' resistance to admitting their crimes. Social gender-role pressures may also cause more discomfort for females than males to disclose pain, discuss sexual matters, and accept legal and social consequences.

Although female sex offender treatment programs have been considered a positive approach by some child abuse experts, importance continues to be given to the legal prosecution of women molesters for the victim's sake. Such action is seen as validating the victim's experience by making clear that the offender's behavior is unacceptable. Research shows that when abuse is reported early, and the victim is supported and protected, the emotional trauma to the child is reduced (McCarty, 1986). Legal prosecution also helps relieve the child's guilt and decreases the likelihood that the abused child will become an abusive parent (Finkelhor et al., 1988). Professionals currently recognize that the offender's punishment provides reward for the victim, but without some form of treatment for the abuser, there is no guaranteed remission of the causes of the abuser's molesting behavior (Lloyd, 1987).

A major legal problem concerning female sex offenders is the criminal justice system's failure to implement treatment programs. Professionals are often uncertain and disagree about the types of programs that address female offenders' rehabilitation needs (Lloyd, 1987). Female offenders confront issues that are different from those of male offenders, including dependency, oppression, and coercion by males to molest. Women offenders require specific treatment orientations that address such issues. Mathews (1987) also reports that female sex offenders frequently have rigid sex-role orientations that cause limited ego or self-development. She emphasizes the need to incorporate developmental, cultural, and stereotypical sex role issues as significant for treatment outcome.

Related experiments with successful outcomes indicate that gender-related programs are required to change female molesting behavior. Mathews (1987) indicates that clinicians in treatment programs must recognize that molesting women suffer not only from guilt about commission of a crime, but also from guilt about a crime that represents a perversion of their role as protective and nurturing mother-figures.

CHAPTER 5

Conclusion

This study has compared historical research on male sex offenders with current case studies of females who have molested female children. The results of this investigation support the cited research focus with the following findings:

FINDING ONE. The comparison of case study information of male and female sex offenders (Table 5) suggests differences between the two genders in the areas of early childhood development, family dynamics, etiologies for abuse, criminal prosecution, and social stereotyping. The findings support the concept that female sex offenders should be perceived as different from male sex offenders. Any analysis of female molesting behavior based on male offender-based research is not applicable to understanding women who molest children.

FINDING TWO. The distortion of early female identity formation contributes to adult molesting behavior. The comparison of characteristic and experiential similarities among women sex offenders in the six core studies suggests that women who sexually molest female children have insufficient early childhood nurturance from their primary caretakers that frustrates the developmental establishment of an autonomous identity. Women who are unable to establish a self-identity will experience feelings of worthlessness and will look to others for confirmation and approval. The inability to establish an identity encourages such women to develop an intense caretaking dependency on others to recreate a self lost at an early age. Westkott (1986) indicates that no amount of caretaking

Table 5
Comparison of Female and Male Offenders

FEMALE	MALE
AVERAGE CHARACTERISTICS	
Feelings of inferiority, dependency, isolation, passivity, subordination, powerlessness; in need of acceptance, nurturance, closeness from others	Feelings of being shy, passive, unassertive, introverted; in need of human attention and acceptance, closeness, and nurturance
CHILDHOOD FAMILY DYNAMICS	
Emotionally, sexually, and/or physically abused, no sense of belonging, lacked attention, approval, respect	Emotionally, sexually, and/or physically abused, familial violence, chaotic childhood, parental substance abuse
RELATIONSHIP WITH PARENTS	
Poor maternal attachment, insufficient emotional nurturance, denied sense of identity and self-realization, increased need for dependency	Denied maternal nurturance, poor sense of self and differentiation, no close relationship with father, experienced parental abandonment/separation or divorce, denied physical affection and modeling of healthy sexuality
COGNITIVE DEVELOPMENT	
Severe ego development disturbances	Lacked essential ego development
SOCIAL SKILLS	
Limited, or lacked personal and situational control	Poor
ADULT RELATIONSHIPS	
Failed and empty	Unsatisfactory, disappointed
INVOLVED IN SUBSTANCE ABUSE	
Frequently	Frequently
VICTIMS MOLESTED	
Mostly prepubertal females	Mostly prepubertal females

Table 5
(Continued)

SEXUALLY MOLESTED FEMALE CHILDREN WITH OTHER ADULTS	
Frequently coerced, forced by others to participate	Felt socially satisfied in initiating sex alone
RELATIONSHIP TO VICTIM	
Higher percentage are mothers	Higher percentage are fathers, step-fathers
NUMBER OF CASES REPORTED	
5% of all sexual abuse cases on females (Russell, 1984); this percentage is not unanimously accepted among researchers	One in every three females has been molested by a male before 18 years of age (Vanderbilt, 1992)
INFLUENCE OF SOCIAL STEREOTYPING	
Women are socially expected to nurture and caretake; they do not have the biological make-up to cause sexual harm to children; more socially unsettling to reveal women as molesters of children	Men are seen as having uncontrollable sexual desires; are encouraged to be dominant and powerful over women and children; are more socially accepted as sex offenders; "less shocking"
MOLESTER CATEGORIES	
Teacher-lover, predisposed, male-coerced (Mathews, et al., 1989)	Fixated, situational (Groth, 1978), rapists, psychopaths (Bierker, 1989)[a]
ETIOLOGIES OF SEXUAL ABUSE	
Biological, learned/behavioral, psychodynamic	Emotional-congruence, sexual arousal, blockage, inhibition (Finkelhor and Araji, 1986)

[a]Indicates that the categories have been applied to both genders

and confirmation from others can compensate for the women's lack of genuine nurturance in childhood or later feelings of worthlessness. They frequently lack an sense of identity and feel unappreciated, unloved, and alienated.

FINDING THREE. Research suggests that a woman's molesting behavior may be theoretically associated with learned/behavioral and psychodynamic influences. The women sex offenders in the six core studies did not molest initially in order to have sex with female children, but to experience emotional contact with another person. The analysis indicates that women offenders also experienced the loss of a psychologically essential relationship, the purpose of which was to provide a sense of self-recognition. The effects of this loss are further enhanced by parental and cultural gender role expectations that generate feelings of isolation, dependence, subordination, and powerlessness. The women sense their alienation from the world as well as from themselves and attempt to confirm their existence by emotionally connecting with a female child who is socially expected to nurture. A woman cannot foresee the pain that she brings upon her "own kind" if she cannot understand or identify the inner loss of her own self. Without a core self from which to operate, the woman sex offender projects onto others her fear of isolation, oppression, and anger.

FINDING FOUR. Gender-related cultural stereotyping encourages women to sexually molest female children. The sexual abuse of female children is considered to be a male crime, and the social system is unprepared and uneducated to understand women's molesting behavior. Social taboos prevent recognition and awareness of women sex offenders because women are not expected to emotionally and physically endanger children. Women who deviate from their cultural role as nurturers and caretakers are considered social misfits and are legally avoided or underemphasized.

FINDING FIVE. The criminal justice system has historically viewed female criminal behavior as less interesting and less important than male crime. As a result, only the most overt acts of female sexual abuse are legally recognized and are explained using theories about male abusers. The legal prosecution of female sex offenders is ambivalent and inconsistent because professionals are not trained to identify and prosecute female sex offenders. The legal system's lack of response to crimes by female sex offenders limits convictions, sentencing, and treatment.

Obvious difficulties hinder the research progress of understanding women who sexually molest female children. Kendall-Tackett and Simon (1987) indicate that adults who were molested as children by both male and female abusers are more likely to reveal molestation by a male long before revealing information about molestation by a female. Women victims often do not report shameful or humiliating crimes (Benedek, 1990), yet reveal that being molested by a female adult was more emotionally damaging than being sexually abused by a male (Renvoize, 1982; Wakefield & Underwager, 1991). Vanderbilt (1991) reports a study of 93 women who had been sexually abused by their mothers. Eighty percent of the women indicated that the abuse was "the most" hidden part of their lives. Only 3% of the women told anyone about the abuse during childhood.

The inability of female victims to expose their female abusers impedes recognizing and treating such offenders. The limited cases of women who molest females are unfortunately classified and analyzed with statistics and research on male sex offenders. Alleviating the suffering of the abused and abusing female will be delayed until professionals are taught to identify women sex offenders and realize that limited case reporting does not mean that female sexual abuse is rare. Research in the following areas would benefit the study and understanding of female sex offenders: an investigation of descriptive definitions of female-child behavior that constitutes molestation; comparative studies of male and female sex offenders against female children designed to explore variable differences and victim consequences; continued explorations of early psychosocial influences on female development that may be related to later molesting behavior; increased awareness of criminal justice inconsistencies in prosecuting and convicting female and male sex offenders; investigation of treatment programs with different gender rehabilitation focus.

REFERENCES

References

Adams, D.B., Gold, A.R., & Burt, A.D. (1978). Rise in female initiated sexual activity at ovulation and its suppression by oral contraceptives. *New England Journal of Medicine, 299,* 1145-1150.

Adler, Z. (1988). Prosecuting child sexual abuse: A challenge to the status quo. In M. Maguire & J. Pointing (Eds.), *Victims of crime: A new deal* (pp. 138-146). Philadelphia: Open University Press.

Alexander, P.C., & Lupfer, S.L. (1987). Family characteristics and long-term consequences associated with sexual abuse. *Archives of Sexual Behavior, 16(3),* 235-245.

Allen, C. (1990). *A comparative analysis of women who sexually abuse children.* Des Moines, IA: University of Iowa Department of Human Development & Family Studies.

Aries, E., & Olver, R. (1985). Sex differences in the development of a separate sense of self during infancy: Directions for future research. *Psychology of Women Quarterly, 9,* 515-532.

Armstrong, L. (1983). *The home front.* New York: McGraw-Hill.

Bardwick, J. (1971). *Psychology of women.* New York: Harper & Row.

Bartky, S.L. (1990). *Femininity and domination: Studies in the phenomenology of oppression.* New York: Routledge.

Beckman, L.J. (1976). Alcoholism problems and women: An overview. In M. Grenblatt, & M. Schuckit (Eds.), *Alcoholism problems in women and children* (pp. 65-96). New York: Grune & Stratton.

Benedek, E.P. (1990). Female offenders. In J. Spurlock & C. Robinowitz (Eds.), *Women's progress, promises, and problems* (pp. 159-171). New York: Plenum.

Berlin, F.S. (1982). Sex offenders: A biomedical perspective. In J. Greer & I. Stuart (Eds.), *Sexual aggression: Current perspectives on treatment* (pp. 83-123). New York: Van Nostrand Reinhold.

Bernard, G., Fuller, A., Robbins, L., & Shaw, T. (1989). *The child molester: An integrated approach to evaluation and treatment.* New York: Brunner/Mazel.

Bierker, S.B. (1989). *About sexual abuse.* Springfield, IL: Charles C. Thomas.

Bishop, F.J. (1978). The abusing parents: Perceptions, memories and pathological identification as precipitants in the attack. In E.J. Anthony, C. Koupernik, & C. Chiland (Eds.), *The child in his family: Vulnerable children* (pp. 239-245). New York: Wiley & Sons.

Bolton, F.G., Morris, L.A., & MacEachron, A.E. (1989). *Males at risk: The other side of sexual abuse.* Newbury Park, CA: Sage.

Boyd, C. (1985). Toward an understanding of mother-daughter identification using concept analysis. *Advances in Nursing Science, 7,* 78-86.

Bradford, J.M.W. (1985). Organic treatments for the male sexual offender. *Behavioral Science & the Law, 3,* 55.

Call, J.D. (1984). Child abuse and neglect in infancy: Sources of hostility with the parent-infant dyad and disorders of attachment in infancy. *Child Abuse & Neglect, 8,* 185-202.

Caplan, P. (1981). *Barriers between women.* New York: Spectrum.

Chasnoff, I.J., Burns, W.J., Schnoll, S.H., Burns, K., Chisum, G., & Kyle-Spore, L. (1986). Maternal-neonatal incest. *American Journal of Orthopsychiatry, 56*(4), 577-580.

Chodorow, N. (1974). Family structure and feminine personality. In M.Z. Rosaldo & L. Lamphere (Eds.), *Women, culture, and society* (pp. 454-468). Stanford, CA: Stanford University Press.

Chodorow, N. (1978a). *The reproduction of mothering.* Berkeley, CA: University of California Press.

Chodorow, N. (1978b). Mothering, object-relations and the female oedipal configuration. *Feminist Studies, 4*(1), 137-158.

Cloninger, C.R., Christiansen, R.D., Reich, T., & Gottesman, I. (1978). Implications of sex differences in the prevalence of antisocial personality, alcoholism and criminality for familial transmission. *Archives of General Psychiatry, 35,* 941-951.

Condy, S.R., Templer, D.I., Brown, R., & Veaco, L. (1987). Parameters of sexual contact of boys with women. *Archives of Sexual Behavior, 16,* 379-394.

Cooper, A.J., Swaminath, S., Baxter, D., Poulin, C. (1990). A female sex offender with multiple paraphilias: A psychologic, physiologic (laboratory sexual arousal) & endocrine case study. *Canadian Journal of Psychiatry, 35,* 334-337.

Cushing, J.G. (1950). Psychopathology of sexual delinquency. *Journal of Criminal Psychopathology, 49,* 26-34.

de Beauvoir, S. (1952). *The second sex.* New York: Random House.

de Young, M. (1982). *Sexual victimization of children.* Jefferson, NC: MacFarland.

Dinnerstein, D. (1976). *The mermaid and the minotaur.* New York: Harper & Row.

Dworkin, A. (1995). Pornography and male supremacy. In G. Dines & J. Humez (Eds.), *Gender, Race & Class in Media* (pp. 237-243). Thousand Oaks, CA: Sage

Eichenbaum, L., & Orbach, S. (1983). *Understanding women.* New York: Basic Books.

Eichholz, A. (1988). Psychohistorical reflections on changing body images for women. In J. Offerman-Zuckerberg (Ed.), *Critical psychophysical passages in the life of a woman: A psychodynamic perspective* (pp. 5-15). New York: Plenum.

Faller, K.C. (1987). Women who sexually abuse children. *Violence & Victims, 2*(4), 263-276.

Faller, K.C. (1988). *Child sexual abuse: An interdisciplinary manual for diagnosis, case management, and treatment.* New York: Columbia University Press.

Fanon, F. (1967). *Black skins, white masks.* New York: Grove Press.

Finkelhor, D. (1984). *Child sexual abuse: New theory and research.* New York: Free Press.

Finkelhor, D., & Araji, S. (1986). Explanations of pedophilia: A four-factor model. *The Journal of Sex Research, 22,* 2, 145-161.

Finkelhor, D., & Russell, D. (1984). Women as perpetrators: Review of the evidence. In D. Finkelhor (Ed.) *Child sexual abuse: New theory and research* (pp. 171-187). Newbury Park, CA: Sage.

Finkelhor, D., Williams, L., & Burns, N. (1988). *Nursery crimes: Sexual abuse in day care.* Newbury Park, CA: Sage.

Fischer, L. (1983). Mothers and mothers-in-law. *Journal of Marriage & the Family, 45,* 187-192.

Flax, J. (1981). The conflict between nurturance and autonomy in mother-daughter relationships and within feminism. In E. Howell & M. Bayes (Eds.), *Women and mental health* (pp. 51-68). New York: Basic Books.

Flor-Henry, P., Lang, R.A., Koles, Z.J., & Frenzel, R.R. (1991). Quantitative EEG studies of pedophilia. *International Journal of Psychophysiology, 10,* 253-258.

Ford, C., & Beach, F. (1951). *Patterns of sexual behavior.* New York: Paul Hoeber.

Forward, S., & Buck, C. (1978). *Betrayal of innocence: Incest and its devastation.* New York: Penguin.

Fraser, M. (1976). *The death of narcissus.* New York: Paul Hoeber.

Freud, S. (1933). *New introductory lectures.* New York: W.W. Norton.

Freund, K., Watson, R., Dickey, R., Rienzo, D. (1991). Erotic gender differentiation in pedophilia. *Archives of Sexual Behavior, 20(6),* 555-566.

Friday, N. (1977). *My mother myself: A daughter's search for identity.* New York: Delacarte.

Fromuth, M.E., & Burkhart, B.R. (1987). Childhood sexual victimization among college men: Definitional and methodological issues. *Violence and Victims, 2,* 241-253.

Gaddini, R. (1983). Incest as a developmental failure. *Child Abuse & Neglect, 7,* 357-358.

Gaffney, G., & Berlin, F. (1984). Is there hypothalamic-pituitary-gonadol dysfunction in pedophilia? *British Journal of Criminology, 145,* 657-660.

Galdston, R. (1965). Observations on children who have been physically abused and their parents. *American Journal of Psychiatry, 122,* 440-443.

Galdston, R. (1981). The domestic dimensions of violence: child abuse. *Psychoanalytic Study of the Child, 36,* 391-414.

Gardiner, J.K. (1987). Self psychology as feminist theory. *Signs: Journal of Women in Culture and Society, 12(4),* 761-780.

Gebhard, P., Gagnon, J., Pomeroy, N., & Christenson, C. (1965). *Sex offenders: An analysis of types.* New York: Harper & Row.

Gillespie, W.H. (1956). The general theory of sexual perversion. *International Journal of psychoanalysis, 37,* 396-403.

Gilligan, C. (1977). In a different voice: Women's conceptions of self and of morality. *Harvard Educational Review, 47,* 481-517.

Gilligan, C. (1982). *In a different voice: Psychological theory and women's development.* Cambridge, MA: Harvard University Press.

Goodwin, J., & DiVasto, P. (1979). Mother-daughter incest. *Child Abuse & Neglect, 3*, 953-957.

Goodwin, J., & DiVasto, P. (1989). Female homosexuality: A sequel to mother-daughter incest. In J.M. Goodwin (Ed.), *Sexual abuse: Incest victims and their families* (pp. 140-146). Chicago: Yearbook Medical.

Gordon, R. (1976). Paedophilia: Normal and abnormal. In W. Kraemer (Ed.), *The forbidden love: The normal and abnormal love of children* (pp. 35-48). London: Sheldon.

Goy, R., & McEwen, B.S. (1977). *Sexual differentiation of the brain.* Cambridge, MA: MIT Press.

Grayson, J. (Ed.). (1989). Female sex offenders. *Virginia Child Protection Newsletter, 28*, 4-13.

Green, A.H., Gaines, R.W., & Sandgrund, A. (1974). Child abuse: Pathological syndrome of family interaction. American Journal of Psychiatry, 131, 882-886.

Greenspan, M. (1983). *A new approach to women and therapy.* New York: New American Library.

Groth, A.N. (1978). Patterns of sexual assault against children and adolescents. In A.W. Burgess, A.N. Groth, L.L. Holmstrom, & S.M. Sgroi (Eds.), *Sexual assault of children and adolescents* (pp. 3-24). Lexington, MA: Lexington Books.

Groth, A.N. (1982). The incest offender. In S.M. Sgroi (Ed.), *Handbook of clinical intervention in child sexual abuse* (pp. 215-239). Lexington, MA: Lexington Books.

Groth, A.N., & Burgress, A.W. (1977). Motivational intent in the sexual assault on children. *Criminal Justice Behavior, 4*, 253-264.

Hammer, S. (1976). *Daughters and mothers: Mothers and daughters.* New York: New American Library.

Hendricks, S.E., Fitzpatrick, D.F., Hartmann, K., Quaife, M.A., Stratbucker, R.A., & Graber, B. (1988). Brain structure and function in sexual molesters of children and adolescents. *Journal of Clinical Psychiatry, 49(3),* 108-112.

Herman, J. (1981). *Father-daughter incest.* Cambridge, MA: Harvard University Press.

Hite, S. (1981). *The Hite report on male sexuality.* New York: Alfred Knopf.

Hockmeyer, A. (1988). Object relations theory and feminism: Strange bedfellows. *Frontiers, 10*(1), 20-28.

Hoffman, L.W. (1972). Early childhood experiences and women's achievement motives. *Journal of Social Issues, 28,* 129-155.

Hollender, J. (1973). Self-esteem and parental identification. *Journal of Genetic Psychology, 122,* 2-7.

Horney, K. (1926). The flight from womanhood: The masculinity complex in women, as viewed by men and by women. *International Journal of Psychoanalysis, 7,* 337-338.

Horney, K. (1942). *Self analysis.* New York: W.W. Norton.

Howells, K. (1981). Adult sexual interest in children: Considerations relevant to theories of aetiology. In M. Cook, & K. Howells (Eds.), *Adult sexual interest in children* (pp. 55-94). New York: Academic Press.

Hucker, S., Langevin, R., Wortzman, G., Bain, J., Handy, L., Chambers, J., & Wright, S. (1986). Neuropsychological impairment in pedophiles. *Canadian Journal of Behavioral Science, 18,* 440-448.

Hutchison, J.B., & Hutchison, R.E. (1990). Sexual development at the neurohormonal level: The role of androgens. In J.R. Feierman (Ed.), *Pedophilia* (pp. 510-543). New York: Springer.

James, B., & Nasjleti, M. (1983). *Treating sexually abused children and their families.* Palo Alto, CA: Consulting Psychologists Press.

Josselson, R. (1987). *Finding herself: Pathways to identity development in women.* San Francisco, CA: Jossey-Bass Publishers.

Jung, C., & Kerearyi, C. (1969). The psychological aspects of the kore. In *Essays on a science of mythology: The myths of the divine child and the mystics of eleusis.* New York: Princeton University Press.

Justice, B., & Justice, R. (1979). *The broken taboo: Sex in the family.* New York: Human Science Press.

Karpman, B. (1954). *The sexual offender and his offenses.* New York: Julian Press.

Kendall-Tackett, K.A., & Simon, A.F. (1987). Perpetrators and their acts: Data from 365 adults molested as children. *Child Abuse & Neglect, 2,* 237-245.

Kinsey, A.C., Pomeroy, W.B., Martin, C.E., & Gebhard, P.H. (1953). *Sexual behavior in the human female.* Philadelphia: Saunders.

Kohut, H. (1971). *The analysis of the self: A systematic approach to psychoanalytic treatment of narcissistic personality disorder.* New York: International Universities Press.

Kohut, H., & Wolf, E. (1978). The disorders of the self and their treatment: An outline. *International Journal of Psycho-Analysis, 59,* 413-425.

Kraemer, W. (1976). *The forbidden love: The normal and abnormal love of children.* London: Sheldon.

Lambert, K. (1976). The scope and dimensions of paedophilia. In W. Kraemer (Ed.), *The forbidden love: The normal and abnormal love of children* (pp. 87-110). London: Sheldon.

Langevin, R., Wortzman, G., Wright, P., & Handy, L. (1989). Studies of brain damage and dysfunction in sex offenders. *Annuals of Sex Research, 2,* 163-179.

Langevin, R., Hucker, S.J., Ben-Aron, M.H., Purins, J.E., & Hook, H.J. (1985). Why are pedophiles attracted to children? Further studies of erotic preference in heterosexual pedophilia. In R. Langevin (Ed.), *Erotic preference, gender identity, and aggression in men: New research studies* (pp. 181-209). Hillsdale, NJ: Erlbaum.

Langevin, R., Paitich, D., Freeman, R., Mann, K., & Handy, L. (1978). Personality characteristics and sexual anomalies in males. *Canadian Journal of Behavorial Science, 10,* 222-238.

Lerner, H. (1985). *The dance of anger.* New York: Harper & Row.

Levin, S.M., Risen, C., & Althof, S. (1990). Essay on the diagnosis and nature of paraphilia. *Journal of Sex & Marital Therapy, 16(2),* 89-102.

Levin, S.M., & Stava, L. (1987). Personality characteristics of sex offenders: A review. *Archives of Sexual Behavior, 16,* 57-79.

Lidz, R.W., & Lidz, T. (1969). Homosexual tendencies in mothers of schizophrenic women. *Journal of Nervous Mental Disorders, 149,* 229-235.

Lidz, T., Fleck, S., & Cornelison, S. (1965). *Schizophrenia and the family.* New York: International Universities Press.

Light, H. (1988). *Alcoholism and women, genetics, and fetal development.* Springfield, IL: Charles C. Thomas.

Lilly, R., Cummings, J.L., Benson, D.F., & Frankel, M. (1983). The human Kluner-Bucy syndrome. *Neurology, 33,* 1141-1145.

Lindberg, F.H., & Disted, L.J. (1985). Post-traumatic stress disorders in women who experienced childhood incest. *Child Abuse & Neglect, 9,* 329-334.

Litwin, D. (1986). Autonomy: A conflict for women. In J. Alpert (Ed.), *Psychoanalysis and women* (pp. 183-213). Hillsdale, NJ: Analytic Press.

Lloyd, C. (1987). Working with the female offender. *British Journal of Occupational Therapy, 50,* 44-46.

Mahler, M. (1968). *On human symbiosis and the vicissitudes of individuation.* New York: International Universities Press.

Mahler, M., Pine, F., & Bergman, A. (1975). *The psychological birth of the human infant.* New York: Basic Books.

Maltz, W., & Holman, B. (1987). *Incest and sexuality: A guide to understanding and healing.* Lexington, MA: Lexington Books.

Marcia, J.E. (1966). Development and validation of ego identity status. *Journal of Personality & Social Psychology, 3,* 551-558.

Marshall, W.L., & Christie, M.M. (1981). Pedophilia and aggression. *Criminal Justice & Behavior, 8(2),* 145-158.

Marvasti, J. (1986). Incestuous mothers. *American Journal of Forensic Psychiatry, 7,* 63-69.

Mathews, R., Matthews, J., Speltz, K. (1989). *Female sexual offenders: An exploratory study.* Orwell, VT: The Safer Society Press.

Mathis, J.L. (1972). *Clear thinking about sexual deviation.* Chicago: Nelson-Hall.

Mayer, A. (1983). *Incest: A treatment manual for therapy with victims, spouses and offenders.* Homes Beach, FL: Learning Publications.

McCarty, L. (1986). Mother-child incest: Characteristics of the offender. *Child Welfare, 65(5),* 447-458.

McIntyre, K. (1981). Role of mothers in father-daughter incest: A feminist analysis. *Social Work, 26,* 462-467.

Meiselman, K.C. (1978). *Incest: A psychological study of causes, effects with treatment considerations.* San Francisco, CA: Jossey-Bass.

Mellar, C.S., Farid, N.R., Craig, D.F. (1988). Female hypersexuality treated with cyproterone acetate. *American Journal of Psychiatry, 145(8),* 1037.

Miller, A. (1981). *The drama of the gifted child*. New York: Basic Books.

Miller, A. (1983). *For your own good. Hidden cruelty in child-rearing: The roots of violence*. New York: Farrar, Straus & Giroux.

Miller, A. (1984). *Thou shalt not be aware: Society's betrayal of the child*. New York: New American Library.

Miller, B.A., Downs, W.R., Gondoli, D.M., & Keil, A. (1987). The role of childhood sexual abuse in the development of alcoholism in women. *Violence and Victims, 2,* 157-172.

Miller, B.L., Cummings, J.L., McIntyre, H., Ebers, G., & Grode, M. (1986). Hypersexuality or altered sexual preference following brain injury. *Journal of Neurology, Neurosurgery, & Psychiatry, 49,* 867-873.

Miller, J.B. (1976, 1986). *Toward a new psychology of women*. 1st and 2nd Edition. Boston: Beacon Press.

Mohr, J., Turner, R., & Jerry, M. (1964). *Pedophilia & exhibitionism*. Toronto, Canada: University of Toronto Press.

Money, J. (1961). Sex hormones and other variables in human eroticism. In W.C. Young (Ed.), *Sex and internal securities* (pp. 1383-1400). Baltimore: Williams & Wilkins.

Money, J. (1981). Paraphilias: Phyletic origins of erotosexual dysfunction. *International Journal of Mental Health, 10,* 75-109.

Money, J. (1990). Pedophilia: A specific instance of new phylism theory as applied to paraphilic lovemaps. In J.R. Feierman (Ed.), *Pedophilia* (pp. 445-463). New York: Springer.

Morgenthaler, F. (1988). *Homosexuality, heterosexuality & perversion*. Hillsdale, NJ: Analytic Press.

Murphy, S.M., Kilpatrick, D.G., Amick-McMullan, A., Veronen, L.J., Paduhovich, J., Best, C.L., Villeponteaux, L.A., & Saunden, B.E. (1988). Current psychological functioning of child sexual assault survivors. *Journal of Interpersonal Violence, 3,* 55-79.

Nadelson, L.L., & Notman, M.T. (1984). Psychodynamics of sexual assault experiences. In I.R. Stuart, & J.G. Greer (Eds.), *Victims of sexual aggression: Treatment of children, women and men* (pp. 3-17). New York: Van Nostrand Reinhold.

Naffin, N. (1981). Theorizing about female crime. In S.K. Mukherjee & J.A. Scutt (Eds.), *Women and crime* (pp. 70-91). Boston: George Allen & Unwin.

National Center on Child Abuse and Neglect (NCCAN). (1988). *Executive summary: Study of national incidence and prevalence of child abuse and neglect.* Washington, DC: U.S. Department of Health and Human Services.

Nelson, S. (1982). *Incest: Fact and Myth. Edinburgh,* Scotland: Stramullion.

O'Connor, A.A. (1987). Female sex offenders. *British Journal of Psychiatry, 150,* 615-620.

Offerman-Zuckerberg, J. (1988). Reflections on the daughter as a projective screen: Mother-daughter boundaries. In J. Offerman-Zuckerberg (Ed.), *Critical psychophysical passages in the life of a woman: A psychodynamic perspective* (pp. 37-48). New York: Plenum.

Owens, T.H. (1984). Personality traits of female psychotherapy patients with a history of incest: A research note. *Journal of Personality Assessment, 48,* 606-608.

Pawlak, A., Boulet, J., & Bradford, J. (1991). Discriminant analysis of a sexual-functioning inventory with intrafamilial and extrafamilial child molesters. *Archives of Sexual Behavior, 20, 8,* 27-34.

Peters, J.J. (1976). Children who are victims of sexual assault and the psychology of offenders. *American Journal of Psychotherapy, 30,* 398-421.

Plummer, K. (1981). Pedophilia: Constructing a sociological baseline. In M. Cook & K. Howells (Eds.), *Adult sexual interest in children* (pp. 222-250). New York: Academic Press.

Pollock-Byrne, J.M. (1990). *Women, prison, and crime.* Pacific Grove, CA: Brooks/Cole.

Quinsey, V. L. (1977). The assessment and treatment of child molesters: A review. *Canadian Psychological Reviews, 18, 3,* 204-222.

Renvoize, J. (1982). *Incest: A family pattern.* London: Routledge & Kegan Paul.

Rich, A. (1976). *Of woman born: Motherhood as experience and institution.* New York: W.W. Norton.

Risen, L.I., & Koss, M.P. (1987). The sexual abuse of boys: Prevalence and descriptive characteristics of childhood victimizations. *Journal of Interpersonal Violence, 2,* 309-323.

Rohsenow, D.J., Corbett, R., & Devine, D. (1986). *Molested as children: The hidden contribution to alcohol and substance abuse.* Paper presented at the annual meeting of the American Medical Society of Alcohol and Other Drug Dependence, San Francisco.

Rose, S. (1991). The contribution of Alice Miller to feminist therapy and theory. *Women & Therapy, 11*(2), 41-53.

Rosen, I. (1979). The general psychoanalytical theory of perversion: A critical and clinical review. In I. Rosen (Ed.), *Sexual deviation,* (pp. 29-64). New York: Oxford University Press.

Rowan, E.L., Rowan, J.B., & Langelier, P. (1990). Women who molest children. *Bulletin of the American Academy of Psychiatry Law, 18*(1), 79-83.

Rush, F. (1980). *The best kept secret: Sexual abuse of children.* Englewood Cliffs, NJ: Prentice Hall.

Russell, D. (1982). The incidence and prevalence of intrafamilial and extrafamilial sexual abuse of female children. *Child Abuse & Neglect, 7,* 133-146.

Russell, D. (1986). *The secret trauma: Incest in the lives of girls and women.* New York: Basic Books.

Sarrel, P.M., & Masters, W.H. (1982). Sexual molestation of men by women. *Archives of Sexual Behavior, 11,* 117-131.

Sax, M., & Deckwitz, S. (1992). When you change the gender, reality changes too. *The Journal of Paedophilia, 2*(8), 3-14.

Sayers, J. (1987). Melanie Klein, psychoanalysis, & feminism. *Feminist Review, 25,* 23-38.

Schwartz, A. (1984). Psychoanalysis and women: A rapprochement. *Women & Therapy, 3*(1), 3-12.

Simari, G.C., & Baskin, D. (1982). Incestuous experiences within homosexual populations: A preliminary study. *Archives of Sexual Behavior, 11,* 329-344.

Socarides, C.W. (1959). Meaning and content of pedophilia perversions. *Journal of the American Psychoanalytic Association, 7,* 84-94.

Sommers-Flanagan, R., & Walters, H.A. (1987). The incest offender, power, and victimization: Scales on the same dragon. *Journal of Family Violence, 2*(2), 163-175.

Spurlock, J., & Robinowitz, C. (Eds.). (1990). *Women's progress, promises and problems.* New York: The Third Press.

Stein, R. (1973). *Incest and human love: The betrayal of the soul in psychotherapy.* New York: The Third Press.

Stoller, R. J. (1975). *Perversion: The erotic form of hatred.* New York: Pantheon.

Sugar, M. (1983). Sexual abuse of children and adolescents. *Adolescent Psychiatry, 11,* 199-211.

Tingle, D., Barnard, G.W., Robbins, L., Newman, G., & Hutchinson, D. (1986). Childhood and adolescent characteristics of pedophiles and rapists. *International Journal of Law and Psychiatry, 9,* 103-116.

Trask, H.K. (1986). Eros and power: *The promise of feminist theory.* Philadelphia: University of Pennsylvania Press.

Travin, S., Cullen, K., & Protter, B. (1990). Female sex offenders: Severe victims and victimizers. *Journal of Forensic Sciences, 35*(1), 140-150.

Vanderbilt, H. (1992, February). Incest: A chilling report. *Lears,* pp. 49-77.

Wahl, C.W. (1960). The psychodynamics of consummated maternal incest. *Archives of General Psychiatry, 8,* 188-193.

Wakefield, H., Rogers, M., & Underwager, R. (1990). Female sexual abusers: A theory of loss. *Issues in Child Abuse Accusations, 2,* 181-195.

Wakefield, H., & Underwager, R. (1991). Female child sexual abusers: A critical view of the literature. *American Journal of Forensic Psychology, 9*(4), 43-69.

Weitzman, L. (1984). Sex-role socialization: A focus on women. In J. Freeman (Ed.), *Women: A feminist perspective* (pp. 157-327). Mountain View, CA: Mayfield Publishing.

Wenet, G., Clark, T., & Hunner, R. (1981). Perspectives on the juvenile sex offender. In R.J. Hunner & E. Walker (Eds.), *Exploring the relationship between child abuse and delinquency* (pp. 145-151). Montclair, NJ: Allonheld, Osmun.

Westkott, M. (1978). Mothers and daughters in the world of the father. *Frontiers, 3*(2), 16-22.

Westkott, M. (1986). *The feminist legacy of Karen Horney.* New Haven, CT: Yale University Press.

Wilking, V.N. (1990). Mothers who abuse their children. In J. Spurlock, & C. Robenowitz (Eds.), *Women's progress, promises and problems* (pp. 143-157). New York: Plenum.

Williams, L.M., & Farrell, R.A. (1990). Legal response to child sexual abuse in day care. *Criminal Justice and Behavior, 17*(3), 284-302.

Wilson, G.D., & Cox, D.N. (1983). Personality of pedophile club members. *Perspectives on Individual Differences, 4,* 323-329.

Wilsnack, S.C. (1976). The impact of sex roles on women's alcohol use and abuse. In M. Greenblatt & M.A. Schuckit (Eds.), *Alcoholism problems in women and children* (pp.37-63). New York: Grune & Stratton.

Winnicott, D.W. (1962). Ego integration in child development. In D.Winnicott *Collected papers: Through pediatrics to psycho-analysis* (pp. 56-63). London: Tavistock.

Winnicott, D.W. (1971). *Playing and reality.* London: Penguin.

Wolfe, F. (1985, March). *Twelve female sexual offenders.* Presented at a conference on "Next steps in research on the assessment and treatment of sexually aggressive persons (paraphiliacs)," St. Louis, MO.

Wolowitz, H. (1972). Hysterical character and feminine identity. In J. Bardwick (Ed.), *Readings on the psychology of women* (pp. 307-314). New York: Harper & Row.

Wood, H.P., & Duffy, E.L. (1966). Psychological factors in alcoholic women. *American Journal of Psychiatry, 123,* 341-345.

Zimberg, S. (1983). Psychotherapy in the treatment of alcoholism. In E. Patterson & E. Kaufman (Eds.), *Encyclopedic handbook of alcoholism* (pp. 999-1010). New York: Gardner.

Zuelzer, M.B., & Reposa, R.E. (1983). Mothers in incestuous families. *International Journal of Family Therapy, 5,* 98-110.

Roadmaps to Recovery: A Guided Workbook for Young People in Treatment by Timothy J. Kahn. (1999). $18.

Web of Meaning: A Developmental-Contextual Approach in Sexual Abuse Treatment by Gail Ryan & Associates. (1999). $22.

Feeling Good Again by Burt Wasserman (1999). A treatment workbook for boys and girls ages 6 and up who have been sexually abused. $16.

Feeling Good Again Guide for Parents & Therapists by Burt Wasserman. (1999). $8.

Cultural Diversity in Sexual Abuser Treatment: Issues and Approaches edited by Alvin Lewis, Ph.D. (1999). $22.

Sexual Abuse in America: Epidemic of the 21st Century by Robert E. Freeman-Longo & Geral T. Blanchard (1998). $20.

Personal Sentence Completion Inventory by L.C. Miccio-Fonseca, PhD (1998). $50, includes ten inventories and user's guide. Additional inventories available in packs of 25 for $25.

When You Don't Know Who to Call: A Consumer's Guide to Selecting Mental Health Care by Nancy Schaufele & Donna Kennedy (1998). $15.

Tell It Like It Is: A Resource for Youth in Treatment by Alice Tallmadge with Galyn Forster (1998). $15.

Back on Track: Boys Dealing with Sexual Abuse by Leslie Bailey Wright and Mindy Loiselle (1997). $14. A workbook for boys ages 10 and up. Foreword by David Calof.

Assessing Sexual Abuse: A Resource Guide for Practitioners edited by Robert Prentky and Stacey Bird Edmunds (1997). $20.

Impact: Working with Sexual Abusers edited by Stacey Bird Edmunds (1997). $15.

Supervision of the Sex Offender by Georgia Cumming and Maureen Buell (1997). $25.

STOP! Just for Kids: For Kids with Sexual Touching Problems Adapted by Terri Allred and Gerald Burns from original writings of children in a treatment program (1997) $15.

A Primer on the Complexities of Traumatic Memories of Childhood Sexual Abuse: A Psychobiological Approach by Fay Honey Knopp & Anna Rose Benson (1997) $25.

The Last Secret: Daughters Sexually Abused by Mothers by Bobbie Rosencrans (1997). $20.

Men & Anger: Understanding and Managing Your Anger for a Much Better Life by Murray Cullen & Rob Freeman-Longo. Revised and updated, new self-esteem chapter. (1996). $15.

When Children Abuse: Group Treatment Strategies for Children with Impulse Control Problems by Carolyn Cunningham and Kee MacFarlane. (1996). $28.

Adolescent Sexual Offender Assessment Packet by Alison Stickrod Gray & Randy Wallace (1992). $8.

The Relapse Prevention Workbook for Youth in Treatment by Charlene Steen (1993). $15.

Pathways: A Guided Workbook for Youth Beginning Treatment by Timothy J. Kahn (Revised Edition 1997). $15.

Pathways Guide for Parents of Youth Beginning Treatment by Timothy J. Kahn (Revised Edition 1997). $8.

Man-to-Man, When Your Partner Says NO: Pressured Sex & Date Rape by Scott A. Johnson (1992). $6.50.

From Trauma to Understanding: A Guide for Parents of Children with Sexual Behavior Problems by William D. Pithers, Alison S. Gray, Carolyn Cunningham, & Sandy Lane (1993). $5.

Empathy and Compassionate Action: Issues & Exercises: A Workbook for Clients in Treatment by Robert Freeman-Longo, Laren Bays, & Euan Bear (1996). Fourth workbook in a series of four for adult sex offenders. $12.

When Your Wife Says No: Forced Sex in Marriage by Fay Honey Knopp (1994). $7.

Female Adolescent Sexual Abusers: An Exploratory Study of Mother-Daughter Dynamics with Implications for Treatment by Marcia T. Turner & Tracey N. Turner (1994). $18.

Protocol for Phallometric Assessment: A Clinician's Guide by Deloris T. Roys & Pat Roys (1994). $10.

Assessments of Sex Offenders by Measures of Erectile Response: Psychometric Properties and Decision Making by William D. Murphy & Howard Barbaree (1988; updated for Safer Society & bound 1994). $10.

Who Am I & Why Am I in Treatment? A Guided Workbook for Clients in Evaluation and Beginning Treatment by Robert Freeman-Longo & Laren Bays (1988; 8th printing 1997) First workbook in a series of four for adult sex offenders. Also available in Spanish. $12.

Why Did I Do It Again? Understanding My Cycle of Problem Behaviors by Laren Bays & Robert Freeman-Longo (1989; 6th printing 1997). Second in the series. $12.

How Can I Stop? Breaking My Deviant Cycle by Laren Bays, Robert Freeman-Longo, & Diane Montgomery-Logan (1990; 5th printing 1997). Third in the series. $12.

The Relapse Prevention Workbook for Youth in Treatment by Charlene Steen (1993). $15.

The Safer Society Press is part of The Safer Society Foundation, Inc., a 501(c)3 nonprofit national agency dedicated to the prevention and treatment of sexual abuse. We publish additional books, audiocassetttes, and training videos related to the treatment of sexual abuse. To receive a catalog of our complete listings, please check the box on the order form (next page) and mail it to the address listed or call us at (802) 247- 3132. For more information on the Safer Society Foundation, Inc., visit our website at **http://www.safersociety.org.***

ORDER FORM

Date _____

ALL BOOKS ARE SHIPPED VIA UNITED PARCEL SERVICE. PLEASE INCLUDE A STREET ADDRESS FOR SHIPPING, AS WE CANNOT SHIP TO A POST OFFICE BOX.

Shipping Address

Name and/or Agency _____

Street Address (NO PO BOX) _____

City _____ State _____ Zip _____

Billing Address (IF DIFFERENT FROM SHIPPING ADDRESS)

Address _____

City _____ State _____ Zip _____

Daytime Phone (_____) _____ PO # _____

Visa or MasterCard # _____ Exp. Date _____

Signature (FOR CREDIT CARD ORDER) _____

☐ Please send me a catalog.   ☐ Do not add me to your mailing list.

QTY	TITLE	UNIT PRICE	TOTAL COST
	Subtotal		
	VT Residents ONLY Add Sales Tax		
	Shipping & Handling		
	TOTAL		

All orders must be prepaid.

Make checks payable to: SAFER SOCIETY PRESS.

All prices subject to change without notice. NO RETURNS.

Bulk discounts available. Please inquire.

MAIL TO:
SaferSocietyPress

PO BOX 340 • BRANDON, VERMONT 05733-0340

Phone orders accepted with MasterCard & Visa. Call (802) 247-3132.

SHIPPING & HANDLING:

1-5 Items — $5	26-30 Items — $18
6-10 Items — $8	31-35 Items — $22
11-15 Items — $10	36-40 Items — $25
16-20 Items — $12	41-50 Items — $30
21-25 Items — $15	51+ Items — $35

Call for quote on rush orders.